Educational Technology: Integrative Approaches

Educational Technology: Integrative Approaches

Edited by
Joey Gallegos

MURPHY & MOORE
www.murphy-moorepublishing.com

Published by Murphy & Moore Publishing,
1 Rockefeller Plaza,
New York City, NY 10020, USA

ISBN: 978-1-63987-179-7

Cataloging-in-Publication Data

Educational technology : integrative approaches / edited by Joey Gallegos.
p. cm.
Includes bibliographical references and index.
ISBN 978-1-63987-179-7
1. Educational technology. 2. Educational innovations. 3. Education--Effect of technological innovations on.
4. Internet in education. 5. Web-based instruction. I. Gallegos, Joey.
LB1028.3 .E38 2022
371.33--dc23

For information on all Murphy & Moore Publications
visit our website at www.murphy-moorepublishing.com

MURPHY & MOORE

Contents

Preface

Over the recent decade, advancements and applications have progressed exponentially. This has led to the increased interest in this field and projects are being conducted to enhance knowledge. The main objective of this book is to present some of the critical challenges and provide insights into possible solutions. This book will answer the varied questions that arise in the field and also provide an increased scope for furthering studies.

The integration of computer software, hardware and educational theory and practice for the facilitation of learning is referred to as educational technology (EdTech). It encompasses theoretical principles from diverse disciplines such as psychology, sociology, education, communication, computer science, and artificial intelligence. Some of the specializations within educational technology are computer-based training, m-learning, learning theory and online learning. This book elucidates the concepts and innovative models around prospective developments with respect to educational technology. There has been rapid progress of educational technologies and their applications are finding their way across multiple curricula and educational boards. The topics covered in this book offer the readers new insights into modern education.

I hope that this book, with its visionary approach, will be a valuable addition and will promote interest among readers. Each of the authors has provided their extraordinary competence in their specific fields by providing different perspectives as they come from diverse nations and regions. I thank them for their contributions.

Editor

1

Technologically-mediated communication: student expectations and experiences in a FOMO society

Angela T. Ragusa

Correspondence:
aragusa@csu.edu.au
School Humanities and Social Sciences, Charles Sturt University, Albury, NSW, Australia

Abstract

While technology enables a wider section of society to access higher education, accessing, as a process, fundamentally differs from acquiring the individual and systemic skills required for online learning. This study presents primary data about perceptions of, and experiences with, online learning in an Australian university from a survey of 289 distance education (DE) students. Epistemologically, it prioritises giving agency and voice to an increasingly disempowered collective, online learners, who often are institutionally pursued for economic advantage, rather than pedagogical interest in serving students' unique, individual needs/preferences. Participants' comparison of face-to-face and online learning experiences allowed for benefits and disadvantages of online learning to emerge from lived-experiences. While a key benefit of online learning was its perceived 'flexibility', findings revealed difference between students' conceptualisation of flexibility and institutional realities. Although DE students longed for non-technologically-medicated communication with peers and lecturers, the process of learning how to become a DE student failed to address students' needs/concerns beyond technical skill acquisition and subject content mastery. Students' 'fear they were missing out' (FOMO) on 'better' internal classroom and learning experiences was a key limitation 85% perceived about DE. Whereas traditional classroom experiences generally were recalled favourably, online learning was described by its shortcomings. Findings demonstrate need for deeper investigation of how/why educational technologies are implemented. Conclusions suggest critical research investigating whether embedded technologies meet student and/or institutional needs and aspirations in globally competitive learning environments may assuage DE's stigma, realign expectations and improve teaching/learning experiences.

Keywords: Distance education, Online learning, Computer-mediated communication, Learning preferences, Isolation

Introduction and literature review

Digital, computer-mediated communication (CMC), or technologically-mediated communication (TMC), is one of the most fundamental social changes characterising society's transition from modernity to post-modernity (García-Jiménez, 2012). TMC affects how we interact as our social order is refashioned from 'structural' to increasingly 'individualistic'. Alongside traditional demographic categories, 'social reality' is shaped by 'new' communication technologies that create more permeable, plastic, and fluid social boundaries facilitated by democratised, pluralised media appearing to support greater public/individual access, while concurrently excluding, marginalising, and maintaining power relations (García-Jiménez, 2012). Higher educational degrees remain one vestige of social attainment, demarcating social status and class as we negotiate new ways of communicating and interacting. Although university degrees increasingly involve TMC, in Australia, the distinction between those obtained 'internally' versus entirely through 'distance education' (DE) persists despite the introduction of 'mixed-mode' courses involving 'on-campus' and 'off-campus' study. Educational reviews note online learning continues to enjoy market expansion (Norton, 2017), yet it was government funding policy change that enabled Australian public universities to increase off-campus offerings and created such growth; "restraints have been removed, and we observe rapid growth in this market" (Kemp & Norton, 2014, p. 58).

In this article, DE refers to degree completion using TMC without 'traditional', face-to-face classrooms and is used interchangeably with the term 'online learning'. Sometimes termed 'online education', DE is a delivery mode that, despite historical persistence and continued growth, retains a minority status. Historical data reveals all 'off-campus' Australian university enrolments between 1950 and 2013 accounted for 9%–18% of total enrolments (Norton & Cherastidtham, 2014). For the most recent year reviewed, 2013, when 'multi-modal' courses are included, DE and mixed-modal study constituted 25% in contrast with 75% of internal, or 'on-campus' study in Australia (Norton & Cherastidtham, 2014). Despite Australian degree and institutional 'quality' being strongly defended by 'online degree' marketing initiatives and university goals that symbolically support meritocratic visions of educational democracy and global access, DE remains socially stigmatised in ways commonly 'known', yet not academically investigated. In contrast, American research illustrates how the social stigma surrounding online degrees disadvantaged graduates. For example, employers chose to hire accounting graduates with lower grades from 'traditional', internal degrees rather than those with higher academic grades who completed online study, irrespective of the perceived quality of the university attended (Grossman & Johnson, 2016). Noting the dearth of research examining hiring managers' perceptions about online degrees, interviews with private-sector hiring managers in Rochester, New York also revealed stigmatised perceptions with 33% having reservations or negative views about online degrees (Cannon, 2014). Even graduates in disciplines at the forefront of online technologies, library science, faced American employers who expressed concern that online degrees are part of educational 'dumbing down' and preferred traditional graduates whom they perceived had better face-to-face skills and experience valuable for working in a library team environment (Chant, 2013).

In contrast with research focusing on employability, the present research explores DE students' experiences with, and perceptions of, studying online, documenting prejudices and benefits for the purpose of enhancing higher education experience and administration for all involved. A myriad of academic disciplines examining the affordances technological innovations grant, or deprive, reveal social interactions mediated by technologies not only have great power to stigmatise, but also to create and recreate the 'self' because who we are is deeply affected by perceptions and social meanings created through social interactions (Giddens, 1991). For centuries social theorists posited 'new' technologies as threats to social cohesion, connection, and functioning, with definitions of 'community' sociologically attached to notions of belonging, shared engagement, identity, and purpose (Chayko, 2014), as a wide array of theorists as diverse as Emile Durkheim and Robert Putnam purport. It is perhaps surprising, therefore, that much empirical and practical focus prioritises comparing and reproducing norms and experiences between online and face-to-face communication, particularly when discussing educational technologies. Bernard et al. (2009) argue direct comparisons of learning-centred interactions and communications between face-to-face and online environments are perhaps inappropriate at best, and misleading at worse, given the perceived change in effective teaching styles afforded by technology. Studies repeatedly associate online and e-learning with an impersonal nature, even as positive and negative emotions are expressed (Zembylas, 2008), in contrast with the highly didactic and content-centred tendencies of traditional face-to-face learning.

Sociologically, demographics have long been used to establish and dispel stereotypical trends across cohorts using various technologies and communication forms. Demographics, however, fail to discern deeper questions examining *what* contemporary online learners construe to be key advantages and challenges of pursuing higher educational degrees when technologically-mediated learning is the *only* communication form offered. Social theorists have long noted the value non-verbal communication norms, symbolic meaning systems, gestures, behaviours, etc., play in negotiating successful social interactions (Garfinkel, 1967; Goffman, 1967). A dearth of research and conceptualisation, however, explores how CMC/TMC, whether synchronous or asynchronous, affect social interactions at micro-sociological levels. Sociological research reviews identify limited application of symbolic interactionism (SI), particularly Erving Goffman's theory, to mediated technologies because its relevance is construed as limited to face to face interactions (Rettie, 2009). Applying and extending SI, Rettie (2009) analytically compared UK interactions using mobile phones with telephones and letters, arguing mobile phones' synchronous nature shares multiple affinities with face-to-face interactions, such as being negotiated social interactions less amenable to being "ignored" (p. 432), in contrast with text-messages and other written forms where one's presentation of 'self' may be more privately controlled. Although relevant for mobile phone users, Rettie (2009) perpetuates theoretical biases and fails to surpass debating a/synchronous communication affordances, returning to classical definitions of 'social situations' to adjudicate micro/macro conceptualisations/applications and conclude synchronous interactions must "create an intersubjective social experience" and foster "collaborative interaction and co-construction of an ongoing shared social situation" (p. 425).

In Australian higher education today, great emphasis is placed on fostering 'interactivity', with CMC/TMCs foregrounded as pathways to *engage* online learners in manners analogous to internal learning. Such focus, however, also reproduces academic debates regarding communication affordances and, practically, produces learning technologies that seek to share greater affinity with face-to-face interactions, rather than innovatively transcend traditional communication norms/processes. CMC/TMC that occur where individuals perceive they have capacity, agency, to co-create online social environments, as embodiments of social order and reality in line with Garfinkel's (1967) classical sociological theory, offer examples where outdated dichotomisation between physical/TM realities may be transcended. Although Rettie (2009, p. 426) purports distinguishing SMS/texting and telephone conversations as a/synchronous communication events by using the SI criterion, "there is an encounter only if there is sustained focused interaction", analytical progress necessitates conceiving interactions occurring within CMC/TMC environments as freed from temporal constraints historically imposed to determine embodiments of 'self'. As Rettie (2009, p. 435) notes, "synchrony is not mere technical affordance, but also depends on social expectations of immediate feedback and sustained, focused attention". Given sociological research documents the centrality of social interactions to higher educational experiences (Ragusa, 2007, 2009, 2010; Crampton & Ragusa, 2012), examining online learners' 'social expectations' with CMC/TMC, rather than debating a/synchronicity, may advance issues of salience to higher education administration, such as 'successful' learning outcomes, degree completion, graduate 'attributes', and 'employability', as well as discerning academic knowledge gained from formal education delivered through different modes (i.e., internal, distance, mixed).

Recent sociological research reveals social interactions resulting from TMC embody a host of social expectations, notably the "social imperative" (Standlee, 2016, p. 15) demanding immediate presence, or, social availability. Social expectations that online communication, whether educational or social, will be received instantly places relentless communication demands, causes difficulty with students' boundary-creation/maintenance, creates dependency, anxiety and, ironically, 'absence' from face-to-face interactions interrupted by TMC's intrusion as 'real-time' conversations are interrupted to respond to a Facebook or other 'instant' TMC/message as "hyper-connection" (Standlee, 2016, p. 19) becomes normative. 'Superconnected' (Baron, 2010), being always 'plugged-in' (Chayko, 2014), and 'fear-of-missing-out' (FOMO) (Przybylski, Murayama, DeHaan, & Gladwell, 2013) are but a few maladaptive responses CMC/TMC yields. While TMC may be 'ignored' as one self-determines when/if response is desirable (Rettie, 2009), more recent research suggests the social expectations and implications arising from 'deviant' CMC/TMC responses share much in common with non-TM social interactions (Chayko, 2014; Przybylski et al., 2013; Standlee, 2016). Put simply, individuals feel compelled to respond to TMC and fear the consequences of not complying with CMC/TMC social norms and expectations.

The present study commenced in light of these insights and sought to produce results of practical relevance to students and teachers using online environments for higher educational purposes. Whereas prior research concentrated on the *quality* of interactions, this article draws attention to prior research finding the *quantity* of online learning interactions may prove worthy of consideration as increased interaction may neither enhance performance, nor student satisfaction. With more than three 'types' of online interaction (email, forums, and lecturers) yielding no further learning advantages, particularly given time and cost considerations (Castaño-Muñoz, Sancho-Vinuesa, & Duart, 2013), assumptions that 'more' communication is better demand critical thought. Further, while commonly assumed younger generations are technologically savvy, and therefore willing/able online learners, prior research finding technology attitudes and learning-resource awareness were greater predictors of usage than age and 86% of students were competent and effective technology users (Concannon, Flynn, & Campbell, 2005) suggests experience is a better predictor of CMC/TMC attitudes/competency than demographics. Thus, the present study uses a qualitative, experience-driven focus to augment the plethora of research arguing the continued relevance of demographically-driven analyses to advance knowledge about educational technologies.

Methods

Students enrolled in a 100-level DE subject were offered the opportunity to voluntarily complete a survey containing open- and close-ended questions for the purpose of exploring students' learning perceptions and lived-experiences. Opportunity was provided to complete the survey electronically or print/mail a hardcopy. Students received neither compensation nor educational privilege for research participation and the research design ensured participants' identity could not be determined. All surveys were submitted to a third party for de-identification and anonymous ID codes were used for data analysis. Both the survey and distribution method received Human Ethics Committee approval by the university. Close-ended questions permitted collection of limited quantitative data which was entered into SPSS for the purpose of demographically describing participants, not to conduct quantitative statistical analysis or determine causality regarding degree perceptions. To identify student perceptions and lived-experiences, a range of open-ended questions were posed. This article presents key qualitative findings for the open-ended survey question, *What do you see as the major advantages and disadvantages of distance education as you have experienced it in this subject?* Although participants' perceptions of DE learning experiences may be illustrative and/or indicative of broader trends, qualitative epistemology restricts extrapolation of findings beyond the present sample and aims to examine emerging themes in-depth rather than be quantitatively representative of broader populations (Cohen, Manion, & Morrison, 2007; Neuman, 2011; Ragusa, 2012). A key advantage of qualitative research is its capacity to advance collective understanding of insights generated by research participants, rather than predetermined by researchers using close-ended answer options, thereby permitting unanticipated ideas to emerge for future examination/verification if localised findings are exhibited more widely, why, and how (Creswell, 2014).

Guided by existing research, theory, and conducted in an economic environment where Australian universities are seeking DE market expansion and growth, this study's research goal sought to document DE students' individualistic expectations and first-hand experiences at an Australian university renowned as a leader in online delivery. Undertaken in a sociocultural environment emphasising individual flexibility, choice, and the ability of technology to 'solve' the social problem of students having insufficient time, infrastructure (i.e., limited physical access to metropolitan or regional universities), and/or capacity to undertake face-to-face university education, the research design was informed by critical grounded theory (CGT). CGT is an ontology gaining increased recognition for its utility in explaining how individuals 'make sense of,' or attribute meaning to, social interactions and phenomena experienced in complex organisations. This approach was chosen for its capacity to surpass the limitations of traditional grounded theory exhibited in Glaser and Strauss' (1967) classical theory, namely uncritically employing an 'a-theortical' approach to social research to conduct inductive research that surpasses limitations imposed by deductive scientific processes.

CGT enabled creating research questions that sought neither to confirm nor reject prior theories/research findings. Rather, it commenced from "critical observations and experiences of a social problem, of an issue or a process that she wishes to explain, because she recognizes the need for social change" (Belfrade, 2017, p. 259). Hence, awareness that prior research found CMC/TMC interactions systemically and individualistically exhibited 'FOMO' and 'superconnection' behaviors informed the data analysis, yet, did not restrict the research design to empirically testing the manifestation of such behaviours/responses. An inductive, grounded approach was applied to enable students to articulate what they considered benefits and disadvantages of online learning in higher education, allowing for fluidity of concepts. Conceptual fluidity was operationalized by creating an iterative coding system that did not categorize individual items as 'good' or 'bad' since the research aim was to identify emerging qualitative trends across participants' responses by generating qualitatively meaningful themes (Bryman, 2012; Corbin & Strauss, 2008). Practically, for example, where students reported "no classes", "flexibility", and "study at my own pace" as either DE 'advantages' or 'disadvantages', these were coded "F" for "flexibility" as a key theme. Thus, while 'flexibility' tended to be perceived an advantage of DE, such perception depended on students' individualistic beliefs and experiences.

In-depth of thematic analysis was made possible by multiple data readings. Initial theme construction guided two further re-readings of all responses, with reflection and revision following each reading until the final thematic coding scheme suitably reflected participants' key perceptions, with great care taken to avoid introducing researcher bias (Marshall & Rossman, 1999). For example, during the second iteration of the coding scheme, 'flexibility' emerged as a theme too simplistic to capture the diversity of responses and experiences/perceptions students conveyed across responses. Whereas initially flexibility appeared to be primarily related to 'time', several examples illustrated that online forums, while able to be accessed from anywhere and at any time, were perceived to permit a different *type* of communication, aside from being temporally different. Indeed, the technologically-mediated nature of online communication was thought by some to create miscommunication, thereby necessitating *more* communication than in face-to-face classrooms and, despite the ability for CMC/TMC to occur at 'any time', inevitably, academic replies to students' online questions were perceived to arrive insufficiently as soon, or immediately, as students wished. Furthermore, depending upon communication proficiency with written expression, some students found online communication more frustrating as they struggled to convey/receive suitable replies from peers/academics. Discursive complexity was one of many examples where a seemingly 'simple' issue, the 'flexibility' afforded by online communication, made the two categories 'advantage' or 'disadvantage' posed in the question unique to individual experiences. Moreover, single students reported times when they both appreciated and despised having 'no classes', so even perceptions of single issues by the same person were at times context-driven and not absolute. For example, some reported the only way they could undertake university study was without having to attend face-to-face lectures even though they felt they were missing out on such experiences as a DE student.

To accommodate such tensions exhibited in the data, analytical priority was given to identification of qualitative content-driven theme construction, rather than dichotomise/categorize responses as 'advantages' or 'disadvantages' in the final coding scheme. Using the example 'flexibility', this practically resulted in allowing responses to be recoded based on individually-described context, rather than use a content analysis process whereby appearance of a single keyword determined which category/code to employ. This process, while more time consuming, ensured the themes better represented the data, enhancing reliability. Three content-driven final coding scheme themes, *Superiority of face-to-face interactions and FOMO, Communication immediacy and learning anywhere,* and *Technologically connected, yet socially isolated* were created to express the major emergent trends across individual responses and document overlap. This method permitted the research focus to remain consistent with the research aim of documenting pervasive issues/perceptions illustrating *why* students were satisfied or dissatisfied, while allowing for divergent perceptions about the same item identified, i.e. 'no classes', to be accurately coded based on students' sentiments/experiences. Findings are presented in the next section using anonymous identification codes to non-exhaustively offer examples of specific surveys and/or data quotes illustrating each theme.

Findings

Demographically, the majority of the 289 students who completed the survey were female (80%). Consistent with broader DE demographic trends, most (87%) were mature-age students (over age 21) and concurrently studying while employed (78%) in full-time (44%) or part-time (34%) jobs while most (62%) also juggled family responsibilities. Of the 56% who were parents, 13% were single-parents. A sizeable group (41%) reported working between 35 and 80 h a week, exceeding the Australian maximum 38-h workweek for full-time employees stipulated by the *Fair Work Act 2009* (NSW). Predominantly (88%) were in their first or second year of their degree, English was largely (97%) their primary language and most (87%) were born in Australia or New Zealand. Birthplaces of the remaining 13% were very diverse, including Europe ($n = 26$), Asia ($n = 7$), North America ($n = 6$), Middle East ($n = 1$) and South Africa ($n = 1$), and 22 distinct ethnicities/cultures were identified.

Thematically, three key trends emerged from qualitative analysis of the open-ended question exploring student perceptions of distance/online learning: a) *Superiority of face-to-face interactions and FOMO,* b) *Communication immediacy and learning anywhere,* and c) *Technologically connected, yet socially isolated.*

Superiority of face-to-face interactions and FOMO

Students overwhelmingly (85%) perceived traditional internal classrooms offered a better outlet for communication than online learning environments. Online education was repeatedly described in contrast to what it lacked. Normative expectations of higher education were guided by, and derived from, internal classroom experiences. *Not being able to attend lectures* (ID86), *lack of face-to-face instruction* (ID88), *no face-to-face interaction* (ID41; ID24), and *no face-to-face discussion* (ID11) are responses exemplifying perceived disadvantages of DE. Further, 64% thought their academic learning would be better if they were in 'traditional' classrooms. *Had I been given the chance to attend classes it would be a great opportunity* (ID69) described a 40-year-old born in Lebanon living in Sydney. The following quote offers insight into criteria students commonly used to evaluate their online learning experiences:

> *Nothing beats the face-to-face communication with student/lecturers or the tutorial/library resources that attending university brings ... the same resources are not available to DE students, especially face-to-face with lecturers. For that reason employers assume obtaining a degree through DE does not carry the same weight.* (ID240).

The perceived disadvantages of online learning, where all communication was technologically-mediated, were complex and seemingly contradictory in several instances. With online interactions the only type of learning-related communication possible, a sense of 'missing out' emerged. Two broad types of 'missing out' were perceived. On one hand, students feared they would *miss out on lectures* (ID101), specifically internal lectures which they thought provided discussion opportunities lacking in DE, even when electronic lectures were provided in their DE subject. *Missing out on conversations about a topic* (ID248) was perceived a major disadvantage of DE despite online conversations about subject-content being made available 24/7 through electronic forum discussion and chat opportunities and provision of teacher-student and student-student online communication/interaction opportunities. Interestingly, this same student exclaimed she *didn't anticipate so many opportunities for online discussion and assistance* (ID248). Although the lecturer was available for the same quantity of time for DE student consultation as for internal students, the perception pervaded across individuals that online communication did not 'count', or qualify as on par with face-to-face interactions. In sum, regardless of pedagogical structure, DE learning opportunities were perceived as quantitatively different.

Communication 'immediacy' and learning 'anywhere'

Students perceived different socio-physical boundaries existed between internal and DE study utilising online learning. DE students perceived internal lectures occurring in fixed times/spaces constituted 'normal' higher education, rather than construed them as an outdated or disadvantageous learning mode. Students unable to meet the demands of internal study exhibited victimised individualism by accepting their personal circumstances were at-fault, rather than expecting universities to better accommodate mature-age students' availability for face-to-face learning. Conversely, online learning was held to disproportionally rigours temporal standards. Despite asynchronous online forums being available 24/7, and synchronous chat available at designated times, the unavailability of on-demand synchronous communication with lecturers to accommodate individual learning needs was highlighted as lacking and disadvantaging students' learning. *Not being able to talk to* [the] *lecturer* (ID247) whenever any student personally desired was a limitation noted by one under-20 Sydneysider. Such sentiments traversed student age, however, as mature-age students, such as a student living on 'the coast' who lamented the *inability to ask 'on the spot' questions* (ID250) when studying by distance, reflected similar perceptions. Although occasionally students listed *lecturer quickness in responses* (ID73) as an advantage of online learning, more commonly the response rate of lecturer-to-student online communication was perceived as too slow. Responses were expected from DE lecturers within minutes of students' typing forum postings or emails. Discourse used, such as needing 'immediate' replies, reflected different communication expectations than those found in traditional classroom environments where hours or days intervened between student/lecturer interactions. *Inability to further clarify immediately* (ID250), *not able to get immediate assistance from a teacher* (ID239), *lack of immediate discussion of material* (ID88), and it *takes time for e-mails/phone call to be returned* (ID254) are examples reflecting expectations of immediate communication with online enrolment.

Sentiments chastising the immediacy of lecturer reply coincided with the prolific identification of *learning at my own pace* (i.e. ID249; ID256; ID258; ID239; ID240; ID245; ID101; ID118) and capacity to *study at home in your own time* (ID246; ID21) as the greatest advantages of DE and online learning, often by the same students. Expectations existed that no rigid time constraints be placed upon students by learning activities; students' time ought not to be obstructed for any reason, particularly demands to participate in synchronous online communication, assessment completion, or exam preparation. Such perceptions reflect online degrees as a consumer product whereby interaction demands, much like customer satisfaction, are perceived unidirectional. Although students associated DE with *learning from anywhere* and perceived advantages included *more freedom, working from home, being with family and pets, ability to complete* [a] *degree in* [a] *rural town* and *not having to sit in noisy, disruptive classroom*[s] (ID255), they were unwilling to accept the many perceived disadvantages of communicating electronically yet simultaneously wanted to be *able to access all the same resources and opportunities* (ID249) as internal students. While eschewing systemic imposition of time constraints, some found DE's flexibility disadvantageous, noting with online there is *less routine, means MORE discipline, less access to library and resources, less socialization* (ID255).

While technology has enabled online learning to grow into mass education, students who modelled communication and interaction experiences on face-to-face classroom experiences were among the most disappointed. A 43-year-old therapist with many caretaker responsibilities for both infirmed parents and children bemoaned, *in my past experience 4–8 years ago the lecturer was supported and seem to know the students. They were flexible for assignments...330 students is too many to do this with. The attention has to be impersonal and patchy* (ID96). In this example, the student's expectations greatly surpassed the institutional time and resource provision conveyed in university online learning policies.

A degree of 'exceptionalism' also emerged whereby online learning was simultaneously thought to require special consideration of individuals' non-academic life commitments and provision of a communication environment on par with internal educational experiences:

> *That you are supported by your lecturer and the university in a staged learning pattern to develop the skills and integrate the knowledge and understand the materials as are the internal students. Recognition needs to be given to the special work and family commitments of distance students over and above those studying internally. To do this you require extensive written materials to work from, guided forums to discuss ideas relevant to that week's material as internal students have in tutorials. Discussion by phone to clarify issues and misunderstandings ... working together to provide alternative views with just as much debate, information and pop quizzes to assess understanding and being on the right track as internal students.* (ID96).

Where face-to-face, traditional classrooms remain normative in guiding learning expectations, re-socialisation may be required to better match student expectations with capacities possible in online higher education learning environments, particularly in a consumer culture:

> *I think my attitude is shaped by the fact that I know I pay the same fees as internal students so I expect similar treatment. Obviously we cannot have face-to-face lectures, but I do expect to receive an experience as close to this as possible...given that most DE students are part-time and time-poor compared to full-time internal students, it seems to be the wrong way around.* (ID73).

Individual experiences, resilience, living conditions, and other factors affected individual attitudes and expectations. In several instances, the same quantity and type of online communication experiences were perceived as vastly different. For example, a single 47-year-old health care worker from New Zealand reported, *I found the online information, lecturer and thoughts of others on the subject inspiring and spurred me to learn more as well as search on the Internet for information* (ID98), much like a 47-year-old male from England who noted no disadvantages and found online communication and learning to be *very satisfying...I have come to really appreciate the value of this Internet campus* despite the subject was his *first foray into Internet study* (ID97). In contrast, a 36-year-old Australian receiving the same online learning experience who worked 60 h a week and had caretaker responsibilities expressed several dissatisfied comments, noting *lack of class/student interaction, lack of teacher input, lack of teacher availability and misinterpretation of what is being said in forums due to lack of face-to-face contact* (ID71). Hence, categorizing specific CMC/TMC and/or educational technologies as 'advantageous' or 'disadvantageous' appears futile given the relevance of individual perceptions, expectations, and experiences with the same DE environment, learning activities, and academic support resulted in highly divergent responses.

Technologically connected, yet socially isolated

Online learning frequently failed to yield a sense of 'connection', despite multiple platforms available for online interactions with peers, academics, and administrative staff. Even when assessments were structured to foster online communication, students expressed *not having a personal connection with peers* (ID249), *no direct contact with lecturer* (ID44), *no face-to-face contact* (ID20; ID22), *no face-to-face access with lecturers* (ID8), and *no personalised teaching* as a 39-year-old full-time social worker, 40-year-old office manager, 35-year-old supervisor, 26-year-old business coordinator and 32-year-old communications officer all commented along with a multitude of others. Although marketed to enable students to combine studying with employment and/or other responsibilities, online communication often was perceived inadequate for learning and/or meaningful connection with peers and lecturers. A 46-year-old female born in Holland expressed frustration with *not being able to interact with others for clarity* (ID50) and a 33-year-old male law enforcement officer born in India described the learning mode as *less humane* (ID57). Neither the provision of lecturer-created online lectures, nor teacher-student and peer-peer online discussions proved sufficient as communicative opportunities to avoid generating the perceived disadvantage that DE offered *no teacher/student relationship* (ID258). This occurred even when individuals 'strongly agreed' to statements such as 'my personality is well-suited to DE' and 'online lectures helped me to learn the information better' and thought *everything was actually quite well set out and I found it simple* (ID258). Indeed, for this 20-year-old male student, like many others, online learning meant, *education for those who lives a great distance from the University* (ID258). For others, such as a 35-year-old Canadian male living in Melbourne, it was not physical geography, but rather the attempt to combine *working 6 days a week in 12 h shifts at the time* (ID87) while undertaking a university degree in order to change careers that proved most challenging and, perhaps unsurprising, led to feeling, *it's tough to stay motivated* (ID87).

DE was undertaken not for its unique capacity, attributes, or difference with face-to-face classrooms, but rather as a 'necessary evil' due to rurality, caretaker responsibilities, financial restraints, and other life circumstances. *Isolation* (i.e. ID258; ID254; ID261; ID267; ID239; ID241; ID68; ID43; ID29; ID21; ID7; ID5 ID1) was a notable disadvantage profusely articulated and transcended individual demographics. Face-to-face interactions were perceived as the only type of communication with capacity to mediate social isolation. Unfortunately, neither the quantity nor type of online communication offered was sufficient to mediate some students' feelings of social isolation, with expressions such as *feeling isolated alone as don't meet fellow students in person* (ID239) conveying the depth of experience. Reflecting on the provision of audio recordings from the same subject's internal lectures, a full-time disability support worker from Sydney described, *I was just an outsider listening to number of interactions between others which I had no part in* (ID261). This student, like others who perceived *loneliness* (ID15) as a key disadvantage, found DE to be a lonely experience, regardless of the quantity and type of CMC/TMC interactions, and elaborated it is *hard to gauge progress without peers around* (ID261).

Online interactions often were considered insufficient to self-assess academic progress or suffice as peer-learning interactions. Comments such as *hard to compare myself to others to see how I'm performing* (ID264) and *no study groups available* (ID101) were offered despite students receiving reports about the cohort's academic performance on assignments, and online discussions, exam preparation, and study groups being offered. Despite most perceived online communication and interactions to be isolating and inferior, with *in-class interaction* [a] *better way to learn* (ID74), the sentiment was not universal. *I found the forum to the best place to learn and to get help when needed* (ID75) wrote a 41-year-old woman born in Bosnia. To her, DE meant *learning independently. I am self-motivated and I like to work at my own pace* (ID75). Likewise, another 41-year-old, Australian-born woman said she *loved...DE and wouldn't have coped emotionally on-campus. I didn't at school!* (ID70). Generally, self-motivated students appeared more satisfied with DE.

Enrolment in online subjects failed to prevent lack of face-to-face interactions to be listed as the 'worst' disadvantage. This occurred irrespective of location, with urbanites as dissatisfied as rural students. *Lack of face-to-face help* (ID244) noted a 30-year-old from Brisbane, *Don't meet actual people/lecturers* wrote a 33-year-old from Sydney and *No one-on-one contact* (ID251) proclaimed a 30-year-old child care worker from Melbourne; the use of multiple/diverse TMC modes were perceived inadequate to meet online students' communication needs and interaction expectations. In contrast with the commonly stereotyped universal appeal of attending face-to-face lectures, virtual classrooms and interactive online teaching platforms were considered suitable for only some types of students. Analysis revealed varied student comfort and confidence with online communication. *I did not post on the forum very much...I needed to be comfortable using the forum* (ID102) and *I was infrequent on chatting on the forum but I was always on looking at people's questions and* [lecturer's] *responses. I wouldn't have been able to complete it* [the subject] *otherwise* (ID87), contrasted with, *I checked the forum nearly every day being a compulsive type!* (ID98), *I access the forum on most days and find it extremely helpful!* (ID72), and *everyday when possible* (ID97). Additionally, 'older' DE students assumed no younger students were studying by distance, despite nearly a third of students enrolled in the subject were under thirty due to their chosen degree offering several subjects only online, students' geographical location, or simply their lifestyle choice. Despite such 'realities', online learning at times was perceived a compensatory offering for seniors, *the University attempts to negate university education being provided only to young school leavers...or even to those that are subconscious of being older than the majority on campus* (ID100). Generational intolerance and stereotyping also emerged, with the following quote demonstrating how TMC may yield qualitatively similar and different types of interactions as face-to-face classrooms:

> *I found the forums to be used by two certain students that seemed to take over the forum and their continually flood of the forums with their thoughts and opinions... the forum has a lot of mature age student use it and it is sad to think that many of us would not post due to these two students. It is also worrying if these two students are mature age as their behavior didn't show that of mature age students.* (ID71).

Discussion and conclusions

Despite communication technologies, economic efficiencies, and geographical restrictions encouraging increased university degree completion entirely through online/distance education, traditional norms associating high quality education with face-to-face learning are perpetuated by employers (Cannon, 2014; Chant, 2013; Grossman & Johnson, 2016), administrators, and researchers (Rettie, 2009), resulting not only in continued comparison of these modes, yet quality being defined by 'traditional' classroom standards. Although other research notes direct comparisons are inappropriate and/or misleading (Bernard et al., 2009), and online education surpasses and/or shares similarities with traditional education (Zembylas, 2008), stereotypes persist about *who* is technologically proficient (Concannon et al., 2005). Furthermore, much practical activity aims to increase students' online interactions despite research finding more TMC may fail to be desirable or useful to learning outcomes because interactions' relevance to learning goals matters most to students (Crampton & Ragusa, 2015). Hence, the present study's goal sought to shift focus away from comparing student demographics and/or study modes towards analysing student perceptions of online learning experiences. This goal permitted examining TMC using a 'micro' sociological lens and in light of known maladaptive psychological responses, namely anxiety stemming from feeling too connected (Baron, 2010; Chayko, 2014; Standlee, 2016) to fearing logging off will result in missing out (FOMO) (Przybylski et al., 2013).

To achieve the research goal, the present qualitative study examined what undergraduates completing an online introductory subject perceived were key advantages and disadvantages of DE based upon their lived-experiences. Thematic analysis permitted identification of three broad themes. The first theme reflected beliefs about the superiority of face-to-face learning interactions with peers and lecturers and a fear-of-missing-out on 'real'/ 'internal' classroom experiences non-DE students were receiving for the same tuition. Second was the perception that TMC, particularly with lecturers, needed to be immediately received by students, yet not reciprocally expected by lecturers of students who were paying customers. The importance of flexibility students' expectations/requests, including the capacity to 'learn anywhere' were valued advantages of DE, yet countered by having to be inconvenienced by 'irritating' TMC from peers. Finally, while students' felt they were always online, technology failed to ameliorate the social isolation online learning encultured. Findings highlight the importance of rejecting notions of who the 'typical' DE learner is and point to the urgent need for systemic consideration of how and what institutional communication practices and preferences are considered most desirable and why. Perceptions of CMC/TMC illustrated normative expectations that online learning ought to mirror stereotypical face-to-face interactions in internal classrooms, regardless of technical capacity or experience. Students' lived-experiences demonstrated online academic communication was perceived enabling degree completion albeit inevitably was an inferior substitute for face-to-face learning, perpetuating broader social norms and biases that CMC/TMC are poor 'substitutes' disadvantaged individuals must try their best to cope with as they 'miss out' on 'real' classroom experiences.

Collectively considered, examples across the three major themes highlight individualistic perceptions about DE and expectations of online learning experiences guided whether students felt they were 'missing out' on 'better' quality internal subjects, or, were advantaged by the unique opportunities afforded by online study. Regardless that, systemically, internal and DE students received the same quantity of academic time, the same learning materials, and the same pedagogical opportunities, beliefs derived from deep-seated social norms that learning occurs best in physical classrooms was mentioned repeatedly by students identifying the absence of face-to-face experiences as the major disadvantage of DE. Without re-socialisation processes in place to counter/disrupt normative biases and stereotypes, namely that 'internal' learning is the golden standard and DE its poor cousin irrespective of empirical evidence, educational technologies will be held accountable to a mythological image of an 'ideal' classroom. DE students overwhelmingly believed technologically-mediated lectures and tutorials, including those involving online discussions, did not produce interactions that enabled debate, clarification, and learning experiences on par with internal education, despite the equal cost of their degree. While universities continue investing in educational technologies aimed at providing 'comparable' learning experiences for internal/online students, findings suggest without equal effort expended to evidence and identify *how* learning content, resources, and interactions are analogous with face-to-face learning, hegemonic assumptions of 'digital dualism' (Jurgenson, 2012) will continue to emphasise differences. Thus, future research is required that evidences the equality of online and internal academic degree content and educational achievement so stereotypes about difference, and subsequent stigmatization of DE, is confirmed or refuted, rather focus on increasing online interactivity or replicating face-to-face interactions in online environments.

Social expectations and norms about educational technologies mirrored social media interactions; online students exhibited heightened expectations of 'immediacy', personalisation, and FOMO in their online study, lending further evidence of a 'superconnected' society where CMC/TMCs produce temporal demands atypical of face-to-face interactions and yield different types of social anxiety (Baron, 2010; Chayko, 2014 Przybylski et al., 2013; Standlee, 2016). With 'soft' social skills, particularly effective communication skills, a highly sought graduate attribute (Nagarajan & Edwards, 2014), findings highlight need to prioritise developing tacit skills required to be 'successful' online communicators, and correspondingly, online learners. Without prior DE experience when admitted, students were left to model prior learning experiences from face-to-face high schools or community colleges. Leaving undergraduates to 'figure out' *how* to be online learners exposes universities to unnecessary risks (i.e. student attrition, 'flaming', stress leave, etc.). With few expectations and little or no experience, it is unsurprising students felt ill-equipped in online interaction skills and findings contribute to research identifying improved access to learning support is a key factor in students' preference for face-to-face over online modes (Bailey, Ifenthaler, Gosper, Kretzschmar, & Ware, 2015; O'Neil & Sai, 2014). Complimenting Lee's (2010) cross-cultural study of North American and Korean students, which found a positive relationship between perceived quality of online support and student satisfaction, students' perceptions and expectations about the quality, and quantity, of online learning support (from peers and lecturers) affected their overall satisfaction; no students who articulated they were dissatisfied with online learning experiences said expectations were met.

In addition to student-identified challenges, discrepancies between individualistic and systemic priorities warrant further consideration. For example, students believed online learning ought to permit completion of assessment items, subjects, and degrees *at their* [students'] *own pace*. This was understood as being around students' personal, work, family, and vacation commitments, an interpretation that differed from university deadlines and policies regarding equity, completion timeframes, and academic workloads. Improved mitigation of competing interests and decreased misinterpretation may be achieved by establishing clearer guidelines that are consistently communicated and applied across subjects, courses, and degrees. Likewise, clearer articulation of what tuition 'pays for' may prevent inaccurate perceptions, and hence customer dissatisfaction, that one learning mode receives 'more' for the money than another. Given the lack of transparency relevant to learning mode expectations, teaching methods, workloads, and assessments were identified as factors affecting enrolment decisions and changes at another large Australian University (Bailey et al., 2015). This study lends additional evidence that ambiguity and varied student/lecturer interpretation about what constitutes effective/sufficient 'online learning' contributes to student dissatisfaction and FOMO. Clear and definitive academic leadership is, therefore, required to clarify what distance, internal, and/or mixed/blended education institutionally *mean* and ought to be provided to students prior to degree commencement as well as extended to staff and students in alignment with institutional goals and capacity.

Perceived difference in the quality of face-to-face and TM-interactions was the greatest, and most consistently agreed upon, disadvantage students noted for online learning; TMC, whether emails, asynchronous/synchronous forums, virtual lectures, phone-calls, or electronic announcements, were deemed inferior to face-to-face conversations. Regardless of the *convenience* (ID13) electronic communication permitted, DE students simply failed to believe interactive online platforms were a suitable substitute for 'real' human interactions. Face-to-face interactions, unlike TMC, were perceived motivational and thus crucial for academic learning. *You have to continually motivate yourself to read and study* (ID10) was the fundamental lesson online students learned. Findings revealed most students felt *internal is better; with distance, you are not pushed to your ability so can slacken off* (ID131), suggesting poor self-motivation may continue underscoring the high online study attrition rates experienced by early online courses (Muilenburg & Berge, 2005). Technological advances appear not to have appropriately addressed this issue as the perception that face-to-face interactions enhance learning motivation perseveres. Nevertheless, this may have less to do with learning mode than with individualistic capacity to personally contextualize a lesson/assessment's importance as Hartnett, St. George, and Dron (2011) found extrinsic motivators, particularly a learning activity's perceived value, were as important as characteristics normally associated with intrinsic motivations (e.g. task enjoyment) often associated with self-efficacy.

To better understand why/how online and face-to-face learning affect academic success in Australia, future researchers may benefit from deeper examination not only of demographics, but also of academic performance, study mode, and degree completion. Community college students studying online have been found more likely to fail or withdraw than those studying internally according to large American studies of 21,000 and 54,000 students (Jaggars & Xu, 2010). Likewise, others found some students initially studying by DE or online in the first two years, such as the students in this study, were less academically prepared than those enrolled in face-to-face classrooms (Shea & Bidjerano, 2014). Further, community college students studying online or completing online coursework were less likely to complete a degree or transfer to a four year college (Xu & Jaggars, 2011). Demographic attributes prior research indicates may increase the likelihood of effective online learning, specifically "highly motivated, "mature age" students" (Bacow, Bowen, Guthrie, Lack, & Long, 2012 p. 18), require deeper examination beyond quantitative description given the present study suggests self-motivated students appeared more 'satisfied,' yet simply being 'mature age' may fail to either increase online learning success or satisfaction. Age-based stereotypes emerged among students that, at times, thwarted positive TMC interactions as students made assumptions about classmates based upon the little demographic information derived from online postings. Thus, in distilling *what* and *how many* communication opportunities to offer, and *for what pedagogical purpose,* age-based stereotyping is exceedingly problematic. Although some students stereotyped others in their own and others' generation, meta-analysis of qualitative comments revealed little variation in technical competency or preference for TMC in online learning, countering notions that younger generations are more technologically able or willing online learners and adding support for the valuable role social attitudes play in willingness to use technology (Concannon et al., 2005).

Consistent with prior research finding 'traditional' internal classroom environments resulted in greater student learning than purely virtual classrooms (Concannon et al., 2005), this research highlighted students' self-reported tendency to 'slacken off' without face-to-face learning. Some perceived certain personality types were better suited to DE, especially those with negative internal classroom experiences, yet the majority felt they had little choice other than online degrees due to life circumstances. This logistical aspect of mode choice has, understandably, been a consistent finding in the literature (Bailey et al., 2015). When logistics is not a determining factor, as was the case for most participants, then students' degree of subject-content interest may affect their satisfaction and expectations given several studies have found students prefer to study topics they find harder or interesting in face-to-face classrooms (Jaggers, 2014; Artino, 2010).

In contrast with suggestions that Internet access has translated into greater interaction in online learning (Bernard et al., 2009), present findings suggest the level of interaction experienced, either peer-peer or student-teacher insufficiently met DE students' expectations. Finding that TMC did not match preferred levels or expectations mirrors Gosper, Malfroy, and McKenzie's (2013) findings from a survey of over 10,000 internal students in three Australian universities. With desire for interaction and connection noted as the major decisive factor for students with the option of studying face-to-face or online (Bailey et al., 2015), TMC is heralded as the primary way to improve DE student engagement at most Australian universities. Indeed, another study from the same institution as the present study found students regarded online tools that promoted interaction with their teacher were the most important among the plethora available (Small, Dowell, & Simmons, 2012). Likewise, absence of suitable levels of interaction with and connection to peers and teachers was described by North American distance students (Otter et al., 2013).

Despite cries for increased/enhanced student-teacher interaction, a contradictory scenario emerged whereby DE students' simultaneously desired more synchronous communication opportunities while eschewing any activity imposing time constraints inhibiting studying at their *own pace.* In reality, provision of multiple TMC platforms and opportunities generated anxiety about how to fit higher communication loads into their already over-loaded lives, aligning with research showing resentment with learning activities, such as synchronous online classrooms or virtual worlds, and frustration, rather than appreciation, from a social group overly preoccupied with maintaining flexibility (Boling, Hough, Krinsky, Saleem, & Stevens, 2012). Thus, a 'catch 22′ scenario emerges whereby institutions are faulted for providing insufficient synchronous communication opportunities and DE students lament the lack of face-to-face engagement experienced in internal classrooms, yet DE students are unwilling to sacrifice flexibility or independent control of their time. Despite the continued growth and ongoing changing nature of DE (Eom, Wen, & Ashill, 2006), findings suggest student satisfaction was increased neither by the quantity nor type of TMC opportunities offered.

Drawing upon DE students' first-hand, lived-experiences with online study, this article documented what learners perceived facilitated or thwarted their learning process and what expectations they held for themselves, their teachers, and higher education institutions more broadly. Findings revealed students thought communicative, not technical, proficiency, mattered most to academic 'success' in online environments. Results suggest organisational and academic quests for 'interactivity' and 'engagement' in online higher education environments (Croxton, 2014; Smith & Winking-Diaz, 2004) may benefit from shifting focus towards creating learning environments that embody effective time management through educational design and organisational health and safety imperatives, rather than demand 'social interaction' through forced online communication. Students perceived too much online communication negatively affected online subject and degree completion. Thus, finding the 'right' balance between 'too much' and 'too little' communication remains a challenge demanding future research. Questioning organisational imperatives for increased online student/teacher interaction, without thorough investigation of its academic purpose, may also assuage and/or prevent negative academic workload implications arising from maladaptive responses to CMC/TMC, namely increased academic stress leave and anxiety encultured by perceptions of '24/7' workloads (Gregory & Lodge, 2015). Educational technologies may facilitate realisation of meritocratic ideals for online higher education (i.e. enhancing flexibility, surpassing sociocultural barriers/inequities, promoting educational pluralisation) by creating adaptive learning environments that proactively create realistic expectations, minimise anxiety-producing behaviours, and promote successful subject, and subsequently degree, completion.

Bridging the many gaps qualitatively manifested – generational, socio-economic, gender, geographical, cultural, and socio-psychological – demands an interdisciplinary lens. Students who disclosed trying to simultaneously cope with mental illnesses, undertake primary caretaker responsibility for parents with dementia or six children, perform 60 h of shift-work weekly, re-integrate into a new culture after migrating, or undertaking a host of other otherwise 'hidden' life activities revealed there is no such thing as a 'normal' distance student, even as many believed internal students had perfectly carefree lives. TMC makes largely invisible our 'real' selves; what is communicated electronically is what the speaker wishes to reveal. Symbolic gestures, expressions, and emotions communicated through the physicality of face-to-face interactions may, therefore, enable students to 'learn' more than academic content. If and how academic learning is differently affected by the 'real' presence of individuals, in contrast with similar but different online expressions, remains unknown. Hence, it is imperative institutions unpack the complex relationship among economic, social, and demographic variables in determining cost-effectiveness of higher education delivery modes, pedagogical quality, and communication norms or guidelines. No economic advantage exists for poorly planned online environments resulting in impoverished student experiences that reduce the likelihood students will continue their degree (Artino, 2010). Technologically-mediated learning environments require deeper critical review and analysis to articulate and understand implications arising from heightened reliance upon, and presumed desirability of, TMC as a principle method of higher education delivery.

Finally, this research suggests the association of 'technology enhanced' education with the development of 'higher order skills' (Hardy & Bower, 2004) may have more to do with the *style* and *purpose* of communicative and interactive activities pursued through learning, rather than a priori aspects of CMC/TMC as inordinately different from face-to-face-interactions. Applying social media theory,'digital dualism' (Jurgenson, 2012) drives many educational technology assumptions and much research. Namely, there is a tendency to accentuate differences between online/offline experiences. If one expects great differences between DE and internal learning, social norms stigmatise DE degrees, and perceptions/expectations of educational technologies are informed by face-to-face-interactions, then academic learning and subject/degree completion may be stymied. Moreover, the affordances of educational technologies may not be fully realised.

Today's service-oriented, knowledge-based society requires high competency in 'soft skills', professionalism in interpersonal relationships, communicative competency, and awareness of cultural norms and their impact (Hendarman & Tjakraatmadja, 2012). The greater interaction deemed necessary for successful online teaching (Desai, Hart, & Richards, 2008; Dixson, Greenwell, Rogers-Stacy, Weister, & Lauer, 2017;

Richardson, 2017) could, therefore, be promoted as an advantage of online education. Creating 'successful' online communicators/learners, however, requires more than skill development. Prior research found having to communicate with peers using 'written discourse', a communication style perceived as a new and unfamiliar, created the greatest anxiety among students new to online learning (Zembylas, 2008). The present study also found students' perceived 'confidence' in their ability to communicate about subject content to peers was a barrier to online participation. Interactive online study may be an effective social environment for developing the communication skills required in today's digital society, yet social norms and perceptions appear to be historically informed. Clearer articulation of how online interactions enable subject content learning and preparedness for contemporary society must be accompanied by research evidencing specific learning modes (i.e., internal and online) achieve didactic outcomes of disciplinary and broader relevance. Comparative analysis of internal and DE students' comprehension of fundamental academic concepts, for example key psychological theories for psychology majors could help dispel or confirm perceptions that delivery mode drives learning outcomes and degree quality. Further, comparison of 'soft skill' acquisition (i.e. writing and communication skills) among modes (internal, mixed, distance) could also identify if and why some modes may be better suited to specific courses, rather than economics driving subject mode and other administrative decisions. By evidencing equity of degree rigour and learning outcomes we may eliminate the stigma pervading online degrees and better ensure hiring managers' preferences are informed by graduates' skills, rather than concerns about degree quality (Cannon, 2014) or perceptions that DE is a 'dumbed down' education option (Chant, 2013). As industry leaders, DE providers must take leadership in evidencing and ensuring equity in the quality, and capacity of, their educational products and graduates.

Acknowledgments

The author would like to acknowledge the research support received by Dr. Andrea Crampton during the research conceptualization process and formally thank the many undergraduate students who shared their 'first hand' experiences and thoughts about challenges and successes with online study for the benefit of future students, higher education providers, and researchers worldwide.

Funding

Not applicable

Declarations

This study was approved by the CSU human ethics committee. There were no competing interests and the study was unfunded. Due to ethics limitations, data is not available for public viewing.

Competing interests

The author declare that he has no competing interests.

References

Artino, A. R. (2010). Online or face-to-face learning? Do exploring the personal factors that predict students' choice of instructional format. *Internet and Higher Education, 13*, 272–276 https://doi.org/10.1016/j.iheduc.2010.07.005.

Bacow, L.S., Bowen, W.G., Guthrie, K.M., Lack, K.A., Long, M.P. (2012). Barriers to adoption of online learning systems in U. S. higher education. Retrieved from: http://www.sr.ithaka.org/wp-content/uploads/2015/08/barriers-to-adoption-of-onlinelearning-systems-in-us-higher-education.pdf. Accessed Apr 2017.

Bailey, M., Ifenthaler, D., Gosper, M., Kretzschmar, M., & Ware, C. (2015). The changing important of factors influencing students' choice of study mode. *Technology, Knowledge and Learning, 20*, 169–184 https://doi.org/10.1007/s10758-015-9253-9.

Baron, N. S. (2010). *Always on: Language in an online and mobile world.* New York: Oxford University Press.

Belfrade, C. (2017). The gentle art of retroduction: Critical realism, cultural political economy and critical grounded theory. *Organization Studies, 38*(2), 251–271 https://doi.org/10.1177/0170840616663239.

Bernard, R. M., Abrami, P. C., Borokhovski, E., Wade, C. A., Tamim, R. M., Surkes, M. A., & Bethel, E. C. (2009). A meta- in distance education. *Review of Educational Research, 79*(3), 1243–1289. 10.3102/0034654309333844.

Boling, E. C., Hough, M., Krinsky, H., Saleem, H., & Stevens, M. (2012). Cutting the distance in distance education: Perspectives on what promotes positive, online learning experiences. *Internet and Higher Education, 15*, 118–126 https://doi.org/10.1016/j.iheduc.2011.11.006.

Bryman, A. (2012). *Social research methods*, (4th ed.,). Oxford: Oxford University Press.

Cannon, T. T. (2014). *Perceptions of hiring managers regarding employment candidates with earned online degrees: Implications for the employability for graduates of online programs, Unpublished doctoral thesis* (). Minneapolis: Capella University.

Castaño-Muñoz, J., Sancho-Vinuesa, T., & Duart, J. M. (2013). Online interaction in higher education: Is there evidence of diminishing returns? *The International Review of Research in Open and Distance Learning, 14*(5), 240–257 http://dx.doi.org/10.19173/irrodl.v14i5.1336.

Chant, I. (2013). As online degrees become more prevalent, questions linger. *Library Journal, 138*(18), 23.

Chayko, M. (2014). Techno-social life: The internet, digital technology, and social connectedness. *Sociology Compass, 8*, 976–991. 10.1111/soc4.12190.

Cohen, L., Manion, L., & Morrison, K. (2007). *Research methods in education*, (6th ed.,). NY: Routledge.

Concannon, F., Flynn, A., & Campbell, M. (2005). What campus-based students think about the quality and benefits of e-learning. *British Journal of Educational Technology, 36*(3), 501–512 https://doi.org/10.1111/j.1467-8535.2005.00482.x.

Corbin, S., & Strauss, A. (2008). *Basics of qualitative research: Techniques and procedures for developing grounded theory*, (3rd ed.,). Thousand Oaks, CA: Sage.

Crampton, A. & Ragusa, A.T. (2012). Communication and education: Finding the balance with 24/7 opportunities for students. International Journal of Technology, Knowledge and Society, Volume 8, Issue 1, pp.33-42. http://www.olt.gov.au/system/files/resources/SD13_2708_Crampton_Report_2015.pdf

Crampton, A & Ragusa, A.T. (2015). Exploring the role of technology in fostering sense of belonging in students studying by distance. Final report to Office of Learning and Teaching. www.olt.gov.au/system/files/resources/SD13_2708_Crampton_Report_2015.pdf.

Creswell, J. W. (2014). *Research design: Qualitative, quantitative and mixed methods approaches*, (4th ed.,). Thousand Oaks, CA: Sage.

Croxton, R. A. (2014). The role of interactivity in student satisfaction and persistence in online learning. *MERLOT Journal of Online Learning and Teaching, 10*(2), 35–50 https://doi.org/10.1016/j.iheduc.2013.10.001.

Desai, M. S., Hart, J., & Richards, T. C. (2008). E-learning: Paradigm shift in education. *Education, 129*(2), 327–334 http://www.sciepub.com/reference/123507.

Dixson, M. D., Greenwell, M. R., Rogers-Stacy, C., Weister, T., & Lauer (2017). Nonverbal immediacy behaviors and online student engagement: Bringing past instructional research into present virtual classroom. *Communication Education, 66*(1), 37–53 https://doi.org/10.1080/03634523.2016.1209222.

Eom, S. B., Wen, J. H., & Ashill, N. (2006). The determinants of students' perceived learning outcomes and satisfaction in university online education: An empirical investigation. *Decision Sciences Journal of Innovation Education, 4*(2), 215–235 https://doi.org/10.1111/j.1540-4609.2006.00114.x.

García-Jiménez, L. (2012). Elements for a social theory of technologically mediated communication: From modernity to postmodernity. *Estudios sobr e el Mensaje Periodístico, 18*(1), 101–114 https://doi.org/10.5209/rev_ESMP.2012.v18.n1.39357.

Garfinkel, H. (1967). *Studies in ethnomethodology*. Englewood Cliffs, NJ: Prentice-Hall.

Giddens, A. (1991). *Modernity and self-identity: Self and society in the late modern age*. Stanford: Stanford University Press.

Glaser, B. G., & Strauss, A. L. (1967). *The discovery of grounded theory: Strategies for qualitative research*. New York: Aldine.

Goffman, E. (1967). *Interaction ritual: Essays on face-to-face behavior*. New York: Doubleday Anchor.

Gosper, M., Malfroy, J., & McKenzie, J. (2013). Students' experiences and expectations of technologies: An Australian study designed to inform planning and development decisions. *Australasian Journal of Educational Technology, 29*(2), 268–282 https://doi.org/10.14742/ajet.127.

Gregory, M. S., & Lodge, J. M. (2015). Academic workload: The silent barrier to the implementation of technology-enhanced learning strategies in higher education. *Distance Education, 36*(2), 210–230 https://doi.org/10.1080/01587919.2015.1055056.

Grossman, A. M., & Johnson, L. R. (2016). Employer perceptions of online accounting degrees. *Issues in Accounting Education, 31*(1), 91–109.

Hardy, K. P., & Bower, B. L. (2004). Instructional and worklife issues for distance learning faculty. In B. L. Bower, & K. P. Hardy (Eds.), *From distance education to e-learning:Lessons along the way*. San Francisco: Jossey-Bass.

Hartnett, M., St. George, A., & Dron, J. (2011). Examining motivation in online distance learning environments: Complex, multifaceted and situational. The International Review of Research in Open and Distance Learning,12(6), 20-37. http://dx.doi.org/10.19173/irrodl.v12i6.1030

Hendarman, A. F., & Tjakraatmadja, J. H. (2012). Relationship among soft skills, hard skills and innovativeness of knowledge workers in the knowledge economy era. *Procedia – Social and Behavioral Sciences, 52*, 35–44 https://doi.org/10.1016/j.sbspro.2012.09.439.

Jaggars, S. S., & Xu, D. (2010). *Online learning in the Virginia community college system (CCRCWorking paper)*. New York, NY: Columbia University, Teachers College, Community College Research Center.

Jaggers, S. S. (2014). Choosing between online and face-to-face courses. *The American Journal of Distance Education, 28*(1), 27–38. http://dx.doi.org/10.1080/08923647.2014.867697.

Jurgenson, N. (2012). When atoms meet bits: Social media, the mobile web and augmented revolution. *FutureInternet, 4*(1), 83–91 https://doi.org/10.3390/fi4010083.

Kemp, D., & Norton, A. (2014). *Review of the demand driven system: Final report*. Australian Government: Department of Education and Training.

Lee, J. (2010). Online support service quality, online learning acceptance, and student satisfaction. *Internet and Higher Education, 13*, 277–283 https://doi.org/10.1016/j.iheduc.2010.08.002.
Marshall, C., & Rossman, G. (1999). *Designing qualitative research*, (3rd ed.,). Thousand Oaks, California: Sage Publications.
Muilenburg, L. Y., & Berge, Z. L. (2005). Student barriers to online learning: A factor analytic study. *Distance Education, 26*(1), 29–48 https://doi.org/10.1080/01587910500081269.
Nagarajan, S., & Edwards, J. (2014). Is the graduate attribute approach sufficient to develop work ready graduates. *Journal of Teaching and Learning for Graduate Employability, 5*(1), 12–28 https://doi.org/10.21153/jtlge2014vol5no1art565.
Neuman, W. L. (2011). *Social research methods*, (7th ed.,). Boston, MS: Pearson Education.
Norton, A., & Cakitaki, B. (2016) Mapping Australian higher education 2016, *Grattan Institute*. https://grattan.edu.au/wp.../08/875-Mapping-Australian-Higher-Education-2016.p.
Norton, A. & Cherastidtham, I. (2014). Mapping Australian higher education, 2014–15. Grattan Institute.
O'Neil, D. K., & Sai, T. H. (2014). Why not? Examining college students' reasons for avoiding an online course. *Higher Education, 68*(1), 1–14 https://doi.org/10.1007/s10734-013-9663-3.
Otter, R. R., Seipel, S., Graeff, T., Alexander, B., Boraiko, C., Gray, J., Petersen, K., & Sadler, K. (2013). Comparing student and faculty perceptions of online and traditional courses. *Internet and Higher Education, 19*, 27–35 https://doi.org/10.1016/j.iheduc.2013.08.001.
Przybylski, A. K., Murayama, K., DeHaan, C. R., & Gladwell, V. (2013). Motivational, emotional, and behavioral correlates of fear of missing out. *Computers in Human Behavior, 29*(4), 1841–1848 https://doi.org/10.1016/j.chb.2013.02.014.
Ragusa, A.T. (2007). The impact of socio-cultural factors in multi-cultural virtual communication environments: A case example from an Australian university's provision of distance education in the global classroom. In St-Amant, K. (Ed.) *Linguistic and Cultural Online Communication Issues in the Global Age* (Chapter 18, pp. 306–27), Idea Group Inc.
Ragusa, A.T. (2009). Peer learning and social interactions in an asynchronous learning environment. *Handbook of Research on Social Interaction Technologies and Collaboration Software: Concepts and Trends, 2 Volumes.* (Chap. 17, Section II). T. Dumova & R. Fiordo (Eds.), Hershey: Information Science Reference.
Ragusa, A. T. (2010). Communication and social interactions in a technologically-mediated world. In A. Ragusa (Ed.), *Interaction in Communication Technologies & Virtual Learning Environments: Human Factors (chapter 1)*, (pp. 1–8). PA: Information Science Reference.
Ragusa, A. T. (2012). *Writing for the social sciences*. NSW: Pearson Education.
Rettie, R. (2009). Mobile phone communication: Extending Goffman to mediated interaction. *Sociology, 43*(3), 421–438 https://doi.org/10.1177/0038038509103197.
Richardson, J. C. (2017). Social presence in relation to students' satisfaction and learning in the online environment: A meta-analysis. *Computers in Human Behaviour, 71*, 402–417 https://doi.org/10.1016/j.chb.2017.02.001.
Shea, P. A., & Bidjerano, T. (2014). Does online learning impede degree completion? A national study of community college students. *Computers & Education, 75*, 103–111 https://doi.org/10.1016/j.compedu.2014.02.009.
Small, F., Dowell, D., & Simmons, P. (2012). Teacher communication preferred over peer interaction. *Journal of International Education in Business*, *5*(2), 114–128. https://doi.org/10.1108/18363261211281735.
Smith, M. C., & Winking-Diaz, A. (2004). Increasing students' interactivity in an online course. *Journal of Interactive Online Learning, 3*(3), 1–25 http://www.ncolr.org/issues/jiol/v2/n3/increasingstudents-interactivity-in-an-online-course. Accessed Apr 2017.
Standlee, A. (2016). Technology and making-meaning in college relationships: understanding hyperconnection. *Qualitative Sociology Review, 12*(2), 6–21. (http://www.qualitativesociologyreview.org/ENG/archive_eng.php)
Xu, D., & Jaggars, S. S. (2011). *Online and hybrid course enrollment and performance in Washington state community and technical colleges (CCRC working paper no. 31)*. New York, NY: Columbia University, Teachers College, Community College Research Center.
Zembylas, M. (2008). Adult learners' emotions in online learning. *Distance Education, 29*(1), 71–87. http://dx.doi.org/10.1080/01587910802004852.

2

Computer-based technology and student engagement

Laura A. Schindler[1*], Gary J. Burkholder[2,3], Osama A. Morad[1] and Craig Marsh[4]

* Correspondence: Laura.schindler@online.liverpool.ac.uk
[1]University of Liverpool Online, Liverpool, UK
Full list of author information is available at the end of the article

Abstract

Computer-based technology has infiltrated many aspects of life and industry, yet there is little understanding of how it can be used to promote student engagement, a concept receiving strong attention in higher education due to its association with a number of positive academic outcomes. The purpose of this article is to present a critical review of the literature from the past 5 years related to how web-conferencing software, blogs, wikis, social networking sites (*Facebook* and *Twitter*), and digital games influence student engagement. We prefaced the findings with a substantive overview of student engagement definitions and indicators, which revealed three types of engagement (behavioral, emotional, and cognitive) that informed how we classified articles. Our findings suggest that digital games provide the most far-reaching influence across different types of student engagement, followed by web-conferencing and *Facebook*. Findings regarding wikis, blogs, and *Twitter* are less conclusive and significantly limited in number of studies conducted within the past 5 years. Overall, the findings provide preliminary support that computer-based technology influences student engagement, however, additional research is needed to confirm and build on these findings. We conclude the article by providing a list of recommendations for practice, with the intent of increasing understanding of how computer-based technology may be purposefully implemented to achieve the greatest gains in student engagement.

Keywords: Student engagement, Web-conferencing, Wikis, Blogs, Social networking, *Facebook*, *Twitter*, Digital games

Introduction

The digital revolution has profoundly affected daily living, evident in the ubiquity of mobile devices and the seamless integration of technology into common tasks such as shopping, reading, and finding directions (Anderson, 2016; Smith & Anderson, 2016; Zickuhr & Raine, 2014). The use of computers, mobile devices, and the Internet is at its highest level to date and expected to continue to increase as technology becomes more accessible, particularly for users in developing countries (Poushter, 2016). In addition, there is a growing number of people who are smartphone dependent, relying solely on smartphones for Internet access (Anderson & Horrigan, 2016) rather than more expensive devices such as laptops and tablets. Greater access to and demand for technology has presented unique opportunities and challenges for many industries, some of which have thrived by effectively digitizing their operations and services (e.g., finance, media) and others that have struggled to keep up with the pace of technological innovation (e.g., education, healthcare) (Gandhi, Khanna, & Ramaswamy, 2016).

Integrating technology into teaching and learning is not a new challenge for universities. Since the 1900s, administrators and faculty have grappled with how to effectively use technical innovations such as video and audio recordings, email, and teleconferencing to augment or replace traditional instructional delivery methods (Kaware & Sain, 2015; Westera, 2015). Within the past two decades, however, this challenge has been much more difficult due to the sheer volume of new technologies on the market. For example, in the span of 7 years (from 2008 to 2015), the number of active apps in Apple's App Store increased from 5000 to 1.75 million. Over the next 4 years, the number of apps is projected to rise by 73%, totaling over 5 million (Nelson, 2016). Further compounding this challenge is the limited shelf life of new devices and software combined with significant internal organizational barriers that hinder universities from efficiently and effectively integrating new technologies (Amirault, 2012; Kinchin, 2012; Linder-VanBerschot & Summers 2015; Westera, 2015).

Many organizational barriers to technology integration arise from competing tensions between institutional policy and practice and faculty beliefs and abilities. For example, university administrators may view technology as a tool to attract and retain students, whereas faculty may struggle to determine how technology coincides with existing pedagogy (Lawrence & Lentle-Keenan, 2013; Lin, Singer, & Ha, 2010). In addition, some faculty may be hesitant to use technology due to lack of technical knowledge and/or skepticism about the efficacy of technology to improve student learning outcomes (Ashrafzadeh & Sayadian, 2015; Buchanan, Sainter, & Saunders, 2013; Hauptman, 2015; Johnson, 2013; Kidd, Davis, & Larke, 2016; Kopcha, Rieber, & Walker, 2016; Lawrence & Lentle-Keenan, 2013; Lewis, Fretwell, Ryan, & Parham, 2013; Reid, 2014). Organizational barriers to technology adoption are particularly problematic given the growing demands and perceived benefits among students about using technology to learn (Amirault, 2012; Cassidy et al., 2014; Gikas & Grant, 2013; Paul & Cochran, 2013). Surveys suggest that two-thirds of students use mobile devices for learning and believe that technology can help them achieve learning outcomes and better prepare them for a workforce that is increasingly dependent on technology (Chen, Seilhamer, Bennett, & Bauer, 2015; Dahlstrom, 2012). Universities that fail to effectively integrate technology into the learning experience miss opportunities to improve student outcomes and meet the expectations of a student body that has grown accustomed to the integration of technology into every facet of life (Amirault, 2012; Cook & Sonnenberg, 2014; Revere & Kovach, 2011; Sun & Chen, 2016; Westera, 2015).

The purpose of this paper is to provide a literature review on how computer-based technology influences student engagement within higher education settings. We focused on computer-based technology given the specific types of technologies (i.e., web-conferencing software, blogs, wikis, social networking sites, and digital games) that emerged from a broad search of the literature, which is described in more detail below. Computer-based technology (hereafter referred to as technology) requires the use of specific hardware, software, and micro processing features available on a computer or mobile device. We also focused on student engagement as the dependent variable of interest because it encompasses many different aspects of the teaching and learning process (Bryson & Hand, 2007; Fredricks, Blumenfeld, & Parks, 1994; Wimpenny & Savin-Baden, 2013), compared narrower variables in the literature such as final grades or exam scores. Furthermore, student engagement has received significant attention over the past several decades due to shifts towards student-centered, constructivist instructional methods (Haggis, 2009; Wright, 2011), mounting pressures to improve teaching and learning outcomes (Axelson & Flick, 2011; Kuh, 2009), and promising studies suggesting relationships between student engagement and positive academic outcomes (Carini, Kuh, & Klein, 2006; Center for Postsecondary Research, 2016; Hu & McCormick, 2012). Despite the interest in student engagement and the demand for more technology in higher education, there are no articles offering a comprehensive review of how these two variables intersect. Similarly, while many existing student engagement conceptual models have expanded to include factors that influence student engagement, none highlight the overt role of technology in the engagement process (Kahu, 2013; Lam, Wong, Yang, & Yi, 2012; Nora, Barlow, & Crisp, 2005; Wimpenny & Savin-Baden, 2013; Zepke & Leach, 2010).

Our review aims to address existing gaps in the student engagement literature and seeks to determine whether student engagement models should be expanded to include technology. The review also addresses some of the organizational barriers to technology integration (e.g., faculty uncertainty and skepticism about technology) by providing a comprehensive account of the research evidence regarding how technology influences student engagement. One limitation of the literature, however, is the lack of detail regarding how teaching and learning practices were used to select and integrate technology into learning. For example, the methodology section of many studies does not include a pedagogical justification for why a particular technology was used or details about the design of the learning activity itself. Therefore, it often is unclear how teaching and learning practices may have affected student engagement levels. We revisit this issue in more detail at the end of this paper in our discussions of areas for future research and recommendations for practice. We initiated our literature review by conducting a broad search for articles published within the past 5 years, using the key words *technology* and *higher education*, in Google Scholar and the following research databases: *Academic Search Complete, Communication & Mass Media Complete, Computers & Applied Sciences Complete, Education Research Complete, ERIC, PsycARTICLES, and PsycINFO.* Our initial search revealed themes regarding which technologies were most prevalent in the literature (e.g., social networking, digital games), which then lead to several, more targeted searches of the same databases using specific keywords such as *Facebook* and *student engagement.* After both broad and targeted searches, we identified five technologies (web-conferencing software, blogs, wikis, social networking sites, and digital games) to include in our review.

We chose to focus on technologies for which there were multiple studies published, allowing us to identify areas of convergence and divergence in the literature and draw conclusions about positive and negative effects on student engagement. In total, we identified 69 articles relevant to our review, with 36 pertaining to social networking sites (21 for *Facebook* and 15 for *Twitter*), 14 pertaining to digital games, seven pertaining to wikis, and six pertaining to blogs and web-conferencing software respectively. Articles were categorized according to their influence on specific types of student engagement, which will be described in more detail below. In some instances, one article pertained to multiple types of engagement. In the sections that follow, we will provide an overview of student engagement, including an explanation of common definitions and indicators of engagement, followed by a synthesis of how each type of technology influences student engagement. Finally, we will discuss areas for future research and make recommendations for practice.

Student engagement

Interest in student engagement began over 70 years ago with Ralph Tyler's research on the relationship between time spent on coursework and learning (Axelson & Flick, 2011; Kuh, 2009). Since then, the study of student engagement has evolved and expanded considerably, through the seminal works of Pace (1980; 1984) and Astin (1984) about how quantity and quality of student effort affect learning and many more recent studies on the environmental conditions and individual dispositions that contribute to student engagement (Bakker, Vergel, & Kuntze, 2015; Gilboy, Heinerichs, & Pazzaglia, 2015; Martin, Goldwasser, & Galentino, 2017; Pellas, 2014). Perhaps the most well-known resource on student engagement is the National Survey of Student Engagement (NSSE), an instrument designed to assess student participation in various educational activities (Kuh, 2009). The NSSE and other engagement instruments like it have been used in many studies that link student engagement to positive student outcomes such as higher grades, retention, persistence, and completion (Leach, 2016; McClenney, Marti, & Adkins, 2012; Trowler & Trowler, 2010), further convincing universities that student engagement is an important factor in the teaching and learning process. However, despite the increased interest in student engagement, its meaning is generally not well understood or agreed upon.

Student engagement is a broad and complex phenomenon for which there are many definitions grounded in psychological, social, and/or cultural perspectives (Fredricks et al., 1994; Wimpenny & Savin-Baden, 2013; Zepke & Leach, 2010). Review of definitions revealed that student engagement is defined in two ways. One set of definitions refer to student engagement as a desired outcome reflective of a student's thoughts, feelings, and behaviors about learning. For example, Kahu (2013) defines student engagement as an "individual psychological state" that includes a student's affect, cognition, and behavior (p. 764). Other definitions focus primarily on student behavior, suggesting that engagement is the "extent to which students are engaging in activities that higher education research has shown to be linked with high-quality learning outcomes" (Krause & Coates, 2008, p. 493) or the "quality of effort and involvement in productive learning activities" (Kuh, 2009, p. 6). Another set of definitions refer to student engagement as a process involving both the student and the university. For example, Trowler (2010) defined student engagement as "the interaction between the time, effort and other relevant resources invested by both students and their institutions intended to optimize the student experience and enhance the learning outcomes and development of students and the performance, and reputation of the institution" (p. 2). Similarly, the NSSE website indicates that student engagement is "the amount of time and effort students put into their studies and other educationally purposeful activities" as well as "how the institution deploys its resources and organizes the curriculum and other learning opportunities to get students to participate in activities that decades of research studies show are linked to student learning" (Center for Postsecondary Research, 2017, para. 1).

Many existing models of student engagement reflect the latter set of definitions, depicting engagement as a complex, psychosocial process involving both student and university characteristics. Such models organize the engagement process into three areas: factors that influence student engagement (e.g., institutional culture, curriculum, and teaching practices), indicators of student engagement (e.g., interest in learning, interaction with instructors and peers, and meaningful processing of information), and outcomes of student engagement (e.g., academic achievement, retention, and personal growth) (Kahu, 2013; Lam et al., 2012; Nora et al., 2005). In this review, we examine the literature to determine whether technology influences student engagement. In addition, we will use Fredricks et al. (2004) typology of student engagement to organize and present research findings, which suggests that there are three types of engagement (behavioral, emotional, and cognitive). The typology is useful because it is broad in scope, encompassing different types of engagement that capture a range of student experiences, rather than narrower typologies that offer specific or prescriptive conceptualizations of student engagement. In addition, this typology is student-centered, focusing exclusively on student-focused indicators rather than combining student indicators with confounding variables, such as faculty behavior, curriculum design, and campus environment (Coates, 2008; Kuh, 2009). While such variables are important in the discussion of student engagement, perhaps as factors that may influence engagement, they are not true indicators of student engagement. Using the typology as a guide, we examined recent student engagement research, models, and measures to gain a better understanding of how behavioral, emotional, and cognitive student engagement are conceptualized and to identify specific indicators that correspond with each type of engagement, as shown in Fig. 1.

Behavioral engagement is the degree to which students are actively involved in learning activities (Fredricks et al., 2004; Kahu, 2013; Zepke, 2014). Indicators of behavioral engagement include time and effort spent participating in learning activities (Coates, 2008; Fredricks et al., 2004; Kahu, 2013; Kuh, 2009; Lam et al., 2012; Lester, 2013; Trowler, 2010) and interaction with peers, faculty, and staff (Coates, 2008; Kahu, 2013;

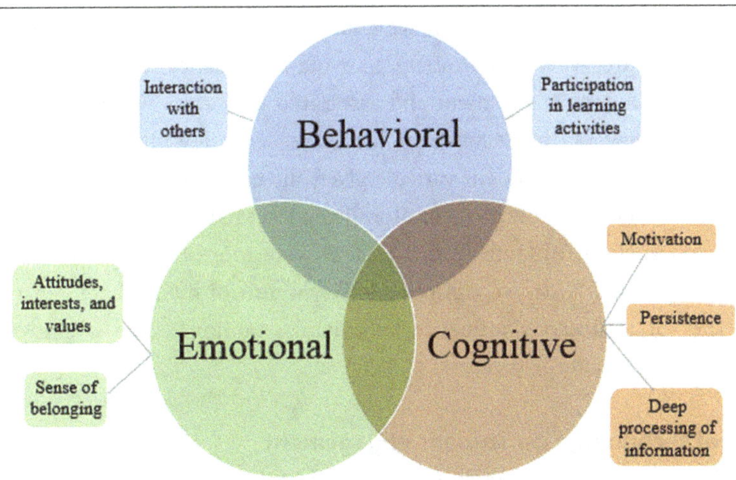

Fig. 1 Conceptual framework of types and indicators of student engagement

Kuh, 2009; Bryson & Hand, 2007; Wimpenny & Savin-Baden, 2013: Zepke & Leach, 2010). Indicators of behavioral engagement reflect observable student actions and most closely align with Pace (1980) and Astin's (1984) original conceptualizations of student engagement as quantity and quality of effort towards learning. Emotional engagement is students' affective reactions to learning (Fredricks et al., 2004; Lester, 2013; Trowler, 2010). Indicators of emotional engagement include attitudes, interests, and values towards learning (Fredricks et al., 2004; Kahu, 2013; Lester, 2013; Trowler, 2010; Wimpenny & Savin-Baden, 2013; Witkowski & Cornell, 2015) and a perceived sense of belonging within a learning community (Fredricks et al., 2004; Kahu, 2013; Lester, 2013; Trowler, 2010; Wimpenny & Savin-Baden, 2013). Emotional engagement often is assessed using self-report measures (Fredricks et al., 2004) and provides insight into how students feel about a particular topic, delivery method, or instructor. Finally, cognitive engagement is the degree to which students invest in learning and expend mental effort to comprehend and master content (Fredricks et al., 2004; Lester, 2013). Indicators of cognitive engagement include: motivation to learn (Lester, 2013; Richardson & Newby, 2006; Zepke & Leach, 2010); persistence to overcome academic challenges and meet/exceed requirements (Fredricks et al., 2004; Kuh, 2009; Trowler, 2010); and deep processing of information (Fredricks et al., 2004; Kahu, 2013; Lam et al., 2012; Richardson & Newby, 2006) through critical thinking (Coates, 2008; Witkowski & Cornell, 2015), self-regulation (e.g., set goals, plan, organize study effort, and monitor learning; Fredricks et al., 2004; Lester, 2013), and the active construction of knowledge (Coates, 2008; Kuh, 2009). While cognitive engagement includes motivational aspects, much of the literature focuses on how students use active learning and higher-order thinking, in some form, to achieve content mastery. For example, there is significant emphasis on the importance of deep learning, which involves analyzing new learning in relation previous knowledge, compared to surface learning, which is limited to memorization, recall, and rehearsal (Fredricks et al., 2004; Kahu, 2013; Lam et al., 2012).

While each type of engagement has distinct features, there is some overlap across cognitive, behavioral, and emotional domains. In instances where an indicator could correspond with more than one type of engagement, we chose to match the indicator to the type of engagement that most closely aligned, based on our review of the engagement literature and our interpretation of the indicators. Similarly, there is also some overlap among indicators. As a result, we combined and subsumed similar indicators found in the literature, where appropriate, to avoid redundancy. Achieving an in-depth understanding of student engagement and associated indicators was an important precursor to our review of the technology literature. Very few articles used the term *student engagement* as a dependent variable given the concept is so broad and multidimensional. We found that specific indicators (e.g., interaction, sense of belonging, and knowledge construction) of student engagement were more common in the literature as dependent variables. Next, we will provide a synthesis of the findings regarding how different types of technology influence behavioral, emotional, and cognitive student engagement and associated indicators.

Influence of technology on student engagement

We identified five technologies post-literature search (i.e., web-conferencing, blogs, wikis, social networking sites, and digital games) to include in our review, based on frequency in which they appeared in the literature over the past 5 years. One commonality among these technologies is their potential value in supporting a constructivist approach to learning, characterized by the active discovery of knowledge through reflection of experiences with one's environment, the connection of new knowledge to prior knowledge, and interaction with others (Boghossian, 2006; Clements, 2015). Another commonality is that most of the technologies, except perhaps for digital games, are designed primarily to promote interaction and collaboration with others. Our search yielded very few studies on how informational technologies, such as video lectures and podcasts, influence student engagement. Therefore, these technologies are notably absent from our review. Unlike the technologies we identified earlier, informational technologies reflect a behaviorist approach to learning in which students are passive recipients of knowledge that is transmitted from an expert (Boghossian, 2006). The lack of recent research on how informational technologies affect student engagement may be due to the increasing shift from instructor-centered, behaviorist approaches to student-centered, constructivist approaches within higher education (Haggis, 2009; Wright, 2011) along with the ubiquity of web 2.0 technologies.

Web-conferencing

Web-conferencing software provides a virtual meeting space where users login simultaneously and communicate about a given topic. While each software application is unique, many share similar features such as audio, video, or instant messaging options for real-time communication; screen sharing, whiteboards, and digital pens for presentations and demonstrations; polls and quizzes for gauging comprehension or eliciting feedback; and breakout rooms for small group work (Bower, 2011; Hudson, Knight, & Collins, 2012; Martin, Parker, & Deale, 2012; McBrien, Jones, & Cheng, 2009). Of the technologies included in this literature review, web-conferencing software most closely mimics the face-to-face classroom environment, providing a space where instructors and students can hear and see each other in real-time as typical classroom activities (i.e., delivering lectures, discussing course content, asking/answering questions) are carried out (Francescucci & Foster, 2013; Hudson et al., 2012). Studies on web-conferencing software deployed *Adobe Connect, Cisco WebEx, Horizon Wimba,* or *Blackboard Collaborate* and made use of multiple features, such as screen sharing, instant messaging, polling, and break out rooms. In addition, most of the studies integrated web-conferencing software into courses on a voluntary basis to supplement traditional instructional methods (Andrew, Maslin-Prothero, & Ewens, 2015; Armstrong & Thornton, 2012; Francescucci & Foster, 2013; Hudson et al., 2012; Martin et al., 2012; Wdowik, 2014). Existing studies on web-conferencing pertain to all three types of student engagement.

Studies on web-conferencing and behavioral engagement reveal mixed findings. For example, voluntary attendance in web-conferencing sessions ranged from 54 to 57% (Andrew et al., 2015; Armstrong & Thornton, 2012) and, in a comparison between a blended course with regular web-conferencing sessions and a traditional, face-to-face course, researchers found no significant difference in student attendance in courses. However, students in the blended course reported higher levels of class participation compared to students in the face-to-face course (Francescucci & Foster, 2013). These findings suggest while web-conferencing may not boost attendance, especially if voluntary, it may offer more opportunities for class participation, perhaps through the use of communication channels typically not available in a traditional, face-to-face course (e.g., instant messaging, anonymous polling). Studies on web-conferencing and interaction, another behavioral indicator, support this assertion. For example, researchers found that students use various features of web-conferencing software (e.g., polling, instant message, break-out rooms) to interact with peers and the instructor by asking questions, expressing opinions and ideas, sharing resources, and discussing academic content (Andrew et al., 2015; Armstrong & Thornton, 2012; Hudson et al., 2012; Martin et al., 2012; Wdowik, 2014).

Studies on web-conferencing and cognitive engagement are more conclusive than those for behavioral engagement, although are fewer in number. Findings suggest that students who participated in web-conferencing demonstrated critical reflection and enhanced learning through interactions with others (Armstrong & Thornton, 2012), higher-order thinking (e.g., problem-solving, synthesis, evaluation) in response to challenging assignments (Wdowik, 2014), and motivation to learn, particularly when using polling features (Hudson et al., 2012). There is only one study examining how web-conferencing affects emotional engagement, although it is positive suggesting that students who participated in web-conferences had higher levels of interest in course content than those who did not (Francescucci & Foster, 2013). One possible reason for the positive cognitive and emotional engagement findings may be that web-conferencing software provides many features that promote active learning. For example, whiteboards and breakout rooms provide opportunities for real-time, collaborative problem-solving activities and discussions. However, additional studies are needed to isolate and compare specific web-conferencing features to determine which have the greatest effect on student engagement.

Blogs

A blog, which is short for Weblog, is a collection of personal journal entries, published online and presented chronologically, to which readers (or subscribers) may respond by providing additional commentary or feedback. In order to create a blog, one must compose content for an entry, which may include text, hyperlinks, graphics, audio, or video, publish the content online using a blogging application, and alert subscribers that new content is posted. Blogs may be informal and personal in nature or may serve as formal commentary in a specific genre, such as in politics or education (Coghlan et al., 2007). Fortunately, many blog applications are free, and many learning management systems (LMSs) offer a blogging feature that is seamlessly integrated into the online classroom. The ease of blogging has attracted attention from educators, who currently use blogs as an instructional tool for the expression of ideas, opinions, and experiences and for promoting dialogue on a wide range of academic topics (Garrity, Jones, VanderZwan, de la Rocha, & Epstein, 2014; Wang, 2008).

Studies on blogs show consistently positive findings for many of the behavioral and emotional engagement indicators. For example, students reported that blogs promoted interaction with others, through greater communication and information sharing with peers (Chu, Chan, & Tiwari, 2012; Ivala & Gachago, 2012; Mansouri & Piki, 2016), and analyses of blog posts show evidence of students elaborating on one another's ideas and sharing experiences and conceptions of course content (Sharma & Tietjen, 2016). Blogs also contribute to emotional engagement by providing students with opportunities to express their feelings about learning and by encouraging positive attitudes about learning (Dos & Demir, 2013; Chu et al., 2012; Yang & Chang, 2012). For example, Dos and Demir (2013) found that students expressed prejudices and fears about specific course topics in their blog posts. In addition, Yang and Chang (2012) found that interactive blogging, where comment features were enabled, lead to more positive attitudes about course content and peers compared to solitary blogging, where comment features were disabled.

The literature on blogs and cognitive engagement is less consistent. Some studies suggest that blogs may help students engage in active learning, problem-solving, and reflection (Chawinga, 2017; Chu et al., 2012; Ivala & Gachago, 2012; Mansouri & Piki, 2016), while other studies suggest that students' blog posts show very little evidence of higher-order thinking (Dos & Demir, 2013; Sharma & Tietjen, 2016). The inconsistency in findings may be due to the wording of blog instructions. Students may not necessarily demonstrate or engage in deep processing of information unless explicitly instructed to do so. Unfortunately, it is difficult to determine whether the wording of blog assignments contributed to the mixed results because many of the studies did not provide assignment details. However, studies pertaining to other technologies suggest that assignment wording that lacks specificity or requires low-level thinking can have detrimental effects on student engagement outcomes (Hou, Wang, Lin, & Chang, 2015; Prestridge, 2014). Therefore, blog assignments that are vague or require only low-level thinking may have adverse effects on cognitive engagement.

Wikis

A wiki is a web page that can be edited by multiple users at once (Nakamaru, 2012). Wikis have gained popularity in educational settings as a viable tool for group projects where group members can work collaboratively to develop content (i.e., writings, hyperlinks, images, graphics, media) and keep track of revisions through an extensive versioning system (Roussinos & Jimoyiannis, 2013). Most studies on wikis pertain to behavioral engagement, with far fewer studies on cognitive engagement and none on emotional engagement. Studies pertaining to behavioral engagement reveal mixed results, with some showing very little enduring participation in wikis beyond the first few weeks of the course (Nakamaru, 2012; Salaber, 2014) and another showing active participation, as seen in high numbers of posts and edits (Roussinos & Jimoyiannis, 2013). The most notable difference between these studies is the presence of grading, which may account for the inconsistencies in findings. For example, in studies where participation was low, wikis were ungraded, suggesting that students may need extra motivation and encouragement to use wikis (Nakamaru, 2012; Salaber, 2014). Findings regarding the use of wikis for promoting interaction are also inconsistent. In some studies, students reported that wikis were useful for interaction, teamwork, collaboration, and group networking (Camacho, Carrión, Chayah, & Campos, 2016; Martínez, Medina, Albalat, & Rubió, 2013; Morely, 2012; Calabretto & Rao, 2011) and researchers found evidence of substantial collaboration among students (e.g., sharing ideas, opinions, and points of view) in wiki activity (Hewege & Perera, 2013); however, Miller, Norris, and Bookstaver (2012) found that only 58% of students reported that wikis promoted collegiality among peers. The findings in the latter study were unexpected and may be due to design flaws in the wiki assignments. For example, the authors noted that wiki assignments were not explicitly referred to in face-to-face classes; therefore, this disconnect may have prevented students from building on interactive momentum achieved during out-of-class wiki assignments (Miller et al., 2012).

Studies regarding cognitive engagement are limited in number but more consistent than those concerning behavioral engagement, suggesting that wikis promote high levels of knowledge construction (i.e., evaluation of arguments, the integration of multiple viewpoints, new understanding of course topics; Hewege & Perera, 2013), and are useful for reflection, reinforcing course content, and applying academic skills (Miller et al., 2012). Overall, there is mixed support for the use of wikis to promote behavioral engagement, although making wiki assignments mandatory and explicitly referring to wikis in class may help bolster participation and interaction. In addition, there is some support for using wikis to promote cognitive engagement, but additional studies are needed to confirm and expand on findings as well as explore the effect of wikis on emotional engagement.

Social networking sites

Social networking is "the practice of expanding knowledge by making connections with individuals of similar interests" (Gunawardena et al., 2009, p. 4). Social networking sites, such as *Facebook, Twitter, Instagram, and LinkedIn,* allow users to create and share digital content publicly or with others to whom they are connected and communicate privately through messaging features. Two of the most popular social networking sites in the educational literature are *Facebook* and *Twitter* (Camus, Hurt, Larson, & Prevost, 2016; Manca & Ranieri, 2013), which is consistent with recent statistics suggesting that both sites also are exceedingly popular among the general population (Greenwood, Perrin, & Duggan, 2016). In the sections that follow, we examine how both *Facebook* and *Twitter* influence different types of student engagement.

Facebook

Facebook is a web-based service that allows users to create a public or private profile and invite others to connect. Users may build social, academic, and professional connections by posting messages in various media formats (i.e., text, pictures, videos) and commenting on, liking, and reacting to others' messages (Bowman & Akcaoglu, 2014; Maben, Edwards, & Malone, 2014; Hou et al., 2015). Within an educational context, *Facebook* has often been used as a supplementary instructional tool to lectures or LMSs to support class discussions or develop, deliver, and share academic content and resources. Many instructors have opted to create private *Facebook* groups, offering an added layer of security and privacy because groups are not accessible to strangers (Bahati, 2015; Bowman & Akcaoglu, 2014; Clements, 2015; Dougherty & Andercheck, 2014; Esteves, 2012; Shraim, 2014; Maben et al., 2014; Manca & Ranieri, 2013; Naghdipour & Eldridge, 2016; Rambe, 2012). The majority of studies on *Facebook* address behavioral indicators of student engagement, with far fewer focusing on emotional or cognitive engagement.

Studies that examine the influence of *Facebook* on behavioral engagement focus both on participation in learning activities and interaction with peers and instructors. In most studies, *Facebook* activities were voluntary and participation rates ranged from 16 to 95%, with an average of rate of 47% (Bahati, 2015; Bowman & Akcaoglu, 2014; Dougherty & Andercheck, 2014; Fagioli, Rios-Aguilar, & Deil-Amen, 2015; Rambe, 2012; Staines & Lauchs, 2013). Participation was assessed by tracking how many students joined course- or university-specific *Facebook* groups (Bahati, 2015; Bowman & Akcaoglu, 2014; Fagioli et al., 2015), visited or followed course-specific *Facebook* pages (DiVall & Kirwin, 2012; Staines & Lauchs, 2013), or posted at least once in a course-specific *Facebook* page (Rambe, 2012). The lowest levels of participation (16%) arose from a study where community college students were invited to use the *Schools App,* a free application that connects students to their university's private *Facebook* community. While the authors acknowledged that building an online community of college students is difficult (Fagioli et al., 2015), downloading the *Schools App* may have been a deterrent to widespread participation. In addition, use of the app was not tied to any specific courses or assignments; therefore, students may have lacked adequate incentive to use it. The highest level of participation (95%) in the literature arose from a study in which the instructor created a *Facebook* page where students could find or post study tips or ask questions. Followership to the page was highest around exams, when students likely had stronger motivations to access study tips and ask the instructor questions (DiVall & Kirwin, 2012). The wide range of participation in *Facebook* activities suggests that some students may be intrinsically motivated to participate, while other students may need some external encouragement. For example, Bahati (2015) found that when students assumed that a course-specific *Facebook* was voluntary, only 23% participated, but when the instructor confirmed that the *Facebook* group was, in fact, mandatory, the level of participation rose to 94%.

While voluntary participation in *Facebook* activities may be lower than desired or expected (Dyson, Vickers, Turtle, Cowan, & Tassone, 2015; Fagioli et al., 2015; Naghdipour & Eldridge, 2016; Rambe, 2012), students seem to have a clear preference for *Facebook* compared to other instructional tools (Clements, 2015; DiVall & Kirwin, 2012; Hurt et al., 2012; Hou et al., 2015; Kent, 2013). For example, in one study where an instructor shared course-related information in a *Facebook* group, in the LMS, and through email, the level of participation in the *Facebook* group was ten times higher than in email or the LMS (Clements, 2015). In other studies, class discussions held in *Facebook* resulted in greater levels of participation and dialogue than class discussions held in LMS discussion forums (Camus et al., 2016; Hurt et al., 2012; Kent, 2013). Researchers found that preference for *Facebook* over the university's LMS is due to perceptions that the LMS is outdated and unorganized and reports that *Facebook* is more familiar, convenient, and accessible given that many students already visit the social networking site multiple times per day (Clements, 2015; Dougherty & Andercheck, 2014; Hurt et al., 2012; Kent, 2013). In addition, students report that *Facebook* helps them stay engaged in learning through collaboration and interaction with both peers and instructors (Bahati, 2015; Shraim, 2014), which is evident in *Facebook* posts where students collaborated to study for exams, consulted on technical and theoretical problem solving, discussed course content, exchanged learning resources, and expressed opinions as well as academic successes and challenges

(Bowman & Akcaoglu, 2014; Dougherty & Andercheck, 2014; Esteves, 2012 Ivala & Gachago, 2012; Maben et al., 2014; Rambe, 2012; van Beynen & Swenson, 2016).

There is far less evidence in the literature about the use of *Facebook* for emotional and cognitive engagement. In terms of emotional engagement, studies suggest that students feel positively about being part of a course-specific *Facebook* group and that *Facebook* is useful for expressing feelings about learning and concerns for peers, through features such as the "like" button and emoticons (Bowman & Akcaoglu, 2014; Dougherty & Andercheck, 2014; Naghdipour & Eldridge, 2016). In addition, being involved in a course-specific *Facebook* group was positively related to students' sense of belonging in the course (Dougherty & Andercheck, 2014). The research on cognitive engagement is less conclusive, with some studies suggesting that *Facebook* participation is related to academic persistence (Fagioli et al., 2015) and self-regulation (Dougherty & Andercheck, 2014) while other studies show low levels of knowledge construction in *Facebook* posts (Hou et al., 2015), particularly when compared to discussions held in the LMS. One possible reason may be because the LMS is associated with formal, academic interactions while *Facebook* is associated with informal, social interactions (Camus et al., 2016). While additional research is needed to confirm the efficacy of *Facebook* for promoting cognitive engagement, studies suggest that *Facebook* may be a viable tool for increasing specific behavioral and emotional engagement indicators, such as interactions with others and a sense of belonging within a learning community.

Twitter

Twitter is a web-based service where subscribers can post short messages, called tweets, in real-time that are no longer than 140 characters in length. Tweets may contain hyperlinks to other websites, images, graphics, and/or videos and may be tagged by topic using the hashtag symbol before the designated label (e.g., #elearning). *Twitter* subscribers may "follow" other users and gain access to their tweets and also may "retweet" messages that have already been posted (Hennessy, Kirkpatrick, Smith, & Border, 2016; Osgerby & Rush, 2015; Prestridge, 2014; West, Moore, & Barry, 2015; Tiernan, 2014;). Instructors may use *Twitter* to post updates about the course, clarify expectations, direct students to additional learning materials, and encourage students to discuss course content (Bista, 2015; Williams & Whiting, 2016). Several of the studies on the use of *Twitter* included broad, all-encompassing measures of student engagement and produced mixed findings. For example, some studies suggest that *Twitter* increases student engagement (Evans, 2014; Gagnon, 2015; Junco, Heibergert, & Loken, 2011) while other studies suggest that *Twitter* has little to no influence on student engagement (Junco, Elavsky, & Heiberger, 2013; McKay, Sanko, Shekhter, & Birnbach, 2014). In both studies suggesting little to no influence on student engagement, *Twitter* use was voluntary and in one of the studies faculty involvement in *Twitter* was low, which may account for the negative findings (Junco et al., 2013; McKay et al., 2014). Conversely, in the studies that show positive findings, *Twitter* use was mandatory and often directly integrated with required assignments (Evans, 2014; Gagnon, 2015; Junco et al., 2011). Therefore, making *Twitter* use mandatory, increasing faculty involvement in *Twitter,* and integrating *Twitter* into assignments may help to increase student engagement.

Studies pertaining to specific behavioral student engagement indicators also reveal mixed findings. For example, in studies where course-related *Twitter* use was voluntary,

45-91% of students reported using *Twitter* during the term (Hennessy et al., 2016; Junco et al., 2013; Ross, Banow, & Yu, 2015; Tiernan, 2014; Williams & Whiting, 2016), but only 30-36% reported making contributions to the course-specific *Twitter* page (Hennessy et al., 2016; Tiernan, 2014; Ross et al., 2015; Williams & Whiting, 2016). The study that reported a 91% participation rate was unique because the course-specific *Twitter* page was accessible via a public link. Therefore, students who chose only to view the content (58%), rather than contribute to the page, did not have to create a *Twitter* account (Hennessy et al., 2016). The convenience of not having to create an account may be one reason for much higher participation rates. In terms of low participation rates, a lack of literacy, familiarity, and interest in *Twitter*, as well as a preference for *Facebook*, are cited as contributing factors (Bista, 2015; McKay et al., 2014; Mysko & Delgaty, 2015; Osgerby & Rush, 2015; Tiernan, 2014). However, when the use of *Twitter* was required and integrated into class discussions, the participation rate was 100% (Gagnon, 2015). Similarly, 46% of students in one study indicated that they would have been more motivated to participate in *Twitter* activities if they were graded (Osgerby & Rush, 2015), again confirming the power of extrinsic motivating factors.

Studies also show mixed results for the use of *Twitter* to promote interactions with peers and instructors. Researchers found that when instructors used *Twitter* to post updates about the course, ask and answer questions, and encourage students to tweet about course content, there was evidence of student-student and student-instructor interactions in tweets (Hennessy et al., 2016; Tiernan, 2014). Some students echoed these findings, suggesting that *Twitter* is useful for sharing ideas and resources, discussing course content, asking the instructor questions, and networking (Chawinga, 2017; Evans, 2014; Gagnon, 2015; Hennessy et al., 2016; Mysko & Delgaty, 2015; West et al., 2015) and is preferable over speaking aloud in class because it is more comfortable, less threatening, and more concise due to the 140 character limit (Gagnon, 2015; Mysko & Delgaty, 2015; Tiernan, 2014). Conversely, other students reported that *Twitter* was not useful for improving interaction because they viewed it predominately for social, rather than academic, interactions and they found the 140 character limit to be frustrating and restrictive. A theme among the latter studies was that a large proportion of the sample had never used *Twitter* before (Bista, 2015; McKay et al., 2014; Osgerby & Rush, 2015), which may have contributed to negative perceptions.

The literature on the use of *Twitter* for cognitive and emotional engagement is minimal but nonetheless promising in terms of promoting knowledge gains, the practical application of content, and a sense of belonging among users. For example, using *Twitter* to respond to questions that arose in lectures and tweet about course content throughout the term is associated with increased understanding of course content and application of knowledge (Kim et al., 2015; Tiernan, 2014; West et al., 2015). While the underlying mechanisms pertaining to why *Twitter* promotes an understanding of content and application of knowledge are not entirely clear, Tiernan (2014) suggests that one possible reason may be that *Twitter* helps to break down communication barriers, encouraging shy or timid students to participate in discussions that ultimately are richer in dialogue and debate. In terms of emotional engagement, students who participated in a large, class-specific *Twitter* page were more likely to feel a sense of community and belonging compared to those who did not participate because they could more easily find support from and share resources with other *Twitter* users

(Ross et al., 2015). Despite the positive findings about the use of *Twitter* for cognitive and emotional engagement, more studies are needed to confirm existing results regarding behavioral engagement and target additional engagement indicators such as motivation, persistence, and attitudes, interests, and values about learning. In addition, given the strong negative perceptions of *Twitter* that still exist, additional studies are needed to confirm *Twitter*'s efficacy for promoting different types of behavioral engagement among both novice and experienced *Twitter* users, particularly when compared to more familiar tools such as *Facebook* or LMS discussion forums.

Digital games

Digital games are "applications using the characteristics of video and computer games to create engaging and immersive learning experiences for delivery of specified learning goals, outcomes and experiences" (de Freitas, 2006, p. 9). Digital games often serve the dual purpose of promoting the achievement of learning outcomes while making learning fun by providing simulations of real-world scenarios as well as role play, problem-solving, and drill and repeat activities (Boyle et al., 2016; Connolly, Boyle, MacArthur, Hainey, & Boyle, 2012; Scarlet & Ampolos, 2013; Whitton, 2011). In addition, gamified elements, such as digital badges and leaderboards, may be integrated into instruction to provide additional motivation for completing assigned readings and other learning activities (Armier, Shepherd, & Skrabut, 2016; Hew, Huang, Chu, & Chiu, 2016). The pedagogical benefits of digital games are somewhat distinct from the other technologies addressed in this review, which are designed primarily for social interaction. While digital games may be played in teams or allow one player to compete against another, the focus of their design often is on providing opportunities for students to interact with academic content in a virtual environment through decision-making, problem-solving, and reward mechanisms. For example, a digital game may require students to adopt a role as CEO in a computer-simulated business environment, make decisions about a series of organizational issues, and respond to the consequences of those decisions. In this example and others, digital games use adaptive learning principles, where the learning environment is re-configured or modified in response to the actions and needs of students (Bower, 2016). Most of the studies on digital games focused on cognitive and emotional indicators of student engagement, in contrast to the previous technologies addressed in this review which primarily focused on behavioral indicators of engagement.

Existing studies provide support for the influence of digital games on cognitive engagement, through achieving a greater understanding of course content and demonstrating higher-order thinking skills (Beckem & Watkins, 2012; Farley, 2013; Ke, Xie, & Xie, 2016; Marriott, Tan, & Marriott, 2015), particularly when compared to traditional instructional methods, such as giving lectures or assigning textbook readings (Lu, Hallinger, & Showanasai, 2014; Siddique, Ling, Roberson, Xu, & Geng, 2013; Zimmermann, 2013). For example, in a study comparing courses that offered computer simulations of business challenges (e.g, implementing a new information technology system, managing a startup company, and managing a brand of medicine in a simulated market environment) and courses that did not, students in simulation-based courses reported higher levels of action-directed learning (i.e., connecting theory to practice in a business context) than students in traditional, non-simulation-based courses (Lu et al., 2014). Similarly, engineering students who participated in a car simulator game, which was designed to help students apply and reinforce the knowledge gained from lectures, demonstrated higher levels of critical thinking (i.e., analysis, evaluation) on a quiz than students who only attended lectures (Siddique et al., 2013).

Motivation is another cognitive engagement indicator that is linked to digital games (Armier et al., 2016; Chang & Wei, 2016; Dichev & Dicheva, 2017; Grimley, Green, Nilsen, & Thompson, 2012; Hew et al., 2016; Ibáñez, Di-Serio, & Delgado-Kloos, 2014; Ke et al., 2016; Liu, Cheng, & Huang, 2011; Nadolny & Halabi, 2016). Researchers found that incorporating gamified elements into courses, such as giving students digital rewards (e.g., redeemable points, trophies, and badges) for participating in learning activities or creating competition through the use of leaderboards where students can see how they rank against other students positively affects student motivation to complete learning tasks (Armier et al., 2016; Chang & Wei, 2016; Hew et al., 2016; Nadolny & Halabi, 2016). In addition, students who participated in gamified elements, such as trying to earn digital badges, were more motivated to complete particularly difficult learning activities (Hew et al., 2016) and showed persistence in exceeding learning requirements (Ibáñez et al., 2014). Research on emotional engagement may help to explain these findings. Studies suggest that digital games positively affect student attitudes about learning, evident in student reports that games are fun, interesting, and enjoyable (Beckem & Watkins, 2012; Farley, 2013; Grimley et al., 2012; Hew et al., 2016; Liu et al., 2011; Zimmermann, 2013), which may account for higher levels of student motivation in courses that offered digital games.

Research on digital games and behavioral engagement is more limited, with only one study suggesting that games lead to greater participation in educational activities (Hew et al., 2016). Therefore, more research is needed to explore how digital games may influence behavioral engagement. In addition, research is needed to determine whether the underlying technology associated with digital games (e.g., computer-based simulations and virtual realities) produce positive engagement outcomes or whether common mechanisms associated with both digital and non-digital games (e.g., role play, rewards, and competition) account for those outcomes. For example, studies in which non-digital, face-to-face games were used also showed positive effects on student engagement (Antunes, Pacheco, & Giovanela, 2012; Auman, 2011; Coffey, Miller, & Feuerstein, 2011; Crocco, Offenholley, & Hernandez, 2016; Poole, Kemp, Williams, & Patterson, 2014; Scarlet & Ampolos, 2013); therefore, it is unclear if and how digitizing games contributes to student engagement.

Discussion and implications

Student engagement is linked to a number of academic outcomes, such as retention, grade point average, and graduation rates (Carini et al., 2006; Center for Postsecondary Research, 2016; Hu & McCormick, 2012). As a result, universities have shown a strong interest in how to increase student engagement, particularly given rising external pressures to improve learning outcomes and prepare students for academic success (Axelson & Flick, 2011; Kuh, 2009). There are various models of student engagement that identify factors that influence student engagement (Kahu, 2013; Lam et al., 2012; Nora et al., 2005; Wimpenny & Savin-Baden, 2013; Zepke & Leach, 2010); however, none include the overt role of technology despite the growing trend and student demands to integrate technology into the learning experience (Amirault, 2012; Cook & Sonnenberg, 2014; Revere & Kovach, 2011; Sun & Chen, 2016; Westera, 2015). Therefore, the primary purpose of our literature review was to explore whether technology influences student engagement. The secondary purpose was to address skepticism and uncertainty about pedagogical benefits of technology (Ashrafzadeh & Sayadian, 2015; Kopcha et al., 2016; Reid, 2014) by reviewing the literature regarding the efficacy of specific technologies (i.e., web-conferencing software, blogs, wikis, social networking sites, and digital games) for promoting student engagement and offering recommendations for effective implementation, which are included at the end of this paper. In the sections that follow, we provide an overview of the findings, an explanation of existing methodological limitations and areas for future research, and a list of best practices for integrating the technologies we reviewed into the teaching and learning process.

Summary of findings

Findings from our literature review provide preliminary support for including technology as a factor that influences student engagement in existing models (Table 1). One overarching theme is that most of the technologies we reviewed had a positive influence on multiple indicators of student engagement, which may lead to a larger return on investment in terms of learning outcomes. For example, digital games influence all three types of student engagement and six of the seven indicators we identified, surpassing the other technologies in this review. There were several key differences in the design and pedagogical use between digital games and other technologies that may explain these findings. First, digital games were designed to provide authentic learning contexts in which students could practice skills and apply learning (Beckem & Watkins, 2012; Farley, 2013; Grimley et al., 2012; Ke et al., 2016; Liu et al., 2011; Lu et al., 2014; Marriott et al., 2015; Siddique et al., 2013), which is consistent with experiential learning and adult learning theories. Experiential learning theory suggests that learning occurs through interaction with one's environment (Kolb, 2014) while adult learning theory suggests that adult learners want to be actively involved in the learning process and be able apply learning to real life situations and problems (Cercone, 2008). Second, students reported that digital games (and gamified elements) are fun, enjoyable, and

Table 1 Summary of Findings by Technology and Engagement Indicator

	Behavioral		Emotional		Cognitive		
	Participation	Interaction	Attitudes, interests, and values	Sense of belonging	Motivation	Persistence	Deep processing of information
Webconferencing	ϕ	√	x	0	x	0	x
Blogs	0	√	√	0	0	0	ϕ
Wikis	ϕ	ϕ	0	0	0	0	x
Facebook	ϕ	√	√	x	0	x	ϕ
Twitter	ϕ	ϕ	0	x	0	0	√
Games	x	0	√	x	√	x	√

√ = three or more articles in support of engagement indicator; x = less than two articles in support of engagement indicator; ϕ = mixed findings across two or more studies; 0 = no studies found interesting (Beckem & Watkins, 2012; Farley, 2013; Grimley et al., 2012; Hew et al., 2016; Liu et al., 2011; Zimmermann, 2013), feelings that are associated with a flow-like state where one is completely immersed in and engaged with the activity (Csikszentmihalyi, 1988; Weibel, Wissmath, Habegger, Steiner, & Groner, 2008). Third, digital games were closely integrated into the curriculum as required activities (Farley, 2013; Grimley et al., 2012, Ke et al., 2016; Liu et al., 2011; Marriott et al., 2015; Siddique et al., 2013) as opposed to wikis, *Facebook*, and *Twitter*, which were often voluntary and used to supplement lectures (Dougherty & Andercheck, 2014 Nakamaru, 2012; Prestridge, 2014; Rambe, 2012).

Web-conferencing software and *Facebook* also yielded the most positive findings, influencing four of the seven indicators of student engagement, compared to other collaborative technologies, such as blogs, wikis, and *Twitter*. Web-conferencing software was unique due to the sheer number of collaborative features it offers, providing multiple ways for students to actively engage with course content (screen sharing, whiteboards, digital pens) and interact with peers and the instructor (audio, video, text chats, breakout rooms) (Bower, 2011; Hudson et al., 2012; Martin et al., 2012; McBrien et al., 2009); this may account for the effects on multiple indicators of student engagement. Positive findings regarding *Facebook*'s influence on student engagement could be explained by a strong familiarity and preference for the social networking site (Clements, 2015; DiVall & Kirwin, 2012; Hurt et al., 2012; Hou et al., 2015; Kent, 2013; Manca & Ranieri, 2013), compared to *Twitter* which was less familiar or interesting to students (Bista, 2015; McKay et al., 2014; Mysko & Delgaty, 2015; Osgerby & Rush, 2015; Tiernan, 2014). Wikis had the lowest influence on student engagement, with mixed findings regarding behavioral engagement, limited, but conclusive findings, regarding one indicator of cognitive engagement (deep processing of information), and no studies pertaining to other indicators of cognitive engagement (motivation, persistence) or emotional engagement.

Another theme that arose was the prevalence of mixed findings across multiple technologies regarding behavioral engagement. Overall, the vast majority of studies addressed behavioral engagement, and we expected that technologies designed specifically for social interaction, such as web-conferencing, wikis, and social networking sites, would yield more conclusive findings. However, one possible reason for the mixed findings may be that the technologies were voluntary in many studies, resulting in lower than desired participation rates and missed opportunities for interaction (Armstrong & Thornton, 2012; Fagioli et al., 2015; Nakamaru, 2012; Rambe, 2012; Ross et al., 2015; Williams & Whiting, 2016), and mandatory in a few studies, yielding higher levels of participation and interaction (Bahati, 2015; Gagnon, 2015; Roussinos & Jimoyiannis, 2013). Another possible reason for the mixed findings is that measures of variables differed across studies. For example, in some studies participation meant that a student signed up for a *Twitter* account (Tiernan, 2014), used the *Twitter* account for class (Williams & Whiting, 2016), or viewed the course-specific *Twitter* page (Hennessy et al., 2016). The pedagogical uses of the technologies also varied considerably across studies, making it difficult to make comparisons. For example, *Facebook* was used in studies to share learning materials (Clements, 2015; Dyson et al., 2015), answer student questions about academic content or administrative issues (Rambe, 2012), prepare for upcoming exams and share study tips (Bowman & Akcaoglu, 2014; DiVall & Kirwin, 2012), complete group work (Hou et al., 2015; Staines & Lauchs, 2013), and discuss course content (Camus et al., 2016; Kent, 2013; Hurt et al., 2012). Finally, cognitive indicators (motivation and persistence) drew the fewest amount of studies, which suggests that research is needed to determine whether technologies affect these indicators.

Methodological limitations

While there appears to be preliminary support for the use of many of the technologies to promote student engagement, there are significant methodological limitations in the literature and, as a result, findings should be interpreted with caution. First, many studies used small sample sizes and were limited to one course, one degree level, and one university. Therefore, generalizability is limited. Second, very few studies used experimental or quasi-experimental designs; therefore, very little evidence exists to substantiate a cause and effect relationship between technologies and student engagement indicators. In addition, in many studies that did use experimental or quasi-experimental designs, participants were not randomized; rather, participants who volunteered to use a specific technology were compared to those who chose not to use the technology. As a result, there is a possibility that fundamental differences between users and non-users could have affected the engagement results. Furthermore, many of the studies did not isolate specific technological features (e.g, using only the breakout rooms for group work in web-conferencing software, rather than using the chat feature, screen sharing, and breakout rooms for group work). Using multiple features at once could have conflated student engagement results. Third, many studies relied on one source to measure technological and engagement variables (single source bias), such as self-report data (i.e., reported usage of technology and perceptions of student engagement), which may have affected the validity of the results. Fourth, many studies were conducted during a very brief timeframe, such as one academic term. As a result, positive student engagement findings may be attributed to a "novelty effect" (Dichev & Dicheva, 2017) associated with using a new technology. Finally, many studies lack adequate details about learning activities, raising questions about whether poor instructional design may have adversely affected results. For example, an instructor may intend to elicit higher-order thinking from students, but if learning activity instructions are written using low-level verbs, such as identify, describe, and summarize, students will be less likely to engage in higher-order thinking.

Areas for future research

The findings of our literature review suggest that the influence of technology on student engagement is still a developing area of knowledge that requires additional research to build on promising, but limited, evidence, clarify mixed findings, and address several gaps in the literature. As such, our recommendations for future areas of research are as follows:

1. Examine the effect of collaborative technologies (i.e., web-conferencing, blogs, wikis, social networking sites) on emotional and cognitive student engagement. There are significant gaps in the literature regarding whether these technologies affect attitudes, interests, and values about learning; a sense of belonging within a learning community; motivation to learn; and persistence to overcome academic challenges and meet or exceed requirements.

2. Clarify mixed findings, particularly regarding how web-conferencing software, wikis, and *Facebook* and *Twitter* affect participation in learning activities. Researchers should make considerable efforts to gain consensus or increase consistency on how participation is measured (e.g., visited *Facebook* group or contributed one post a week) in order to make meaningful comparisons and draw conclusions about the efficacy of various technologies for promoting behavioral engagement. In addition, further research is needed to clarify findings regarding how wikis and *Twitter* influence interaction and how blogs and *Facebook* influence deep processing of information. Future research studies should include justifications for the pedagogical use of specific technologies and detailed instructions for learning activities to minimize adverse findings from poor instructional design and to encourage replication.
3. Conduct longitudinal studies over several academic terms and across multiple academic disciplines, degree levels, and institutions to determine long-term effects of specific technologies on student engagement and to increase generalizability of findings. Also, future studies should take individual factors into account, such as gender, age, and prior experience with the technology. Studies suggest that a lack of prior experience or familiarity with *Twitter* was a barrier to *Twitter* use in educational settings (Bista, 2015, Mysko & Delgaty, 2015, Tiernan, 2014); therefore, future studies should take prior experience into account.
4. Compare student engagement outcomes between and among different technologies and non-technologies. For example, studies suggest that students prefer *Facebook* over *Twitter* (Bista, 2015; Osgerby & Rush, 2015), but there were no studies that compared these technologies for promoting student engagement. Also, studies are needed to isolate and compare different features within the same technology to determine which might be most effective for increasing engagement. Finally, studies on digital games (Beckem & Watkins, 2012; Grimley et al., 2012; Ke et al., 2016; Lu et al., 2014; Marriott et al., 2015; Siddique et al., 2013) and face-to-face games (Antunes et al., 2012; Auman, 2011; Coffey et al., 2011; Crocco et al., 2016; Poole et al., 2014; Scarlet & Ampolos, 2013) show similar, positive effects on student engagement, therefore, additional research is needed to determine the degree to which the delivery method (i.e.., digital versus face-to-face) accounts for positive gains in student engagement.
5. Determine whether other technologies not included in this review influence student engagement. *Facebook* and *Twitter* regularly appear in the literature regarding social networking, but it is unclear how other popular social networking sites, such as *LinkedIn, Instagram,* and *Flickr,* influence student engagement. Future research should focus on the efficacy of these and other popular social networking sites for promoting student engagement. In addition, there were very few studies about whether informational technologies, which involve the one-way transmission of information to students, affect different types of student engagement. Future research should examine whether informational technologies, such as video lectures, podcasts, and pre-recorded narrated Power Point presentations or screen casts, affect student engagement. Finally, studies should examine the influence of mobile software and technologies, such as educational apps or smartphones, on student engagement.

6. Achieve greater consensus on the meaning of student engagement and its distinction from similar concepts in the literature, such as social and cognitive presence (Garrison & Arbaugh, 2007)

Recommendations for practice

Despite the existing gaps and mixed findings in the literature, we were able to compile a list of recommendations for when and how to use technology to increase the likelihood of promoting student engagement. What follows is not an exhaustive list; rather, it is a synthesis of both research findings and lessons learned from the studies we reviewed. There may be other recommendations to add to this list; however, our intent is to provide some useful information to help address barriers to technology integration among faculty who feel uncertain or unprepared to use technology (Ashrafzadeh & Sayadian, 2015; Hauptman, 2015; Kidd et al., 2016; Reid, 2014) and to add to the body of practical knowledge in instructional design and delivery. Our recommendations for practice are as follows:

1. Consider context before selecting technologies. Contextual factors such as existing technological infrastructure and requirements, program and course characteristics, and the intended audience will help determine which technologies, if any, are most appropriate (Bullen & Morgan, 2011; Bullen, Morgan, & Qayyum, 2011). For example, requiring students to use a blog that is not well integrated with the existing LMS may prove too frustrating for both the instructor and students. Similarly, integrating *Facebook*- and *Twitter*-based learning activities throughout a marketing program may be more appropriate, given the subject matter, compared to doing so in an engineering or accounting program where social media is less integral to the profession. Finally, do not assume that students appreciate or are familiar with all technologies. For example, students who did not already have *Facebook* or *Twitter* accounts were less likely to use either for learning purposes and perceived setting up an account to be an increase in workload (Bista, 2015, Clements, 2015; DiVall & Kirwin, 2012; Hennessy et al., 2016; Mysko & Delgaty, 2015, Tiernan, 2014). Therefore, prior to using any technology, instructors may want to determine how many students already have accounts and/or are familiar with the technology.
2. Carefully select technologies based on their strengths and limitations and the intended learning outcome. For example, *Twitter* is limited to 140 characters, making it a viable tool for learning activities that require brevity. In one study, an instructor used *Twitter* for short pop quizzes during lectures, where the first few students to tweet the correct answer received additional points (Kim et al., 2015), which helped students practice applying knowledge. In addition, studies show that students perceive *Twitter* and *Facebook* to be primarily for social interactions (Camus et al., 2016; Ross et al., 2015), which may make these technologies viable tools for sharing resources, giving brief opinions about news stories pertaining to course content, or having casual conversations with classmates rather than full-fledged scholarly discourse.

3. Incentivize students to use technology, either by assigning regular grades or giving extra credit. The average participation rates in voluntary web-conferencing, *Facebook*, and *Twitter* learning activities in studies we reviewed was 52% (Andrew et al., 2015; Armstrong & Thornton, 2012; Bahati, 2015; Bowman & Akcaoglu, 2014; Divall & Kirwin, 2012; Dougherty & Andercheck, 2014; Fagioli et al., 2015; Hennessy et al., 2016; Junco et al., 2013; Rambe, 2012; Ross et al., 2015; Staines & Lauchs, 2013; Tiernan, 2014; Williams & Whiting, 2016). While there were far fewer studies on the use of technology for graded or mandatory learning activities, the average participation rate reported in those studies was 97% (Bahati2015; Gagnon, 2015), suggesting that grading may be a key factor in ensuring students participate.
4. Communicate clear guidelines for technology use. Prior to the implementation of technology in a course, students may benefit from an overview the technology, including its navigational features, privacy settings, and security (Andrew et al., 2015; Hurt et al., 2012; Martin et al., 2012) and a set of guidelines for how to use the technology effectively and professionally within an educational setting (Miller et al., 2012; Prestridge, 2014; Staines & Lauchs, 2013; West et al., 2015). In addition, giving students examples of exemplary and poor entries and posts may also help to clarify how they are expected to use the technology (Shraim, 2014; Roussinos & Jimoyiannis, 2013). Also, if instructors expect students to use technology to demonstrate higher-order thinking or to interact with peers, there should be explicit instructions to do so. For example, Prestridge (2014) found that students used *Twitter* to ask the instructor questions but very few interacted with peers because they were not explicitly asked to do so. Similarly, Hou et al., 2015 reported low levels of knowledge construction in *Facebook*, admitting that the wording of the learning activity (e.g., explore and present applications of computer networking) and the lack of probing questions in the instructions may have been to blame.
5. Use technology to provide authentic and integrated learning experiences. In many studies, instructors used digital games to simulate authentic environments in which students could apply new knowledge and skills, which ultimately lead to a greater understanding of content and evidence of higher-order thinking (Beckem & Watkins, 2012; Liu et al., 2011; Lu et al., 2014; Marriott et al., 2015; Siddique et al., 2013). For example, in one study, students were required to play the role of a stock trader in a simulated trading environment and they reported that the simulation helped them engage in critical reflection, enabling them to identify their mistakes and weaknesses in their trading approaches and strategies (Marriott et al., 2015). In addition, integrating technology into regularly-scheduled classroom activities, such as lectures, may help to promote student engagement. For example, in one study, the instructor posed a question in class, asked students to respond aloud or tweet their response, and projected the *Twitter* page so that everyone could see the tweets in class, which lead to favorable comments about the usefulness of *Twitter* to promote engagement (Tiernan, 2014).
6. Actively participate in using the technologies assigned to students during the first few weeks of the course to generate interest (Dougherty & Andercheck, 2014; West et al., 2015) and, preferably, throughout the course to answer questions, encourage dialogue, correct misconceptions, and address inappropriate behavior (Bowman & Akcaoglu, 2014; Hennessy et al., 2016;

Junco et al., 2013; Roussinos & Jimoyiannis, 2013). Miller et al. (2012) found that faculty encouragement and prompting was associated with increases in students' expression of ideas and the degree to which they edited and elaborated on their peers' work in a course-specific wiki.

7. Be mindful of privacy, security, and accessibility issues. In many studies, instructors took necessary steps to help ensure privacy and security by creating closed *Facebook* groups and private *Twitter* pages, accessible only to students in the course (Bahati, 2015; Bista, 2015; Bowman & Akcaoglu, 2014; Esteves, 2012; Rambe, 2012; Tiernan, 2014; Williams & Whiting, 2016) and by offering training to students on how to use privacy and security settings (Hurt et al., 2012). Instructors also made efforts to increase accessibility of web-conferencing software by including a phone number for students unable to access audio or video through their computer and by recording and archiving sessions for students unable to attend due to pre-existing conflicts (Andrew et al., 2015; Martin et al., 2012). In the future, instructors should also keep in mind that some technologies, like *Facebook* and *Twitter*, are not accessible to students living in China; therefore, alternative arrangements may need to be made.

Conclusion

In 1985, Steve Jobs predicted that computers and software would revolutionize the way we learn. Over 30 years later, his prediction has yet to be fully confirmed in the student engagement literature; however, our findings offer preliminary evidence that the potential is there. Of the technologies we reviewed, digital games, web-conferencing software, and *Facebook* had the most far-reaching effects across multiple types and indicators of student engagement, suggesting that technology should be considered a factor that influences student engagement in existing models. Findings regarding blogs, wikis, and *Twitter*, however, are less convincing, given a lack of studies in relation to engagement indicators or mixed findings. Significant methodological limitations may account for the wide range of findings in the literature. For example, small sample sizes, inconsistent measurement of variables, lack of comparison groups, and missing details about specific, pedagogical uses of technologies threaten the validity and reliability of findings. Therefore, more rigorous and robust research is needed to confirm and build upon limited but positive findings, clarify mixed findings, and address gaps particularly regarding how different technologies influence emotional and cognitive indicators of engagement.

Abbreviation

LMS: Learning management system

Acknowledgements

Not applicable.

Funding

This research was supported in part by a Laureate Education, Incl. David A. Wilson research grant study awarded to the second author, "A Comparative Analysis of Student Engagement and Critical Thinking in Two Approaches to the Online Classroom".

Authors' contributions

The first and second authors contributed significantly to the writing, review, and conceptual thinking of the manuscript. The third author provided a first detailed outline of what the paper could address, and the fourth offer provided input and feedback through critical review. All authors read and approved the final manuscript.

Competing interests

The authors declare that they have no competing interests.

Author details

[1]University of Liverpool Online, Liverpool, UK. [2]Laureate Education, Inc., Baltimore, USA. [3]Walden University, Minneapolis, USA. [4]University of Lincoln, Lincoln, UK.

References

Amirault, R. J. (2012). Distance learning in the 21st century university. *Quarterly Review of Distance Education, 13*(4), 253–265.

Anderson, M. (2016). *More Americans using smartphones for getting directions, streaming TV*. Washington, D.C.: Pew Research Center Retrieved from http://www.pewresearch.org/fact-tank/2016/01/29/us-smartphone-use/.

Anderson, M., & Horrigan, J. B. (2016). *Smartphones help those without broadband get online, but don't necessary bridge the digital divide*. Washington, D.C.: Pew Research Center Retrieved from http://www.pewresearch.org/fact-tank/2016/10/03/smartphones-help-those-without-broadband-get-online-but-dont-necessarily-bridge-the-digital-divide/.

Andrew, L., Maslin-Prothero, S., & Ewens, B. (2015). Enhancing the online learning experience using virtual interactive classrooms. *Australian Journal of Advanced Nursing, 32*(4), 22–31.

Antunes, M., Pacheco, M. R., & Giovanela, M. (2012). Design and implementation of an educational game for teaching chemistry in higher education. *Journal of Chemical Education, 89*(4), 517–521. doi:10.1021/ed2003077.

Armier, D. J., Shepherd, C. E., & Skrabut, S. (2016). Using game elements to increase student engagement in course assignments. *College Teaching, 64*(2), 64–72 https://doi.org/10.1080/87567555.2015.1094439.

Armstrong, A., & Thornton, N. (2012). Incorporating Brookfield's discussion techniques synchronously into asynchronous online courses. *Quarterly Review of Distance Education, 13*(1), 1–9.

Ashrafzadeh, A., & Sayadian, S. (2015). University instructors' concerns and perceptions of technology integration. *Computers in Human Behavior, 49*, 62–73. doi:10.1016/j.chb.2015.01.071.

Astin, A. W. (1984). Student involvement: A developmental theory for higher education. *Journal of College Student Personnel, 25*(4), 297–300.

Auman, C. (2011). Using simulation games to increase student and instructor engagement. *College Teaching, 59*(4), 154–161. doi:10.1080/87567555.

Axelson, R. D., & Flick, A. (2011). Defining student engagement. *Change: The magazine of higher learning, 43*(1), 38–43.

Bahati, B. (2015). Extending student discussions beyond lecture room walls via Facebook. *Journal of Education and Practice, 6*(15), 160–171.

Bakker, A. B., Vergel, A. I. S., & Kuntze, J. (2015). Student engagement and performance: A weekly diary study on the role of openness. *Motivation and Emotion, 39*(1), 49–62. doi:10.1007/s11031-014-9422-5.

Beckem, J. I., & Watkins, M. (2012). Bringing life to learning: Immersive experiential learning simulations for online and blended courses. *Journal if Asynchronous Learning Networks, 16*(5), 61–70 https://doi.org/10.24059/olj.v16i5.287.

Bista, K. (2015). Is Twitter an effective pedagogical tool in higher education? Perspectives of education graduate students. *Journal of the Scholarship Of Teaching And Learning, 15*(2), 83–102 https://doi.org/10.14434/josotl.v15i2.12825.

Boghossian, P. (2006). Behaviorism, constructivism, and Socratic pedagogy. *Educational Philosophy and Theory, 38*(6), 713–722 https://doi.org/10.1111/j.1469-5812.2006.00226.x.

Bower, M. (2011). Redesigning a web-conferencing environment to scaffold computing students' creative design processes. *Journal of Educational Technology & Society, 14*(1), 27–42.

Bower, M. (2016). A framework for adaptive learning design in a Web-conferencing environment. *Journal of Interactive Media in Education, 2016*(1), 11 http://doi.org/10.5334/jime.406.

Bowman, N. D., & Akcaoglu, M. (2014). "I see smart people!": Using Facebook to supplement cognitive and affective learning in the university mass lecture. *The Internet and Higher Education, 23*, 1–8. doi:10.1016/j.iheduc.2014.05.003.

Boyle, E. A., Hainey, T., Connolly, T. M., Gray, G., Earp, J., Ott, M., et al. (2016). An update to the systematic literature review of empirical evidence of the impacts and outcomes of computer games and serious games. *Computers & Education, 94*, 178–192. doi:10.1016/j.compedu.2015.11.003.

Bryson, C., & Hand, L. (2007). The role of engagement in inspiring teaching and learning. *Innovations in Education and Teaching International, 44*(4), 349–362. doi:10.1080/14703290701602748.

Buchanan, T., Sainter, P., & Saunders, G. (2013). Factors affecting faculty use of learning technologies: Implications for models of technology adoption. *Journal of Computer in Higher Education, 25*(1), 1–11.

Bullen, M., & Morgan, T. (2011). Digital learners not digital natives. *La Cuestión Universitaria, 7*, 60–68.

Bullen, M., Morgan, T., & Qayyum, A. (2011). Digital learners in higher education: Generation is not the issue. *Canadian Journal of Learning and Technology, 37*(1), 1–24.

Calabretto, J., & Rao, D. (2011). Wikis to support collaboration of pharmacy students in medication management workshops – a pilot project. *International Journal of Pharmacy Education & Practice, 8*(2), 1–12.

Camacho, M. E., Carrión, M. D., Chayah, M., & Campos, J. M. (2016). The use of wiki to promote students' learning in higher education (Degree in Pharmacy). *International Journal of Educational Technology in Higher Education, 13*(1), 1–8 https://doi.org/10.1186/s41239-016-0025-y.

Camus, M., Hurt, N. E., Larson, L. R., & Prevost, L. (2016). Facebook as an online teaching tool: Effects on student participation, learning, and overall course performance. *College Teaching, 64*(2), 84–94 https://doi.org/10.1080/87567555.2015.1099093.

Carini, R. M., Kuh, G. D., & Klein, S. P. (2006). Student engagement and student learning: Testing the linkages. *Research in Higher Education, 47*(1), 1–32. doi:10.1007/s11162-005-8150-9.

Cassidy, E. D., Colmenares, A., Jones, G., Manolovitz, T., Shen, L., & Vieira, S. (2014). Higher Education and Emerging Technologies: Shifting Trends in Student Usage. *The Journal of Academic Librarianship, 40*, 124–133. doi:10.1016/j.acalib.2014.02.003.

Center for Postsecondary Research (2016). Engagement insights: Survey findings on the quality of undergraduate education. Retrieved from http://nsse.indiana.edu/NSSE_2016_Results/pdf/NSSE_2016_Annual_Results.pdf.

Center for Postsecondary Research (2017). About NSSE. Retrieved on February 15, 2017 from http://nsse.indiana.edu/html/about.cfm

Cercone, K. (2008). Characteristics of adult learners with implications for online learning design. *AACE Journal, 16*(2), 137–159.

Chang, J. W., & Wei, H. Y. (2016). Exploring Engaging Gamification Mechanics in Massive Online Open Courses. *Educational Technology & Society, 19*(2), 177–203.

Chawinga, W. D. (2017). Taking social media to a university classroom: teaching and learning using Twitter and blogs. *International Journal of Educational Technology in Higher Education, 14*(1), 3 https://doi.org/10.1186/s41239-017-0041-6.

Chen, B., Seilhamer, R., Bennett, L., & Bauer, S. (2015). Students' mobile learning practices in higher education: A multi-year study. In *EDUCAUSE Review* Retrieved from http://er.educause.edu/articles/2015/6/students-mobile-learning-practices-in-higher-education-a-multiyear-study.

Chu, S. K., Chan, C. K., & Tiwari, A. F. (2012). Using blogs to support learning during internship. *Computers & Education, 58*(3), 989–1000. doi:10.1016/j.compedu.2011.08.027.

Clements, J. C. (2015). Using Facebook to enhance independent student engagement: A case study of first-year undergraduates. *Higher Education Studies, 5*(4), 131–146 https://doi.org/10.5539/hes.v5n4p131.

Coates, H. (2008). *Attracting, engaging and retaining: New conversations about learning.* Camberwell: Australian Council for Educational Research Retrieved from http://research.acer.edu.au/cgi/viewcontent.cgi?article=1015&context=ausse.

Coffey, D. J., Miller, W. J., & Feuerstein, D. (2011). Classroom as reality: Demonstrating campaign effects through live simulation. *Journal of Political Science Education, 7*(1), 14–33.

Coghlan, E., Crawford, J. Little, J., Lomas, C., Lombardi, M., Oblinger, D., & Windham, C. (2007). ELI Discovery Tool: Guide to Blogging. Retrieved from https://net.educause.edu/ir/library/pdf/ELI8006.pdf.

Connolly, T. M., Boyle, E. A., MacArthur, E., Hainey, T., & Boyle, J. M. (2012). A systematic literature review of empirical evidence on computer games and serious games. *Computers & Education, 59*, 661–686. doi:10.1016/j.compedu.2012.03.004.

Cook, C. W., & Sonnenberg, C. (2014). Technology and online education: Models for change. *ASBBS E-Journal, 10*(1), 43–59.

Crocco, F., Offenholley, K., & Hernandez, C. (2016). A proof-of-concept study of game-based learning in higher education. *Simulation & Gaming, 47*(4), 403–422. doi:10.1177/1046878116632484.

Csikszentmihalyi, M. (1988). The flow experience and its significance for human psychology. In M. Csikszentmihalyi & I. Csikszentmihalyi (Eds.), *Optimal experience: Psychological studies of flow in consciousness* (pp. 15–13). Cambridge, UK: Cambridge University Press.

Dahlstrom, E. (2012). *ECAR study of undergraduate students and information technology, 2012* (Research Report). Retrieved from http://net.educause.edu/ir/library/pdf/ERS1208/ERS1208.pdf

de Freitas, S. (2006). Learning in immersive worlds: A review of game-based learning. Retrieved from https://curve.coventry.ac.uk/open/file/aeedcd86-bc4c-40fe-bfdf-df22ee53a495/1/learning%20in%20immersive%20worlds.pdf.

Dichev, C., & Dicheva, D. (2017). Gamifying education: What is known, what is believed and what remains uncertain: A critical review. *International Journal of Educational Technology in Higher Education, 14*(9), 1–36. doi:10.1186/s41239-017-0042-5.

DiVall, M. V., & Kirwin, J. L. (2012). Using Facebook to facilitate course-related discussion between students and faculty members. *American Journal of Pharmaceutical Education, 76*(2), 1–5 https://doi.org/10.5688/ajpe76232.

Dos, B., & Demir, S. (2013). The analysis of the blogs created in a blended course through the reflective thinking perspective. *Educational Sciences: Theory & Practice, 13*(2), 1335–1344.

Dougherty, K., & Andercheck, B. (2014). Using Facebook to engage learners in a large introductory course. *Teaching Sociology, 42*(2), 95–104 https://doi.org/10.1177/0092055x14521022.

Dyson, B., Vickers, K., Turtle, J., Cowan, S., & Tassone, A. (2015). Evaluating the use of Facebook to increase student engagement and understanding in lecture-based classes. *Higher Education: The International Journal of Higher Education and Educational Planning, 69*(2), 303–313 https://doi.org/10.1007/s10734-014-9776-3.

Esteves, K. K. (2012). Exploring Facebook to enhance learning and student engagement: A case from the University of Philippines (UP) Open University. *Malaysian Journal of Distance Education, 14*(1), 1–15.

Evans, C. (2014). Twitter for teaching: Can social media be used to enhance the process of learning? *British Journal of Educational Technology, 45*(5), 902–915 https://doi.org/10.1111/bjet.12099.

Fagioli, L., Rios-Aguilar, C., & Deil-Amen, R. (2015). Changing the context of student engagement: Using Facebook to increase community college student persistence and success. *Teachers College Record, 17*, 1–42.

Farley, P. C. (2013). Using the computer game "FoldIt" to entice students to explore external representations of protein structure in a biochemistry course for nonmajors. *Biochemistry and Molecular Biology Education, 41*(1), 56–57 https://doi.org/10.1002/bmb.20655.

Francescucci, A., & Foster, M. (2013). The VIRI classroom: The impact of blended synchronous online courses on student performance, engagement, and satisfaction. *Canadian Journal of Higher Education, 43*(3), 78–91.

Fredricks, J., Blumenfeld, P., & Paris, A. (2004). School engagement: Potential of the concept, state of the evidence. *Review of Educational Research, 74*(1), 59–109. doi:10.3102/00346543074001059.

Gagnon, K. (2015). Using twitter in health professional education: A case study. *Journal of Allied Health, 44*(1), 25–33.

Gandhi, P., Khanna, S., & Ramaswamy, S. (2016). Which industries are the most digital (and why?). Retrieved from https://hbr.org/2016/04/a-chart-that-shows-which-industries-are-the-most-digital-and-why.

Garrison, D. R., & Arbaugh, J. B. (2007). Researching the community of inquiry framework: Review, issues, and future directions. *The Internet and Higher Education, 10*(3), 157–172 http://dx.doi.org/10.1016/j.iheduc.2007.04.001.

Garrity, M. K., Jones, K., VanderZwan, K. J., de la Rocha, A. R., & Epstein, I. (2014). Integrative review of blogging: Implications for nursing education. *Journal of Nursing Education, 53*(7), 395–401. doi:10.3928/01484834-20140620-01.

Gikas, J., & Grant, M. M. (2013). Mobile computing devices in higher education: Student perspectives on learning with cellphones, smartphones & social media. *The Internet and Higher Education, 19*, 18–26 http://dx.doi.org/10.1016/j.iheduc.2013.06.002.

Gilboy, M. B., Heinerichs, S., & Pazzaglia, G. (2015). Enhancing student engagement using the flipped classroom. *Journal of Nutrition Education and Behavior, 47*(1), 109–114 http://dx.doi.org/10.1016/j.jneb.2014.08.008.

Greenwood, S., Perrin, A., & Duggan, M. (2016). *Social media update 2016*. Washington.: Pew Research Center Retrieved from http://www.pewinternet.org/2016/11/11/social-media-update-2016/.

Grimley, M., Green, R., Nilsen, T., & Thompson, D. (2012). Comparing computer game and traditional lecture using experience ratings from high and low achieving students. *Australasian Journal of Educational Technology, 28*(4), 619–638 https://doi.org/10.14742/ajet.831.

Gunawardena, C. N., Hermans, M. B., Sanchez, D., Richmond, C., Bohley, M., & Tuttle, R. (2009). A theoretical framework for building online communities of practice with social networking tools. *Educational Media International, 46*(1), 3–16 https://doi.org/10.1080/09523980802588626.

Haggis, T. (2009). What have we been thinking of? A critical overview of 40 years of student learning research in higher education. *Studies in Higher Education, 34*(4), 377–390. doi:10.1080/03075070902771903.

Hauptman, P.H. (2015). *Mobile technology in college instruction. Faculty perceptions and barriers to adoption* (Doctoral dissertation). Retrieved from ProQuest. (AAI3712404).

Hennessy, C. M., Kirkpatrick, E., Smith, C. F., & Border, S. (2016). Social media and anatomy education: Using twitter to enhance the student learning experience in anatomy. *Anatomical Sciences Education, 9*(6), 505–515 https://doi.org/10.1002/ase.1610.

Hew, K. F., Huang, B., Chu, K. S., & Chiu, D. K. (2016). Engaging Asian students through game mechanics: Findings from two experiment studies. *Computers & Education, 93*, 221–236. doi:10.1016/j.compedu.2015.10.010.

Hewege, C. R., & Perera, L. R. (2013). Pedagogical significance of wikis: Towards gaining effective learning outcomes. *Journal of International Education in Business, 6*(1), 51–70 https://doi.org/10.1108/18363261311314953.

Hou, H., Wang, S., Lin, P., & Chang, K. (2015). Exploring the learner's knowledge construction and cognitive patterns of different asynchronous platforms: comparison of an online discussion forum and Facebook. *Innovations in Education and Teaching International, 52*(6), 610–620. doi:10.1080/14703297.2013.847381.

Hu, S., & McCormick, A. C. (2012). An engagement-based student typology and its relationship to college outcomes. *Research in Higher Education, 53*, 738–754. doi:10.1007/s11162-012-9254-7.

Hudson, T. M., Knight, V., & Collins, B. C. (2012). Perceived effectiveness of web conferencing software in the digital environment to deliver a graduate course in applied behavior analysis. *Rural Special Education Quarterly, 31*(2), 27–39.

Hurt, N. E., Moss, G. S., Bradley, C. L., Larson, L. R., Lovelace, M. D., & Prevost, L. B. (2012). The 'Facebook' effect: College students' perceptions of online discussions in the age of social networking. *International Journal for the Scholarship of Teaching & Learning, 6*(2), 1–24 https://doi.org/10.20429/ijsotl.2012.060210.

Ibáñez, M. B., Di-Serio, A., & Delgado-Kloos, C. (2014). Gamification for engaging computer science students in learning activities: A case study. *IEEE Transactions on Learning Technologies, 7*(3), 291–301 https://doi.org/10.1109/tlt.2014.2329293.

Ivala, E., & Gachago, D. (2012). Social media for enhancing student engagement: The use of facebook and blogs at a university of technology. *South African Journal of Higher Education, 26*(1), 152–167.

Johnson, D. R. (2013). Technological change and professional control in the professoriate. *Science, Technology & Human Values, 38*(1), 126–149. doi:10.1177/0162243911430236.

Junco, R., Elavsky, C. M., & Heiberger, G. (2013). Putting Twitter to the test: Assessing outcomes for student collaboration, engagement and success. *British Journal of Educational Technology, 44*(2), 273–287. doi:10.1111/j.1467-8535.2012.01284.x.

Junco, R., Heibergert, G., & Loken, E. (2011). The effect of Twitter on college student engagement and grades. *Journal of Computer Assisted Learning, 27*(2), 119–132. doi:10.1111/j.1365-2729.2010.00387.x.

Kahu, E. R. (2013). Framing student engagement in higher education. *Studies in Higher Education, 38*(5), 758–773. doi:10.1080/03075079.2011.598505.

Kaware, S. S., & Sain, S. K. (2015). ICT Application in Education: An Overview. *International Journal of Multidisciplinary Approach & Studies, 2*(1), 25–32.

Ke, F., Xie, K., & Xie, Y. (2016). Game-based learning engagement: A theory- and data-driven exploration. *British Journal of Educational Technology, 47*(6), 1183–1201 https://doi.org/10.1111/bjet.12314.

Kent, M. (2013). Changing the conversation: Facebook as a venue for online class discussion in higher education. *Journal of Online Learning & Teaching, 9*(4), 546–565 https://doi.org/10.1353/rhe.2015.0000.

Kidd, T., Davis, T., & Larke, P. (2016). Experience, adoption, and technology: Exploring the phenomenological experiences of faculty involved in online teaching at once school of public health. *International Journal of E-Learning, 15*(1), 71–99.

Kim, Y., Jeong, S., Ji, Y., Lee, S., Kwon, K. H., & Jeon, J. W. (2015). Smartphone response system using twitter to enable effective interaction and improve engagement in large classrooms. *IEEE Transactions on Education, 58*(2), 98–103 https://doi.org/10.1109/te.2014.2329651.

Kinchin. (2012). Avoiding technology-enhanced non-learning. *British Journal of Educational Technology, 43*(2), E43–E48.

Kolb, D. A. (2014). *Experiential learning: Experience as the source of learning and development* (2nd ed.). Upper Saddle River: Pearson Education, Inc..
Kopcha, T. J., Rieber, L. P., & Walker, B. B. (2016). Understanding university faculty perceptions about innovation in teaching and technology. *British Journal of Educational Technology, 47*(5), 945–957. doi:10.1111/bjet.12361.
Krause, K., & Coates, H. (2008). Students' engagement in first-year university. *Assessment and Evaluation in Higher Education, 33*(5), 493–505. doi:10.1080/02602930701698892.
Kuh, G. D. (2009). The National Survey of Student Engagement: Conceptual and empirical foundations. *New Directions for Institutional Research, 141*, 5–20.
Lam, S., Wong, B., Yang, H., & Yi, L. (2012). Understanding student engagement with a contextual model. In S. L. Christenson, A. L. Reschly, & C. Wylie (Eds.), *Handbook of Research on Student Engagement* (pp. 403–419). New York: Springer.
Lawrence, B., & Lentle-Keenan, S. (2013). Teaching beliefs and practice, institutional context, and the uptake of Web-based technology. *Distance Education, 34*(1), 4–20.
Leach, L. (2016). Enhancing student engagement in one institution. *Journal of Further and Higher Education, 40*(1), 23–47.
Lester, D. (2013). A review of the student engagement literature. *Focus on Colleges, Universities, and Schools, 7*(1), 1–8.
Lewis, C. C., Fretwell, C. E., Ryan, J., & Parham, J. B. (2013). Faculty use of established and emerging technologies in higher education: A unified theory of acceptance and use of technology perspective. *International Journal of Higher Education, 2*(2), 22–34 http://dx.doi.org/10.5430/ijhe.v2n2p22.
Lin, C., Singer, R., & Ha, L. (2010). Why university members use and resist technology? A structure enactment perspective. *Journal of Computing in Higher Education, 22*(1), 38–59. doi:10.1007/s12528-010-9028-1.
Linder-VanBerschot, J. A., & Summers, L. L. (2015). Designing instruction in the face of technology transience. *Quarterly Review of Distance Education, 16*(2), 107–118.
Liu, C., Cheng, Y., & Huang, C. (2011). The effect of simulation games on the learning of computational problem solving. *Computers & Education, 57*(3), 1907–1918 https://doi.org/10.1016/j.compedu.2011.04.002.
Lu, J., Hallinger, P., & Showanasai, P. (2014). Simulation-based learning in management education: A longitudinal quasi-experimental evaluation of instructional effectiveness. *Journal of Management Development, 33*(3), 218–244. doi:10.1108/JMD-11-2011-0115.
Maben, S., Edwards, J., & Malone, D. (2014). Online engagement through Facebook groups in face-to-face undergraduate communication courses: A case study. *Southwestern Mass Communication Journal, 29*(2), 1–27.
Manca, S., & Ranieri, M. (2013). Is it a tool suitable for learning? A critical review of the literature on Facebook as a technology-enhanced learning environment. *Journal of Computer Assisted Learning, 29*(6), 487–504. doi:10.1111/jcal.12007.
Mansouri, S. A., & Piki, A. (2016). An exploration into the impact of blogs on students' learning: Case studies in postgraduate business education. *Innovations in Education And Teaching International, 53*(3), 260–273 http://dx.doi.org/10.1080/14703297.2014.997777.
Marriott, P., Tan, S. W., & Marriot, N. (2015). Experiential learning – A case study of the use of computerized stock market trading simulation in finance education. *Accounting Education, 24*(6), 480–497 http://dx.doi.org/10.1080/09639284.2015.1072728.
Martin, F., Parker, M. A., & Deale, D. F. (2012). Examining interactivity in synchronous virtual classrooms. *International Review of Research in Open and Distance Learning, 13*(3), 227–261.
Martin, K., Goldwasser, M., & Galentino, R. (2017). Impact of Cohort Bonds on Student Satisfaction and Engagement. *Current Issues in Education, 19*(3), 1–14.
Martínez, A. A., Medina, F. X., Albalat, J. A. P., & Rubió, F. S. (2013). Challenges and opportunities of 2.0 tools for the interdisciplinary study of nutrition: The case of the Mediterranean Diet wiki. *International Journal of Educational Technology in Higher Education, 10*(1), 210–225 https://doi.org/10.7238/rusc.v10i1.1341.
McBrien, J. L., Jones, P., & Cheng, R. (2009). Virtual spaces: Employing a synchronous online classroom to facilitate student engagement in online learning. *International Review of Research in Open and Distance Learning, 10*(3), 1–17 https://doi.org/10.19173/irrodl.v10i3.605.
McClenney, K., Marti, C. N., & Adkins, C. (2012). *Student engagement and student outcomes: Key findings from "CCSSE" validation research.* Austin: Community College Survey of Student Engagement.
McKay, M., Sanko, J., Shekhter, I., & Birnbach, D. (2014). Twitter as a tool to enhance student engagement during an interprofessional patient safety course. *Journal of Interprofessional Care, 28*(6), 565–567 https://doi.org/10.3109/13561820.2014.912618.
Miller, A. D., Norris, L. B., & Bookstaver, P. B. (2012). Use of wikis in pharmacy hybrid elective courses. *Currents in Pharmacy Teaching & Learning, 4*(4), 256–261. doi:10.1016/j.cptl.2012.05.004.
Morley, D. A. (2012). Enhancing networking and proactive learning skills in the first year university experience through the use of wikis. *Nurse Education Today, 32*(3), 261–266.
Mysko, C., & Delgaty, L. (2015). How and why are students using Twitter for #meded? Integrating Twitter into undergraduate medical education to promote active learning. *Annual Review of Education, Communication & Language Sciences, 12*, 24–52.
Nadolny, L., & Halabi, A. (2016). Student participation and achievement in a large lecture course with game-based learning. *Simulation and Gaming, 47*(1), 51–72. doi:10.1177/1046878115620388.
Naghdipour, B., & Eldridge, N. H. (2016). Incorporating social networking sites into traditional pedagogy: A case of facebook. *TechTrends, 60*(6), 591–597 http://dx.doi.org/10.1007/s11528-016-0118-4.
Nakamaru, S. (2012). Investment and return: Wiki engagement in a "remedial" ESL writing course. *Journal of Research on Technology in Education, 44*(4), 273–291.
Nelson, R. (2016). Apple's app store will hit 5 million apps by 2020, more than doubling its current size. Retrieved from https://sensortower.com/blog/app-store-growth-forecast-2020.
Nora, A., Barlow, E., & Crisp, G. (2005). Student persistence and degree attainment beyond the first year in college. In A. Seidman (Ed.), *College Student Retention* (pp. 129–154). Westport: Praeger Publishers.
Osgerby, J., & Rush, D. (2015). An exploratory case study examining undergraduate accounting students' perceptions of using Twitter as a learning support tool. *International Journal of Management Education, 13*(3), 337–348. doi:10.1016/j.ijme.2015.10.002.

Pace, C. R. (1980). Measuring the quality of student effort. *Current Issues in Higher Education, 2*, 10–16.

Pace, C. R. (1984). *Student effort: A new key to assessing quality*. Los Angeles: University of California, Higher Education Research Institute.

Paul, J. A., & Cochran, J. D. (2013). Key interactions for online programs between faculty, students, technologies, and educational institutions: A holistic framework. *Quarterly Review of Distance Education, 14*(1), 49–62.

Pellas, N. (2014). The influence of computer self-efficacy, metacognitive self-regulation, and self-esteem on student engagement in online learning programs: Evidence from the virtual world of Second Life. *Computers in Human Behavior, 35*, 157–170. doi:10.1016/j.chb.2014.02.048.

Poole, S. M., Kemp, E., Williams, K. H., & Patterson, L. (2014). Get your head in the game: Using gamification in business education to connect with Generation Y. *Journal for Excellence in Business Education, 3*(2), 1–9.

Poushter, J. (2016). *Smartphone ownership and internet usage continues to climb in emerging economies*. Washington, D. C.: Pew Research Center Retrieved from http://www.pewglobal.org/2016/02/22/smartphone-ownership-and-internet-usage-continues-to-climb-in-emerging-economies/.

Prestridge, S. (2014). A focus on students' use of Twitter - their interactions with each other, content and interface. *Active Learning in Higher Education, 15*(2), 101–115.

Rambe, P. (2012). Activity theory and technology mediated interaction: Cognitive scaffolding using question-based consultation on "Facebook". *Australasian Journal of Educational Technology, 28*(8), 1333–1361 https://doi.org/10.14742/ajet.775.

Reid, P. (2014). Categories for barriers to adoption of instructional technologies. *Education and Information Technologies, 19*(2), 383–407.

Revere, L., & Kovach, J. V. (2011). Online technologies for engagement learning: A meaningful synthesis for educators. *Quarterly Review of Distance Education, 12*(2), 113–124.

Richardson, J. C., & Newby, T. (2006). The role of students' cognitive engagement in online learning. *American Journal of Distance Education, 20*(1), 23–37 http://dx.doi.org/10.1207/s15389286ajde2001_3.

Ross, H. M., Banow, R., & Yu, S. (2015). The use of Twitter in large lecture courses: Do the students see a benefit? *Contemporary Educational Technology, 6*(2), 126–139.

Roussinos, D., & Jimoyiannis, A. (2013). Analysis of students' participation patterns and learning presence in a wiki-based project. *Educational Media International, 50*(4), 306–324 https://doi.org/10.1080/09523987.2013.863471.

Salaber, J. (2014). Facilitating student engagement and collaboration in a large postgraduate course using wiki-based activities. *International Journal of Management Education, 12*(2), 115–126. doi:10.1016/j.ijme.2014.03.006.

Scarlet, J., & Ampolos, L. (2013). Using game-based learning to teach psychopharmacology. *Psychology Learning and Teaching, 12*(1), 64–70 https://doi.org/10.2304/plat.2013.12.1.64.

Sharma, P., & Tietjen, P. (2016). Examining patterns of participation and meaning making in student blogs: A case study in higher education. *American Journal of Distance Education, 30*(1), 2–13 http://dx.doi.org/10.1080/08923647.2016.1119605.

Shraim, K. Y. (2014). Pedagogical innovation within Facebook: A case study in tertiary education in Palestine. *International Journal of Emerging Technologies in Learning, 9*(8), 25–31. doi:10.3991/ijet.v9i8.3805.

Siddique, Z., Ling, C., Roberson, P., Xu, Y., & Geng, X. (2013). Facilitating higher-order learning through computer games. *Journal of Mechanical Design, 135*(12), 121004–121010.

Smith, A., & Anderson, M. (2016). *Online Shopping and E-Commerce*. Washington, D.C.: Pew Research Center Retrieved from http://www.pewinternet.org/2016/12/19/online-shopping-and-e-commerce/.

Staines, Z., & Lauchs, M. (2013). Students' engagement with Facebook in a university undergraduate policing unit. *Australasian Journal of Educational Technology, 29*(6), 792–805 https://doi.org/10.14742/ajet.270.

Sun, A., & Chen, X. (2016). Online education and its effective practice: A research review. *Journal of Information Technology Education: Research, 15*, 157–190.

Tiernan, P. (2014). A study of the use of Twitter by students for lecture engagement and discussion. *Education and Information Technologies, 19*(4), 673–690 https://doi.org/10.1007/s10639-012-9246-4.

Trowler, V. (2010). *Student engagement literature review*. Lancaster: Lancaster University Retrieved from http://www.lancaster.ac.uk/staff/trowler/StudentEngagementLiteratureReview.pdf.

Trowler, V., & Trowler, P. (2010). *Student engagement evidence summary*. Lancaster: Lancaster University Retrieved from http://eprints.lancs.ac.uk/61680/1/Deliverable_2._Evidence_Summary._Nov_2010.pdf.

van Beynen, K., & Swenson, C. (2016). Exploring peer-to-peer library content and engagement on a student-run Facebook group. *College & Research Libraries, 77*(1), 34–50 https://doi.org/10.5860/crl.77.1.34.

Wang, S. (2008). Blogs in education. In M. Pagani (Ed.), *Encyclopedia of Multimedia Technology and Networking* (2nd ed., pp. 134–139). Hershey: Information Sciences Reference.

Wdowik, S. (2014). Using a synchronous online learning environment to promote and enhance transactional engagement beyond the classroom. *Campus — Wide Information Systems, 31*(4), 264–275. doi:10.1108/CWIS-10-2013-0057.

Weibel, D., Wissmath, B., Habegger, S., Steiner, Y., & Groner, R. (2008). Playing online games against computer-vs. human-controlled opponents: Effects on presence, flow, and enjoyment. *Computers in Human Behavior, 24*(5), 2274–2291 https://doi.org/10.1016/j.chb.2007.11.002.

West, B., Moore, H., & Barry, B. (2015). Beyond the tweet: Using Twitter to enhance engagement, learning, and success among first year students. *Journal of Marketing Education, 37*(3), 160–170. doi:10.1177/0273475315586061.

Westera, W. (2015). Reframing the role of educational media technologies. *Quarterly Review of Distance Education, 16*(2), 19–32.

Whitton, N. (2011). Game engagement theory and adult learning. *Simulation & Gaming, 42*(5), 596–609.

Williams, D., & Whiting, A. (2016). Exploring the relationship between student engagement, Twitter, and a learning management system: A study of undergraduate marketing students. *International Journal of Teaching & Learning in Higher Education, 28*(3), 302–313.

Wimpenny, K., & Savin-Baden, M. (2013). Alienation, agency, and authenticity: A synthesis of the literature on student engagement. *Teaching in Higher Education, 18*(3), 311–326. doi:10.1080/13562517.2012.725223.

Witkowski, P., & Cornell, T. (2015). An Investigation into Student Engagement in Higher Education Classrooms. *InSight: A Journal of Scholarly Teaching, 10*, 56–67.

Wright, G. B. (2011). Student-centered learning in higher education. *International Journal of Teaching and Learning in Higher Education, 23*(3), 92–97.

Yang, C., & Chang, Y. (2012). Assessing the effects of interactive blogging on student attitudes towards peer interaction, learning motivation, and academic achievements. *Journal of Computer Assisted Learning, 28*(2), 126–135 https://doi.org/10.1111/j.1365-2729.2011.00423.x.

Zepke, N. (2014). Student engagement research in higher education: questioning an academic orthodoxy. *Teaching in Higher Education, 19*(6), 697–708 http://dx.doi.org/10.1080/13562517.2014.901956.

Zepke, N., & Leach, L. (2010). Improving student engagement: Ten proposals for action. *Active Learning in Higher Education, 11*(3), 167–177. doi:10.1177/1469787410379680.

Zickuhr, K., & Raine, L. (2014). *E-reading rises as device ownership jumps.* Washington, D.C.: Pew Research Center Retrieved from http://www.pewinternet.org/2014/01/16/e-reading-rises-as-device-ownership-jumps/.

Zimmermann, L. K. (2013). Using a virtual simulation program to teach child development. *College Teaching, 61*(4), 138–142. doi:10.1080/87567555.2013.817377.

3

University students' self-regulated learning using digital technologies

Carmen Yot-Domínguez and Carlos Marcelo*

* Correspondence: marcelo@us.es
Universidad de Sevilla, Pirotecnia s/n
C.P, 41013 Sevilla, Spain

Abstract

Analysing the process by which students—whether at university or not—manage and facilitate their own learning has been a recurrent educational research problem. Recently, the question arises about how the development of strategies taking place during the aforementioned process could be made easier by using technologies. In an effort to know whether university students really use digital technologies to plan, organize and facilitate their own learning, we have proposed three research questions. Which technologies do university students use to self-regulate their learning? What self-regulated learning strategies do they develop using technologies? What profiles could be identified among students based on their use of self-regulation strategies with technology? To answer these questions, the "Survey of Self-regulated Learning with Technology at the University" was designed. Information from a sample group with 711 students from various universities located in the region of Andalusia (Spain) was collected with this survey. The results indicate that university students, even when they are frequent users of digital technology, they tend not to use these technologies to regulate their own learning process. Of all technologies analysed, Internet information search and instant communication tools are used continually. In turn, the most generalised self-regulation learning strategies are those relative to social support. Nevertheless, students differ from each other regarding their use and frequency. There are groups of students who make use of self-regulation strategies when learning with technologies. In this regard, two distinctive groups of students have been identified, who show differentiated self-regulated levels.

Keywords: Higher education, Self-regulated learning, Technology, Digital native

Introduction

Today, one of the most extended myths is that young people are regular and skilled in the use of digital technologies because they were born in the last two decades. Prensky's work (Prensky, 2001) is considered a classic as he coined the term "*digital natives*" to refer to a new generation that has grown up with technologies and for which the term "*new*" almost seems senseless.

Although refuted (Bennett et al., 2008), this idea continues to be present in our society. We assume that young people use and process technologies with greater ease than those known as "*digital immigrants*". Nevertheless, numerous studies (Jones et al., 2010; Kennedy et al., 2008) have proven that the "*Net generation*" is not consistent according to the technological knowledge that users have and the use they make of these technologies.

This research seeks to find out whether university students really use digital technologies to plan, organize and facilitate their own learning. We explore not only the type of technologies they use but also the learning strategies for which they are used. We are especially interested in independent and self-regulated learning strategies that students develop from their own educational learning process.

The self-regulated learning (SRL) concept arose in the 1980s as a research problem and, for decades, it has continued to be important for researchers and teachers (Zimmerman & Schunk, 2011). One reason that explains the interest in SRL lies in the fact that we live in a society where life-long learning is increasingly important and informal learning environments requiring self-regulation skills proliferate (Beishuizen & Steffens, 2011). The university is responsible for motivating students to continually want to learn more. Developing independent learners is also one of the objectives that university studies are currently pursuing. The importance of the matter is justified because academic success is influenced by the students' ability to learn independently of the support offered by instructors (Kingsbury, 2015).

SRL-related research explains the processes by which students take control of their own learning and the strategies they develop to favour this learning. One of the initial aspects that characterises SRL is that the learner begins his/her search based on personal initiative, perseverance and adaptive skills (Zimmerman, 2009). To learn, students use a variety of strategies to regulate certain cognitive, motivational and behavioural aspects as well as certain environmental characteristics (Pintrich, 1999a, b ; Zimmerman and Martinez Pons, 1986).

According to Zimmerman's (1998) cyclic model, within a social cognitive perspective, self-regulation is a self-directed learning process that occurs in three successive phases. These are forecast (processes that precede the learning effort), execution control (processes that occur during learning) and self-reflection (processes that occur after learning). During the initial phase, students approach the learning activity analysis; they assess their ability to successfully accomplish and establish goals and plans to complete the process (Panadero & Alonso Tapia, 2014). During the second phase, the two main processes that students use are self-control and self-observation. Self-control involves a variety of strategies including self-instruction, seeking help or self-consequences (Dabbagh & Kitsantas, 2013). Furthermore, self-observation (observation and performance follow-up and results) implies two types of actions: self-monitoring (comparison of the actions carried out or the resulting products with criteria that assess the quality of what is being undertaken) and self-recording (record of actions while being executed to promote in-depth review). Lastly, the self-reflection phase involves those processes that follow the learning effort. At this point, students judge their learning and draw up reasons to justify the results obtained. One way to do this is through self-assessments (Zimmerman & Moylan, 2009).

Pintrich (2004) breaks down this central phase into two: forethought, planning, and activation (phase 1), monitoring (phase 2), control (phase 3) and reaction and reflection (phase 4). He completes his process model with another component that identifies the strategy types participating in the SRL. The SRL dimensions that arise are: metacognitive regulation (commitment with the learning goal, planning and follow-up), cognition regulation (use of cognitive strategies), motivation regulation (adjustment of mood, making learning attractive), behavioural regulation (time and effort management) and environmental regulation (seeking material and social resources). Motivational or volitional control strategies were studied independently (Pintrich, 1999) while the last two were considered, initially, under the same category (Pintrich, 1999a). The final version of the model contemplates the fourteen self-regulated learning strategies identified by Zimmerman & Martinez Pons (1986).

Developing this self-regulation cycle could be facilitated by technologies. Kitsantas & Dabbagh (2011) acknowledge that 2.0 social software technologies (communications tools, resource and experience exchange tools and social network tools) have ample potential to encourage self-regulation but empiric research in this area is still very limited. Kitsantas (2013) has described how certain technologies support each of the three phases presented above. This is carried out to orient teachers about how to facilitate self-regulation of learning.

Digital technologies represent an open gateway to new learning alternatives and options that favour the acquisition of self-regulation skills (Bernacki et al., 2011; Schneckenberg et al., 2011). At the same time, in technology-based learning experiences, using SRL is essential (Winters et al., 2008). The relation between SRL strategies and technologies may even be casual, as seen in the work by Valentín et al. (2013).

A number of studies have analysed the presence of technologies in the university student learning processes, either in formal or informal learning situations (Corrin et al., 2010; Margaryan et al., 2011). These help to determine which range of technologies are used but not which learning purposes are pursued with the use of each one. This is how Lai & Gu (2011) adopted SRL as a theoretical framework for understanding how university students use technologies. These authors were concerned with the use of technology outside the classroom for self-regulating learning. They found, in line with the aforementioned studies, that students have limited knowledge regarding the use of technology for learning. Despite this fact, students selectively use a variety of technologies to self-regulate their learning.

However, after reviewing all these previous studies, we still know very little about technology mediated SRL processes undertaken by university students. This leads us to the following questions: Which technologies do university students use to self-regulate their learning? Which SRL strategies do they develop using technologies? What profiles could be identified among students based on their use of self-regulation strategies with technology?

Method

To respond to these questions, we have designed the Survey of Self-regulated Learning with Technology at the University (SRLTU). This survey incorporates some initial questions (sex, age, university where the students are studying and the degrees currently studied) and 33 items that refer to various SRL strategies that may be performed using technologies. These items were assessed on a scale of 1 (*Never*) to 5 (*Always*) depending on the frequency with which they are carried out. As shown in Table 1, we used these items to analyse the level at which the different SRL strategies were used, which corresponded to the phases control of execution and self-reflection. The items also facilitate the analysis of the type of technology students use to learn.

Table 1. SRL strategies and technologies associated with SRLTU items. Classification of SRLTU items according to the Zimmerman and Pintrich models

Technology	Items	Strategies	Zimmerman (1989,1990)	Pintrich, 1999a, b
1. Communication Tools: WhatsApp, Line, Skype, Google Talk.	12, 13	Exchange information Solve doubts Discussion	Social support	Resource Management (Social)
2. Repositories: Slideshare, Instagram, Pinterest, Issuu, Calameo, Youtube, iTunes, iVoox.	3, 5, 6, 20, 21	Review of specific material obtained for studies	Record review	Metacognitive (Regulation)
	31	Be informed	Search for information	Metacognitive (Planning)
	15, 28, 29	Share one's own productions and material	Social support	Resource Management (Social)
3. Social Networks: Twitter, Facebook.	1	Comment information	Organise and transform	Cognitive (Formulation and Organisation)
	18	Information Exchange	Social support	Resource Management (Social)
	17	Be informed	Search for information	Metacognitive (Planning)
4. Production and Storage Tools in the cloud: wikis & blogs, Dropbox, Google + .	4, 11	Team work	Social support	Resource Management (Social)
	14	Comment information	Organise and transform	Cognitive (Formulation and Organisation)
	33	Be informed	Search for information	Metacognitive (Planning)
5. Social Markers & RSS: Delicious, Sage.	26, 27	Record Information Receive Information	Search for information	Metacognitive (Planning)
6. Multimedia Resources: podcast, video.	2	Listen to the previously recorded lesson	Record review	Metacognitive (Regulation)
	7	Self-listening	Memorisation	Cognitive (Essay)
	22	Self-observation	Save records	Metacognitive (Follow Up)
7. Assessment Tools: ExamTime, Google Application Forms.	23, 24	Verify learning	Self-Assessment	Metacognitive (Follow Up)
8. Internet: Wikipedia or online dictionaries; translators; Google academic, Dialnet.	9	Translate information	Organise and Transform	Cognitive (Formulation and Organisation)
	8, 32	Locate information	Search for information	Metacognitive Planning)
9. Management tools: Cmap, MindManager; RefWorks, Mendeley; Viper.	10,16, 25	Create concept maps, Draft texts managing bibliography Draft texts and verify plagiarism	Organise and Transform	Cognitive (Formulation and Organisation)
10. Other Technology: specific apps (Kalkulilo, Whiteboard Lite) & organisers (Google Calendar, EverNote).	30	Resolve academic activities making them more attractive		Volitional verification (Task Verification)
	19	Manage academic activities	Establish goals and plan	Resource Management (Time and Effort)

The research team collected the learning strategies that young people could independently develop with the various technologies currently available to them. Within a week, each member was responsible for reviewing the statement for the various strategies suggested and to determine whether or not this extensively addressed the objective of the study. All contributions made were taken into consideration. When the final draft of the strategies was ready, the self-regulating learning models of Zimmerman and Pintrich were used (because these have been widely recognized and both are very similar when explaining self-regulated learning) to confirm that these were pertinent and diversified. Likewise, it was verified that all of them could analyse the use of the different digital technologies. That is why the technologies mentioned in the different strategies were identified and classified in categories.

Once the survey was drafted, it was validated by a group of eight university students. Later, it was developed using the online e-survey service and distributed to the university teachers from ten universities in Andalusia. These teachers were asked to inform their students about the survey.

The quantitative data that we collected was analysed using SPSS statistical software. E-survey generates an Excel spread sheet with all the cases and answers for each variable. Any errors contained were corrected before importing the information to SPSS to work with it. Essentially, the numerous response intents that did not materialize were eliminated.

In order to measure the survey's reliability, a Cronbach's Alfa coefficient was calculated. The internal consistency was .877.

According to the first research problem, this study is interested in gathering information about the digital technologies that university students use for independent learning. Thus, we began by identifying the many digital technologies available to any of the students mentioned in the SRLTU. These technologies were grouped into the ten categories indicated in Table 1. Then, the average frequency of use of each was calculated.

Our next interest focused on how students use technologies to support their learning strategies. To answer this question, we performed a *factor analysis* of the 33 survey items. In keeping with *Bartlett's test* (p = .000) and the *Kaiser-Meyer-Olkin index* (.886), the data was adjusted for the application of the factor analysis. A *varimax rotation* was used to analyse the principal components. This exploratory analysis determined that the number of factors should be 9, and would therefore explain a variation of 54.904% of the data. To shape the factors, factorial loads greater than 0.40 were considered. Then, the mean and standard deviation were calculated for each factor. Descriptive statistics were also used to individually interpret the level of use for the items.

Lastly, we wanted to delve into the possibilities of identifying differentiated university student profiles based on the SRL strategies they develop with digital technologies. Other studies have identified student profiles based on their use of technologies (Lorenzo Romero et al., 2014) and the self-regulation learning skills they have (Barnard Brak et al., 2010; Ning & Downing, 2015; Valle et al., 2008.

For this, a *cluster analysis* was carried out based on the frequency with which the students made use of each factor. First, a *hierarchy analysis* was performed with the nearest *neighbour method* to detect outliers. Three participants were withdrawn from the analysis as they were atypical cases. Then, following the *Ward method*, we determined that the number of conglomerates should be 4. Lastly, a *k-means analysis* was performed considering the identified number. In the results, reference is made only to the two conglomerates of students with the greatest difference between them.

Sample

The sample was made up by 711 university students from the various universities located in the region of Andalusia (Spain). Of these, 38.3% were male and 61.2% female, and 59.8% of the participants were between 21 and 25 years of age while 27% were under 21.

The university students belonged to various Andalusian universities. Forty three percent of the participants were from the University of Seville, 18.7% from the University of Granada, 12% from the University of Cordoba and 11.5% from the University of Cadiz. A lower percentage was associated with the Universities of Malaga (0.1%) Almeria (0.7%), Jaen (3.2%), Pablo de Olavide (Seville) (3.2%) and Huelva (6.5%). The students were from several fields: 51.2% were studying social sciences, 18.6% engineering and architecture, 13.5% health sciences and 11.7% science. Only 4.5% of the students were from the field of arts and humanities.

Results

Which technologies do university students use to self-regulate their learning?

As shown in Fig. 1, it can be stated that students do use digital technologies in SRL, but their use is limited.

Of all technologies, only three of these reached an average level of use ($2.5 \leq M \geq 3.5$). These were: tools to search for information on Internet such as search engines or data

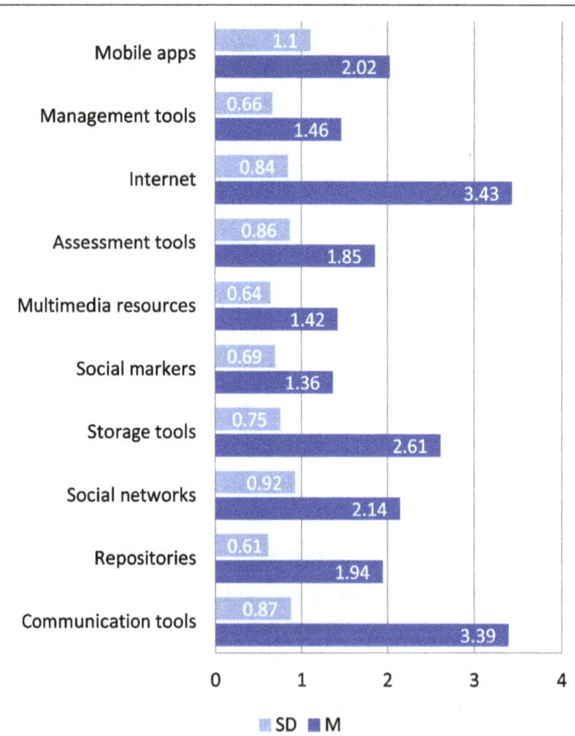

Fig. 1 Means and standard deviations of the use of digital technologies. The first grouped bar chart shows, first of all, the average frequency with which university students use the different digital technologies. According to the frequency of use indicated by the students of the sample, the graph also shows the standard deviation for each of the digital technologies. Since these are measures of central tendency and dispersion, they help distinguish the role of technologies nowadays in the self-regulation of learning. They show the current state of the technologies that are or are not used by university students to self-regulate learning

bases (M = 3.43 SD = .84), communication tools such as WhatsApp or Google Talk (M = 3.39 SD = .87) and 2.0 production and cloud storage tools such as wikis or Google + (M = 2.61 SD = .75). However, these fail to have the same degree of penetration in the students' study routine. More than 60% of the students use the first two to some degree, although in most cases it is only occasional use (42.8%, 50.4%). Less than 40% use production and cloud storage tools with some frequency. Our results coincide with those of other researchers (Gallardo et al., 2015; Kennedy et al., 2008; Margaryan et al., 2011). Web search tools and instant messaging are among the most frequently used technologies for informal learning situations or university academic life.

Regarding all other digital technologies, the degree to which these are used is low or very low ($M \leq 2.5$). Among the less used are social markers and Really Simple Syndication (RSS) feeds (M = 1.36 SD = .69). Seventy percent of the students have never used them. Multimedia resources (podcasts and videos), management tools (concept map creation and literature management or plagiarism verification) or repositories (videos, images, podcasts, presentations or learning objects) are not used for SRL support either. The same holds true for assessment tools, social networks, professional apps and personal organisers.

In line with previous studies, our results show that university students are not inclined to using technologies when regulating their own learning process, even when they are regular users of digital technologies for social, personal and leisure activities, among others. In part, this is explained by their limited view that technologies have in learning. Although students know how to use technologies, they are lacking in how to efficiently use them to support their own learning process (Littlejohn et al., 2010).

When focusing on social networks, these have a low level of use. According to Gosper et al. (2013), students frequently use this technology in every-day life. However, they are unwilling to use it for learning as it is not perceived as a tool with a high educational potential. Email is perceived as more efficient when solving academic issues (Vrocharidou & Efthymiou, 2012); therefore, it is used more often (Dahlstrom et al., 2013). Social applications, such as Facebook, are relegated almost exclusively to non-academic purposes (Swanson & Walker, 2015).

For students to further adopt digital technologies that favour their own learning, they need information about how to use them, even when their degree of digital competence is high (Deepwell & Malik, 2008). As set forth by Lai et al. (2012), support, advice and motivation from teachers becomes crucial.

What SRL strategies do university students develop using technologies?

Each of the resulting factors is described herein, focusing on the degree to which students use the various SRL strategies.

Factor 1. Share information. In the first factor, we located SRL strategies that belong to several of the categories considered in the models by Zimmerman and Pintrich (see Table 1). The items are characterised by the students' concern about broadcasting and sharing the documents that they draw up for class. These documents may have varied formats, such as presentations, books, blogs or electronic addresses. When deciding to share digital resources, students show a high degree of self-regulation, as by broadcasting their work, they run the "risk" of others criticizing their work. This is especially clear when students use blogs to express their opinions and where anyone may make a comment. In this sense, our results are coherent with those of Baggetun & Wasson (2006) when analysing the contribution of blogs to SRL. They pointed out that the nature of an open, written environment forces the recognition that SRL is not limited to the individual sphere, it also acquires collectively (collective self-regulation).

The factor "frequency of use" was very low (M = 1.37 SD = .57) among the students: 87.1% of the students had never used social markers to store and share information, 86.5% had never had a blog to publish considerations and 82.1% had never made their work available to others by means of an electronic format for reuse (Table 2).

Factor 2. Active presence. The second factor is linked to strategies in which the learning objectives are sought through an active presence on the web. Not only is the web an extensive library to search for information, it is also a space for interaction to construct social learning. Social networks as well as micro blogging services have proven to be a new means of communication that supports informal learning (Ebner et al., 2010; Vivian, 2011). Students use these resources to discuss topics they are studying, exams and assessments, share information, ideas, feelings and opinions or exchange study resources (texts, photos, videos). Such resources favour reflective thoughts, collaborative learning, the reception of feedback and coaching from others (Gao et al., 2012; Nosko & Wood, 2011). Their contribution is not only limited to academic development; it is also useful for personal, social and professional development (Wong et al., 2012).

As shown in Table 3, university students use digital technologies very little to promote their presence before others (M = 2.08 SD = .86). Nevertheless, from the set of strategies, one is implemented more often than the rest. This is the case because 29.9% of the students regularly consult updates relative to study contents distributed via social networks. Of these, 11.3% do it more frequently.

Factor 3. Documentation and classification. Searching for and classifying information is an essential aspect of university work. Today's students are ever more accustomed to using specific tools that help them to locate, organize and recover the information they need. This is not the case when it comes to relying upon these tools to manage and correctly use the sources in their academic work (He et al., 2012). Students prefer digital documents available online. Students see Internet, and more specifically search engines and academic databases, as the starting point when it comes to searching for information (Dilek-Kayaoglu, 2014). However, they need further information about how

Table 2 Factorial loads, means and standard deviations of SRLTU items for the first factor, "Share information"

	Factorial load	*M*	SD
28. When designing a multimedia presentation, I share it through repositories such as Slideshare.	.754	1.53	.99
29. I turn my work and notes into an e-book (Issuu, Calameo…) to facilitate its distribution.	.659	1.32	.83
26. I use social markers to register information found on Internet.	.619	1.20	.63
14. I have a blog where I comment topics regarding contents.	.598	1.24	.72
25. Before turning in my work, I verify its originality using anti-plagiarism software.	.544	1.39	.90
10. When studying, I create concept maps with specific software.	.451	1.54	.98

Table 3 Factorial loads, means and standard deviations of SRLTU items for the second factor, "Active presence"

	Factorial load	*M*	SD
18. I'm a member of groups on social networks that discuss, exchange information, etc., about content-related topics.	.739	2.13	1.36
17. I look up content-related information, news, etc., distributed on social networks.	.679	2.68	1.32
15. I share pictures on Instagram, Pinterest… about practical work carried out for the subjects.	.544	1.93	1.18
1. I discuss the information facilitated by teachers during class using Twitter, Facebook…	.487	1.62	.98

to correctly cite and reference these sources (Imler & Hall, 2009). Our results prove this, as 40.1% of the students search for information in databases with high or very high frequency. Yet, with the same frequency, only 7.2% store and classify such sources using citation management tools and recover the information when producing reports, essays, etc (Table 4).

Factor 4. Superficial use with limited information processing. Students resort to online encyclopaedias and dictionaries, as opposed to hard copies, when faced with the need to look up the definition of a concept (He et al., 2012). More specifically, they resort to Wikipedia when they need to quickly inquire about an unknown fact or topic or for in-depth information regarding a given topic (Lim, 2009). The strategies considered under this factor are those that help reach an understanding of the information handled when studying or during other academic activities. They refer to the use of Wikipedia and online dictionaries as well as e translators for purely apparent purposes and for a low level of information processing. The result is that students very frequently use both. More than 50% of the students frequently use online translators and more than 60% resort to Wikipedia. In this sense, the factor turns into the only one that reaches the highest level of use (M = 3.65 SD = .94) (Table 5).

Factor 5. Expansion and in-depth information. The fifth factor takes us closer to the pro-active attitude of students who are unhappy studying with only what their teachers provide. By contrast, students embark upon a richer and more independent learning process facilitated by digital technologies (video, blogs, presentations, etc.). Students like to use pre-recorded classes when preparing classes or while studying (Gorissen et al., 2012). Currently, they also rely on the slides presented by teachers (Parson et al., 2009). Our results reveal that, at some stage, 58.1% of those surveyed view videos related to the contents they are studying and 64.6% review multimedia presentations that they have found on their own accord. Students work directly on multimedia resources that have not necessarily been provided by the teacher (Table 6).

Factor 6. Monitoring and feedback. Unlike the previous factor, this one includes those strategies that pursue learning through listening. Using podcasts, students may relive

Table 4 Factorial loads, means and standard deviations of SRLTU items for the third factor, "Documentation and classification"

	Factorial load	*M*	SD
8. I locate scientific, content-related texts in specialised data bases (Google scholar, Dialnet…).	.752	2.99	1.39
16. I use citation management tools such as RefWorks, Mendeley... when I need to draft reports or essays.	.578	1.47	.98

Table 5 Factorial loads, means and standard deviations of SRLTU items for the factor "superficial use with limited information processing"

	Factorial load	*M*	SD
9. I use web translators to understand content-related texts written in other languages	.695	3.45	1.29
32. I resort to Wikipedia or any other online dictionary when I need to clarify a content-related topic or concept.	.550	3.85	1.15

master classes with the opportunity to listen to them on more than one occasion whilst they take and check their notes. Consequently, this leads to good learning results (McKinney et al., 2009; Scutter et al., 2010). Also, academic success rates increase if students create their own audio productions, given the fact that they are involved in transforming and communicating or sharing information with others (Heilesen, 2010). Considering the massive volume of information available on the web, such presentations are a perfect complement to the information received (Hew, 2009). Based on the above, the factor is made up of those strategies that, in Zimmerman's model, respond to the review of recorded information and memorisation, which feed mainly off podcasts. However, limited use is made of all these strategies. Therefore, 84.5% of students have never downloaded podcasts for playback when studying and 75.8% have not recorded themselves for self-examination (Table 7).

Factor 7. Personal management. The strategies grouped together in this factor refer to student time and information management: the need to have immediate access to the most recently published information in sources of interest, to count on the material produced by teachers to help them when studying, to solve proposed academic activities in the most efficient and attractive manner possible and to distribute the time available for this and studying. Once again, all of the strategies included in this factor have a very low level of use: 73.1% of the students have never syndicated to electronic sources and 63.7% have never or hardly ever organised their agenda using management software (Table 8).

Factor 8. Self-evaluation. Self-evaluation is a relevant portion in the SRL process as it encourages one to ponder his/her own learning (Ibabe and Jauregizar, 2010). This is the case to such a point that it has been considered one of the central strategies in the last SRL phase. Zimmerman defined it as such and Pintrich considered it among the metacognitive strategies, more specifically follow-up. Self-evaluation is the activity through which students verify their own level of learning, as they must carry out self-correction exercises or digital tests on line. Despite its importance for SRL, it is not widely used by students ($M = 1.85$ $SD = .86$): 90.2% of the students never or hardly ever practiced

Table 6 Factorial loads, means and standard deviations of SRLTU items for the factor "expansion and in-depth information"

	Factorial load	*M*	SD
31. I follow Youtube video channels where there are videos related to the topics I'm studying.	.783	1.97	1.27
5. When studying, I search for content-related videos on Youtube, Vimeo…	.643	2.83	1.28
33. I follow blogs by experts who publish content-related work.	.521	2.04	1.27
3. When studying, I look for multimedia, content-related presentations (Slideshare, Prezi...).	.444	2.95	1.27

Table 7 Factorial loads, means and standard deviations of SRLTU items for the sixth factor, "Monitoring and feedback"

	Factorial load	*M*	SD
7. I record my own content-related podcasts to use them when I'm studying.	.676	1.29	.79
2. I record the teacher's presentations with my mobile device.	.668	1.54	.94
6. When studying, I listen to content-related podcasts found on iTunes, iVoox…	.590	1.24	.67
22. When preparing a presentation, a practical exam…. I record myself using a handheld device.	.430	1.45	.95

with simulated online exams, and even when 40.9% have at some point practiced with self-correction activities, 58.4% make little or very little use of them (Table 9).

Factor 9. Collaborative learning. Collaborating or simply interacting with classmates is the aim of the strategies included in the last of the factors. They all correspond to a specific category of those considered in Zimmerman's (social support) model as well as Pintrich's (social resource management). Although self-regulation learning is an individual characteristic, it is no longer questionable if a student community offers an adequate environment for developing SRL (Beishuizen, 2008). This factor illustrates how certain digital technologies favour social learning, as would be the case of *cloud computing* technologies (Denton, 2012). Unlike the rest of the factors, two of the strategies included are of very frequent use: 74.1% of the students frequently interact with their classmates outside the classroom using instant messaging apps, and 63.4% regularly share material via the cloud for studying or working together (Table 10).

Ultimately, the factor analysis provides new aspects for organising SRL strategies as put forward by Zimmerman (1989, 1990) or Pintrich (1999a, b). Those identified have been updated with the incorporation of digital technologies on behalf of the students.

What profiles could be identified among students based on their use of self-regulation strategies with technology?

The description of each of the factors proves that some of the technology-based SRL strategies are more frequent than others among university students. Herein, the descriptions of the two antagonistic student profiles identified evidence that Andalusian university students do not use technology-based SRL strategies in the same manner. It is noteworthy that a large number of young people implement limited strategies without a high level of usage.

Table 8 Factorial loads, means and standard deviations of SRLTU items for the factor "personal management"

	Factorial load	*M*	SD
19. I use programmes such as Google Calendar, EverNote… to handle my academic activity agenda.	.646	2.23	1.52
21. I download content-related material through my institution's repository of learning objects (RODAS, RiUMA, etc.) or from open learning resource libraries such as Universia.	.579	2.22	1.45
27. I use Really Simple Syndication (RSS) feeds to receive updated information about topics I am interested in.	.533	1.51	1.01
30. I use specific apps (such as scientific calculator Kaljulilo, Whiteboard Lite…) to solve problems and exercises included in the subjects.	.454	1.82	1.23

Table 9 Factorial loads, means and standard deviations of SRLTU items for the eighth factor, "Self-evaluation"

	Factorial load	*M*	SD
24. I look for content-related, self-evaluation exercises online and I use them to prepare for exams.	.700	*2.36*	1.28
23. I create online exam samples (ExamTime, Google Forms...) and I share them with my classmates when preparing exams.	.515	*1.35*	.82

The first profile characterises students with a greater level of self-regulation learning and the use of technologies (see Fig. 2). They represent 84 students, which is 11.86% of the respondents. Of these, 65.5% are female, and 59.5% are between 21 and 25 years of age while 17.9% are under 20. They stand out because they have the greatest mean frequency of implementation in all the factors, including those with a low level of use as in the case of sharing information and monitoring and feedback. They are students who use a variety of technologies for discussion, request help from peers, exchange material and collaborate with classmates when studying or preparing classwork. They are more familiar with handling instant messaging (IM) apps (M = 4.78 SD = .47) but they do not forsake videoconference tools (M = 3.43 SD = 1.31) for communication. They frequently use online translators, (M = 4.12 SD = .97), encyclopaedias and dictionaries (M = 4.11 SD = 1.00) to help process information that they do not understand. They are used to searching the web for multimedia resources such as videos (M = 4.10 SD = 1.05) and presentations (M = 4.02 SD = 1.04) that allow them to expand and delve into the information received in the classroom.

The second profile, on the other hand, refers to students with a lower level of use of self-regulation learning strategies involving technologies (see Fig. 2). This group includes 238 students, which corresponds to 33.62% of the respondents. Of these, 62.2% are between 21 and 25 years of age. This group of students shows an intermediate level regarding the use of strategies for the superficial use of information and collaborative learning factors. Most of them actively use instant messaging apps to communicate with their classmates (M = 4.27 SD = 1.07). They are frequent Wikipedia users (M = 3.41 SD = 1.21).

Discussion

This study adopts the theoretical models regarding self-regulation learning developed by Zimmerman and Pintrich for the interpretation of the use that Andalusian university students make of digital technologies to favour learning. We have moved away from limiting the focus of this work on the type of technologies used in their learning processes, whether this is due to individual initiatives, independently of classroom

Table 10 Factorial loads, means and standard deviations of SRLTU items for the factor "Collaborative learning"

	Factorial load	*M*	SD
4. I share material with my classmates using Dropbox, Google+	.754	3.72	1.22
11. I produce collaborative work using tools such as wikis, Google Drive...	.753	3.44	1.38
12. I interact outside the classroom with classmates using apps (WhatsApp, Line...) and we exchange information, solve doubts, etc.	.597	4.59	.82
13. I communicate with my classmates via videoconference (Skype, Google Talk...) to solve or discuss topics related to the subjects.	.562	2.19	1.34

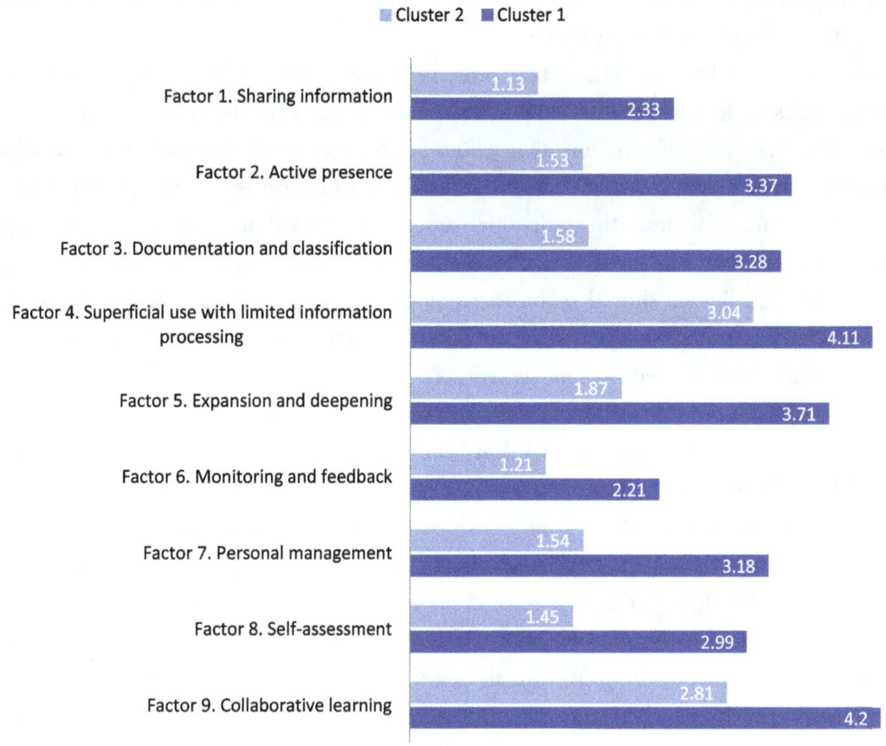

Fig. 2 Final cluster centres. The second grouped bar chart shows the final cluster centres of each of the two groups of students identified with more antagonistic behaviours in each of the factors generated from the principal component analysis. These central values help describe the composition of the clusters

demands or the frequency with which students use these technologies. This research is more focused on determining which type of SRL strategies university students use digital technologies for.

We can state that Andalusian university students make limited use of learning technologies. Most of the technologies that we considered could be useful to assist them in studying are, in practice, excluded. Internet search engines or databases and instant communication tools are the most generalised and used continually by the respondents. These coincide with those identified by Kennedy et al. (2008) as the resources that students generally want to use in their studies. Despite the time elapsed since this work was presented, we agree with Mirriahi & Alonzo (2015) that the type of technology that students handle for learning has remained practically unchanged over the years.

On the other hand, we maintain that university students carry out varied actions to self-regulate learning using technologies. This coincides with the conclusions reached by Chaves et al. (2016). Based on the most used technologies, the most generalized SRL strategies are those relative to social support. As shown in the cluster analysis, even the group of students with a lesser level of use of self-regulation learning strategies with technologies uses them regularly.

The selected profiles show that university students do not have a uniform behaviour when it comes to SRL and technologies. New lines of work are now open. It will be interesting to deepen into how students organize and manage their learning using technologies, and the reasons that explain the varied uses of SRL strategies with technologies. Observation and interviews allow us to learn and trace processes, learning dilemmas and styles among students.

According to Winne (1995), SRL is principally comprised of knowledge, beliefs and learned skills. It forms incrementally as learners engage with instructional experiences where they receive information that is useful to construct knowledge about what productive self-regulation is, and when and how it can be used. Consequently, future research should look into the individual differences regarding a learner's knowledge base about SRL, and knowledge about when and under what conditions that knowledge is engaged. Equally, we should reconsider going over at least one of the questions that Boekaerts & Cascallar (2006) address: "*What can teachers do to help students self-regulate their learning, motivation and effort?*"

Upon analising the learning activities that instructors at Andalusian universities design and implement (Authors, 2015), it becomes apparent that if students do not use digital technologies to regulate their own learning, it is because teachers neither require nor encourage their use. There is no reason why students who use digital resources on a regular basis in their personal and social life should not use them when studying or learning. We therefore highlight the need for university teachers to incorporate digital technologies, because our students must learn to use the technological and conceptual tools that workers use in professional careers. Failing to do so translates into the perpetuation of the gap between industry and education (Feiman & Buchmann, 1983): the university world and the labour and social world.

University teachers need to create learning environments that favour independent and self-regulated learning, in which students have opportunities to seek challenges, to reflect on their progress, and to take responsibility and pride in their accomplishments (Paris & Paris, 2001). Research is appearing, not only to highlight teaching methods that can improve academic self-regulation but also to present teaching models that promote SRL using new ICTs as support (Cazan, 2013; Núñez et al., 2011).

New technologies are being incorporated into the design of intervention programs to promote SRL within the university context (Cerezo et al., 2010). For example, there are a growing number of learning designs that seek to achieve balance between self-regulated, personalised learning and scaffolding/support through the use of Web 2.0 and social software tools (McLoughlin & Lee, 2010). Dabbagh & Kitsantas (2012) described one of the possible pedagogical frameworks that teachers can use to demonstrate to students how to use social media to foster SRL.

If we propose to research how students become masters of their own learning processes and teachers contribute to it, we have to reconsider the methodology followed in the data collection phase of this research (Zimmerman, 2008). At the same time, we must surpass an important limitation encountered in the interpretation of our findings. Future research should consider expanding the size and diversity of the student sample, while also taking the teacher population into account.

Beyond what is presented herein, this work is useful to expand our understanding of how SRL takes place with technologies. The factor analysis used to aid the presentation of the results facilitates a way to interpret SRL strategies that is different from the models presented by Zimmerman and Pintrich. The resulting factors constitute categories that are useful to classify the set of SRL strategies that university students develop by means of technologies. Each of the factors groups together strategies that seek the same learning objective through pedagogical affordances of technology (information, relationship or personal management, monitoring, etc.). Following the models by Zimmerman and Pintrich only allows us to recognize SRL strategies based on technologies that respond to the aspect of social support or management of resources (social) and self-assessment or follow-up.

Consistent with our results, previous studies have evidenced that different technological tools (e.g., collaborative and communication tools, content creation and delivery tools) supported different SRL processes (Dabbagh & Kitsantas, 2005). In keeping with this, SRL strategies need to be explained in a way that differs from the time when the technological component was not included to facilitate the task (Lai & Gu, 2011).

Conclusions

This work addresses a set of SRL strategies that university students may implement using digital technologies. The strategies identified are consistent with what has been pointed out in the research literature. These strategies range from the simplest activities, such as reading, classifying, using or sharing information, to others with a higher level of intentionality and cognitive complexity, such as monitoring, self-assessment or personal management.

Of them all, we highlight a group of strategies that show the appropriation of digital technologies for a more connected learning model. We are referring to those strategies that we have called "active presence". These prove university students' interest in sharing and exchanging their own digital contents, creating opinions, etc. Ultimately, this demonstrates that young people need to have a personal presence on the network and favours collaborative learning. Students project their learning well beyond the physical academic space to be able to learn with their fellow classmates by using digital technologies.

Therefore, the results show a university student profile that usually fails to consider it necessary, or lacks adequate training, to incorporate digital technologies into their own academic learning process. Students make limited use of SRL strategies with technologies. They state that the digital technologies they use have more to do with simple activities such as searching, storing or sharing information. These activities, although necessary for the learning process, are limited when not complemented with others that support understanding, monitoring or self-assessment of the actual student throughout the learning process.

As a final conclusion, university teachers must favour self-regulation of learning, offer the students the opportunities to discover the usefulness of digital technologies and foster their incorporation into the actual learning process.

Funding
Consejería de Innovacion, Ciencia y Empresa. Junta de Andalucía.

Availability of data and materials
Not applicable

Ethics approval and consent to participate
Not applicable

Competing interests
Not applicable

References

Marcelo, C., Yot, C., & Mayor, C. (2015). University Teaching with Digital Technologies. *Comunicar, 23*(45), 117-124. doi: 10.3916/C45-2015-12.

Baggetun, R., & Wasson, B. (2006). Self-regulated learning and open writing. *European Journal of Education, 41*(3/4), 453–472. doi:10.1111/j.1465-3435.2006.00276.x.

Barnard Brak, L., Lan, W. Y., & Paton, V. O. (2010). Profiles in self-regulated learning in the online learning environment. *International Review of Research in Open and Distance Learning, 11*(1), 61–80.

Beishuizen, J. (2008). Does a community of learners foster self-regulated learning? *Technology, Pedagogy and Education, 17*(3), 183–193. doi:10.1080/14759390802383769.

Beishuizen, J., & Steffens, K. (2011). A conceptual framework for research on self-regulated learning. In R. Carneiro, P. Lefrere, K. Steffens, & J. Underwood (Eds.), *Self-regulated learning in technology enhanced learning environments*, (pp. 3–19). The Netherlands: Sense Publishers.

Bennett, S. J., Maton, K. A., & Kervin, L. K. (2008). The "digital natives" debate: A critical review of the evidence. *British Journal of Educational Technology, 39*(5), 775–786. doi:10.1111/j.1467-8535.2007.00793.x.

Bernacki, M. L., Aguilar, A. C., & Byrnes, J. P. (2011). Self-regulated learning and technology- enhanced learning environments: An opportunity-propensity analysis. In G. Dettori, & D. Persico (Eds.), *Fostering self-regulated learning through ICT*, (pp. 1–26). Hersey, PA: IGI Global Publishers.

Boekaerts, M., & Cascallar, E. (2006). How far have we moved toward the integration of theory and practice in self-regulation? *Educational Psychology Review, 18*(3), 199–210. doi:10.1007/s10648-006-9013-4.

Cazan, A. M. (2013). Teaching self-regulated learning strategies for psychology students. *Procedia. Social and Behavioral Sciences, 78*, 743–747. doi:10.1016/j.sbspro.2013.04.387.

Cerezo, R., Núñez, J. C., Rosário, P., Valle, A., Rodríguez, S., & Bernardo, A. B. (2010). New media for the promotion of self-regulated learning in higher education. *Psicothema, 22*(2), 306–315.

Chaves, E., Trujillo, J. M., & López, J. A. (2016). Acciones para la autorregulación del aprendizaje en entornos personales. *Pixel-Bit. Revista de Medios y Educación*, (48), 67–82. doi:10.12795/pixelbit.2016.i48.05.

Corrin, L., Bennett, S., & Lockyer, L. (2010). Digital natives: Everyday life versus academic study. In *Paper presented at the 7th International Conference on Networked Learning*. Aalborg: Denmark.

Dabbagh, N., & Kitsantas, A. (2005). Using web-based pedagogical tools as scaffolds for self-regulated learning. *Instructional Science, 33*(5), 513–540. doi:10.1007/s11251-005-1278-3.

Dabbagh, N., & Kitsantas, A. (2012). Personal learning environments, social media, and self-regulated learning: A natural formula for connecting formal and informal learning. *Internet and Higher Education, 15*(1), 3–8. doi:10.1016/j.iheduc.2011.06.002.

Dabbagh, N., & Kitsantas, A. (2013). Using learning management systems as Metacognitive tools to support self-regulation in higher education contexts. In R. Azevedo, & V. Aleven (Eds.), *International handbook of Metacognition and learning technologies*, (pp. 197–211). New York: Springer.

Dahlstrom, E., Walker, J. D., & Dziuban, C. (2013). *ECAR study of undergraduate students and information technology*. Louisville, CO: EDUCAUSE Center for Analysis and Research.

Deepwell, F., & Malik, S. (2008). On campus, but out of class: An investigation into students' experiences of learning technologies in their self-directed study. *ALT-J, Research in Learning Technology, 16*(1), 5–14. doi:10.3402/rlt.v16i1.10881.

Denton, D. W. (2012). Enhancing instruction through constructivism, cooperative learning, and cloud computing. *TechTrends, 56*(4), 34–41. doi:10.1007/s11528-012-0585-1.

Dilek-Kayaoglu, H. (2014). Information-seeking behavior of undergraduate, graduate, and doctoral students: A survey of Istanbul University, Turkey. In J. N. Gathegi, Y. Tonta, S. Kurbanoğlu, U. Al, & Z. Taşkın (Eds.), *Challenges of information management beyond the cloud*, (pp. 123–136). Berlin: Springer.

Ebner, M., Lienhardt, C., Rohs, M., & Meyer, I. (2010). Microblogs in higher education. A chance to facilitate informal and process-oriented learning? *Computers & Education, 55*(1), 92–100. doi:10.1016/j.compedu.2009.12.006.

Feiman, S., & Buchmann, M. (1983). *Pitfall of experience in teacher preparation*. Michigan: Institute for Research on Teaching Retrieved from http://files.eric.ed.gov/fulltext/ED237504.pdf.

Gallardo, E., Marqués, L., & Bullen, M. (2015). Students in higher education: Social and academic uses of digital technology. *RUSC. Universities and Knowledge Society Journal, 12*(1), 25–37. doi:10.7238/rusc.v12i1.2078.

Gao, F., Luo, T., & Zhang, K. (2012). Tweeting for learning: A critical analysis of research on microblogging in education published in 2008–2011. *British Journal of Educational Technology, 43*(5), 783–801. doi:10.1111/j.1467-8535.2012.01357.x.

Gorissen, P., van Bruggen, J., & Jochems, W. (2012). Students and recorded lectures: Survey on current use and demands for higher education. *Research in Learning Technology, 20*, 297–311. doi:10.3402/rlt.v20i0.17299.

Gosper, M., Malfroy, J., & McKenzie, J. (2013). Students' experiences and expectations of technologies: An Australian study designed to inform planning and development decisions. *Australasian Journal of Educational Technology, 29*(2), 268–283. doi:10.1234/ajet.v29i2.127.

He, D., Wu, D., Yue, Z., Fu, A., & Vo, K. T. (2012). Undergraduate students' interaction with online information resources in their academic tasks. A comparative study. *ASLIB Proceedings*, *64*(6), 615–640. doi:10.1108/00012531211281715.

Heilesen, S. B. (2010). What is the academic efficacy of podcasting? *Computers & Education*, *55*(3), 1063–1068. doi:10.1016/j.compedu.2010.05.002.

Hew, K. F. (2009). Use of audio podcast in K-12 and higher education: A review of research topics and methodologies. *Educational Technology Research and Development*, *57*(3), 333–357. doi:10.1007/s11423-008-9108-3.

Ibabe, I., & Jauregizar, J. (2010). Online self-assessment with feedback and metacognitive knowledge. *Higher Education*, *59*(2), 243–258. doi:10.1007/s10734-009-9245-6.

Imler, B., & Hall, R. A. (2009). Full-text articles: Faculty perceptions, student use, and citation abuse. *Reference Services Review*, *37*(1), 65–72. doi:10.1108/00907320910935002.

Jones, C., Ramanau, R., Cross, S., & Healing, G. (2010). Net generation or digital natives: Is there a distinct new generation entering university? *Computers & Education*, *54*(3), 722–732. doi:10.1016/j.compedu.2009.09.022.

Kennedy, G. E., Judd, T. S., Churchward, A., Gray, K., & Krause, K. L. (2008). First year students' experiences with technology: Are they really digital natives? *Australasian Journal of Educational Technology*, *24*(1), 108–122. doi:10.14742/ajet.v24i1.1233.

Kingsbury, M. (2015). Encouraging independent learning. In H. Fry, S. Ketteridge, & S. Marshal (Eds.), *A handbook for teaching and learning in higher education: Enhancing academic practice*, (pp. 169–179). New York: Routledge.

Kitsantas, A. (2013). Fostering college students' self- regulated learning with learning technologies. *Hellenic Journal of Psychology*, *10*, 235–252.

Kitsantas, A., & Dabbagh, N. (2011). The role of web 2.0 technologies in self-regulated learning. *New Directions for Teaching and Learning*, (126), 99–106. doi:10.1002/tl.448.

Lai, C., & Gu, M. (2011). Self-regulated out-of-class language learning with technology. *Computer Assisted Language Learning*, *24*(4), 317–335. doi:10.1080/09588221.2011.568417.

Lai, C., Wang, Q., & Lei, J. (2012). What factors predict undergraduate students' use of technology for learning? A case from Hong Kong. *Computers & Education*, *59*(2), 569–579. doi:10.1016/j.compedu.2012.03.006.

Lim, S. (2009). How and why do College students use Wikipedia? *Journal of the American Society for Information Science and Technology*, *60*(11), 2189–2202. doi:10.1002/asi.21142.

Littlejohn, A., Margaryan, A., & Vojt, G. (2010). Exploring students' use of ICT and expectations of learning methods. *Electronic Journal of e-Learning*, *8*(1), 13–20.

Lorenzo Romero, C., Alarcón del Amo, M. C., & Gómez Borja, M. A. (2014). Learning styles and web technology use in business and economics university students. *Procedia. Social and Behavioral Sciences*, *141*, 1281–1290. doi:10.1016/j.sbspro.2014.05.221.

Margaryan, A., Littlejohn, A., & Vojt, G. (2011). Are digital natives a myth or reality? University students' use of digital technologies. *Computers & Education*, *56*(2), 429–440. doi:10.1016/j.compedu.2010.09.004.

McKinney, D., Dyck, J. L., & Luber, E. S. (2009). iTunes university and the classroom: Can podcasts replace professors? *Computers & Education*, *52*(3), 617–623. doi:10.1016/j.compedu.2008.11.004.

McLoughlin, C., & Lee, M. J. W. (2010). Personalised and self-regulated learning in the web 2.0 era: International exemplars of innovative pedagogy using social software. *Australasian Journal of Educational Technology*, *26*(1), 28–43

Mirriahi, N., & Alonzo, D. (2015). Shedding light on students' technology preferences: Implications for academic development. *Journal of University Teaching & Learning Practice*, *12*(1), 1–14.

Ning, H. K., & Downing, K. (2015). A latent profile analysis of university students' self-regulated learning strategies. *Studies in Higher Education*, *40*(7), 1328–1346. doi:10.1080/03075079.2014.880832.

Nosko, A., & Wood, E. (2011). Learning in the digital age with SNSs: Creating a profile. In B. White, I. King, & P. Tsang (Eds.), *Social media tools and platforms in learning environments*, (pp. 399–418). Berlin: Springer-Verlag.

Núñez, J. C., Cerezo, R., Bernardo, A., Rosário, P., Valle, A., Fernández, E., & Suárez, N. (2011). Implementation of training programs in self-regulated learning strategies in Moodle format: Results of a experience in higher education. *Psicothema*, *23*(2), 274–281.

Panadero, E., & Alonso Tapia, J. (2014). How do students self-regulate? Review of Zimmerman's cyclical model of self-regulated learning. *Anales de Psicología*, *30*(2), 450–462. doi:10.6018/analesps.30.2.167221.

Paris, S. G., & Paris, A. H. (2001). Classroom applications of research on self-regulated learning. *Educational Psychologist*, *36*(2), 89–101. doi:10.1207/S15326985EP3602_4.

Parson, V., Reddy, P., Wood, J., & Senior, C. (2009). Educating an iPod generation: Undergraduate attitudes, experiences and understanding of vodcast and podcast use. *Learning, Media and Technology*, *34*(3), 215–228. doi:10.1080/17439880903141497.

Pintrich, P. R. (1999a). Taking control of research on volitional control: Challenges for future theory and research. *Learning and Individual Differences*, *11*(3), 335–354. doi:10.1016/S1041-6080(99)80007-7.

Pintrich, P. R. (1999b). The role of motivation in promoting and sustaining self-regulated learning. *International Journal of Educational Research*, *31*(6), 459–470. doi:10.1016/S0883-0355(99)00015-4.

Pintrich, P. R. (2004). A conceptual framework for assessing motivation and self-regulated learning in college students. *Educational Psychology Review*, *16*(4), 385–407. doi:10.1007/s10648-004-0006-x.

Prensky, M. (2001). Digital natives, digital immigrants. *On the Horizon*, *9*(5), 1–6. doi:10.1108/10748120110424816.

Schneckenberg, D., Ehlers, U., & Adelsberger, H. (2011). Web 2.0 and competence-oriented design of learning. Potentials and implications for higher education. *British Journal of Educational Technology*, *42*(5), 747–762. doi:10.1111/j.1467-8535.2010.01092.x.

Scutter, S., Stupans, I., Sawyer, T., & King, S. (2010). How do students use podcasts to support learning? *Australasian Journal of Educational Technology*, *26*(2), 180–191. doi:10.14742/ajet.v26i2.1089.

Swanson, J. A., & Walker, E. (2015). Academic versus non-academic emerging adult college student technology use. *Technology, Knowledge and Learning*, *20*(2), 147–158. doi:10.1007/s10758-015-9258-4.

Valentín, A., Mateos, P. M., González Tablas, M. M., Pérez, L., López, E., & García, I. (2013). Motivation and learning strategies in the use of ICTs among university students. *Computers & Education*, *61*, 52–58. doi:10.1016/j.compedu.2012.09.008.

Valle, A., Núñez, J. C., Cabanach, R. G., González, J. A., Rodríguez, S., Rosário, P., Cerezo, R., & Muñoz, M. A. (2008). Self-regulated profiles and academic achievement. *Psicothema, 20*(4), 724–731.

Vivian, R. (2011). University students' informal learning practices using Facebook: Help or hindrance? In R. Kwan, C. McNaught, P. Tsang, F. Lee Wang, & K. Cheong Li (Eds.), *Enhancing learning through technology. Education unplugged: Mobile technologies and web 2.0*, (pp. 254–267). Berlin: Springer.

Vrocharidou, A., & Efthymiou, I. (2012). Computer mediated communication for social and academic purposes: Profiles of use and university students' gratifications. *Computers & Education, 58*(1), 609–616. doi:10.1016/j.compedu.2011.09.015.

Winne, P. H. (1995). Inherent details in self-regulated learning. *Educational Psychologist, 30*(4), 173–187. doi:10.1207/s15326985ep3004_2.

Winters, F. I., Greene, J. A., & Costich, C. M. (2008). Self-regulation of learning within computer-based learning environments: A critical analysis. *Educational Psychology Review, 20*(4), 429–444. doi:10.1007/s10648-008-9080-9.

Wong, K., Kwan, R., Leung, K., & Wang, F. L. (2012). Exploring the potential benefits of Facebook on personal, social, academic and career development for higher education students. In S. K. S. Cheung, J. Fong, L. F. Kwok, K. Li, & R. Kwan (Eds.), *Hybrid learning*, (pp. 253–264). Berlin: Springer.

Zimmerman, B. J. (1989). A social cognitive view of self-regulated academic learning. *Journal of Educational Psychology, 81*(3), 329–339.

Zimmerman, B. J. (1990). Self-regulated learning and academic achievement: An overview. *Educational Psychologist, 25*(1), 3–17.

Zimmerman, B. J. (1998). Developing self-fulfilling cycles of academic regulation: An analysis of exemplary instructional models. In D. H. Schunk, & B. J. Zummerman (Eds.), *Self-regulated learning. From teaching to self-reflective practice*, (pp. 1–19). New York: The Guilford Press.

Zimmerman, B. J. (2008). Investigating self-regulation and motivation: Historical background, methodological developments, and future prospects. *American Educational Research Journal, 45*(1), 166–183. doi:10.3102/0002831207312909.

Zimmerman, B. J. (2009). Theories of self-regulated learning and academic achievement: An overview and analysis. In B. J. Zimmerman, & D. H. Schunk (Eds.), *Self-regulated learning and academic achievement, Theoretical Perspectives* (pp. 1–38). New York: Routledge.

Zimmerman, B. J., & Martinez Pons, M. (1986). Development of a structured interview for assessing student use of self-regulated learning strategies. *American Educational Research Journal, 23*(4), 614–628. doi:10.3102/00028312023004614.

Zimmerman, B. J., & Moylan, A. R. (2009). Self-regulation: Where metacognition and motivation intersect. In D. J. Hacker, J. Dunlosky, & A. C. Graesser (Eds.), *Handbook of Metacognition in education*, (pp. 299–315). New York: Routledge.

Zimmerman, B. J., & Schunk, D. H. (2011). Self-regulated learning and performance. In B. J. Zimmerman, & D. H. Schunk (Eds.), *Handbook of self-regulation of learning and performance*, (pp. 1–12). New York: Routledge.

4

Student use and perception of technology enhanced learning in a mass lecture knowledge-rich domain first year undergraduate module

Daniel J. Peart*, Penny L. S. Rumbold, Karen M. Keane and Linda Allin

* Correspondence:
Daniel.peart@northumbria.ac.uk
Department of Sport, Exercise and Rehabilitation, Faculty of Health and Life Sciences, Northumbria University, Newcastle-upon-Tyne, UK

Abstract

The purpose of this study was to examine student use and perceptions of technology enhanced learning tools (TELTs), including their value for learning. Students enrolled onto a 12-week undergraduate science module had access to four TELTs each week, (i) a recording of the lecture (Panopto™), (ii) an animated mini review of the lecture (ShowMe), (iii) a multiple choice quiz hosted on Blackboard® (MCQ), and (iv) a module Twitter feed. Ninety-five students completed a survey at the end of the module, which included quantitative and qualitative questions, to examine whether they perceived the TELT to be useful for their learning. Analysis of the quantitative data suggest that Twitter was used significantly less than the other three TELTs ($p < 0.001$) with less people agreeing that it helped their learning ($p < 0.001$), whilst ShowMe and MCQ had a greater occurrence of an 'agree' rating compared to Twitter and Panopto ($p \leq 0.002$). A thematic analysis of the qualitative responses identified assessment as a common theme across all four TELTs, being a positive factor for Panopto, ShowMe and MCQ, but negative for Twitter. Students highlighted ShowMe as being particularly useful for simplifying information. Based on this study TELTs similar to ShowMe (i.e. animations) are most recommended as this was one of the two highly rated TELTs (alongside MCQ), but may have more potential for crossover with other subjects, and students found it useful for more than just assessment.

Keywords: Social network, Animations, Assessment, Tel, E learning

Introduction

Technology enhanced learning (TEL) has the potential to enhance the student experience by facilitating self-paced learning, lowering inhibition thresholds for asking questions, and allowing access to learning on an as-and-when basis (Kamath, 2015), all of which are factors that may contribute to informal and incidental learning outside of the formal learning space (Peart et al., 2014). There is a body of research examining the role of the teacher in facilitating TEL, and a reservation or anxiety from staff has been described with respect to the technology acceptance model (Blackwell et al., 2014; Gong et al., 2004; Louw, 2015; Teo et al., 2008). Such problems may present a barrier to the promotion of TEL to support student learning. However, an aspect that has been less researched is the contribution of students to the impact of TEL, and in particular their perspectives on TEL tools (TELT). There is a wealth of information on student perceptions of a selection of 'learning objects' (LO) and 'web based learning tools' (WBLT) (Cochrane, 2005; R. Kay, 2011; R. H. Kay & Knaack, 2009; Nurmi & Jaakkola, 2006; Vargo et al., 2003). Such studies can provide a useful insight for LO and WBLT developers, but the implication from a teaching perspective is somewhat limited unless the teacher is likely to use that very specific tool in their teaching. For example Cochrane (2005) evaluated two audio engineering LOs (interactive mixing desk and microphone chooser) and Nurmi and Jaakkola (2006) evaluated three LOs to teach fractions, the Finnish language and electrical DC circuits. Such tools are typically designed to be used in the classroom, and as a result do not promote extra-curricular and informal/incidental learning.

It may be more beneficial from a teaching perspective to understand the benefits of more generic TELTs, which staff can have more control over, implemented over a longer period of time. However current examples are limited, and are focused primarily upon an institution virtual learning environment (VLE) or social networking. Šumak et al. (2011) collated Electrical Engineering and Computer Science students' perceptions of using a general virtual VLE (Moodle) and reported that perceived usefulness was a strong predictor of intention to use the VLE. This again has limited scope today as the use of a VLE is now commonplace within Higher Education. However, the identification of perceived usefulness as a predictor of acceptance is important as it can direct research to now determine what characteristics students consider useful, or indeed how students define 'useful'. Junco et al. (2011) incorporated Twitter into a semester long module for pre-health professional majors, where students were encouraged to continue class discussions, organise study groups, and connect with each other and with staff. They concluded that the use of Twitter successfully increased student engagement, which may present a promising development for a wide range of teachers as the uses could be incorporated into any subject of study. However, the authors did not provide any data on the student perception of the use of Twitter, therefore it is unclear *why* the students engaged with Twitter, and without knowing this it is difficult to predict what other TELTs may be well accepted.

Lecture capture is another example of a generic TELT available to teaching staff. A narrative review identified that students use lecture capture to review content, but there is mixed evidence as to its effect on student grades and attendance (Karnad, 2013). This practice has been examined specifically in higher education science students, namely in the areas of veterinary medicine (Danielson et al., 2014) and pharmacy (Marchand et al., 2014). Danielson et al. (2014) reported that students perceived lecture capture to be most useful for learning in content driven lecture sessions compared to group work sessions, particularly for reviewing segments flagged in their notes, recapping a fast lecture, studying for examinations, and reviewing content missed due to absence. Staff agreed lecture capture to be beneficial for students to review lecture content, but identified reduced attendance as a risk. Marchand et al. (2014) also identified reduced attendance as a concern for staff, however neither study reported actual attendance data so it is unknown if the staff concerns were realised. In a letter to the editor Lach and McCarthy (2015) challenged the findings of Marchand et al. (2014) stating that attendance should not be a concern, as attendance is not a learning outcome and does not guarantee that learning will occur. They argue that staff focusing on the possible negative effect upon attendance may shadow the opportunities afforded by technology.

A form of TELT currently more researched in younger ages is the use of electronic whiteboards to simplify and share information (Castek & Beach, 2013; Maher, 2013). The potential for these to support learning in higher education has received little attention in the literature, other than being described as a useful tool for in the moment teaching (Archibald et al., 2014). Using such a tool to deliver a short summary video of the lecture may act to reinforce learning from the lecture, rather than replace it. Simplifying the lecture content in such a way may also help students direct their learning, and has been proposed as a way to help students overcome troublesome knowledge, as they present scientific mechanisms in the absence of other barriers such new terminology (Peart et al., 2014).

An understanding of student perceptions of different TELTs could be of benefit for a number of reasons; (i) identification of shared characteristics between well perceived TELTs may help predict what tools are likely to work in future, (ii) targeting particular types of TELTs may act to reduce staff anxiety by reducing choice and preventing over saturation with TELTs, (iii) contribute to the planning of departmental and institutional TEL strategies. The objective of this study was to integrate four different TELTs that the teaching staff could control into a semester long undergraduate sport and exercise science module, with the aim of examining student use and perceptions of the TELTs. Of particular interest was their views on accessibility, use and value for learning.

Method

Participants

The study focused on a 12-week Level 4 (first year Undergraduate) module called Energetics of Exercise, which included 210 students from BSc Applied Sport and Exercise Science, BSc Sport, Exercise and Nutrition and BSc Psychology with Sport Sciences. The summative assessment for the module consisted of three multiple-choice examinations throughout the semester. All procedures were approved by the institution's ethics committee, and all participants were provided with verbal and written information to ensure informed consent.

Experimental approach

The module was delivered primarily in a traditional manner with a one-hour lecture each week accompanied by 2 hours of additional contact time in a seminar, laboratory, or computer class. Alongside this traditional approach all of the students, irrespective of whether they chose to take part in the study, also had voluntary access to four different TELTs to support their learning each week. The TELTs were chosen with the intention of each serving a different function, to allow an insight into for what purpose students accessed the TELTs, as opposed to which TELT they preferred for a given purpose. It was also deemed important that the student could use each in his or her own time without the reliance of another person.

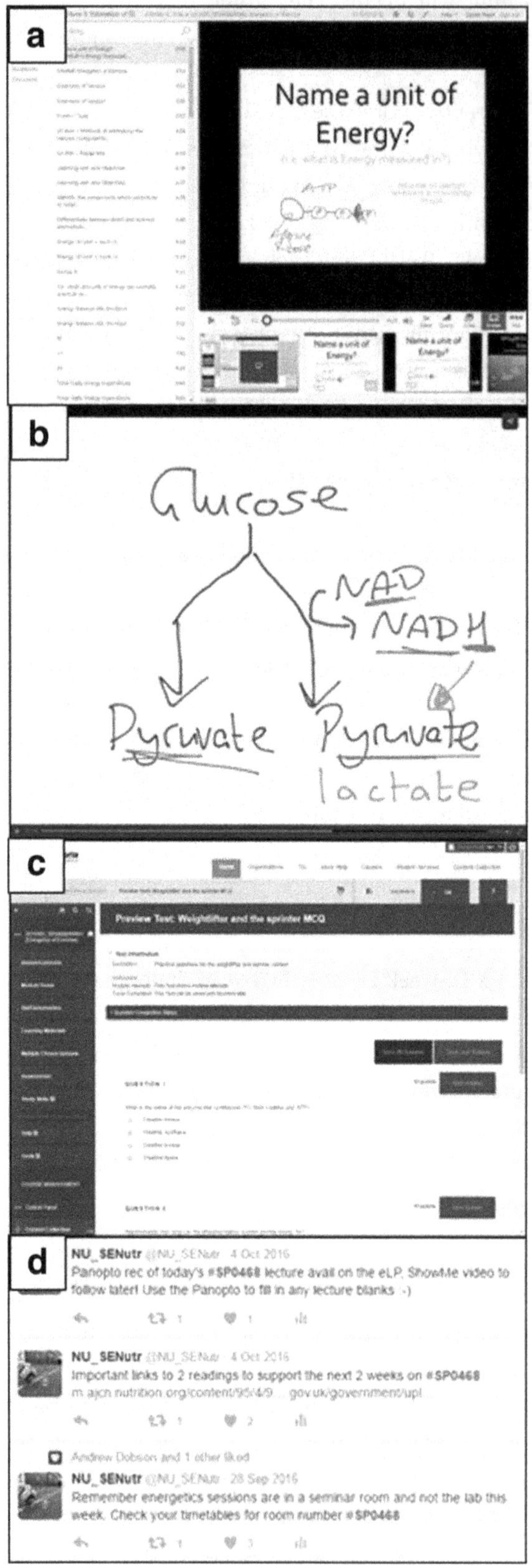

Fig. 1 Screenshots of Panopto (**a**), ShowMe (**b**), MCQ (**c**) and Twitter (**d**)

1. A Panopto™ recording of the lecture which allowed the students to download a video file (Fig. 1a). This was chosen as a simple TELT that would require no technological knowledge or extra-curricular effort from the staff, with the purpose of allowing students to recap the lecture content.
2. An animated mini review of the lecture using an interactive whiteboard mobile application (ShowMe), which consisted of a < 5-min video developed by the lecturer, focusing on what the lecturer deemed to be the essential part of the lecture (Fig. 1b). It was anticipated that the students would use these videos to recap on the main points as a start of, or alternative to, further reading.
3. A multiple choice quiz (MCQ) hosted on the VLE (Blackboard®) (Fig. 1c). Devised by the lecturer, these quizzes mimicked the summative assessment for the module to provide the students an opportunity for formative assessment.
4. A module Twitter feed sharing relevant information (Fig. 1d). Previous studies have identified Twitter as a tool to facilitate student engagement in a course, and encourage student discussion (Gikas and Grant, 2013; Junco et al., 2011).

Survey design and analysis

Student perceptions of the four TELTs were collected via an online survey in week twelve of the module (95 respondents). The survey used was adapted from the technology acceptance model (TAM) survey (Šumak et al., 2011) and a similar learning technology survey from Rossing et al. (2012) to include quantitative (7-point likert scale) and qualitative responses (Table 1). Questions that were deemed the most appropriate to the current study, with a focus on their use were selected from each of these inventories, and as the inventories were adapted both internal reliability and construct validity were checked. Both measurements were found to be satisfactory, determined by a Cronbach Alpha score > 0.7, and the average variance extracted >0.5. Given this, the median response for the six questions was taken as the overall score. This overall score

Table 1 A representation of the questions included in the online questionnaire

Why did you access X?
□ To recap weekly content □ To prepare for the exam □ For general interest □ I did not use it □ Other....
How did you access X?
□ Phone/tablet □ PC/Laptop □ I did not use it □ Other....
Where did you access X?
□ At University □ At home □ While travelling □ I did not use it □ Other....

Question	I strongly disagree	I disagree	I somewhat disagree	Cannot decide	I somewhat agree	I agree	I strongly Agree
I find X useful for learning.	□	□	□	□	□	□	□
X helped me develop confidence in the subject area.	□	□	□	□	□	□	□
I find X easy to use.	□	□	□	□	□	□	□
Using X is a bad idea (negative)	□	□	□	□	□	□	□
X makes learning more interesting.	□	□	□	□	□	□	□
I would like to use X in future modules	□	□	□	□	□	□	□

What in particular did you find useful about X?
Is there a way that the use of X could be improved?

(X denotes where the name of the relevant TELT was inserted)

was then classified as *'did not use', 'disagree'* (1–2), *'unsure'* (3–5), and *'agree'* (6–7). A contingency table analysis with post-hoc tests on the adjusted residuals was used to compare the ratings of each TELT. To account for multiple comparisons the threshold for significance was $p < 0.003$. All statistical analysis was performed using PASW Statistics 22.0 for Windows (SPSS, Inc., Chicago, IL, USA). The qualitative data was analysed via a thematic analysis, with raw quotes from the survey added to first order themes that sat under the common second order themes of 'positives' and 'improvements'.

Results

Data describing the use of each TELT is displayed in Table 2. Significant cells in the contingency table were 'Twitter – did not use' ($p < 0.001$), 'Twitter – agree' ($p < 0.001$), 'ShowMe – agree' ($p = 0.002$) and 'MCQ – agree' ($p < 0.001$) (Table 2). These results suggest that Twitter was used significantly less than the other three TELTs with less people agreeing that it helped, whilst ShowMe and MCQ had a greater occurrence of an 'agree' rating compared to Twitter and Panopto.

A thematic analysis has been presented in Table 4. One main finding was that a first order theme shared across all TELTs was that of assessment preparation. This theme was identified as a positive for Panopto (*'helped prepare for the exam'*), ShowMe (*'can pick out main points for exam revision'*) and MCQ (*'helped to know what to expect on the exam'*). Specific reasons for these TELTs being perceived as useful for assessment could have been to help check understanding (MCQ; *'helps you find out what you actually know'*), tailor and personalise the delivery (Panopto; *'can jump to specific points'*) and provide information in a different format (ShowMe; *'easier to understand than the lectures'*). Conversely the theme of assessment was identified as an area for improvement with Twitter ('*not clearly linked to the exams'*). In fact, the only positive theme for Twitter was convenience (*'easy to access links'*).

Discussion

The purpose of this study was to implement different TELTs into the delivery of a first year undergraduate science module, and collect student perceptions of their use and perceived value for learning. It was found that approximately 80% of the students surveyed accessed Panopto, ShowMe and MCQ to support their learning. However less

Table 2 Frequency of student responses on whether each TELT was useful to support their learning. Agree = median score 6–7; unsure = median score 3–5; Disagree = median score 1–2

TELT		Did not use	Disagree	Unsure	Agree
Panopto		21	2	27	45
	Adj. residual	*−2.1*	*−0.2*	*1.0*	*1.1*
Show Me		21	1	20	53
	Adj. residual	*−2.1*	*−1.0*	*−1.0*	*3.1**
MCQ		19	1	16	59
	Adj. residual	*−2.6*	*−1.0*	*−2.1*	*4.5**
Twitter		55	5	31	4
	Adj. residual	*6.7**	*2.1*	*2.1*	*−8.7**

X^2 (9, $N = 380$) = 87.76, $p < 0.001$
* $p \leq 0.002$

than half of the cohort accessed Twitter, significantly less than the other three methods. Furthermore, only 4% of students agreed that it helped them with their studies, which is again in stark contrast to the other three methods (Table 2). This is despite students identifying it as a convenient way to get information (Table 4). Previous authors have advocated the use of Twitter to support Higher Education students, including Junco et al. (2011) who observed greater levels of engagement in students assigned to a Twitter group as opposed to a control. Gikas and Grant (2013) also reported generally positive student perceptions of using Twitter, including being able to embed learning within their normal lives and the ability to have discussions with classmates. Interestingly interaction was a theme under suggested improvements in the current study, with students commenting that *'everyone should follow each other'* and that they should *'share content'*. A possible reason for the lack of interaction was a lack of student awareness, with one student commenting an improvement would be to *'make students more aware'*. However, the way in which staff made students aware of Twitter was no different to the other TELTs. Furthermore staff regularly updated the Twitter feed with both course specific information and relevant sources for further learning e.g. recent articles linked to that week's course content, but no students posted their own tweets. The fact that Twitter was accessed more on mobile devices may suggest that it was used more for keeping up to date rather than active engagement. Of note is that the intervention implemented by Junco and colleagues used Twitter as a sole source of information (e.g. discussion board, announcements page, reading lists etc.), with no competing TELTs being used simultaneously. It may be that the use of Twitter in the current study was influenced by the fact that the traditional VLE was also being used for the roles described by Junco et al. (2011), or that three other TELTs were available at the same time so students directed their attention elsewhere. These factors may have had more of an influence if students were unfamiliar with the workings of Twitter.

A possible reason for the other three TELTs being used by a greater proportion of students is the perceived link to assessment, with the thematic analysis identifying this as a positive theme for ShowMe, MCQ and Panopto, but an area for improvement for Twitter (Table 4). Furthermore, ShowMe and MCQ had a greater proportion of students 'agree' compared to Panopto (Table 2), which may again be linked to assessment as these were the two TELTs used predominantly to help prepare for the examination (Table 3). A reason for ShowMe being rated higher than Panopto may be due to the delivery of information. Whilst students liked being able to alter the delivery and pace of the lecture using Panopto, the ShowMe videos offered an alternative delivery that helped to simplify content (Table 4). Moreover, the delivery on ShowMe was suggested to be convenient and time efficient for the student. The use of the ShowMe App has been described in past work as a way for students to create notes and share ideas at primary and secondary level (Castek & Beach, 2013; Maher, 2013). It has also been suggested to be popular for clinical teaching within medical residences, specifically for annotating notes and producing quick diagrams for 'in the moment' teaching (Archibald et al., 2014). This latter point is the most related to the use of the App in this study i.e. to simplify information. Research has highlighted the use of animations in other formats as a positive way to support science teaching, with authors reporting enhanced self-efficacy and enjoyment in elementary schools

Table 3 A summary of student access to the TELTs

	Panopto	ShowMe	MCQ	Twitter
Why did you access X?				
To recap weekly content	7 (7%)	44 (46%)	37 (39%)	7 (7%)
To prepare for the examination	7 (7%)	63 (66%)	74 (78%)	7 (7%)
For general interest	10 (11%)	5 (5%)	11 (12%)	10 (11%)
How did you access X?				
Phone/tablet	16 (17%)	26 (27%)	27 (28%)	16 (17%)
PC/laptop	10 (11%)	64 (67%)	72 (76%)	10 (11%)
Where did you access X?				
At University	8 (8%)	40 (42%)	39 (41%)	8 (8%)
At home	21 (22%)	64 (67%)	72 (76%)	21 (22%)
While travelling	2 (2%)	3 (3%)	5 (5%)	2 (2%)

Table 4 Thematic analysis of qualitative responses for each TELT

Raw Quotes	First Order	Second Order	TELT
Able to pause at any point to make notes/Can jump to specific points	Tailor lecture delivery and pacing	Positive	Panopto
Good for exam revision/Helped prepare for the exam	Assessment		
Microphone poor/Missing video/Logging in was difficult	Technology limitations	Improvements	
A good quick recap/It condenses all of the information/ Short and concise/Straight to the point/Short, sharp and accurate summary	Time efficient	Positive	ShowMe
Gives step by step views/Makes complicated information compact and easy to understand/The verbal and visual information at the same time is useful/Simplifies lectures/ Easier to understand than the lectures	Delivery of information		
Easy to use/Easy to find the information	Convenient		
Can pick out main points for exam revision	Assessment		
Some videos too short/Lecturer sometimes quiet/ Sometime talk too fast	Lecturer delivery	Improvements	
Useful to see the types of questions/Good tool for revision/ You can practice for the exam/Prepared you for the exam/ Helped to know what to expect on the exam	Assessment	Positive	MCQ
Helps recap/Helps you find out what you actually know/ Helped check where I may have been wrong with my notes/ Shows what you know and what you don't/Can track my learning	Confirming understanding		
More questions/Links to webpages relating to the subject area/Not just multiple choice questions/A variety of questions	Content	Improvements	
Easy to use/Easy to access links	Convenience	Positive	Twitter
Everyone should follow each other/Should share content/ Make students more aware	Interaction	Improvements	
Give more examples/Have a specific page/Make more links available /	Content		
Not clearly linked to the exams	Assessment		

(Barak et al., 2011), and improved retention of information in university students (Lin & Atkinson, 2011). Of note is that the animations used by Barak et al. (2011) and Lin and Atkinson (2011) were specific LOs used in a formal learning environment, whereas the current study is novel in that the animations were produced by the teaching staff and could be accessed outside of the formal learning environment. It is advised that those looking to implement a similar strategy to the current study consider their clarity of speech when producing the videos, as this was commented on by some students (Table 4).

It is perhaps clear why the MCQ was rated highly by the students, as it mimicked the summative assessment of the module. Some of the comments in the 'confirming understanding' theme suggest it may have also been of benefit for formative feedback (*'can track my learning'*) (Table 4), however what is unclear is whether this TELT would have been perceived as useful if the mode of summative assessment had been different i.e. an essay or report. Another factor that may explain the positive perception of the MCQs is that this was the only TELT that required the student to take an active part. However no students alluded to this in the questionnaires.

As students appeared to be extrinsically motivated by assessment, TELTs were not used a lot for general interest (Table 3). All of the TELTs had the capacity to be used on mobile devices, however they were used primarily on PCs/laptops (Table 3). This may suggest that the potential for incidental or informal learning was not enhanced by using the TELTs. Each TELT was accessed mostly at home, therefore perhaps promoting extra-curricular study as it was hoped that the ShowMe videos would, but still in a formal and structured fashion. However, these points are speculative as we have no comparison to their learning habits prior to the study. Furthermore 'general interest' is quite vague and open to individual interpretation. Perhaps this would have been better termed 'further study' or 'further understanding'.

In summary the current study has identified shared characteristics between the TELTs that students engage with and perceive to be useful. Such characteristics include links to the summative assessment and offering an alternative method of content delivery to the traditional lecture. Previous research has shown that time is a barrier for staff to incorporate TELTs into their teaching (Reed, 2014), so an appropriate practical message may be to start with one type of TELT. Based on this study TELTs similar to the ShowMe App are most recommended as this was one of the two highly rated TELTs (alongside MCQ), but has more scope for crossover with other subjects as the students found it useful for more than just assessment. Moreover the lecturer has full control over the content, so can make each animation specific to the current topic of study. Further work should look at the potential transfer of animations for learning in other subject disciplines, and investigate if there are any alternative TELTs for meeting the same purpose of simplifying information. It should be considered that this paper describes only those students that completed the survey (45% response rate), and the perceptions of the other students enrolled on the module are unknown. Furthermore, we cannot discount that using the TELTs in combination may have influenced the perception of each TELT, and we relied upon student self-reported usage for each TELT. Future work should monitor the actual use of the TELTs using tracking statistics, and look to examine predictive validity of student perceptions of TELTs to gain more insight into what student perception means for learning and academic performance, and what the implications are for teaching staff.

Acknowledgements
The authors wish to thank the students that took the time to complete the survey.

Authors' contributions
DP conceived the study, and DP, PR and LA designed the study. DP, PR and KK taught on the module and implemented the protocol. All authors reviewed the results and DP performed the final analysis. All authors approved the final version of the manuscript.

Funding
The authors received no funding for this study.

Competing interests
The authors declare that they have no competing interests.

References
Archibald, D., Macdonald, C. J., Plante, J., Hogue, R. J., & Fiallos, J. (2014). Residents' and preceptors' perceptions of the use of the iPad for clinical teaching in a family medicine residency program. *BMC Medical Education, 14*(1), 174.

Barak, M., Ashkar, T., & Dori, Y. J. (2011). Learning science via animated movies: Its effect on students' thinking and motivation. *Computers & Education, 56*(3), 839–846.

Blackwell, C. K., Lauricella, A. R., & Wartella, E. (2014). Factors influencing digital technology use in early childhood education. *Computers & Education, 77*, 82–90.

Castek, J., & Beach, R. (2013). Using apps to support disciplinary literacy and science learning. *Journal of Adolescent & Adult Literacy, 56*(7), 554–564.

Cochrane, T. (2005). Interactive QuickTime: Developing and evaluating multimedia learning objects to enhance both face-to-face and distance e-learning environments. *Interdisciplinary Journal of Knowledge and Learning Objects, 1*(1), 33–54.

Danielson, J., Preast, V., Bender, H., & Hassall, L. (2014). Is the effectiveness of lecture capture related to teaching approach or content type? *Computers & Education, 72*, 121–131.

Gikas, J., & Grant, M. M. (2013). Mobile computing devices in higher education: Student perspectives on learning with cellphones, smartphones & social media. *The Internet and Higher Education, 19*, 18–26.

Gong, M., Xu, Y., & Yu, Y. (2004). An enhanced technology acceptance model for web-based learning. *Journal of Information Systems Education, 15*(4), 365–374.

Junco, R., Heiberger, G., & Loken, E. (2011). The effect of twitter on college student engagement and grades. *Journal of Computer Assisted Learning, 27*(2), 119–132.

Kamath, A. (2015). A review of use of eLearning in pharmacology. *International Journal of Integrative Medical Sciences, 2*(9), 157–162.

Karnad, A. (2013). *Student use of recorded lectures: A report reviewing recent research into the use of lecture capture technology in higher education, and its impact on teaching methods and attendance.* London: London School of Economics and Political Science.

Kay, R. (2011). Evaluating learning, design, and engagement in web-based learning tools (WBLTs): The WBLT evaluation scale. *Computers in Human Behavior, 27*(5), 1849–1856.

Kay, R. H., & Knaack, L. (2009). Assessing learning, quality and engagement in learning objects: The learning object evaluation scale for students (LOES-S). *Educational Technology Research and Development, 57*(2), 147–168.

Lach, M. K., & McCarthy Jr., B. C. (2015). Student and faculty member perspectives on lecture capture in pharmacy education. *American Journal of Pharmaceutical Education, 79*(8), 126.

Lin, L., & Atkinson, R. K. (2011). Using animations and visual cueing to support learning of scientific concepts and processes. *Computers & Education, 56*(3), 650–658.

Louw, A. (2015). Developing a lecturer workshop for using tablets in the classroom. *International Journal of Teaching and Learning in Higher Education, 27*(3), 294–309.

Maher, D. (2013). Pre-service primary teachers' use of iPads to support teaching: Implications for teacher education. *Educational Research for Social Change, 2*(1), 48–63.

Marchand, J.-P., Pearson, M. L., & Albon, S. P. (2014). Student and faculty member perspectives on lecture capture in pharmacy education. *American Journal of Pharmaceutical Education, 78*(4), 74.

Nurmi, S., & Jaakkola, T. (2006). Effectiveness of learning objects in various instructional settings. *Learning, Media and Technology, 31*(3), 233–247.

Peart, D. J., Johnstone, S., Brown, J., & Bangani, P. (2014). Supporting teaching and learning in biosciences with mobile technology: Staff and student perspectives. *The Journal of Research in Higher and Further Education, 2*(1), 5–10.

Reed, P. (2014). Staff experience and attitudes towards technology enhanced learning initiatives in one Faculty of Health & life sciences. *Research in Learning Technology, 22*, 22770.

Rossing, J. P., Miller, W. M., Cecil, A. K., & Stamper, S. E. (2012). iLearning: The future of higher education? Student perceptions on learning with mobile tablets. *Journal of the Scholarship of Teaching and Learning, 12*(2), 1–26.

Šumak, B., Heričko, M., Pušnik, M., & Polančič, G. (2011). Factors affecting acceptance and use of Moodle: An empirical study based on TAM. *Informatica, 35*(1), 91–100.

Teo, T., Lee, C. B., & Chai, C. S. (2008). Understanding pre-service teachers' computer attitudes: Applying and extending the technology acceptance model. *Journal of Computer Assisted Learning, 24*(2), 128–143.

Vargo, J., Nesbit, J. C., Belfer, K., & Archambault, A. (2003). Learning object evaluation: Computer-mediated collaboration and inter-rater reliability. *International Journal of Computers and Applications, 25*(3), 198–205.

5

Magnetic and multistable: reinterpreting the affordances of educational technology

Jesper Aagaard

Correspondence:
jaagaard@psy.au.dk
Department of Psychology and Behavioral Sciences, Aarhus University, 8000 Aarhus C, Denmark

Abstract

The concept of affordances has become a popular analytical tool in educational technology. The present article, however, argues that the current understanding of affordances does not adequately address the use of educational technology and instead advocates a phenomenological reinterpretation. The article first introduces Gibson's concept of affordances and describes how scholars in the field of educational technology have invoked this concept to compile lists of technical action possibilities. It then argues that affordances do not just 'offer' a range of action possibilities; they actively 'invite' certain actions. To explore how such behavioral invitations manifest themselves in the everyday use of educational technologies, the article introduces the analytical concepts of multistability, relational strategy, and mediation and uses these concepts to analyze the affordances of laptops in the classroom. It is argued that laptops act as powerful attentional magnets that often invite students to become distracted. Theoretical and practical implications are discussed.

Keywords: Affordance, Educational technology, Habit, Multistability, Phenomenology

Introduction

In the past few years, Gibson's (2015) concept of *affordances* has become a popular tool in the field of educational technology (e.g., Conole & Dyke, 2004, Dalgarno & Lee, 2010, Song, 2011, Bower & Sturman, 2015). Although sympathetic to the general thrust of this ecological approach, the present article argues that employing a quasi-objectivist conceptualization of affordances as 'action possibilities' does not adequately address the everyday use of educational technologies. Instead, the article advocates a phenomenological approach that retains Gibson's direct realism, but adds concern for the so-called invitation character (*Aufforderungscharakter*) of affordances: Affordances do not simply *offer* a range of action possibilities; they actively *invite* certain actions. It is argued that this approach brings us closer to students' actual experiences of using digital technologies. The article first introduces Gibson's original notion of affordances and describes how scholars in the field of educational technology have used this concept as shorthand for 'action possibilities'. It then describes Hubert Dreyfus' critique of affordances and his phenomenological rehabilitation of their invitation character. To explore how such invitations manifest themselves in the everyday use of educational technologies, the article then introduces the analytical concepts of multistability, relational strategy, and mediation. Finally, these concepts are used to analyze the affordances of a ubiquitous educational technology: The laptop. Drawing on empirical research, it is shown that laptops often invite students to become distracted and that students take precautions such as closing the lids of their laptops to resist this powerful invitation.

Gibson's concept of affordances

The concept of affordances originally stems from Gibson's (2015) ecological psychology. In his ecological studies of visual perception, Gibson's starting point was the active and mobile perceiver: "One sees the environment not just with the eyes but with the eyes in the head on the shoulder of a body that gets about" (p. 211). Based on such active exploration, the perceiver picks up information that is directly specified in the ambient optical array. This direct realism lead Gibson and his wife Eleanor Gibson (1955) to argue that information does not need to be stored in memory, since it is accessible in the environment. Accordingly, perception learning can (and should) be explained without invoking mentalist concepts: Perceptual learning does not happen through a mental *enrichment* of bare sensations with memory traces, but through an ever finer *differentiation* of previously vague impressions (this point applies across all perceptual systems, and the Gibsons gave the example of a wine connoisseur who is able to discriminate between claret, burgundy, and chianti). "Perceptual learning, then, consists of responding to variables of physical stimulation not previously responded to" (p. 34). This point dovetails with Latour's (2004) conceptualization of having a body as *learning to be affected*, which is exemplified through the perfume industry's use of odor kits to train apprentices in differentiating subtle fragrances. Ultimately, Gibson taught us that perceptual learning means learning to be affected by the world, getting increasingly attuned to its meaningful differences. His ecological psychology thereby stood in stark contrast to prevailing psychological theories, which understood the world as an aggregate of brute matter that human minds endow with meaning.

Gibson's project was to turn psychology's focus from the inner recesses of the mind to the richly textured and meaningful human environment. According to Gibson (2015), this environment consists of directly perceivable *affordances*, which he defined as follows: "The affordances of the environment are what it offers the animal, what it provides or furnishes, either for good or ill" (p. 119). Affordances are always taken with reference to an agent, which means that they are relative to species, physiology, development, and culture. To me, the pencil on my desk is not a brute chunk of wood and graphite, but a meaningful artifact that affords writing. Although still a meaningful artifact, the same pencil would not afford writing to a baby or a dog. Affordances are in turn enabled by an artifact's materiality such as its shape, size, rigidity, and so forth. If my pencil were broken, for instance, it would no longer afford writing, but it might still afford bookmarking or backscratching. Gibson further emphasized that all objects afford a multitude of actions: "The fact that a stone is a missile does not imply that it cannot be other things as well. It can be a paperweight, a bookend, a hammer, or a pendulum bob" (p. 126). Finally, to protect the concept of affordances from the perceived dualism of Gestalt theory, Gibson denied that affordances are defined in terms of their invitation character (*Aufforderungscharakter*) and described them as real and permanent features of the environment: "An affordance is not bestowed upon an object by a need of an observer and his act of perceiving it. The object offers what it does because it is what it is" (p. 130).

Affordances in educational technology

The concept of affordances has since been imported to the field of educational technology. Articles using an affordance-based framework are often built around the question: "What is the affordance of educational technology *X*?" (see e.g., Conole & Dyke, 2004, Dalgarno & Lee, 2010, Song, 2011, Bower & Sturman, 2015). When attempting to answer this question, scholars tend to use the concept of affordances as shorthand for 'action potentials' (Bower, 2008), 'possibilities for action' (Hammond, 2010), or 'action possibilities' (Antonenko, Dawson, & Sahay, 2017). In adherence to the idea of affordances as real and permanent features of the environment, such action possibilities are understood as technical features of educational technologies that enable and constrain certain actions. Conole and Dyke (2004), for instance, argue that digital educational technologies offer a wealth of action possibilities including access to rapidly changing information, exposure to diversity, and communication and collaboration. Bower (2008) similarly presents an extensive classification system for affordances that includes no less than 11 different categories: Media affordances (e.g., write-ability), spatial affordances (e.g., move-ability), temporal affordances (e.g., playback-ability), navigation affordances (e.g., search-ability), emphasis affordances (e.g., highlight-ability), synthesis affordances (e.g., combine-ability), access-control affordances (e.g., share-ability), technical affordances (e.g., speed), usability (e.g., intuitiveness), aesthetics (e.g., appeal), and, finally, reliability (e.g., robustness). Bower argues that singling out such inherent technical properties helps us avoid "any contextual biases that could be caused by the experience or culture of the user" (p. 5). While such lists may indeed contain very real and permanent technical features, they do raise the question of whether (and how) such 'action possibilities' are utilized in educational practice. In other words, do such deliberately decontextualized lists help us understand the everyday use of educational technologies?

In an article explicitly dismissing the usefulness of affordances in educational technology, Martin Oliver (2005) criticizes affordance lists for being confused and inconsistent. Unless one succumbs to an essentialist and positivist epistemology, he argues, cataloging possible affordances is a purely speculative endeavor: "'Possible' leaves nothing substantial to work with, unless a definitive list of possibilities can be constructed from the properties of each element separately, and their various interactions" (p. 403). Oliver goes on to dismiss the use of affordances *tout court*, since Gibson explicitly dismissed the mental realm and therefore provided unsatisfactory explanations for human learning. The concept of affordance may be adequate for species-level generalities, Oliver argues, but "people and learning are beyond it" (p. 412).[1] Jan Derry (2007) likewise protests the use of affordances in educational technology because of its roots in Gibson's direct realism. Drawing on the philosophy of John McDowell, Derry argues that direct perception cannot be transferred from the 'straightforward' question of animal perception to the 'complex' issue of human learning, because the distinctive feature of human engagement with the world is that it is conceptually mediated. Human beings are able to determine something *as* something (e.g., a door *as* a door) due to our enculturation into a conceptually structured space of reasons without which we would respond causally to our environment like a fire alarm responds to smoke. In both cases, Gibson's direct realism is critiqued for disregarding a 'higher' human level of cognition. While I agree that itemizing technical features does not tell us much about how educational technologies are actually used in everyday practice, I do not subscribe to these mentalist critiques of the concept of affordances for reasons that will soon become clear. In what follows, I instead present a phenomenological approach to affordances that maintains Gibson's direct realism, but substitutes abstract 'action possibilities' with concrete use. The purpose of this reorientation is to shift focus from technical *possibilities* to what is *actually* going in the day-to-day realities of educational practice.

The phenomenology of responsiveness

Acclaimed phenomenologist Hubert Dreyfus has forcefully rejected McDowell's idea of a conceptually structured space of reasons as relying on a misleading myth of the mental (see Schear, 2013). According to Dreyfus (2007), humans absorbed in everyday coping experience the world nonconceptually, which means that we do not experience doors *as* doors, we just go through them. When pressing into possibilities, there is no conceptuality, no mindedness, and we simply move towards things that attract or repulse us. In making this argument, Dreyfus launches an interesting critique of affordances: Gibson's concept is not misleading due to its lack of conceptuality, but due to its peculiar status as "objective facts about what affords what" (p. 356). When responding to situations, however, we do not act on objective affordance-facts, but on *solicitations*, a Gestaltist term Dreyfus picks to convey how our surroundings are directly perceived as 'suggesting' or 'calling for' certain responses.[2] A handrail, for instance, suggests grinding to the savvy skater, while an extraordinary event calls for pictures. While Gibson's affordance-facts are somehow *out there*, at a distance from us, solicitations move us to act by drawing us in or pushing us away. The world of everyday coping, then, is not a disenchanted world of affordance-facts, but a vibrant web of attractions and repulsions. "Instead of the affordance-facts", Dreyfus argues, "it is the affordance's solicitations - such as the attraction of an apple when I'm hungry - to which I am directly open" (p. 357). Dreyfus thereby rehabilitates the invitation character of affordances: Affordances are magnetic entities that do not just *offer* a range of action possibilities, but actively *invite* specific actions (and repel others).

Dreyfus' reinterpretation of affordances is based on Maurice Merleau-Ponty's (2002) phenomenology of perception, which, like Gibson's ecological psychology, stresses the active, mobile, and embodied nature of perception. Also like Gibson, Merleau-Ponty argues that perception has no room for mediational epistemology and puts us in direct contact with the world (Dreyfus & Taylor, 2016). Finally, the Gibsonian idea that all experience is projected back into the world as increasingly rich differentiation is echoed in Merleau-Ponty's notion of an *intentional arc* (for examples of such Merleau-Pontyian connoisseur perception, see Ihde, 2015), but Merleau-Ponty (2002) crucially adds that our experiences invest the world with functional significances that pull us in certain directions: "The light of a candle changes its appearance for a child when, after a burn, it stops attracting the child's hand and becomes literally repulsive" (p. 60). The child experiences the hotness of the flame by burning her finger and this embodied understanding is henceforth present in her comportment towards lit candles. This example may imply a rather reflex-like notion of learning, but Merleau-Ponty's theoretical apparatus extends all the way to typing, sewing, and other forms of skillful coping

(Dreyfus, 2014) that solicit intuitive responses from involved agents. Phenomenology thus dispels the voluntarist dogma of most psychology: We often *feel immediately drawn* to act in certain ways (Dreyfus & Kelly, 2007).[3] "The body is no more than an element in the system of the subject and his world, and the task to be performed elicits the necessary movements from him by a sort of remote attraction" (Merleau-Ponty, 2002, p. 122). The question is how such solicitations manifest themselves in the everyday use of educational technologies. Here it is relevant to look at a contemporary school of thought called postphenomenology.

Studying human-technology-world relations

While naked perception involves a direct and unmediated 'human-world' relation, the use of technology extends this intentional relation into a 'human-technology-world' relation (Verbeek, 2005). Postphenomenology is a philosophy of technology that is concerned with such relations. It has its roots in classical phenomenology, but also draws on American pragmatism. As Ihde (2009) explains, the term postphenomenology was coined to sever connections to later Heidegger's one-size-fits-all account of Technology and to Husserl's subjectivist notion of consciousness. Instead, postphenomenology examines specific technologies in their particularities and subscribes to Merleau-Ponty's strong sense of embodiment. In short, it is empirical and materialist rather than metaphysical and idealist (Scharff, 2012). Some of its key concepts are multistability, relational strategy, and mediation. Firstly, a principal tenet of postphenomenology is the notion of *multistability,* which alludes to an artifact's various partially determined trajectories in different contexts (Rosenberger, 2016). Even the simplest technology has no singular, stable essence, but can be taken up for different purposes or 'stabilities' in different contexts. This idea mirrors Gibson's notion that any object affords a multitude of actions. A pencil, for instance, is typically or canonically (Costall, 2012) used for writing, but can also be used for backscratching or even for stabbing someone. There is no 'essential' use of a pencil. As Ihde (1990) puts it: "A technological object, whatever else it is, *becomes* what it 'is' through its uses", (p. 70). The idea of multistability thus acts as an antidote to readings that perceive technologies solely in terms of their intended use, what is also known as the designer fallacy (Ihde, 2008).

Secondly, to explain how certain stabilities take precedence over others, Rosenberger (2009) introduces the concept of a *relational strategy,* which he defines as "the particular configuration of bodily habits, intentions, and conceptions that make it possible for a person to take up a particular stable relation" (p. 176). Learning to write with a pencil not only means learning the alphabet, it also includes learning the tripod grip (holding the pencil with ones thumb and index finger), adopting the right posture, and learning to draw the letters. As any child versed in the art of filling out worksheets knows, mastering this technique takes hard work. Over time, some relational strategies take deeper roots than others, and technologies are mostly encountered in terms of one's dominant strategy: If one usually writes with pencils, a pencil is directly perceived as a writing tool rather than, say, a backscratching device (Rosenberger, 2017a). Finally, the concept of *mediation* designates how technologies shape the human-world relation: Technologies do not afford action possibilities to preexisting subjects with fixed goals, but subtly invite (Verbeek, 2005) and facilitate (Rosenberger, 2014a) certain comportments while inhibiting and foreclosing others. Returning to our example, it has been shown that using a pencil to take lecture-notes yields better results than using a laptop (Mueller & Oppenheimer, 2014). In a postphenomenological account, this is because the slowness of pencil note-taking invites students to rephrase and condense the presented material, whereas the compositional speed of a laptop invites students to transcribe material verbatim (Aagaard, 2015b). Nothing in the laptop *determines* that it be used for transcription, however, and we must not understand invitations as lodged 'inside' artifacts: Technologies can only be understood in terms of the concrete relations that we have to them. Let us now apply this postphenomenological approach to the domain of educational technology.

The magnetism of educational technologies

In this section, I want to look at the affordances of a ubiquitous educational technology: The laptop.

I will draw on results from my empirical study of educational technology use in a Danish business college (see Aagaard, 2015a, 2017a). When spending time in educational practice, one quickly discovers that the popular image of laptops and other forms of information and communication technology (ICT) as benevolent forces that connect us to the world, break down traditional barriers, and afford 'anytime/anywhere learning' (Wright & Parchoma, 2011) fails to recognize the deeply ambivalent nature of importing such digital technologies into the classroom: Not only do laptops afford so-called 'technologically-enhanced learning', they also afford classroom distraction (Aagaard, 2017a). In other words, just as laptops open up the possibility of bringing the world into the classroom, they also constitute a backdoor through which students may occasionally escape. Acknowledging such multistability helps us avoid the ICT educator's fallacy, which refers to the mistaken assumption that digital devices introduced into the classroom will be taken up for the precise purposes that designers and curriculum developers envision (Rosenberger, 2017b). With multistability thus established, an important question becomes how the relational strategies that students have developed in the course of their everyday lives intertwine with their educational use of these devices.

During interviews, students described being drawn to distraction in ways that bypass their conscious decision-making: They often experience a *habitual distraction* in the form of a prereflective attraction towards certain frequently visited, but educationally irrelevant websites like Facebook (the following is based on Aagaard, 2015a). Due to deeply sedimented relational strategies that have been built, maintained, and solidified in the course of their everyday lives, the action of logging onto Facebook has become embodied in students' hands and fingers and now occurs habitually. "It's just F, A, and Enter", as the student Karen said. Succumbing to this habitual distraction is deceptively easy, since it occurs independently of students' conscious willpower. Jacob put it like this: "You're looking out of the window and going, 'Oh, it's raining', and then you look back, and now you're on Facebook. If you stop listening for *one* second, you're already on Facebook". This, of course, does not mean that digital distraction is *never* a conscious choice, but deliberate use of Facebook is limited to visits that involve a specific purpose. "If I'm there thinking that I'm going to go on Facebook, that's because I just have to write to someone or make an appointment", said Dan. "Otherwise, it's a habit". To resist this solicitation and obstruct the habitual slide into distraction, students described occasionally closing the lids of their laptops.

> Jesper: Why can't you just refrain from looking at it?
>
> Carol: Well it's standing right in front of me, and then you might look down for a second and you're just caught by Facebook. Then you sort of forget the other thing you're supposed to focus on.
>
> Jesper: So unless you physically shut down the screen, it's simply too tempting?
>
> Carol: Yes, it is for me. Maybe not for everybody.

Although relational strategies spring from purpose- and meaningful activity, prolonged sedimentation thus seem to make them manifest with a degree of automaticity and stubbornness that challenges our conventional, humanist conceptions of agency and intentionality: Sometimes our habitual use of technologies inclines us do things *we do not intend to do.* Discussing distracted driving, Rosenberger (2014b) similarly notes that: "Like the way those who habitually bite their nails will be on occasion surprised to look down and find they are once again biting their nails, drivers may slide inadvertently and unconsciously into the distracting habits of the phone" (p. 43). The phenomenon of distraction obviously predates the advent of laptops in the classroom, but the idea of magnetic affordances or 'invitations' suggests that digital distraction may differ from existing forms of unmediated distraction like staring blankly into space, since laptops actively shape the relation between students and their classrooms: "When a lesson is experienced as boring, this may to a certain extent be *because* technological alternatives are constantly available and ready to be utilized at a whim" (Aagaard, 2015a, p. 95). This point raises important questions about the role of technology in the classroom (for an in-depth discussion of this issue, see Aagaard, 2017b).

Conclusion

In this article, I have tried to read James J. Gibson's concept of affordances through a phenomenological lens. The benefit of this theoretical reinterpretation is threefold: First, by insisting that affordances actively invite certain actions, phenomenology dispels the awkward idea of 'affordance-facts' that has lead educational researchers to compile strangely detached lists of technical features. Secondly, phenomenology helps us analyze expressly multistable objects like digital technologies that have no canonical affordances (Costall, 2012). As Cutting (1982) argues, a sheet of paper, another quintessentially multistable artifact, affords an endless amount of action possibilities including writing, drawing, wadding up, cutting, photocopying, burning, and so on. "To be sure, it does not afford flying to Baghdad upon", he continues, "but the exclusion of a large domain of behaviors does not diminish the fact that an infinity remain" (p. 216). But does that mean is it up to us to *decide* which of these affordances are utilized? By focusing on our habitualized use of technological artifacts, phenomenology helps us circumvent such potential voluntarism. Finally, granting analytical priority to habits belies phenomenology's roots in the mundane aspects of everyday life. In the field of educational technology, this self-conscious immersion in routine and repetition guarantees a much-needed fidelity to the 'state-of-the-actual' (Selwyn, 2010), to what is *actually* going in the day-to-day realities of educational practice. In other words, while the laptop surely provides a wealth of technical 'action possibilities,' decontextualized analyses that treat affordances as quasi-objectivist features of the world cannot tell us *which* of these affordances will be utilized in practice or *how*. To do so, we must understand affordances as magnetic and multistable. Ultimately, a phenomenological approach to affordances help us do so and thereby provides a critical and empirically based approach to educational technology, which counterbalances the currently reigning techno-optimism ("technologies will save our educational system") without lapsing into technological instrumentalism ("technologies will be what we make of them"). This tactic not only suggests that we place less faith (and money) in the idea of ICT as some sort of educational panacea; it also urges us to discuss the downsides and drawbacks of our current technohabits.

Endnotes

[1]Oliver (2005) ultimately suggests analyzing technologies as *texts*, but I have difficulties discerning this approach from plain affordance-analyses: In an analysis of the virtual world *Second Life*, Oliver (2013) attributes to a red rug on a green field the affordance of 'visible demarcation' between inside (speaking) and outside (listening) positions for student avatars. In a corresponding textual analysis, he concludes: "Having taken away the physical structures usually associated with formal education (the spatial demarcation of conventional institutions) some students were not sure how they should react [...] This led to problems, which the rug was created to address" (p. 40).

[2]Elsewhere, Dreyfus (1991) distinguishes actions that are *logically* and *physically* possible from the smaller subset of actions that are *existentially* possible in a specific situation – one's so-called "live options" (p. 190). This Heideggerian distinction supplements the Merleau-Pontyian contrast between affordance-facts and solicitations that is being made here.

[3]Withagen, de Poel, Araújo, and Pepping (2012) also argue that affordances can invite behavior, but insist that their argument differs from phenomenology, since affordances do not generally invite behavior. In a later article, however, the authors seem to have warmed to phenomenology and insist that, "an ecological account of agency should do justice to this phenomenological insight – affordances are not mere possibilities for action but generally invite us" (Withagen, Araújo, & de Poel, 2017, p. 16).

Acknowledgements
None.

Funding
Not applicable.

Authors' contributions
Conceptualized and wrote the article.

Competing interests
The author declares that he has no competing interests.

References

Antonenko, P., Dawson, K., & Sahay, S. (2017). A Freamework for Algning needs, abilities and affordances to inform design and practice of educational technologies. *British Journal of Educational Technology, vol., 48*(4), 916–927.

Aagaard, J. (2015a). Drawn to Distraction: A Qualitative Study of Off-Task Use of Educational Technology. *Computers & Education, vol. 87*, 90–97.

Aagaard, J. (2015b). Media Multitasking, Attention, and Distraction: A Critical Discussion. *Phenomenology and the Cognitive Sciences, vol. 14*(4), 885–896.

Aagaard, J. (2017a). Breaking Down Barriers: The Ambivalent Nature of Technologies in the Classroom. *New Media & Society, vol. 19*(7), 1127–1153.

Aagaard, J. (2017b). *Digital Distraction: A Qualitative Exploration of Media Multitasking*. PhD Dissertation. Aarhus: Aarhus University

Bower, M. (2008). Affordance analysis–matching learning tasks with learning technologies. *Educational Media International, vol., 45*(1), 3–15.

Bower, M., & Sturman, D. (2015). What are the educational affordances of wearable technologies? *Computers & Education, vol., 88*, 343–353.

Conole, G., & Dyke, M. (2004). What are the affordances of information and communication technologies? *Research in Learning Technology, 12*(2), 113–124.

Costall, A. (2012). Canonical affordances in context. *AVANT: Trends in Interdisciplinary Studies, 3*(2), 85–93.

Cutting, J. (1982). Two ecological perspectives: Gibson vs. Shaw and Turvey. *The American Journal of Psychology, 95*(2), 199–222.

Dalgarno, B., & Lee, M. (2010). What are the learning affordances of 3-D virtual environments? *British Journal of Educational Technology, 41*(1), 10–32.

Derry, J. (2007). Epistemology and conceptual resources for the development of learning technologies. *Journal of Computer Assisted Learning, 23*(6), 503–510.

Dreyfus, H. (1991). *Being-in-the-world: A commentary on Heidegger's being and time, division I*. Cambridge: MIT Press.

Dreyfus, H. (2007). The return of the myth of the mental. *Inquiry, 50*(4), 352–365.

Dreyfus, H. (2014). *Skillful coping: Essays on the phenomenology of everyday perception*. Oxford: Oxford University Press.

Dreyfus, H., & Kelly, S. D. (2007). Heterophenomenology: Heavy-handed sleight-of-hand. *Phenomenology and the Cognitive Sciences, 6*(1–2), 45–55.

Dreyfus, H., & Taylor, C. (2016). *Retrieving realism*. Cambridge: Harvard University Press.

Gibson, J. J. (2015). *The ecological approach to visual perception: Classic edition*. New York: Psychology Press.

Gibson, J. J., & Gibson, E. (1955). Perceptual learning: Differentiation or enrichment? *Psychological Review, 62*(1), 32–41.

Hammond, M. (2010). What is an affordance and can it help us understand the use of ICT in education? *Education and Information Technologies, 15*(3), 205–217.

Ihde, D. (1990). *Technology and the Lifeworld: From garden to earth*. Indianapolis: Indiana University Press.

Ihde, D. (2008). *Ironic Technics*. New York: Automatic Press/VIP.

Ihde, D. (2009). *Postphenomenology and Technoscience: The Peking University lectures*. Albany: SUNY Press.

Ihde, D. (2015). Foreword: Is there a bat problem for Postphenomenology? In J. K. Friis, & R. Crease (Eds.), *Technoscience and Postphenomenology: The Manhattan papers*. Lanham: Lexington Books.

Latour, B. (2004). How to talk about the body? The normative dimension of science studies. *Body and Society, 10*(2–3), 205–229.

Merleau-Ponty, M. (2002). *Phenomenology of perception*. London: Routledge Classics.

Mueller, P., & Oppenheimer, D. (2014). The pen is mightier than the keyboard: Advantages of longhand over laptop note taking. *Psychological Science, 25*(6), 1159–1168.

Oliver, M. (2005). The problem with affordance. *E-Learning and Digital Media, 2*(4), 402–413.

Oliver, M. (2013). Learning technology: Theorising the tools we study. *British Journal of Educational Technology, 44*(1), 31–43.

Rosenberger, R. (2009). The sudden experience of the computer. *AI & SOCIETY, 24*(2), 173–180.

Rosenberger, R. (2014a). Multistability and the Agency of Mundane Artifacts: From speed bumps to Subway benches. *Human Studies, 37*(3), 369–392.

Rosenberger, R. (2014b). The phenomenological case for stricter regulation of cell phones and driving. *Techné, 18*(1/2), 20–47.

Rosenberger, R. (2016). Notes on a nonfoundational phenomenology of technology. *Foundations of Science*. Advance online publication. https://doi.org/10.1007/s10699-015-9480-5.

Rosenberger, R. (2017a). On the everyday hermeneutics of things: Or, the philosophy of fire hydrants. *AI & SOCIETY, 32*(2), 233–241.

Rosenberger, R. (2017b). The ICT Educator's fallacy. *Foundations of Science, 22*(2), 395–399.

Scharff, R. (2012). Ihde's Postphenomenological Heidegger. *Continental Philosophy Review, 45*(2), 297–306.

Schear, J. (2013). *Mind, reason, and being-in-the-world: The McDowell-Dreyfus debate*. London: Routledge.

Selwyn, N. (2010). Looking beyond learning: Notes towards the critical study of educational technology. *Journal of Computer Assisted Learning, 26*(1), 65–73.

Song, Y. (2011). What are the affordances and constraints of handheld devices for learning in higher education. *British Journal of Educational Technology, 42*(6), E163–E166.

Verbeek, P. P. (2005). *What things do: Philosophical reflections on technology, agency, and design*. Penn State: Penn State University Press.

Withagen, R., Araújo, D., & de Poel, H. (2017). Inviting affordances and agency. *New Ideas in Psychology, 45*, 11–18.

Withagen, R., de Poel, H., Araújo, D., & Pepping, G. J. (2012). Affordances can invite behavior: Reconsidering the relationship between affordances and agency. *New Ideas in Psychology, 30*(2), 250–258.

Wright, S., & Parchoma, G. (2011). Technologies for Learning? An actor-network theory critique of 'affordances' in research on mobile learning. *Research in Learning Technology, 19*(3), 247–258.

6

The contributions of mixed insights to advancing technology-enhanced formative assessments within higher education learning environments: an illustrative example

Cheryl Poth

Correspondence: cpoth@ualberta.ca
Department of Educational Psychology, University of Alberta, Edmonton, Alberta, Canada

Abstract

Technology-enhanced formative assessment (TEFA) represents strategies for improving student learning and motivation, yet researchers point to methodological issues underpinning claims of effectiveness. This mixed methods paper, using an empirical example, illustrates the novel contributions of mixed insights in informing the implementation of two TEFA classroom strategies. An embedded mixed methods case study design bounded by an 8-week undergraduate course across three terms was used to answer the following research question: How can a mixed methods approach examining the influences to and effects of involvement in TEFA offset the weaknesses inherent to either qualitative or quantitative data and guide collection, analysis, and integration? A qualitative dominant crossover mixed analysis strategy generated four novel mixed insights from the integration of 175 classroom-based observations, 26 instructional team meeting summaries, and 274 end-of-course student questionnaires. These are represented in a case summary and joint displays: influences on involvement, effects on learning, accessibility of feedback, and impacts on instruction. The mixed insights have important implications for theory, research, and practice related to TEFA strategies and highlight the contribution that mixed methods approaches can have in advancing educational technology in higher education.

Keywords: formative assessment, case study, educational technology, joint display, higher education learning environment, mixed methods research

Introduction

There is growing evidence of the usefulness and, indeed, unrealized potential of mixed methods research for tackling complex problems (Mertens, 2015; Poth, in press). Complex research problems address societal issues involving multiple, interacting influences with no known solution or established methods and expertise for studying the interrelated contexts in which they take place. An increased use of mixed methods research in such projects around the world, funded by diverse sectors is captured in studies measuring prevalence across a variety of disciplines and journals (Molina-Azorin & Fetters,

2016). The motivations for its use vary greatly, yet the rationale underlying my working definition of mixed methods research emphasizes designed to generate previously inaccessible insights by integrating qualitative and quantitative data. Mixed methods research requires the integration of both quantitative and qualitative data, and assumes that their collective contribution mitigates inherent weaknesses in either type of data. There exists an untapped potential for mixed methods research to contribute to advancements within the field of educational technology in higher education. This potential is especially evident under conditions of research complexity. Thus, my experiences as a mixed methods researcher, educational technology adopter, higher education instructor, and classroom assessment expert provide the impetus for my desire to contribute to the discourse around the use of mixed methods research within the field of educational technology in higher education. I do so through this paper focused on technology-enhanced formative assessments (TEFA).

Emergence of technology-enhanced formative assessments

Newer theories recognize the learning progression as inherently complex — learning is situated in and influenced by the dynamic contexts in which it takes place, with outcomes that are challenging to predict (Wiliam, 2016). We are only beginning to recognize the prominence of features present in the learning environment that explicitly check for understanding and then support learning through adjustments in instruction. General agreement exists that formative assessment represents such classroom strategies whereby instructors, students, and peers elicit, interpret, and apply evidence of student learning for the purpose of supporting learning and adjusting instruction (e.g., Shepard, Hammerness, Darling-Hammong, Rust, Snowden, et al., 2005; Wiliam, 2016). Developing ways for students and instructors to access this information through TEFA is viewed as a necessary and practical means of improving the quality of higher education teaching and learning environments (Maier, Wolf, & Randler, 2016).

The inclusion of technologies in higher education teaching and learning environments has been revolutionizing the ways in which instructors and students interact. Indeed, in online environments there has been debate about the differences in effectiveness between synchronous and asynchronous interactions. On-demand access has led to the creation of masses of digitized lectures and learning activities and a marked increase in research that is assessing student experience and impacts on learning; for example, there has been an exploration of alternative means of assessment in massive open online courses, MOOCs (Sánchez-Vera & Prendes-Espinosa, 2015). Less is known about how technologies are shaping the experiences of instructors and students in the real-time classroom environments.

Among the key TEFA strategies included in face-to-face classroom implementations are audience response system (ARS) and practice quizzes because research has established both the feasibility of implementation and the impact on student experience within higher education contexts (e.g., Maier et al., 2016; Wieman, 2010). A remote device is used to offer ARS by the instructors whereas the two practice quizzes are offered through the online class learning management system (LMS). In this paper, we present a case study in which the university has adopted the use of Moodle as the campus-wide LMS. The aim of the practice quizzes was to provide students with examples of the type of items, scope of content, and the level of cognition required for their midterm and final exams. ARS and practices quizzes are unique in their capacity to provide students with immediate feedback based on their anonymous answers to closed questions and in showing them a graph of classmates' answers afterward. The individual and aggregate class results can also be accessed by the instructor so that they can vary or remediate instruction if necessary. In so doing, the TEFA strategies adhered to principles of formative assessment: students are actively involved, students' learning benefits, access to feedback is timely, and adjustments to instruction are evident (Wiliam, 2016).

Formative assessment represents effective strategies for improving student motivation and learning, yet key methodological issues exist with the evidence that underpins claims of effectiveness (e.g., Bennett, 2011). First there are the difficulties with establishing the causal effect of formative assessments on student achievement and the expanded research focus; different meta-analyses have shown varying effect sizes that are often attributed to learning content, feedback procedures, or learner characteristics (Black & Wiliam, 1998; Kingston & Nash, 2011). Calls for research exploring the holistic interaction (and effects) among learners and the learning environment afforded by TEFA remain unanswered (Kay & LeSage, 2009). Second, the validity and reliability of many studies have been limited in their measurement of only students' perceptions of engagement and learning by the use of only one or two quantitative items (Offerdahl & Tomanek, 2011) and because they rely on anecdotal data which draws strong criticism (Ha & Finkelstein, 2013). A more rigorous approach is necessary to capture educational benefits and challenges reflective of all involved in TEFA. The purpose of the research reported in this paper was to generate a comprehensive understanding of influences to and effects of involvement in two TEFA strategies within a higher education learning environment through the integration of multiple perspectives. Specifically related to their involvement in the two TEFA strategies across three terms, students were asked directly, classroom interactions were observed, and instructor viewpoints were sought.

Tapping the potential of mixed methods research

Mixed methods research has emerged as an approach for generating insights from the integration of qualitative and quantitative data that otherwise would have been inaccessible. Researchers point to mixed methods research as offering more comprehensive evidence because it mitigates, to a large extent, the limitations of relying on either quantitative or qualitative data sources alone (Bryman, 2006). The rationale for the use of mixed methods research in the present study is that it offsets strengths and weaknesses (Plano Clark & Ivankova, 2016). This is especially noteworthy when working under research conditions such as the present study's: addressing complex problems that require new ways of study beyond our existing mixed methods research practices. "Business as usual will not lead to effective use of research to address wicked [complex] problems" (Mertens, 2015, p. 5). This call to action for the community of mixed methods researchers was recently followed up in an article inspired by the taskforce report for the Mixed Methods International Research Association in their description of the future of mixed methods research as kaleidoscopic, with its "seemingly unpredictable patterns full of rich possibilities for diversity and potential to provide opportunities to see things that have not yet been seen" (Mertens, Bazeley, Bowleg, Fielding, Maxwell, et al., 2016; p. 222).

As mixed methods researchers, our responses to complex problems pose dilemmas and offer opportunities. All too often, our responses involve attempts to reduce, control, or simply ignore the effects of complexity rather than considering new approaches including adopting new research designs and integration strategies. The time has come for mixed methods research to guide work within the field of educational technology—to address some of the dilemmas and harness some of the opportunities afforded by mixed methods research under conditions of complexity within higher education teaching and learning environments. Thus, this mixed methods study offers an innovative perspective from which to examine the influences to and effects of two TEFA strategies through the integration of both instructor and student perspectives within an undergraduate course. The present paper illustrates, using an empirical example, the contributions of a mixed methods research approach can have in generating mixed insights on two TEFA strategies: the implementation of the audience response system and practice quizzes.

Methods

Yin (2014) identifies a case study as useful for documenting implementation of an intervention — in this case, an instructional intervention embedding opportunities for engaging with TEFA strategies — within a real-life course context, making it the most appropriate methodology for my research. According to Creswell and Plano Clark (2018), the mixed methods case study design involves embedding both qualitative and quantitative data into a case (Fig. 1). In the present study, quantitative data were embedded within a qualitative case study bounded by the duration of the 8-week course repeated over three terms, and bounded by those involved in the course. A unique aspect of the research was the concurrent timing of the multiple sources of data collected from convenience samples representing differing perspectives. This sampling strategy was necessary for this mixed methods study rather than the matched samples often involved in embedded case study designs. This design helped to capture the

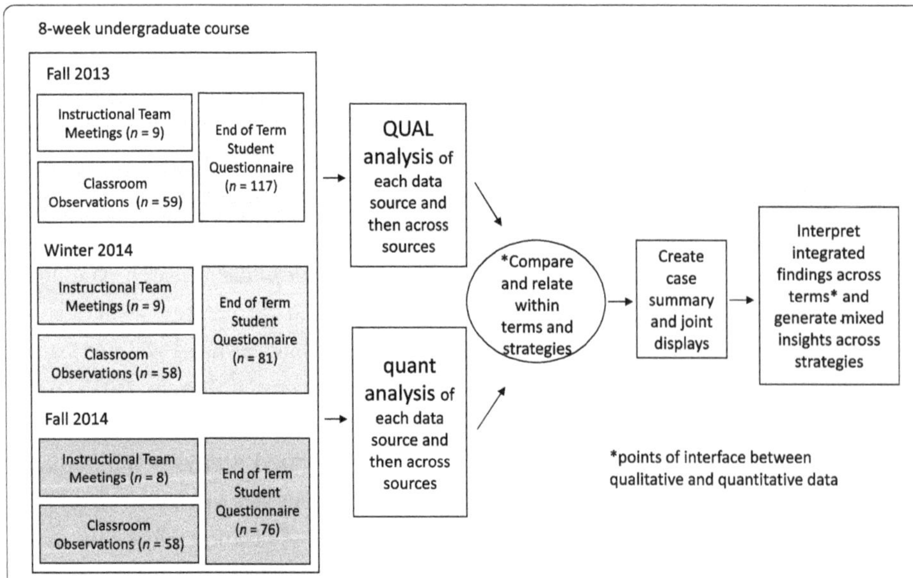

Fig. 1 Mixed methods case study design

perspectives of instructional team members and what has been documented related to the influences and effects of TEFA strategies on students. As well, there are two points of interface between the qualitative and quantitative data: first within the teaching terms for each TEFA strategy and then across terms and TEFA strategies.

Ethical considerations

The study design and procedures were reviewed and approved by the university's institutional review board and the researcher undertook all appropriate measures to ensure informed consent, protect participant confidentiality, and mitigate power issues. An external research assistant recruited participants. Informed consent was indicated by signing consent forms (instructional team) or by the overt action of choosing to complete the online questionnaire (students). To further mitigate potential power issues between instructors and graduate students under their supervision as teaching assistants as well as between instructional team members and the undergraduate students enrolled in their classes, all data collection activities were embedded within the course activities and data was collected anonymously. The researchers did not have access to the data until submission of the course grades for undergraduate students and performance evaluations for instructors and teaching assistants.

Study context

The selection of ARS and practice quizzes for this study was pragmatic as they were the only TEFA strategies that were implemented across the three terms. The undergraduate course involved large class-sized, face-to-face lectures. An instructional team approach had initially been adopted within the course in 2010 as a collaborative milieu wherein educational responsibility for the organization, instruction, and assessment was shared among an instructional team — often including an instructor and graduate teaching assistants (GTA) (Zhou, Kim, & Kerekes, 2011). The author played a dual role as a researcher and instructor in this research. A full description of the aims and activities involved in the team-instruction approach used in the current study is provided elsewhere (Yapp & Poth, 2013). The team approach meant that the instructional team members were involved in all aspects of the course and fostered mutual respect for individual contributions of team members. The implementation of the two TEFA strategies aligned well with the instructional team's focus on trying new ways of enhancing student access to immediate feedback and integrating technology. At the beginning of the study, the instructional team had been working together for 2 years and had already been monitoring and integrating student feedback into their instructional decisions. Among the roles and responsibilities for team members were:

- Planning; for example, preparing course materials and embedding feedback mechanisms,
- Delivery; for example, collecting data and interacting with students), and
- Development; for example, participating in weekly team meetings and leading review of data findings).

Each member was tasked with individual and shared responsibilities and allocated time to contribute their ideas and perspectives with the understanding that learning was a key aspect of the work. The team philosophy was based on the idea that, together, the team could attain more than each individual could separately to respond to emerging student needs.

Participants

The required undergraduate course is offered each term through the Faculty of Education at a research-intensive western Canadian university. All members of the instructional team and students enrolled across three terms (Fall 2013, Winter 2014, and Fall 2014) were invited to participate. In all, the study involved a convenience sample of 11 members of the instructional team (one coordinator, tjree instructors, and seven GTAs) and 274 students who completed questionnaires (45% response rate). The overall student sample reported the following demographic characteristics (see Table 1 for each term): 73.6% female; 65% completing an elementary-teacher program stream (as opposed to the secondary-teacher program stream); and 77.1% being enrolled in the 4-year Bachelor of Education program (as opposed to the 2-year post-graduate program). Every class and team meeting that took place during the time bounded by the case study was also included.

Data sources and collection procedures

The three data sources and methods included 26 instructional team meeting summaries, 274 student questionnaires, and 175 instructional class observations.

Instructional team meeting summaries

Throughout each term, the instructional team members met weekly to discuss and make decisions related to course planning, delivery, and adjustments. A protocol was developed to guide note-taking during the meeting for the purpose of documenting team meeting interactions, reports of students' involvement in TEFA strategies and emerging issues, and meeting outcomes from decisions. These meeting notes were primarily qualitative in nature.

Student questionnaires

At the end of each term, a web-based questionnaire was administered to students anonymously using an online survey delivery system: SurveyMonkey. The five-part questionnaire (measuring participation in TEFA, examining TEFA uses, documenting participant demographics, assessing course experiences, and determining assessment preferences) was developed by the research team with assistance from a measurement expert. It included both quantitative and qualitative questions for a total of 35 items with comments available for the majority.

Table 1 Student demographics

	% Overall ($n = 274$)	% Fall 2013 ($n = 117$)	% Winter 2014 ($n = 81$)	% Fall 2014 ($n = 76$)
Female	73.7	70.0	76.5	76.3
Elementary program stream	65.3	64.1	61.7	71.0
Two-year post-graduate program	77.4	73.5	80.0	80.2

Class observations

Throughout each term, a class observation guided by a protocol was completed by a GTA who attended each lecture for the dual purposes of documenting emergent issues and class interactions focused on student involvement in TEFA strategies as well as course delivery as a means of assessing instructional fidelity across sections of the same course. The protocol consisted of 14 dichotomous (yes/no) items (e.g., Were opportunities provided for students to use the audience response system?) and two open-ended questions about emergent issues and questions students asked during class. Protocol training was provided and inter-rater reliability was assessed among multiple GTAs during the first two classes until 90% reliability was reached.

Data analysis and integration procedures

The data analysis and integration procedures involved the separate analysis of each data type (i.e., qualitative and quantitative data) within each source and then across data sources.

Qualitative data analysis

The qualitative data analysis was undertaken using a computer assisted qualitative data analysis software: *NVivo©*. This involved the thematic analysis of comments generated by the student questionnaires, classroom observations, and team instructional meetings within each term. The iterative process followed the activities described by the data analysis spiral supplemented by the taking of memos (Creswell & POth 2017). An independent researcher not involved in the study worked with the study researcher separately to highlight the text into large meaning units and make initial notes. This helped build consensus and enhance reliability among the coders by establishing descriptions of initial categories and codes that were eventually applied across all qualitative data sources. After applying the codes, the coders met to discuss the coding and refined codes until inter-rater reliability reached 90%. They then identified nine thematic codes and finalized the codebook. The codebook consisted of five columns: category, codes, definition (i.e., what the code means), anti-definition (i.e., what the code does not mean), and examples of verbatim quotes that represent the code.

Quantitative data analysis

The separate quantitative data analysis involved eliminating missing data by using listwise deletion of questionnaire and classroom observation items and then generating descriptive statistics (mean, standard deviation, and frequency) using SPSS Statistics 20 software within each data source and terms. The differences across terms related to rates of participation and demographics were subsequently explored with a Kruskal-Wallis test. Post-hoc Mann–Whitney U analysis was done on a significant Kruskal-Wallis test to identify areas of difference.

Integration

Qualitative themes and quantitative results were compared via a qualitative dominant crossover mixed analysis (Onwuegbuzie & Hitchcock, 2015). To do this, the case summaries were generated to represent the areas of convergence and divergence highlighted by the basic type of qualitative dominant crossover mixed analysis where the nine qualitative thematic categories were used as the organizational framework on which to integrate the quantitative findings. The integration across three instructional terms and two TEFA strategies revealed four mixed insights. Several strategies served to enhance reliability in the analysis procedures and generate multiple sources of validity evidence for the mixed insights. Key among these efforts is the use of multiple qualitative coders; visual plotting of the generation of the mixed insights from the qualitative dominant crossover analysis strategy (Fig. 2); and provision of integrated findings through the case summary and joint displays (Tables 1 and 2).

Summary of the case

At the pre-term instructional team meeting for the Fall 2013 term, evidence of enthusiasm was apparent in the summary description that all tasks were complete and "course materials and activities were ready to go." The ARS implementation seemed to be going well during the first few weeks: classroom observations captured an increasing rate of student involvement and interest in the ARS activities, and several team members expressed satisfaction with the overall regularity of student participation they had observed in the classroom. The team had even observed student uses of the information gleaned from the ARS activities and saw the instructors consider how this information could inform instructional changes. For example, the third instructional team meeting summary captured the discussions about students asking to review particular content areas that they had found confusing, which led to the instructional team adding examples to the subsequent lecture notes. By the midpoint of the term, classroom observations and team members reported having reached "a plateau" described as participation consistently estimated to be the majority of students attending class yet no visible increases in rates of participation across more than two classes. Interestingly, concern with student participation became a consistent subject during subsequent instructional team meetings because GTAs and instructors both observed a slight decrease in frequency of participation in the latter half of the term.

The initial very high rate of participation in the practice quizzes (87% completed both) reported by students at the end of the Fall 2013 term was familiar to members of the instructional team. This is because the team had advertised this activity as being

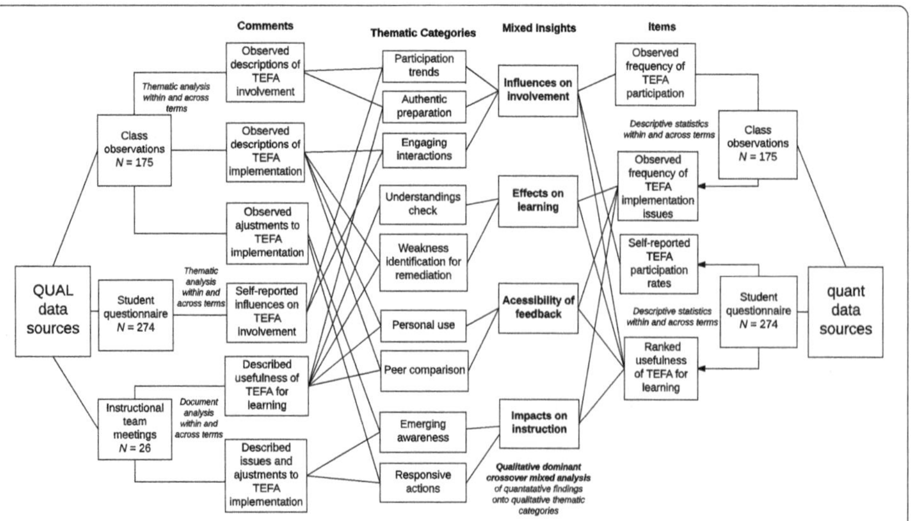

Fig. 2 Study's data collection, analysis, and integration

Table 2 Audience response systems joint display

Mixed Insights	Thematic Categories	% Fall 2013 ($n = 117$)	% Winter 2014 ($n = 81$)	% Fall 2014 ($n = 76$)
Influences on involvement	Participation trends (Use/ purchase rates)	72.6/61.5 High yet decreasing frequency	67.9/61.7 Lower and inconsistent use	75.0/65.8 Higher and consistent use
	Authentic preparation	85.6 "the questions were hard but good practice"	83.3 "made me think about exam items"	86.4 "I learned what questions to expect"
	Engaging interactions*	84.4 "It created more interactions"	66.7 "I wish I had more chances"	80.3 "I enjoyed these activities"
Effects on learning	Understandings check	94.4 "fun way to confirm understanding"	90.0 "I thought I knew more"	97.0 "I was surprised at what I knew"
	Weakness identification for remediation*	92.2 "now I know what I did not know"	76.7 "I need to study more"	92.4 "I know what to study"
Accessibility of feedback	Personal use	94.4 "I like that no one knows my answer"	90.0 "I know quickly if I am right"	97.0 "telling me right away"
	Peer comparisons*	85.6 "want to know how class is doing"	68.3 "I knew as much as others"	86.4 "I was lagging behind others"
Impacts on instruction	Emerging awareness	Cost barrier yet participation independent "I learned as much from watching as if I had used one."	Ongoing resistance to purchase yet want more often "I will not pay to participate"	Multiple platforms challenging "more expertise needed"
	Responsive actions	Sought lower cost options & revised lecture content	Offered cost-effective alternatives Increased frequency of classroom use	Continued to explore options & revisit content

Note. * Denotes a statistically significant difference across terms ($p < 0.05$)

helpful for exam preparation and students had already confirmed their participation verbally in class. Whereas some comments were general, stating they " ... liked the practice exams ... ," others explained the students use prior to a summative exam saying, "exam practice [quizzes] [are] excellent study tool[s]" and "It gave me an idea of what types of questions would be asked." Unanticipated by the instructional team were the anecdotal comments describing the single attempt for each practice quiz as limiting its benefit.

At the post-term meeting for the Fall 2013 term, team members seemed to be surprised by the questionnaire results: students' high participation rate in audience response technology activities (72.6%) was viewed by the instructional team as encouraging, yet the lower rate of purchase of the stand-alone remote (61.5%) was unexpected. It became clear that students most often cited cost ($40) as a barrier to purchasing the remote. However, this did not seem to impact their participation in the ARS activities. Indeed, several students reported engaging in the ARS activities regardless of whether they were individually able to contribute to the group response using the remote; one student noted, "I learned as much from watching the [ARS] questions as if I had [been] using one." Also noted in the summary was a lengthy discussion about the contrast between what could be considered the high rate of students' self-reported participation at the end of the first term with the decreasing pattern of participation observed by instructional team members as well as discussion of how cost might be addressed.

The team members seemed initially skeptical that though the TEFA strategies were viewed as useful for learning, the effect for the ARS was not dependent on participation with remote. The uncertainty was evident in the meeting summaries where the GTAs voiced a concern that students were not buying the remote, "if they don't buy it how can they learn from it?" The questionnaire results revealed that the vast majority of students during the Fall 2013 term reported using the TEFA strategies foremost for an understanding check of course content (94.4% for ARS and 94.0% for practice quizzes) and for areas of weakness identification for remediation (92.2% for ARS and 96.6% for practice quizzes). This is compared with fewer, yet still more than 80% of respondents agreeing that the TEFA strategies were useful for providing peer comparisons, authentic preparation, and engaging interactions. Further, students attributed their enjoyment of ARS activities to the ability to respond anonymously for guiding personal use of the information (94%); one student expressed it was a "fun way to check my own understanding." Similarly, from the instructional team perspective, the ARS activities were thought to enable student access to data related to individual understandings of course content that could then be compared with their peers, if desired. Team instructional meeting summaries captured the persistent concern that a potential cumulative effect of the ever-decreasing use during the term had resulted in fewer students using the ARS remote over time and thus hampered the ability for students to compare with classmates. Thus, two members were tasked with seeking less expensive alternatives to the remote.

The questionnaire findings also indicated that timing of the students completing the practice quizzes influenced their perceptions of their usefulness in supporting learning their own learning (96.6%). Whereas the majority of students reported use of the practice quizzes at the end of studying as a final check of their understanding of the material, another group of students used the practice quizzes before beginning to study as a means of focusing their efforts on areas of weakness. Clearly students valued the on-demand aspects of the practice quizzes saying, "by doing it more than once, I can see how I am improving". Specifically, students attributed not being able to complete the quiz multiple times to a perception of limited usefulness evidenced by a lower rate of participation in the end-of-term practice quiz compared with that offered at the middle of the term (88.9 and 94% respectively). The student's desire for greater access to the practice quizzes were echoed across the team meeting summaries. Unanimous agreement among the instructional team about the lack of pedagogical reasons to limit access to the practice quizzes led to allowing multiple attempts during the Winter 2014 term.

At the pre-term instructional team meeting for the Winter 2014 term, the GTAs reported that serendipitously, a more-cost-effective, phone-based application using the same system as the remote was now available for a quarter of the cost — just $10. One team member had examined its viability including ease of access and compatibility for use along with the remote and consensus was reached to offer the options in tandem. The ARS implementation across the two platforms (i.e., stand-alone remote and phone-based application) seemed to go really well for the first 2 weeks of class; classroom observations indicated the majority of students attending class were participating. However, following the third class, the classroom observations and team members reported a marked decrease in ARS participation and one of the GTAs was assigned to further investigate.

Interestingly, this timing was found to coincide with the end of the free trial of the phone-based application. A further trend that was noted across the classroom observations with some consistency was the increased interest for ARS activities as practicing exam-type items. This lead to discussions at subsequent team meetings about why this might be the case rather than using the questions for an understanding check, and team members were tasked with talking with students informally. The following meeting for one of these instances provided information that students reported primary interest in the ARS activities as a practice to the exam, "I like knowing what the exam questions might look like".

The initial high rate of participation in the practice quizzes (84% completed both) was reported by students at the end of the Winter 2014 term. These students described the practice quizzes as generally useful for exam preparation and specifically for identifying areas of weakness, yet raised concerns about the lack of access to the correct answers. Representative comments include "I have yet to do the final exam practice quiz, however I do intend to do it prior to the final exam. I just want to review my notes and study before I take it to see what I need to look over again" and, the practice exams " ... guide studying and evaluate which sections of the course [I] needed to revisit". At the same time, additional LMS features were being introduced that would provide students access to more information than whether the item had been answered correctly or not. One team member was tasked with examining potential applications of those practice quiz features.

At the post-term meeting for the Winter term 2014, the team members reviewed the questionnaire results that initially seemed puzzling related to participation and usefulness of the TEFA strategies. Together, the rates of purchase of the remote and app during the second term remained at similar rates to the first term (61%), yet there was a small decline (five percentage points) in overall participation to 67.9%. A reasonable explanation advanced by the instructional team for the lower rate of purchase (1.2%) of the phone-based application by students was that some students may be used to accessing apps for free or for modest costs and thus be unwilling to pay $10 for the phone-based app. Another difference was the extent of agreement related to the usefulness of the TEFA strategies; particularly for the ARS.

An understanding check of course content remained the most useful for both strategies (90% for ARS and 92.6% for practice quizzes) followed by authentic preparation (83.3% for ARS and 92.6% for practice quizzes). Indeed, the ability to receive personalized feedback immediately was reported as being useful by the vast majority of students (90.0% for ARS and 92.6% for practice quizzes). There was less agreement between the perceived usefulness of strategies such as weakness identification for remediation (92.6% for the practice quizzes compared with 76.7% for ARS). This is compared with fewer, yet still more than 60% of respondents for ARS and 80% of respondents for practice quizzes agreeing that the TEFA strategies were useful for providing peer comparisons and engaging interactions. These results lead to team discussions to consider how the ARS activities could be more engaging. One member took on the task of developing more frequent opportunities for ARS to be used in subsequent lectures.

A new LMS feature allowed team members to give students access to the total number of correct responses for each attempt during Winter 2014 and these effects were discussed at the post-term team meeting. Similar to the preceding terms, students consistently reported a high rate of participation in the practice quizzes for exam preparation either at the beginning of the studying process or to confirm exam readiness. An unanticipated outcome was that these students also desired access to the correct answers, saying, "[t]he practice quizzes would be more beneficial if they had answers." The team meeting summaries documented the struggle the instructional team experienced while attempting to resolve the dilemma: while students might benefit from immediate access to the answers, students might equally benefit from having to find the answer themselves. Ultimately one team member was tasked with creating a feature allowing students to review their incorrect items using prompts that would ultimately unveil the correct answer.

At the pre-term instructional team meeting for the Fall 2014 term, further discussions ensued, which lead them to offer both ARS platforms and open and on-demand access to the practice quizzes during this term. Through the classroom observations, the team members noted consistent participation in the ARS and practice quizzes and did not note any problems with the compatibility of the platforms or quiz access. The review of questionnaire results at the end of the term showed a small increase in overall participation rates (up seven percentage points from the previous term, to 75%) and purchase rates (up four percentage points from the previous term, to 65.8%). The team members noted surprise that despite the lower cost of the phone-based application ($10), the rate of purchase was higher for stand-alone remotes (44.7%) than it was for the phone-based apps (21.1%). The team members reported similar perceived usefulness of ARS activities across platforms. Indeed, the vast majority of students reported TEFA strategies as most useful for an understanding check of course content (97% for ARS and 93.4% for practice quizzes) and weakness identification for remediation (92.4% for ARS and 93.4% for practice quizzes). Further, more than 80% of respondents agreed that the TEFA strategies were useful for providing peer comparisons, authentic preparation, and engaging interactions. It is also key to note that the vast majority of students found the ability to respond anonymously and receiving immediate feedback from the TEFA strategies as highly useful (97% for ARS and 93.4% for practice quizzes). The final integration across three instructional terms and two TEFA strategies revealed four mixed insights.

Integrated findings and discussion

The integrated findings across terms summarized in joint displays (see Tables 2 and 3) and differences between fall and winter terms that were statistically significant; this was also noted in the qualitative data. Four mixed insights were generated and are discussed across the two TEFA strategies and terms: influences on involvement, effects on learning, accessibility of feedback, and impacts on instruction.

Influences on involvement

The consistent higher participation trends in the practice quizzes than in the ARS may be associated with the reported access barriers of the costs of the remote and phone app reported by students across the terms. Common across both the ARS and practice quizzes was the consistent perceived usefulness of the TEFA strategies for practicing the types of items expected on the exams. Overall, the students seem more focused on the usefulness of the TEFA strategies for preparing for the exam than on engaging with the activity for enjoyment. Interestingly, the analysis across terms revealed differences between fall and winter that were statistically significant ($H = 6.003$, $p = 0.05$) in the students' perceptions about the

Table 3 Practice quizzes joint display

Mixed Insights	Thematic Categories	% Fall 2013 ($n = 117$)	% Winter 2014 ($n = 81$)	% Fall 2014 ($n = 76$)
Influences on involvement	Participation trends (Middle/ end)	94.0/88.9 High completion rates of both (87.1) yet decreasing use	91.4/91.4 High completion rates of both (84.0) and use	98.7/89.5 Highest completion rates of both (88.2) yet decreasing use
	Authentic preparation	95.7 "... gave me an idea of types of questions asked."	92.6 "good preparation exercise for final exam"	96.6 "I do it prior to the final exam for practice"
	Engaging interactions	81.2 "it was a good way to study"	82.7 "...liked the practice activity..."	82.3 "I'm glad I did the quizzes"
Effects on learning	Understandings check	94.0 "...are excellent study tool telling me what I know"	92.6 "I used it before I started studying"	93.4 "after studying I wanted to know what I knew"
	Weakness identification for remediation	96.6 "...guide studying which sections of content to revisit."	92.6 "definitely helped me to see what I needed to study"	93.4 "I liked seeing how much more I know now"
Accessibility of feedback	Personal use	96.6 "I saw what I knew immediately"	92.6 "glad to know my score right away"	93.4 "could see what I learned easily"
	Peer comparisons	81.2 "I like to see how my peers did"	88.9 "I was similar to my peers"	88.2 "Others scored way better"
Impacts on instruction	Emerging awareness	Access limited to single attempt "... do it more so I can know if I am improving"	Feedback limited to number correct "want to know answers"	Need access early in the term "I want to do the quizzes when I wanted"
	Responsive actions	Access opened to multiple attempts	Access to total and correct answers	Opened access at start of term

ARS providing engaging interactions. The qualitative comments and observations provide some context for this finding because in the fall terms, the students described the effects for the ARS on learning was not dependent on participation with the remote whereas these understandings were not evident in the winter term. Further, the consistent 20 percentage point differences in participation rates between ARS and practice quizzes are noteworthy because even though students also reported access barriers for the practice quizzes related to number of attempts and information they could access, the rates of participation for practice quizzes were higher. These findings may reflect the social context in which each of the TEFA takes place — whereas the ARS occurs within the classroom context as a group, the practice quizzes are completed online, independently — and eventually on demand — so they may garner greater participation. These findings align with the suggestion that practice quizzes foster interaction among students and between students and instructors (Sancho & Escudero, 2012) as well as favourable experiences (Blanco & Ginovart, 2013).

Effects on learning

The consistently high levels of agreement in the ratings, observations, and comments about the usefulness across terms related to both the practice quizzes provides evidence of the TEFA strategies as effective for supporting learning. Overall, the students seem focused on the usefulness of the TEFA strategies for both checking understandings and identifying areas of weakness for further study. Interestingly, the analysis across terms revealed differences between fall and winter that were statistically significant ($H = 9.036$, $p = 0.011$) in the students' perceptions about the ARS for identifying areas of weakness for remediation. The qualitative comments and observations provide some context for this finding because in the fall terms, the students described needing to study "more" but not necessarily knowing what to study. These findings based on several groups of students begin to address the concerns with previous ARS studies that relied on small sample sizes highlighted by Ha and Finkelstein (2013). To compare, the practice quizzes seemed to support students' study efforts related to specific content. These findings may reflect the timing of participation in each TEFA strategy. Whereas the ARS were embedded throughout the term, the practice quizzes were generally taken during exam preparation and thus students might be more focused on particular content. These findings suggest that practice quizzes provide students the opportunity to regulate their own learning but that this learning is predicated on access to information beyond whether their answers are correct. Indeed, the work of Sancho and Escudero (2012) supports this line of thinking —that practice quizzes provide the opportunity for immediate feedback to inform students about how they are performing related to the course expectations yet these activities are most useful when they can be completed on-demand and aligned with students' needs.

Accessibility of feedback

The usefulness of the TEFA strategies for providing timely access to feedback is reflected in the consistently high levels of agreement in the ratings, observations, and comments across terms. Overall, the students seem focused on the usefulness of the feedback provided by the TEFA strategies for both personal use and peer comparisons. Interestingly, the analysis across terms revealed differences between fall and winter that were statistically significant ($H = 11.498$, $p = 0.003$), in the students' perceptions about the ARS for comparing with peers. The qualitative comments and observations provide some context for this finding because in the fall terms, the students, observations, and team meetings described the instructors as immediately responding to the group's ARS results whereby the instructor response was not evident in the winter term.

These findings may reflect the instructional use of the feedback provided by each TEFA strategy. The classroom observations provide further evidence of the instructors' use of individuals' formative results and comparisons within and across groups. Whereas the instructor could make explicit the use of the ARS in class and impact the students directly, the feedback practice quizzes was generally taken into account for the following term and thus was less visible. These findings begin to address the underpresented issue in the ARS literature described by Ha and Finkelstein (2013) related to the instructors' specific formative use and how students perceive the usefulness of the information for their own learning.

Impacts on instruction

The analysis across terms and strategies generated understandings about the instructional adjustments that were evidence-based decisions. As the team became aware of emerging issues, they would discuss them at the team meetings, and then seek further information in the classroom observations, anecdotally from students, and in the end-of-term student questionnaires. For the ARS, the cost to purchase a remote was an early and recurring issue over the three terms. Even after offering a lower-cost alternative (i.e., phone based apps), ongoing resistance to any cost was apparent. Interestingly, the qualitative data revealed that participation in the activities of the ARS was not dependent upon purchase of the remote. These findings begin to shed much needed light as described by Offerdahl and Tomanek (2011) on the impact of ARS on instructors' thought processes and actions resulting from the implementation of such activities. Students described learning as much from observing the activities as they did from participating, which was not apparent in the quantitative findings alone. Gaining understandings of the participation rates also lead the team to increase the frequency of use in the classroom both because the students were benefiting from and enjoying the interactions, and to justify the cost for many students. In comparison, the adjustments to the practice quizzes responded to demands for unlimited access and greater specificity in the feedback provided. As new understandings emerged about the role of peer comparisons, the team gave access to class results on practice quizzes.

Implications and limitations

The mixed insights offer important implications in terms of advancing theory, research, and practice related to TEFA strategies and highlight the contribution that mixed methods approaches can have in advancing educational technology in higher education. First, in terms of theory and research and specifically to how the two strategies examined in this paper (ARS and on-demand practices quizzes) support learning from the perspectives of the instructional team and students. From a theoretical perspective, this study points to educational technology as an important mediator for creating significant classroom-based learning experiences. Specifically, this study points to the effectiveness of the TEFA strategies for supporting student motivation, student use for directing their own learning, and team use for informing instructional adjustments that have effects for students immediately and in the future. The advancements made by Ha and Finkelstein (2013) are an excellent starting place for further quantitative study of the student perspective of the impact of ARS and its use for informing instructional decisions. It is important not to exclude other types of my consideration of effectiveness in this study, for example while peer interactions are often less timely than ARS or practice quizzes, written peer feedback remains a useful tool for supporting learning (Ion, Barrera-Corominas, & Tomàs-Folch, 2016).

From the examination of the illustrative example of two effective TEFA strategies, it seems that assessing the impacts and influences of educational technology in higher education teaching and learning contexts is also complex and thus theory and research in this area needs to heed the same calls as the field of mixed methods research does more generally. This includes not only continuing to refine theory in light of new and emerging understandings but also to continue to develop new TEFA strategies and ways of capturing the influence and effects of these strategies through the use of mixed methods. Indeed, this reflects the thinking highlighted by Li (2014) that technology-enhanced learning will need to take into account the interrelated relationships among the learner, the learning context, the technology, and (I would argue) the instructor. The use of a mixed methods research approach to the case study impacted this research in three important ways: First, the integration of qualitative and quantitative data at two points of interface generated rich understandings specific to each term and then the cross-analysis of terms and strategies allowed for new trends and differences to be noted. Second, the integration of multiple perspectives provided access to new understandings that had been previously inaccessible; notably the instructional adjustments and the reasons underpinning the adjustments. Third, the integration of multiple data sources enhanced validity evidence as it allowed for triangulation within the descriptive case summary and, specifically, the qualitative findings provided context for participation trends that had previously not been captured across terms. By capturing the implementation processes over time and across different groups of students rather than simply the outcomes from one term, I offer an illustrative example of an embedded mixed methods case study design reflective of the necessary openness to emerging and innovative ways that are appropriate for the complex conditions under which research is undertaken.

In terms of practice, this study points to three areas to consider when implementing TEFA strategies; frequency of use, cost to students, and ease of on-demand access. Instructors adopting educational technology in their higher education teaching and learning environments need to be aware of the literature guiding implementation of TEFA and the influences of their own assessment experiences on their instructional practices. This is because researchers have established that instructors' classroom assessment practices are influenced by their attitudes, prior experiences, knowledge, skills, and motivation related to the nature of assessment and learning (Calderhead, 1996). Meaningful learning interactions incorporating educational technology and formative assessments require appropriate structures (Sorensen & Takle, 2005). Thus, more comprehensive understandings related to influences on involvement, effects on learning, accessibility of feedback, and impacts on instructors could influence future implementations of TEFA and thus have important practice consequences and impacts on classroom teaching and learning environments.

To provide guidance to educational technology researchers in higher education, I designed this research with dimensions of high quality research in mixed methods (Collins, 2015) and the criteria for publishing (Onwuegbuzie & Poth 2016; Fetters & Freshwater, 2015) in mind. Based on these standards, this research represents high quality mixed method research in the following five ways: the use of literature to clearly justify a mixed methods approach for generating mixed insights; the detailed descriptions of the procedures to create transparency of the methodology used in the case study; the mixing strategy used to address the convergent purpose underpinning the intentional integration; the procedures and practices for maintaining ethical standards, rigor, and complexity built into the design itself; and validity evidence gathered to support the findings from each strand separately as well as the mixed insights.

The results need to be interpreted with the following two limitations in mind: First, the design is somewhat unique in that it used a convenience concurrent mixed sampling strategy with involvement in the case study because of the relationship between the qualitative data collected from observations and team meetings and the quantitative data collected from student questionnaires. The use of a convenience sample meant that the individuals were available and willing to participate — similar to the concurrent implementation described by Teddlie and Yu (2007). The data captured the key perspectives for the case study and met the minimum sample size recommendations was met (Collins, 2010). Second, the results of the quantitative strand may be underrepresented in the crossover mixed analysis. For example, in the crossover analysis I chose to focus on items rather than means or relationships at the scale level. This was done because the items had been researcher-created and may have simplified the quantitative perspective through the use of item-level descriptive statistics. Future research could use a similar design with established constructs.

Conclusions

This study illustrates the contributions of novel mixed insights about the influences to and effects of an audience response system as a TEFA strategy with the educational significance important for educational policies and practices enhancing teaching and student engagement in higher education. Specifically, this empirical case study which focused on ARS and practice quizzes generated novel insights about the TEFA strategy's effectiveness in supporting instructional adjustments and peer comparisons that had not been previously documented, and it provided further understandings of the effectiveness of features such as timely and specific feedback, authentic practice, and engaging interactions. The inclusion of TEFAs within higher education classrooms requires new approaches both in the ways people teach and the ways people learn. For instructors, modeling the desirability and usefulness of feedback for informing adjustments on the go helps students to see the value of such information. For students, embracing the opportunities to guide their own learning is a necessary and appropriate transition in the current higher education context.

The mixed insights were not previously accessible using either qualitative or quantitative research approaches; indeed, the mixed methods approach integrating the instructional team and student perspectives was essential. In short, from the results presented in this paper, I advocate TEFA strategies as an important contributor towards creating continuous assessment systems where learning and assessment go hand in hand and students are provided the opportunity to drive their own learning. And consequently, it is hoped that this study will stimulate further investigations of the impacts of additional TEFA strategies.

Abbreviations

ARS: Audience response system; GTA: Graduate teaching assistant; LMS: Learning management system; TEFA: Technology-enhanced formative assessment

Acknowledgements

The author would like to thank Alvin Yapp and Erin Sulla for their assistance collecting data, as well as Lia Daniels for her contributions in the larger project and Adrienne Montgomery for helpful comments during the draft stages of this manuscript.

Funding

This work was supported by a Social Sciences and Humanities Research Council of Canada (SSHRC) Standard Grant (410-2011-0095) and a University of Alberta Teaching and Learning Enhancement Fund Grant (RES0004915).

Authors' contributions

Not applicable

Competing interests

The author declares that she has no competing interests.

References

Bennett, E. G. (2011). Formative assessment: A critical review. *Assessment in Education: Principles, Policy and Practice, 18*(1), 5–25. https://doi.org/10.1080/0969594X.2010.513678.

Black, P., & Wiliam, D. (1998). Assessment and classroom learning. *Assessment in Education: Principles, Policy, and Practice, 5*(1), 7–74.

Blanco, M., & Ginovart, M. (2013). On how Moodle quizzes can contribute to the formative e-assessment of first-year engineering students in mathematics courses. *Universities and Knowledge Society Journal, 9*, 354–370.

Bryman, A. (2006). Integrating quantitative and qualitative research: How is it done? *Qualitative Research Journal, 6*(1), 97–113. https://doi.org/10.1177/1468794106058877.

Calderhead, J. (1996). Teachers' beliefs and knowledge. In D. C. Berliner, & R. C. Calfee (Eds.), *Handbook of educational psychology*, (pp. 709–725). New Yoyk: Simon & Schuster Macmillan.

Collins, K. (2010). Advanced sampling designs in mixed research: Current practices and emerging trends in the social and behavioral sciences. In A. Tashakkori, & C. Teddlie (Eds.), *Sage handbook of mixed methods in Social & Behavioral Research*, (2nd ed., pp. 353–378). Thousand Oaks: Sage.

Collins, N. K. (2015). Validity in multimethod and mixed research. In S. Hesse-Biber, & B. Johnson (Eds.), *The Oxford handbook of multimethod and mixed methods research inquiry*, (pp. 240–256). New York: Oxford University Press.

Creswell, J., & Poth, C. (2017). *Qualitative inquiry and research design: Choosing among five approaches* (4th ed.). Thousand Oaks, CA: Sage.

Creswell, J., & Plano Clark, V. (2018). *Designing and conducting mixed methods research*, (3rd ed.,). Thousand Oaks: Sage.

Fetters, M., & Freshwater, D. (2015). The 1 + 1 = 3 integration challenge. *Journal of Mixed Methods Research, 9*, 115–117. https://doi.org/10.1177/1558689815581222.

Ha, J. H., & Finkelstein, A. (2013). Understanding the effects of professors' pedagogical development with clicker assessment and feedback technologies and the impact on students' engagement and learning in higher education. *Computers & Education, 65*, 64–76. https://doi.org/10.1016/j.compedu.2013.02.002.

Ion, G., Barrera-Corominas, A., & Tomàs-Folch, M. (2016). Written peer-feedback to enhance students' current and future learning. *International Journal of Educational Technology in Higher Education, 13*(15), 1–11. https://doi.org/10.1186/s41239-016-0017-y.

Kay, R. H., & LeSage, A. (2009). Examining the benefits and challenges of using audience response systems: A review of the literature. *Computers & Education, 53*(3), 819–827. dx.doi.org. https://doi.org/10.1016/j.compedu.2009.05.001.

Kingston, N., & Nash, B. (2011). Formative assessment: A meta-analysis and a call for research. *Educational Measurement: Issues and Practice, 30*(4), 28–37.

Li, Z. (2014). Rethinking the relationship between learner, learning contexts, and technology: A critique and exploration of Archer's morphogenetic approach. *Learning, Media and Technology, 41*, 501–520. https://doi.org/10.1080/17439884.2014.978336.

Maier, W., Wolf, N., & Randler, C. (2016). Effects of a computer-assisted formative assessment intervention based on multiple-tier diagnostic items and different feedback types. *Computers & Education, 95*, 85–98. https://doi.org/10.1016/j.compedu.2015.12.002.

Mertens, D. M. (2015). Mixed methods and wicked problems. *Journal of Mixed Methods Research, 9*, 1–6. https://doi.org/10.1177/1558689814562944.

Mertens, D. M., Bazeley, P., Bowleg, L., Fielding, N. G., Maxwell, J. A., Molina-Azorin, J. F., & Niglas, K. (2016). Expanding thinking through a kaleidoscopic look into the future: Implications of the mixed methods international research Association's task force report on the future of mixed methods research. *Journal of Mixed Methods Research, 10*, 221–227. https://doi.org/10.1177/1558689816649719.

Molina-Azorin, J. F., & Fetters, M. (2016). Mixed methods research prevalence studies: Field specific studies on the state of the art in mixed methods research. *Journal of Mixed Methods Research, 10*(2), 123–128. https://doi.org/10.1177/1558689816636707.

Offerdahl, E. G., & Tomanek, D. (2011). Changes in instructors' assessment thinking related to experimentation with new strategies. *Assessment & Evaluation in Higher Education, 36*(7), 781–795 dx.doi.org/10.1080/02602938.2010.488794.

Onwuegbuzie, A., & Hitchcock, J. H. (2015). Advanced mixed analysis approaches. In S. Hesse-Biber, & B. Johnson (Eds.), *The Oxford handbook of multimethod and mixed methods research inquiry*, (pp. 275–295). New York: Oxford University Press.

Onwuegbuzie, A., & Poth, C. (2016). Editors' afterword: Toward evidence-based guidelines for reviewing mixed methods research manuscripts submitted to journals. *International Journal of Qualitative Methods, 15*, 1–13. https://doi.org/10.1177/1609406916628986.

Poth, C. (in press). The curious case of complexity: Implications for mixed methods research practices. *International Journal of Multiple Research Approaches*.

Plano Clark, V. L., & Ivankova, N. V. (2016). *Mixed methods research: A guide to the field*. Thousand Oaks: Sage.

Sánchez-Vera, M. M., & Prendes-Espinosa, M. P. (2015). Beyond objective testing and peer assessment: Alternative ways of assessment in MOOCs. RUSC. *Universities and Knowledge Society Journal, 12*(1), 119–130 http://dx.doi.org/10.7238/rusc.v12i1.2262.

Sancho, T., & Escudero, N. (2012). A proposal for formative assessment with automatic feedback on an online mathematics subject. *Universities and Knowledge Society Journal, 9*, 240–260 http://dx.doi.org/10.7238/rusc.v9i2.1285.

Shepard, L. A., Hammerness, K., Darling-Hammong, L., Rust, F., Snowden, J. B., Gordon, E., … Pacheco, A. (2005). Assessment. In L. Darling-Hammong, & J. Bransford (Eds.), *Preparing teachers for a changing world: What teachers should learn and be able to do*, (pp. 275–326). San Francisco: Jossey Bass.

Sorensen, E. K., & Takle, E. S. (2005). Investigating knowledge building dialogues in networked communities of practice. A collaborative learning endeavor across cultures. *Interactive Educational Multimedia, 10*, 50–60.

Teddlie, C., & Yu, F. (2007). Mixed methods sampling: A typology with examples. *Journal of Mixed Methods Research, 1* 77–100. https://doi.org/10.1177/2345678906292430.

Wieman, C. (2010). Why not try a scientific approach to science education? In J. C. Hughes, & J. Mighty (Eds.), *Taking stock: Research on teaching and higher learning in education*, (pp. 175–190). Montreal: McGill-Queen's University Press.

Wiliam, D. (2016). *Leadership for teacher learning*. West Palm Beach: Learning Sciences International.
Yapp, A., & Poth, C. (2013). Evaluating the impact of formative assessment on large class learning environments: Integrating multiple perspectives. Paper presented at the annual meeting of the Canadian Evaluation Society, Toronto, ON.
Yin, R. K. (2014). *Case study research: Design and method*, (5th ed.,). Thousand Oaks: Sage.
Zhou, G., Kim, J., & Kerekes, J. (2011). Collaborative teaching of an integrated methods course. *International Electronic Journal of Elementary Education*, *3*, 123–138.

7

Three paradoxes in the approach to educational technology in the education studies of the Spanish universities

Joan Ferrés, Maria-Jose Masanet* and Julio-César Mateus

* Correspondence: mjose.masanet@upf.edu
MEDIUM Research Group, Communication Department, Universitat Pompeu Fabra, C/ Roc Boronat, 138, 08018 Barcelona, Spain

Abstract

The education studies of the Spanish universities are not alien to technological innovations, but their approach to them tends to be basically instrumental. Neuroscience's contributions about the functioning of the minds that interact with these technologies give new perspectives to the academic world; perspectives that are necessary for optimizing teaching-learning processes. This article analyses the recent scientific production on ICT and innovation in Spanish higher education, as well as the Spanish university teaching guides of education degree subjects about technologies. This critical analysis is organized around three paradoxes related to information, rationality and critical sense. Comparing the analysis results with the discoveries of neuroscience during the last decades reveals limits and contradictions in those areas that tend to be considered strongest in the technology-education relationship. We draw conclusions for revising the parameters for the approach to ICT in university education.

Keywords: ICT, Innovation, Higher education, Neuroscience, Educational technology, Spain, Media education, Storytelling, Entertainment, Emotions

Introduction

The objective of this article is to discuss from a critical perspective the instrumental approach that prevails in the academic field of educational technology in Spanish universities. The critical analysis is based on neuroscience findings on the functioning of the minds that interact with technologies.

The definition of educational technology — or *edtech* — is ambiguous, but there is a consensus that it constitutes a field of study related to the use of technology to improve the quality of learning (AECT Definition and Terminology Committee, 2008). Academic attention generally focuses on use and appropriation, omitting more complex interactions between the users' minds and the technologies, especially in relation to emotions and tastes. In this article we focus on the face-to-face or blended educational process, excluding the virtual, in Spanish higher education. Although the real impacts on learning are still questionable, the market for educational technologies continues to grow. Most universities around the world allocate large budgets to purchasing and maintaining technology and the virtualization of their services and management processes. Several reports evidence the increasing trends towards mobile-learning, cloud-computing, and the Internet of Things (IoT), as well as the use of new and more powerful mobile devices in the classroom (Adams Becker et al., 2017).

In Spain, according to the latest report by the ICT Sectoral Commission of the Conference of Deans of Spanish Universities (CRUE) access to technologies is a reality: virtual teaching, software license management for teaching and support for computer classrooms for teaching are implemented in a practical way in all universities, automated management in universities is already fully consolidated, and more than 80% of classrooms throughout the country have an Internet connection and multimedia projector (Gómez, 2016).

Faced with the unstoppable technologizing of higher education, the limited effects on the educational process are explained away by the lack of digital skills or institutional policies of the universities themselves: lack of incentives and time for teachers, as well as a very high learning curve (Sutton & DeSantis, 2016). There is also sufficient evidence of the importance of intrinsic factors such as the teachers' subjectivity in the process of integrating technology in the classroom. In this sense, the teachers' beliefs, conceptions and approaches to the use of technologies are decisive for the success of this process (Englund, Olofsson, & Price, 2016).

In this scenario, terms such as innovation or disruption abound in teaching plans and are discursively associated with the use of technologies without a clear explanation of how they relate or what role they play in these processes: "Many universities recognise the need to innovate, but there is no decisive leadership to tackle the actions of change that innovation requires" (Casas & Stojanovic, 2013: 249). As Sevillano-García and Vázquez-Cano (2015) warn in a study on mobile devices in Spanish universities, "viewing each technological breakthrough as the quintessence of educational innovation is a mistake; other variables must also be considered, such as existing context and culture, educational practices and relations, and the way those involved conceive of teaching-learning processes" (107).

A recent study in the education studies of the Spanish universities concluded that teachers perceive that digital devices can be useful and functional from a didactic perspective. For instance, when they are used to conduct videoconferences, to manage ubiquitously chats and academic forums related to the subjects, or to encourage the participation of students in academic life. The creation and visualization of videos is a didactic activity that mobile digital devices favor in the current mobile and ubiquitous context of Higher Education (Vázquez-Cano, 2015). However, this instrumental dimension is not enough to transform traditional education the way ed-tech is capable of, by expanding this instrumental approach.

In short, despite the motivating power of technologies, the lack of clarity in the ICT strategies and projects in higher education is an urgent challenge that must be addressed. This article draws attention to the prevalence of the instrumental approach to technologies and the absence of other essential dimensions linked to neuroscientific findings.

We speak of paradoxes because, comparing the academic approach to technologies in Spanish universities with neuroscience findings on the human mind, we discover that behind the most powerful and relevant academic concepts (information society, cognition and critical thinking) hide shortcomings that prevent more effective and more integrative education (entertainment and storytelling, emotion and critical attitude). In this context, we propose the following specific objectives:

SO1: Determine the attention given to the areas of information and entertainment in the Spanish university approach to educational technology.
SO2: Determine the attention given to the cognitive and emotional areas in the Spanish university approach to educational technology.
SO3: Analyse whether critical sense is related to knowledge or attitude in the Spanish university approach to educational technology.

With this we aim explore which areas are more present in the selected documents, whether there is a significant disproportion between them and whether some are invisible or are practically not considered at all, thus demonstrating the seriousness of these deficiencies.

To organise this article, we propose three paradoxes related to informational, cognitive and critical areas, discussed based on the available literature.

The dichotomies between information and entertainment, between motives and emotions and between criticism and critical attitude are not presented for the defense of one option against the other, but to emphasize the need for the integration of complementary poles and, therefore, to draw attention to the need to cover the gaps to optimize the teaching-learning processes.

Contextualising the three paradoxes

The inadequacy of the informational

To start, the discoveries of neuroscience on the functioning of the human brain reveal that stories are much more effective than explicit information for motivating people (Keysers, 2011; Ramachandran, 2011; Salmon, 2008). This is assumed and applied by professionals of persuasive communication in all fields, from advertising and marketing to politics and business communication. Increasingly more people focus their communication strategies on the potential of storytelling (Heath & Heath, 2007; Lehrer, 2010; Salmon, 2008).

While discourse only activates the cerebral cortex (rational brain), stories activate the cortex by triggering the perceptive, motor and emotional systems in an integral way through mirror neurons (Ramachandran, 2011; Rizzolatti & Sinigaglia, 2006); hence, their motivating potential.

The paradox is that, in the academic world, the informational competence of students is focussed almost exclusively on their ability to search for, analyse, select, filter, contrast, organize, synthesize, use and communicate information, while persuasive communication professionals avoid using information and focus on stories and storytelling. In short, the new generations of citizens leave the educational environment without specific preparation for dealing with communication strategies that are increasingly present in the environment in which they move.

The inadequacy of the cognitive

The polarization of the academic world towards the cognitive aspects could be justified by arguing that students live a very intense emotional relationship with the technologies outside the classroom and that the objective of the education system is to counterbalance this by incorporating the rational, reflective dimension.

This seemingly reasonable argument crashes headlong with the more recent contributions of neuroscience in relation to brain functioning, especially from the point of view of the mental processes underlying decision-making.

Today it is known that the emotional brain is essential for the correct functioning of the rational brain: "Emotions are the foundation of everything we do, even reasoning" (Maturana & Bloch, 1998: 137). "Certain aspects of the process of emotion and feeling are indispensable for rationality" (Damasio, 1996: 10). "The limbic system (the emotional brain) is the brain's power plant" (Carter, 2002: 54). Perhaps the most radical expression in this respect comes from Jonah Lehrer (2010): "Reason without emotion is impotent" (idem: 26). And even more emphatically: "If it weren't for our emotions, reason wouldn't exist at all" (Lehrer, 2010: 13).

The forcefulness of these quotes should lead university teachers to question whether the difficulties they encounter in obtaining rational attitudes and behaviours from students are not largely a consequence of their inability as educational professionals to elicit emotional responses from them.

The inadequacy of critical thinking

There is often criticism that the instrumental approach dominates the panorama of education technology. However, this happens because it is the most comfortable approach: Firstly because technology, being a material, specific and visible product, is easier to evaluate than an abstract and intangible process. Secondly, because its materiality becomes a result in itself: a classroom set up with screens and devices is a modern and innovative space per se. Thirdly, because the idea persists that technologies are neutral, and thus are subordinated to the use given to them, which puts them above any questioning, usually associated with resistance to change or little clarity about the specific advantages they offer beyond the initial novelty of their incorporation. As a recent article in *The Economist* (2017) notes: "education technology (edtech) has repeated the cycle of hype and flop, even as computers have reshaped almost every other part of life. One reason is the conservatism of teachers and their unions. But another is that the brain-stretching potential of edtech has remained unproven".

From this comfortable approach "the processes of innovation through ICTs that have been implemented in university institutions have tended to focus on the translation of materials and tools into digital formats. That is to say, most curricular materials have been digitised without transforming the foundations of the dominant educational paradigm" (Gómez, 2014: 51). In this regard, Steven Johnson (2010) believes that innovation can only occur in an environment that facilitates relationships between people and diverse materials that can be explored and recombined. The university system, like the school system, is usually rigid, based on the principles of repetition and vertical control, and against risk or error, concepts outlawed from academic vocabulary. The projects to incorporate technologies in education therefore prefer the product to the process, with the aim of efficiency based on the transmission of contents.

Finally, Neuroscience experts implicitly highlight the shortcomings of the academic world when they affirm that "consciousness can only be understood by studying the unconscious processes that make it possible" (LeDoux, 1999: 32). Screens are an excellent opportunity to access the unconscious, a prerequisite for in-depth understanding (Keysers, 2011; Mlodinow, 2013; Van Praet, 2012).

Method

As we explained in the introduction, the main objective of this article is to critically analyse the approach to educational technology in education studies in Spanish universities. We started with three research hypotheses:

H1: Educational technology in education studies in Spain focussed on the information field, and entertainment is barely present if not completely excluded.
H2: Educational technology in education studies in Spain is directed far more at the cognitive than the emotional.
H3: Educational technology in education studies in Spain relates critical sense to knowledge more than attitude.

To confirm or refute these hypotheses, we carried out a thematic content analysis (Andreu, 2002). Two types of documents were analysed. Firstly, 50 articles and communications published in the last 5 years in the academic reference indexes that focus on the use of technologies in the university education context. These documents had been compiled and analysed in an earlier research project that aimed to evaluate the scientific production on the use of technologies in the education field (Mateus, Aran-Ramspott & Masanet, 2017). They include scientific articles and communications about experiences and research carried out in Spanish universities, based on self-reported initiatives such as innovations in the integration of educational technologies. To carry out this systematic review, the following inclusion criteria were used: range of years (2012–2016); publication in the chosen indexes (Web of Science, Scopus and Google Scholar); and inclusion in its metadata (titles, abstracts and keywords) of ed-tech related words. The result of this analysis was 50 items (42 of them belonging to scientific journals and the remaining eight to proceedings). Secondly, we analysed 194 teaching guides for education technology subjects taught in Spanish education faculties (pre-primary, primary, pedagogy and social education). These guides are part of a previous study that analysed media education in Spanish universities (Ferrés & Masanet, 2015). Teaching guides for university subjects are the documents that specify the objectives, the skills the students need to acquire, the theoretical programme and practical activities, methodology, bibliography and teaching techniques. The teaching guides are based on the principles of the convergence process for the creation of a European Higher Education Area, which is governed by the Declaración de Bolonia (1999). Here we focus only on the teaching guides for education studies because it is compulsorily for these studies to include educational technology subjects, considering that the objective of these studies is to prepare teachers for their future educational work with children and adolescents, who need to be competent for life in a media environment.

These two types of documents are an appropriate sample for the first objective of the article, which is to identify the actions performed in the context of educational technology in Spanish universities. Despite these two informative products being different in terms of origin and objectives -one is institutional and the other one comes from the research field-, they are the only official documents available. On the other hand, if the results from these two informative products are similar it should confirm the validity of the hypothesis raised.

To carry out the analysis, we first identified a series of semantic fields and terms linked to these fields, updating those used in previous studies (Ferrés & Masanet, 2015; Ferrés, Masanet & Marta-Lazo, 2013) (see Table 1).

These semantic fields have been created following basic guidelines developed from neuroscience findings on the functioning of the human brain that demonstrate the need to work with emotions, entertainment and attitudes in an educational context, as discussed earlier.

Secondly, the word frequency in all the articles, communications and teaching guides was determined with the *software* for qualitative analysis NVivo Pro. Based on these frequencies and their distribution by semantic fields we studied each document individually to analyse and verify the context in which these terms were expressed. Thirdly, the results were presented quantitatively with word clouds. Finally, the analysis results of the documents were contrasted with some of the discoveries that neuroscience has made during the last decades in relation to decision-making processes. The critical analysis is based on three key areas: information, rationality and critical sense. In order to do so, we used the rhetorical figure of the paradox.

Results

The paradox of information

In 2006, with the appearance of the Organic Law of Education (LOE), digital competence became part of the prescriptive curriculum linked to the treatment of information. Digital literacy was structured from the outset around two central poles: the technological and the informational.

Already in 2001 the definition of digital literacy proposed by UNESCO referred to the set of skills, knowledge and attitudes that a person needs to be able to develop functionally within the Information Society. UNESCO followed experts who, at the end of the last century, expressed themselves along the same lines, demanding digital literacy "to enable students to understand and use information sources presented through computers" (Gilster, 1997: 6).

Table 1 Distribution of terms by semantic fields (We searched for all words in Spanish, English, Catalan and Galician, as well as all variations of gender and number and their respective conjugations)

Semantic Field	Terms linked to the Semantic Field
Rational	know, reason, reflection, knowledge, information, comprehension, understanding, opinion, thought, analysis, concept
Emotional	emotion, feeling, motivation, attitude, desire, pleasure, empathy, taste, unconscious, subconscious
Information / Knowledge	information, knowledge, concept, comprehension, understanding
Entertainment	entertainment, free-time, leisure, fun, storytelling, story, game, gamification, simulation
Critical linked to knowledge	critical thinking, critical understanding, critical analysis, critical reading, critical interpretation
Critical linked to attitude	critical attitude, critical posture, critical behaviour, critical use, critical commitment

Source: Adapted from Ferrés & Masanet, 2015

The academic world has readily accepted technologies as support for the Information and Knowledge Society and as an opportunity to enhance the information competence of citizens.

In this reductionist polarization of technology to information, it is forgotten that in people's daily lives, entertainment and the relationships and interactions with others are as much or more important than the information. This is even more true for children and young people.

The academic world is comfortable with concepts like Information Society or Knowledge Society because they are part of its domain, its tradition:

> Policy decision makers in many countries began [since 1990] adopting the rhetoric of the information society, the knowledge society, and twenty-first century skill requirements. The United Nations Educational, Scientific, and Cultural Organization (UNESCO, 1999) on "Task Force on Education for the Twenty-First Century," the European Union's project, i2010, on "A European Information Society for Growth and Employment" (i2010, 2007), and the "Okinawa Charter on the Global Information Society" of the G8 world leaders (G8, 2000) all reflect the movement at all levels of policy making (Anderson, 2008: 9)

In the same way, UNESCO's last world education report titled *Rethinking Education: Towards a global common good?* (UNESCO, 2015) states thatthe challenge becomes

> how to teach learners to make sense of the vast amount of information they encounter everyday, identify credible sources, assess the reliability and validity of what they read, question the authenticity and accuracy of information, connect this new knowledge with prior learning and discern its significance in relation to information they already understand (41).

But at the same time, feels uncomfortable with the phenomenon of entertainment because it considers it outside its interests, irrelevant in socialization processes and, although it does not explicitly confess this, because it does feel competent to deal with it.

In the 50 articles on technological innovation analysed there are 1468 references to terms belonging to the semantic field of information. In contrast, there are only 253 references to the semantic field of entertainment. Only 17 of the 50 articles (34.00%) contain concepts related to entertainment, fun or leisure (a total of 49 references). These documents are linked to educational innovation, thus many of the educators intend to innovate by linking technology strictly to the informational. Terms related to stories and narrative (a total of 63 references) only appear in 12 of the 50 documents (24.00%), which implies that 76.00% of the authors make no reference at all to *storytelling*. Finally, 28 of the 50 articles (56.00%) contain concepts related to game, gamification and simulation (141 references). In this case the percentage is higher than the previous, but it is also important to highlight that 60 of the 141 references are included in just one document. Therefore, a single document incorporates 42.55% of these references.

In the 194 teaching guides of technology subjects in Spanish university education faculties there are 1817 references to terms linked to the semantic field of information, while there are only 189 references to terms linked to the semantic field of entertainment. Only

20 of the 194 teaching guides (10.31%) explicitly refer to the concepts of entertainment, fun or leisure (27 references), which means that 89.69% of the teachers who teach these subjects can be competent in the digital age without considering the dimension of entertainment.

The case of terms related to stories and narrative in the teaching guides follows a similar pattern to that of the articles and communications. There are only 102 references distributed in 42 of the 194 documents (21.65%), implying that 78.35% of authors do not include any technology teaching guidelines that reference storytelling. Finally, the case of terms related to game, gamification and simulation is similar to the previous ones. There are only 60 references distributed in 40 documents (20,62%).

The analysis of these documents shows that concepts such as gaming, gamification, simulation or virtual reality that connect with the sphere of the emotional and entertainment and that could contribute to enhance learning appear rarely, which agrees with the results of other studies around the Spanish university in which it is clear that the incorporation of these concepts is still in the minority and has significant gaps (Llorens-Largo et al., 2015; Peñalba, 2017).

Figure 1 illustrates the disproportion between the references to terms from the fields of information and entertainment. As it can be seen, references to entertainment are practically non-existent, given the low number found in the entire set of documents. In short, we speak of the informational paradox not only because this disproportion in academic attention between information and entertainment conflicts with people's daily practices, and particularly those of children and young people, but also because of the relevance of persuasive and emotional strategies such storytelling presented at the beginning.

Fig. 1 Cloud of informational and entertainment fields in articles and guides. Source: Own Creation

The paradox of the cognitive

In both the analysis of the 50 documents on educational innovation using technologies and in the 194 teaching guides of the technology-related subjects in Spanish education faculties, we discover a polarization towards the cognitive and rational, and a significant, if not total, marginalization of the emotional dimension.

In the 50 documents on educational innovation there are 2649 references to terms linked to the cognitive-rational semantic field and only 245 references to terms linked to the semantic field of emotion. There are only six explicit references to emotions, which means that 45 of the 50 documents (90%) do not make a single direct reference to emotions. It would seem that the aim is to innovate while totally marginalizing this dimension, intentionally or not.

In the entire set of articles and communications there are 80 references to motivation, but there are 18 documents (36%) that do not contain a single reference to this concept. Bearing in mind that these are texts focused on university educational innovation through technology, this lack is alarming, since the students' motivations are a key aspect for learning.

In the 194 university teaching guides analysed, there are 6068 references to terms related to the cognitive-rational semantic field and only 396 references to terms related to the semantic field of emotion. There are only 78 direct references to emotions, and these are distributed among 41 guides (21.13%). Therefore, there are 153 teaching guides (78.87%) in which there is not a single reference to concepts related to emotions.

Regarding motivation, in the set of guides there are 33 references to motivation, but there are 169 documents (87.11%) that do not make a single reference to this concept. Being teaching guides for technology subjects, this absence is worrying, since almost 90% of the guides do not make any reference to the students' motivations, a key aspect in the educational process.

Figure 2 confirms that the cognitive-rational field goes far beyond the emotional in the number of mentions. As the word cloud shows, the terms from the semantic field of emotion are barely visible.

The paradox of criticism

A further step in our research was aimed at detecting which conception of critical sense underlies the documents analysed. To achieve this, we analysed contextually with which noun the adjective "critical" was associated in each case. We were primarily interested in detecting whether the critical sense was related to the cognitive or the emotional. In other words, with thought or attitude.

In some cases the associated terms are ambiguous from this point of view. For example, when we talk about critical capacity, critical perspective, critical sense, critical awareness, and critical factors, among others. Or simply when critical is used as a noun: criticism, critics. In other cases the term is associated with concepts that are clearly cognitive: critical analysis, critical view, critical reading, critical understanding, critical reflection, critical evaluation, critical look, critical approach, and, above all, critical thinking. Finally, some associations can be related to the emotional: critical attitude, critical commitment, critical posture, critical use.

Fig. 2 Cloud of cognitive-rational and emotional fields in articles and guides. Source: Own Creation

Of the 50 documents dealing with education technology innovation only 23 include the concept of critical (46%), and in these there are only 55 references to critical. Of these 55 references, most are associated with terms from the cognitive field and very few with the emotional field. For example, there is much talk about critical thinking or analysis (8 references) while there is not a single reference to "critical attitude".

On the other hand, in 52 of the 194 teaching guides (26.80%) there is no reference to critical. And in the 142 guides (73.20%) where references do appear (a total of 613 references) these are polarized towards the cognitive field. If we combine the three most-used terms of the cognitive field (critical analysis, critical incorporation and critical vision) we obtain a total of 170 references. However, combining the three most-used terms in the emotional field (critical attitude, critical posture and critical use) we only obtain 37 references.

In Fig. 3 we can see the disproportion between the terms associated with critical. As in the previous clouds, we are working with articles, communications and teaching guides.

This lack is particularly serious in the light of statements by neuroscience experts: "Emotions create a fury of activity dedicated to a single goal. Thoughts, unless they activate the emotional mechanisms, do not do this" (LeDoux, 1999: 337).

Thoughts and knowledge do not motivate if they do not turn into feelings. Knowing that you are going to die 1 day does not impel you to review your life and your value system. You only do this when you have an accident or when a loved one dies; that is, when knowledge is accompanied by feelings.

Fig. 3 Cloud terms associated with the adjective "critical" in articles and guides. Source: Own creation

Neurobiologist Donald Calne states that "the essential difference between reason and emotion is that while emotion leads to action, reason leads to drawing conclusions" (quoted by Roberts, 2005: 42). If we intend to achieve the transformation of the students, e critical thinking, critical understanding, critical reading or critical analysis should be just a step. The main objective of education should be a critical attitude, understanding attitude as a *drive*, an impulse, a willingness to act.

Of course, there can be no critical attitude without critical thinking, but critical thinking is insufficient if education is intended to enhance the personal autonomy and social commitment of citizens.

As already stated, in the set of 50 documents on educational innovation the concept of critical is referenced 55 times; however, in these references, self-criticism is referred to only twice. Similarly, in the set of 194 teaching guides the term critical appears 613 times, and only 16 of these refer to self-criticism.

These data reveal another significant lack in Spanish university education. If criticism is almost always only heterocritical (we must learn to criticize messages, products, information, and news, among others), it is because knowledge does not include self-knowledge. No account is taken of the great challenge already proposed by the Ancient Greek aphorism of the Delphic oracle considered the principle of wisdom: "know thyself." In the Information and Knowledge Society, no attention is given to information and knowledge about oneself.

Every effort is made to take advantage of the screens as windows, as an opportunity to access the external reality, to accumulate information and knowledge about the world, and hardly any effort is made to take advantage of the possibilities of the screens as mirrors, as an opportunity to find yourself, and especially as an opportunity to access your own unconscious, the dark side of yourself, the most latent contradictions.

Discussion

Two conclusions emerge from the considerations made so far: it is necessary to include new contents in the educational treatment of technologies, and it is necessary to change the point of view from which contents are treated.

Concerning the new contents, as we indicated at the beginning of the article, the development of personal autonomy and social commitment requires, in addition to the mastery of technology, the knowledge and capacity to manage the mental processes of the people who use these technologies. It is not possible to use the technologies to their full potential without a deep knowledge of the mechanisms that govern the minds of those who interact with them.

The knowledge and capacity to manage emotions in their cognitive dimension and from their motivating potential (Damasio, 1996, 2005; LeDoux, 1999) are essential for ensuring both the effectiveness of educational communication and facilitating understanding of the socializing and educational force that screens have, even when this is not their objective or their intention (Ferrés, 2014; Bueno, 2017; Mora, 2013).

The knowledge and capacity to manage mirror neurons, one of the most transcendental discoveries of neuroscience during the last decades (Keysers, 2011; Ramachandran, 2011; Rizzolatti & Sinigaglia, 2006), are essential for understanding the processes of teaching by imitation or models, the processes of empathy and the socialization strategies of stories, through identification and projection mechanisms.

Still in relation to the incorporation of new content, together with the actual information, we need to pay attention to the field of entertainment and particularly to storytelling, both so that the students understand how they are socialized through media stories and so that teachers can take full advantage of educational communication by incorporating these resources.

Concerning the need to change the point of view, in education it is necessary to take a step towards emphasizing attitudes more than knowledge. In other words, we should approach thoughts and knowledge only as a preliminary step towards attitudes. There is often talk of the need to turn information into knowledge. In fact, it is necessary to go one step further and add the requirement of turning knowledge into attitudes.

We conclude by saying that the reflections and contributions that have been made here are largely the result of the research that the authors of the article have carried out in recent years in the media education field (Mateus, Aran-Ramspott & Masanet, 2017; Ferrés & Masanet, 2015; Ferrés, Masanet & Marta-Lazo, 2013.; Ferrés & Masanet, 2017).

Limitations and further research

In this article, we have focused only on teaching guides and published work in the last years corresponding to education studies, therefore its results cannot be generalized to all higher education. Perhaps the polarization in the cognitive, the rational and the informative is not exclusive of the subjects or academic fields linked to technology exclusively, but a tendency of education in general. It would have to be confirmed in later investigations. Likewise, future work must integrate qualitative methodologies that allow a better understanding of the subjective view of the teachers who use educational technologies.

Acknowledgements
Not applicable.

Funding
This work was funded by the R + D + i project "Media literacy in the emerging digital media in university environments" (EDU2015-64015-C3-2-R) of the Ministry of Economy and Competitiveness of Spain.

Authors' contributions
All authors read and approved the final manuscript.

Authors' information
Joan Ferrés holds a Ph.D in Information Sciences (Autonomous University of Barcelona), a Degree in Information Sciences (Autonomous University of Barcelona) and a Degree of Teacher in Primary Education (Barcelona University). He is Associate Professor (tenure) at the Department of Communication of the University Pompeu Fabra (Barcelona, Spain). Researcher specialized in media literacy, communication and education and emotional competence. He has been the PI of different projects related with media literacy as *Undergraduate teaching faced with the audiovisual communication competence in a digital environment* and *Evaluation of the media competence of Spanish citizenship*.
Maria-Jose Masanet holds a Ph.D. in Social Communication (Universitat Pompeu Fabra, 2015), a Degree in Audiovisual Communication (Universitat Pompeu Fabra, 2008), a MA in Social Communication ((Universitat Pompeu Fabra, 2009) and a MA in Secondary Education (Universitat Politècnica de Catalunya, 2011). She is researcher at the Pompeu Fabra University. Her main research lines are related with media literacy, adolescence and youth, series, gender and the representation of sexuality and love relationships in the media. She has published the book *La educación Mediática en la Universidad Española* (Gedisa, 2015) with Dr. Joan Ferrés. She has been visiting researcher at the Loughborough University (2013), at the Universidad Central de Venezuela (2014), at the Université Sorbonne Nouvelle Paris 3 (2015) and at the Centre de Liaison de l'Enseignement et des Médias d'Information (2015) and at the Ghent University (2016).
Julio-César Mateus holds a Master in Advanced Studies in Social Communication (Universitat Pompeu Fabra), a Master's Degree in Communication and Education (Universitat Autònoma de Barcelona) and a B.A. in Communication (University of Lima). He studies the PhD Program in Communication (UPF). As a fellow of the Department of Communication, he collaborates in research projects and develops his doctoral thesis on media education in teacher training. He has taught in the degree of Communication of the University of Lima, the Master in ICT and Education of the Pontificia Universidad Católica and in the Department of Social and Political Sciences of the University of the Pacific, in Peru. He is guest professor of the Master in Communication at Casagrande University, in Ecuador.

Competing interests
The authors declare that they have no competing interests.

References
Adams Becker, S., Cummins, M., Davis, A., Freeman, A., Hall Giesinger, C., & Bueno, D. (2017). *Neurociència per a educadors*. Barcelona: Associació de Mestres Rosa Sensat.
AECT Definition and Terminology Committee (2008). Definition. In A. Januszewski, & M. Molenda (Eds.), *Educational technology: A definition with commentary*. New York: Lawrence Erlbaum.
Anderson, R. E. (2008). Implications of the information and knowledge society for education. In J. Voogt, & G. Knezek (Eds.), *International handbook of information technology in primary and secondary education*, (pp. 5–22). Boston: Springer.
Andreu, J. (2002). Las técnicas de Análisis de Contenido: Una revisión actualizada, *Centro de Estudios Andaluces*. Retrieved from: http://public.centrodeestudiosandaluces.es/pdfs/S200103.pdf. Accessed 20 Feb 2018
Bueno, D. (2017). Neurociència per a educadors. Barcelona: Associació de Mestres Rosa Sensat.
Carter, R. (2002). *El nuevo mapa del cerebro*. Barcelona: RBA Ediciones de Librerías, Col. Integral.
Casas, M., & Stojanovic, L. (2013). Innovation in Ibero-American Universities. *Universities and Knowledge Society Journal (RUSC)*, *10*(1), 240–253. https://doi.org/10.7238/rusc.v10i1.1345.
Damasio, A. (1996). *El error de Descartes*. Barcelona: Crítica.
Damasio, A. (2005). *En busca de Spinoza. Neurobiología de la emoción y los sentimientos*. Barcelona: Crítica.
Declaración de Bolonia (1999). Declaración conjunta de Ministros Europeos de Educación. Retrieved from: https://www.eurashe.eu/library/modernising-phe/Bologna_1999_Bologna-Declaration.pdf. Accessed 20 Feb 2018

Englund, C., Olofsson, A. D., & Price, L. (2016). Teaching with technology in higher education: Understanding conceptual change and development in practice. *Higher Education Research & Development, 36*(1), 73–87. https://doi.org/10.1080/07294360.2016.1171300.

Ferrés, J. (2014). *Las pantallas y el cerebro emocional*. Barcelona: Gedisa.

Ferrés, J., & Masanet, M-J. (eds.) (2015). *La educación mediática en la universidad española*. Barcelona: Gedisa.

Ferrés, J., & Masanet, M.-J. (2017). Communication Efficiency in Education: Increasing Emotions and Storytelling. Comunicar, 25(52), 51–60. https://doi.org/10.3916/C52-2017-05.

Ferrés, J., Masanet, M-J., & Marta-Lazo, C. (2013). Neurociencia y educación mediática: carencias en el caso español. *Historia y Comunicación Social, 18*(3), 129-144

Gilster, P. (1997). *Digital Literacy*. New York: Wiley.

Gómez, F. (2014). Educational innovation through ICTs in the university setting. What do students think of these practices? *Revista de Universidad y Sociedad del Conocimiento (RUSC), 11*(1), 49–60. https://doi.org/10.7238/rusc.v11i1.1657.

Gómez, J. (Ed.) (2016). *UNIVERSITIC 2016. Análisis de las TIC en las Universidades Españolas*. Madrid: Crue Universidades Españolas.

Heath, C., & Heath, D. (2007). *Made to stick: Why some ideas survive and others die*. New York: Random House.

Johnson, S. (2010). *Where good ideas come from: The natural history of innovation*. New York: Penguin.

Keysers, C. (2011). *The empathic brain. How the discovery of mirror neurons changes our understanding of human nature*. Amsterdam: Social Brain Press.

LeDoux, J. (1999). *El cerebro emocional*. Barcelona: Ariel/Planeta.

Lehrer, J. (2010). *How we decide*. Boston: Houghton Mifflin Harcourt.

Llorens-Largo, F., Gallego-Durán, F. J., Villagrá-Arnedo, C. J., Compañ-Rosique, P., Satorre-Cuerda, R., & Molina-Carmona, R. (2015). *Lecciones aprendidas gamificando cuando aún no se llamaba gamificación*, (pp. 214–219). Madrid: III Congreso Internacional sobre Aprendizaje, Innovación y Competitividad Recuperado de: https://goo.gl/NZR7UA (07/04/17).

Mateus, J. C., Aran-Ramspott, S., & Masanet, M-J. (2017). Revisión de la literatura sobre dispositivos móviles en la universidad española. RIED. *Revista Iberoamericana de Educación a Distancia, 20*(2), 49–72. https://doi.org/10.5944/ried.20.2.17710

Maturana, H., & Bloch, S. (1998). *Biología del Emocionar y Alba Emoting. Respiración y emoción*. Santiago de Chile: Dolmen.

Mlodinow, L. (2013). *Subliminal: cómo tu inconsciente gobierna tu comportamiento*. Barcelona: Crítica.

Mora, F. (2013). *Neuroeducación. Solo se aprende aquello que se ama*. Madrid: Alianza.

Peñalba, S. (2017). *Los profesores universitarios españoles ante la gamificación. Una perspectiva educomunicativa. Master Thesis*. Huelva: Universidad Internacional de Andalucía y Universidad de Huelva.

Ramachandran, V. S. (2011). *The tell-tale brain*. New York: W.W. Norton & Company.

Rizzolatti, G., & Sinigaglia, C. (2006). *Las neuronas espejo. Los mecanismos de la empatía emocional*. Barcelona: Paidós.

Roberts, K. (2005). *Lovemarks. El futuro más allá de las marcas*. Barcelona: Urano.

Salmon, C. (2008). *Storytelling. La máquina de fabricar historias y formatear las mentes*. Barcelona: Península.

Sevillano-García, M. L., & Vázquez-Cano, E. (2015). The impact of digital mobile devices in higher education. *Educational Technology & Society, 18*(1), 106–118.

Sutton, K., & DeSantis, J. (2016). Beyond change blindness: Embracing the technology revolution in higher education. *Innovations in Education and Teaching International, 54*(3), 1–6. https://doi.org/10.1080/14703297.2016.1174592.

The Economist. (2017). Together, technology and teachers can revamp schools. *The Economist*. Retrieved from https://www.economist.com/news/leaders/21725313-how-science-learning-can-get-best-out-edtech-together-technology-and-teachers-can. Accessed 20 Feb 2018

UNESCO (1999). Task force on education for the twenty-first century. Retrieved from: http://www.unhas.ac.id/rhiza/arsip/pembelajaran/unesco.html (20/02/2018).

UNESCO (2015). *Rethinking education: Towards a global common good?* Paris: UNESCO Retrieved from http://unesdoc.unesco.org/images/0023/002325/232555e.pdf (26/01/2018).

Van Praet, D. (2012). *Unconscious branding. How neuroscience can empower (and inspire) marketing*. New York: Palgrave MacMillan.

Vázquez-Cano, E. (2015). El reto de la formación docente para el desarrollo de una metodología ubicua en la Educación Superior. *Perspectiva Educacional, 54*(1), 149–162. https://doi.org/10.4151/07189729-Vol.54-Iss.1-Art.236.

8

Dawn or dusk of the 5th age of research in educational technology? A literature review on (e-)leadership for technology-enhanced learning in higher education (2013-2017)

Deborah Arnold* and Albert Sangrà

* Correspondence: darnold@uoc.edu
Universitat Oberta de Catalunya, Rambla del Poblenou 156, 08018 Barcelona, Spain

Abstract

The aim of this article is to establish the extent to which the concept of e-leadership has taken off as a lens through which to study leadership for technology-enhanced learning (TEL) in higher education. Building on a previous study conducted in 2013, this article thus covers an exploratory review of the literature for the period 2103-2017. It analyses 49 articles which explore both the specific concept of e-leadership as well as other work dealing more generally with leadership and organisational change for TEL in higher education. The findings show that while none of the empirical studies identified in the literature refer explicitly to e-leadership, there are a number of interesting insights to be found in the theoretical articles. The results also highlight the widely different interpretations and applications of the concept of e-leadership and the consequent need for the definition to be refined. The paper concludes with recommendations for further multidisciplinary research at the intersection of the fields of educational technology and educational management, focusing on values, strategy, organisation and leadership interactions at meso level, the economy and public policy at macro level, and teaching and learning at the micro level, as well as for research in Leadership Development for TEL.

Keywords: e-leadership, higher education, technology-enhanced learning, online learning, distributed leadership, change management

Introduction

Technology has been part of the educational landscape for decades, and one could argue that even chalk and the blackboard are forms of technology appropriated for learning, as indeed are books. However, within the scope of this paper, the term technology is used to refer to digital technology as "a system that combines computers, telecommunications, software and rules and procedures or protocols" and media (text, graphics, audio and video, which involve the creation, communication and interpretation of meaning (Bates, 2015). Technology-Enhanced Learning (TEL) is to be understood as the use of technology in any teaching and learning situation, on a continuum from face-to-face to fully online learning (Bates & Sangrà, 2011). The rapid pace of development of digital technologies has already disrupted many industries and sectors, most notably the music industry (Moreau, 2013; Rogers, 2013), hotels and taxis

(D'Emidio, Dorton, & Duncan, 2015; Suzor & Wikstrom, 2016) and it is not infrequent to hear claims that the next area to be seriously challenged will be that of higher education (HE) (Barber, Donnelly, & Rizvi, 2013; Craig, 2015; Lucas Jr., 2016; Shirky, 2012), though Selwyn (2013) offers a critical analysis, as do Weller and Anderson (2013).

Universities in general, and European universities in particular, have survived in their more or less current form for several hundred years, yet currently face a number of challenges: the wide availability of knowledge on the web, massification and greater diversity of students, a decline in public funding coupled with rising student debt in many countries (Barber et al., 2013; Boyer, 2016; Staley & Trinkle, 2011). While technology is not the only solution to these challenges, it has been suggested that HE leaders need to develop a better understanding of the potential of TEL coupled with a high level of strategic thinking (Bates & Sangrà, 2011).

This is often associated with the theory of e-leadership, initially developed by Avolio, Kahai, and Dodge (2001) in the context of the business world, where e-leadership is defined as "a social influence process embedded in both proximal and distal contexts mediated by AIT [Advanced Information Technology] that can produce a change in attitudes, feelings, thinking, behavior, and performance." (Avolio, Sosik, Kahai, & Baker, 2014) as updated from the initial definition (Avolio et al., 2001).

This study aims to establish the extent to which the concept of e-leadership has taken off as a lens through which to study leadership for TEL in HE. The approach taken is that of an exploratory literature review in that it aims to identify what research has been published in the period 2013-2017 in terms of theory, empirical evidence and research methods with respect to the topic in question. It is situated at the intersection of different disciplinary fields: leadership within the wider field of management and business studies, and TEL within the education and educational research field. It is thus necessary to establish the current state of knowledge at this point of overlap. As Jameson (2013) states:

> ...the many scholarly educational research and professional communities that span the liminal edges bordering the two fields of educational technology and leadership do not, for the most part, relate to or recognise each other's work very much. (Jameson, 2013, pp. 891-892).

In addition to answering the primary research question of establishing the extent to which e-leadership has taken off as a lens through which to study leadership for TEL in HE, the results are also analysed in terms of the following secondary research questions:

- What is the geographical distribution of research in the field? Is it concentrated in a particular region and, if so, are there any gaps to be filled?
- In which disciplinary fields (journals) are these studies being published?
- What thematic trends can be identified in comparison with those identified by Jameson (2013)?
- What populations within HE (formal leaders, teachers, students,...) are being studied with respect to leadership for TEL? Are they considered in isolation or as part of a wider multi-stakeholder perspective?
- What is the level of analysis (project level, single institution, multiple institutions)?
- What methodologies are being applied?

Finally, if we understand leadership as a highly context-dependent social influence process, where there is a need to investigate "real organizational life" (Alvesson, 2017, p. 11) the last three questions are taken in combination to explore how this is taken into account through the methodology, the populations studied and the level of analysis.

The place of leadership in the literature on TEL and online learning

Examining the developments within TEL research over time, Winn (2002) defines four ages of such research as (1) instructional design with a focus on content; (2) differentiated message design focused on format, (3) simulation with a focus on learner control, interaction, scaffolding of student learning and constructivist principles; (4) a focus on technology-supported artificial learning environments, distributed cognition and the social nature of learning in communities. In the period 2002-2014, Baydas, Kucuk, Yilmaz, Aydemir, and Goktas (2015) identify a focus mainly on learning approaches/ theories and (online) learning environments, albeit in a literature review restricted to two UK journals (BJET, the British Journal of Educational Technology and ETR&D, Educational Technology Research and Development).

In the field of distance and online education, Zawacki-Richter and Naidu (2016) identify waves of alternating institutional and individual research over the past 35 years from articles published in the journal Distance Education: professionalization and institutional consolidation (1980–1984), instructional design and educational technology (1985–1989), quality assurance in distance education (1990–1994), student support and early stages of online learning (1995–1999), the emergence of the virtual university (2000–2004), collaborative learning and online interaction patterns (2005–2009), and interactive learning, MOOCs and OERs (2010–2014). It would thus seem that the next institutional wave is somewhat overdue.

Indeed, in an extensive literature review covering the period 2000 to 2013, in both the management and the education fields, Jameson (2013) concludes with a call for a 5th age in educational technology research, where e-leadership in higher education is the focus.

Updating Jameson's 2013 literature review

In order to bring the literature review up to date and provide a current picture of the state of the art, searches were carried out in four major databases between October 2017 and February 2018, for the period 2013-2017.

Method

Jameson used the following combinations of search terms:

A) e-leadership AND "higher education" AND "educational technology"
B) leadership AND "higher education" AND "educational technology".

For the purposes of updating the literature review for the period 2013-2017, these same combinations were used in ISI Web of Science, Scopus, ERIC (selected for their relevance to the field) and Google Scholar (selected in order to widen the search as far as possible).

In order to check for results which may not have been found through the two aforementioned combinations and, given the complexity of conducting literature review in the field of educational technology due to the wide variety of terms used by researchers and practitioners (Pretto & Curró, 2017), a concept map (Keeble & Kirk, 2007) was created in order to delimit the study (Fig. 1). The central topic of (e-)leadership was broken down into three main components in order to:

- identify synonyms or alternative terms relevant for extending the search, in particular with respect to TEL;
- identify key authors from both the leadership and TEL fields for the theoretical background;
- to delimit the study in terms of education sector (HE) and to facilitate exclusion of non-relevant results.

With respect to these exclusions, a prior initial search resulted in a high number of results pertaining to school leadership, leadership education programmes, health leadership and virtual team leadership, all of which were deemed out of scope for this literature review.

Finally, the concept map included an identification of populations in HE concerned with TEL leadership, as both leaders and followers, as well as of the different levels of analysis. These last two areas were used to categorise the results in the analysis phase.

In referring to the challenges of conducting literature reviews in the IT, ICT and educational technology fields, Pretto and Curró (2017) draw attention to the need for judicious selection of key search terms. With respect to educational technology, the authors list commonly-used alternatives such as technology-enhanced learning (TEL), digital technologies, instructional technology, blended learning, online learning, digital learning, while Wheeler (2012) identifies the use of TEL, e-learning and digital learning. Bayne (2015) points out that TEL is quite specific to the UK, with some usage in European contexts, and that on a global scale the terms 'instructional technology', 'educational technology' and 'e-learning' still dominate. While the importance of assumptions behind the use of particular terms needs to be recognised, as highlighted by both Pretto & Curró and Bayne, a full analysis of these is beyond the scope of this current study.

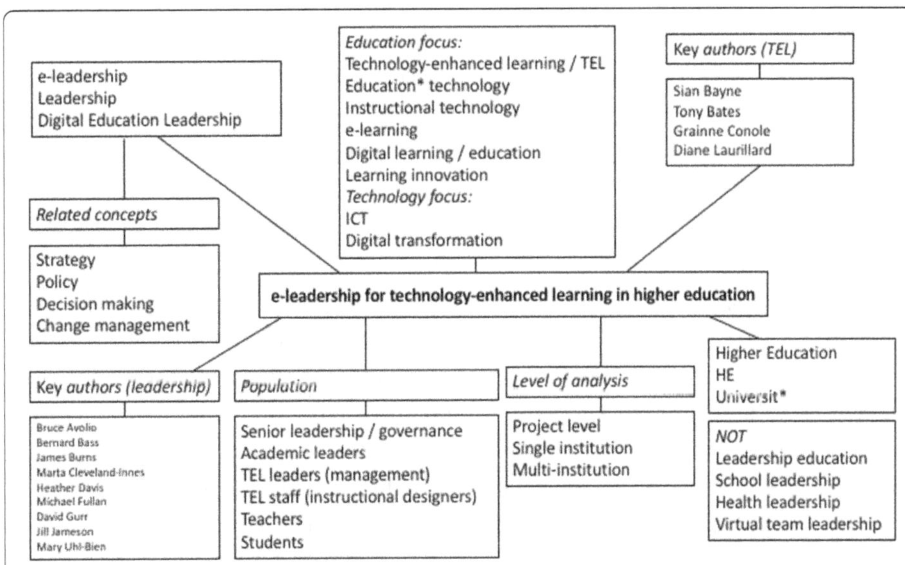

Fig. 1 Concept map for literature review

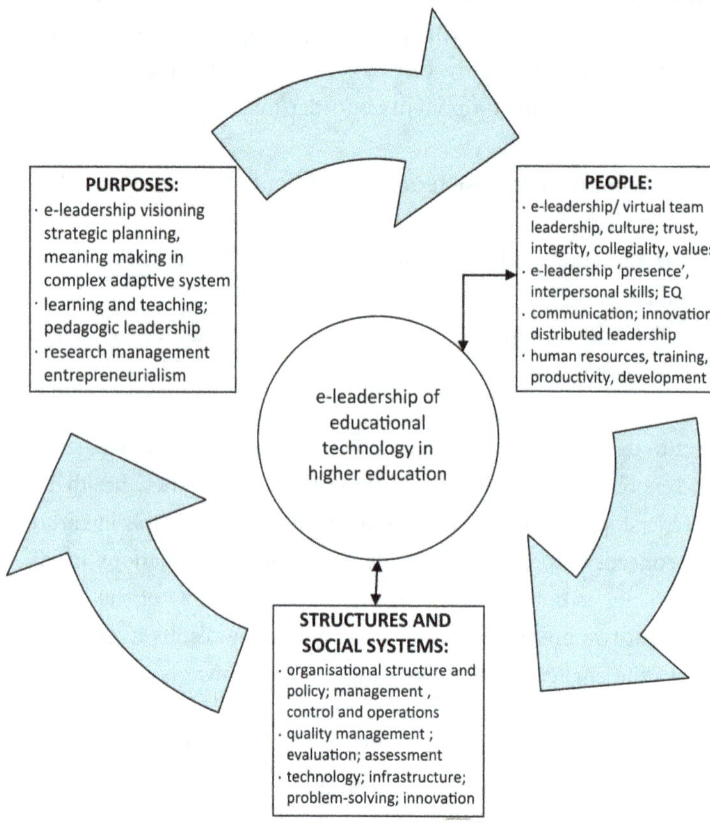

Fig. 2 e-Leadership framework for educational technology in higher education (Jameson, 2013, p. 911)

Finally, in addition to the aforementioned concept map, the TEL e-leadership framework developed by Jameson (Fig. 2) was taken as the basis for conducting a trend analysis, checking for reference to the existing concepts as well as for additional themes emerging from the literature in the period 2013-2017.

Results

Overall, the search resulted in the following initial results (Table 1).

A total of 843 results were screened based on title, keywords and abstract (where available). The results from all searches were first winnowed down to exclude those not covering leadership or related concepts at all. A second winnowing excluded results which were considered off-topic, dealing with schools, the health sector, gaming or information systems. The Google Scholar search proved the most challenging, as despite the inclusion of higher education and an attempt to filter out books and schools, these still appeared in the results, alongside results pertaining to business. Another issue with the Google Scholar search was in bringing up results which had clearly not been peer-reviewed and the impossibility of defining this in the search criteria. Given the time frame for this study, it was only feasible to screen the first search for "e-leadership" AND "higher education" AND "education* technology" within the first 100 results obtained via Google Scholar, and the first 20 results of the other searches.

The final results, after identifying duplicates obtained via different searches and across the different databases, are as follows:

Table 1 Search results for peer-reviewed articles since and including 2013

Search combination	Database used			
	ISI Web of Science	Scopus	ERIC	Google Scholar
e-leadership AND "higher education" AND "education* technology"	1	1	3	250
e-leadership AND "higher education"	3	2	7	929
leadership AND "higher education" AND "education* technology"	7	10	29	19 200
Leadership AND "higher education" AND "TEL"	0	0	2	16 800
Leadership AND "higher education" AND "ICT"	7	17	15	15 000
Leadership AND "higher education" AND "e-learning"	10	18	28	16 400
Leadership AND "higher education" AND "digital"	20	3	37	17 000
Leadership AND "higher education" AND "technology-enhanced learning"	2	1	2	5 520
Leadership AND "higher education" AND "instructional technology"	0	1	2	10 800
Leadership AND "higher education" AND "learning innovation"	1	1	8	3 100
Leadership AND "higher education" AND "digital transformation"	1	1	0	1 100
"Digital transformation" AND "higher education"	5	3	2	1 500
Leadership AND "higher education" AND "technology"	27	110	116	24 500
TOTAL number of results screened	84	168	251	340

Forty-nine articles, 48 of which we can be confident have been peer-reviewed. The non-peer-reviewed result is a concept paper (Brown, Czerniewicz, Huang, & Mayisela, 2016) retained for its highly relevant selection and analysis of digital education leadership competency and literacy frameworks. Identified via the Google Scholar search, its status was checked in ERIC which only produced it as a result after including non-reviewed papers in the search.

After detailed analysis of the main body of the articles, and in particular of the methodology section where present, the results were classified according to the following three categories: empirical studies (where clearly-defined populations were studied according to recognised research methodologies); theoretical analyses (reviews of leadership and related theories, applied to higher education but with no empirical study); and opinion pieces (articles expressing author's opinions based on personal experience with no or only nominal reference to underlying theory). These categories can be related to the main types of scientific publication, where empirical studies come under the umbrella of research papers or original research, theoretical analyses belong to the 'review article' category and opinion pieces can be considered as viewpoints (Öchsner, 2013). As such viewpoints or opinion papers are not always peer-reviewed, the status of all results obtained in this category was double-checked in ERIC, confirming that they had indeed been peer-reviewed.

The non-empirical studies (theoretical articles and opinion pieces) were included in this literature review to give a fuller picture of the type of research being published in the field of (e)-leadership for technology-enhanced learning in higher education. More specifically, theoretical articles can provide insights into how scholars are approaching the question from a broader angle, and opinion pieces can give insights into the preoccupations of leaders and other stakeholders as they reflect on challenges and leadership practice from a strategic or organisational perspective.

The 49 results are thus comprised of:

- 27 empirical studies (ES), one of which from 2013 had already been identified by Jameson (Garrison & Vaughan, 2013)
- 16 theoretical analyses (TA)
- 6 opinion pieces (OP)

Figure 3 below presents the number and type of results per year of publication.

While empirical studies are the most widely represented in total over the 5-year period (55%), no obvious trend in the development of such research can be detected in the results, apart from a peak in 2015. Theoretical analyses, which often propose models that have not been tested empirically, appear to be relatively popular forms of presenting research about e-leadership in higher education (33%), followed by opinion pieces (12%).

Two major differences with respect to Jameson's 2000-2013 literature review should be noted here: firstly, the inclusion of opinion pieces which reflect how and where (e-) leadership is being written about in relation to TEL in HE, and secondly that only results pertaining to higher education were retained, whereas Jameson included results from other phases of education due to the lack of results obtained for HE.

Detailed presentation of results

The following three tables present a summary of the results, organised into the three categories. The tables provide the reference of the publication, information about location, population, context and methodology together with a summary of the findings (Tables 2, 3, and 4).

Analysis of results

From the three aforementioned tables, the empirical studies were analysed from the perspectives of geographical location, methodologies used and populations studied in relation to leadership, in order to answer the corresponding secondary research questions indicated earlier. Additional analysis identified the leadership theories or terms associated with leadership for the overall results. A series of concept matrices (Webster & Watson, 2002) were used in order to perform this analysis, to identify themes and trends and to produce the associated tables and figures.

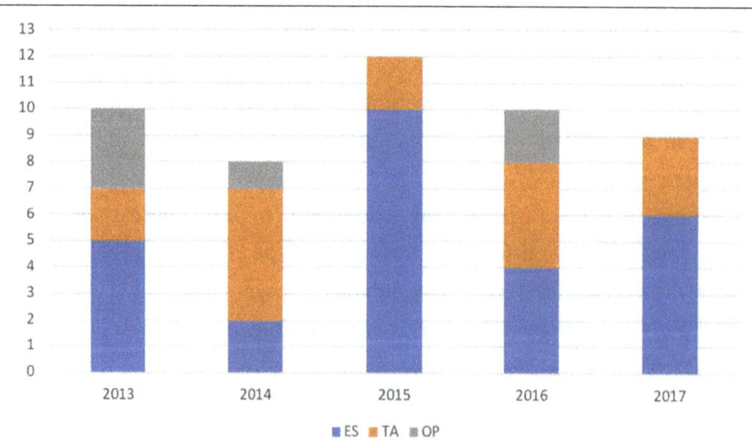

Fig. 3 Number and type of results per year

Table 2 Results: Empirical studies

Empirical studies 2013-2017	Location / population / methodology	Findings
Akcil et al. (2017). An Examination of Open and Technology Leadership in Managerial Practices of Education System. *EURASIA Journal of Mathematics Science and Technology Education*, *13*(1), 119–131.	Location not specified / 153 education managers / quantitative analysis of survey data.	Finds that technology acceptance and self-efficacy in technological development have influence on forming digital citizenship; and that digital citizenship and self-efficacy in technological leadership have influence on forming open leadership.
Ashbaugh (2013). Expert Instructional Designer Voices: Leadership Competencies Critical to Global Practice and Quality Online Learning Designs. *Quarterly Review of Distance Education*, *14*(2), 97–118.	US/Canada / 6 expert instructional designers / phenomenological study, Delphi-style, narrative inquiry study.	Concludes that leadership from instructional designers has the potential for significant impact on the quality of online higher educational products. Provides a Model of Leadership for Instructional Design - Competencies / Attributes / Duties => Strategy, Vision, Personality (Interpersonal Skills), Productivity, Emotional/Psychological Strength, Values, Duties.
Bälter (2017). Moving Technology-Enhanced-Learning Forward: Bridging Divides through Leadership. *International Review of Research in Open and Distributed Learning*, *18*(3).	Sweden / 12 participants (PhD students, teachers, support staff) / explorative case study, qualitative analysis of interviews	Existence of divides between academic subjects and competences, mistrust of support staff due to divides relating to academic level, divides in attitudes towards teaching. Proposes the application of Appreciative Inquiry as a leadership strategy to bridge these divides (Orr & Cleveland-Innes, 2015).
Bervell and Umar (2017). A Decade of LMS Acceptance and Adoption Research in Sub-Sahara African Higher Education: A Systematic Review of Models, Methodologies, Milestones and Main Challenges. *EURASIA Journal of Mathematics, Science and Technology Education*, *13*(11), 7269–7286.	Sub-Sahara Africa / meta-analysis of 31 studies / quantitative	Among the challenges identified in the 31 studies, Leadership/ management support and policy (11.7% each) were found to be in joint 4rd place after IT infrastructure (21.7%), skills and training (21.7%) and system related challenges (13.3%). Concludes with recommendations for leadership and management of higher education institutions to allocate funds towards a more intentional ICT infrastructural development and periodic skills training in LMS usage, coupled with a definite policy framework, as well as to sensitize instructors and students on the benefits, usefulness and importance of using LMS in instructional delivery.
Bogler et al. (2013). Transformational and Passive Leadership. *Educational Management Administration & Leadership*, *41*(3), 372–392.	Israel / single HEI (Open Uni) / students (n=1270) / quantitative study	Examines the effects of transformational and passive leadership styles of university instructors on students' satisfaction and learning outcomes, using Full Range Leadership Theory. Satisfaction was linked to a high score for transformational leadership associated with a low score for passive leadership. Highlights the fact that perception of the leader might be more significant than the actual behaviour of the (online instructor) leader.

Table 2 Results: Empirical studies *(Continued)*

Empirical studies 2013-2017	Location / population / methodology	Findings
Brown (2013). Large-scale innovation and change in UK higher education. *Research in Learning Technology, 21*, 1–14.	UK / 5 HEIs / methodology not stated	Analyses 5 curriculum redesign projects in the light of current theories and models of change management (formulated as top-down, bottom-up, distributed leadership). Argues for collaborative approaches to project management as opposed to top-down bottom-up approaches.
Burnette (2015). Negotiating the mine field: Strategies for effective online education administrative leadership in higher education institutions. *The Quarterly Review of Distance Education, 16*(3), 13–35.	USA / Online Education Administrators, multiple HEIs (n=12) / Qualitative inquiry	Identifies two main political challenges faced by online education administrators: being bound by tradition and struggling for authority. Also identifies the strategies used to overcome these challenges: building relationships, building trust and credibility, finding common ground, empowering faculty and using data to drive change.
Ciabocchi et al. (2016). A Study of Faculty Governance Leaders' Perceptions of Online and Blended Learning. *Online Learning, 20*(3), 52–73.	USA / faculty governance / online survey (n=129) + follow-up questions by email to 9 self-selected participants	Provides insights into the perceptions of faculty governance on matters related to online and blended learning: focus on teaching, quality and approval, staff development, overuse of adjuncts.
Cifuentes and Vanderlinde (2015). ICT Leadership in Higher Education: A Multiple Case Study in Colombia. *Media Education Research Journal*, 133–141.	Colombia / ICT leaders & team members, faculty / Multiple case study / Mixed methods (semi-structured interviews, focus groups, document analysis, survey (n=348)	Identifies the main struggles of ICT leaders as a lack of institutional regulations and the challenge of bringing about educational change in the face of reluctance. Concludes the need for distributed leadership.
Davis and Higgins (2015). Researching Possible Futures to Guide Leaders Towards More Effective Tertiary Education. *Journal of Open, Flexible and Distance Learning, 19*(2), 8–24.	New Zealand / 16 local and international experts / Scenario building: semi structured interviews, document analysis brainstorming workshops	Created a collective scenario organised around tensions between facing academia/the disciplines and facing employers and the professions, and standardised versus customised education. 4 scenarios: articulation, supermarket, quality-branded, self-determined.
Díaz and Báez (2015). Exploración de la capacidad de liderazgo para la incorporación de TICC en educación: validación de un instrumento. *RELATEC - Revista Latinoamericana de Tecnología Educativa, 14*(3), 35–47.	Mexico / 6 experts (5 Mexico + 1 USA) / rating of items => Quantitative analysis using Content Validity Index (CVI).	Validated an instrument to explore leadership capabilities for ICT in education, consisting of 31 items divided into four variables: digital competence, visionary leadership, strategic leadership and contextual intelligence.
Domingo-Coscollola et al. (2016). Do It Yourself in Education: Leadership for Learning across Physical and Virtual Borders. *International Journal of Educational Leadership and Management, 4*(1), 5–29.	Spain, Finland, Czech Republic / Schools and Higher Education, teachers, students and parents / Qualitative – document analysis, focus groups	Finds that HE teachers have more freedom than school teachers to innovate in the classroom but that highly-fragmented curricula and rigid timetables represent barriers. Focuses on teachers leading learning rather than institutional governance.
Garrison and Vaughan (2013). Institutional change and leadership associated with blended learning innovation: Two case studies. *The Internet and Higher Education, 18*, 24–28.	Canada / two case studies / practical inquiry, community of inquiry	Documents two cases of the development of blended learning from the point of view of institutional change and leadership. Concludes the need for committed collaborative leadership engaging all levels of the institution, with clear vision, specific action plans, teaching recognition and adequate resource allocation.

Table 2 Results: Empirical studies *(Continued)*

Empirical studies 2013-2017	Location / population / methodology	Findings
Holt et al. (2015). Framing and enhancing distributed leadership in the quality management of online learning environments in higher education. Distance Education, 35(3), 382–399.	Australia, national project / senior leaders at each partner institution / semi-structured interviews	Examines leaders' understandings of distributed leadership in the context of quality management of Open Learning Environments. Confirms the existence of a gap between the existence of distributed leadership, and the acceptance of its meaning and value. Concludes the need for deliberative formal top-level leadership commitment and action in order to instil distributed leadership.
Inayatullah and Milojevic (2014). Augmented reality, the Murabbi and the democratization of higher education: alternative futures of higher education in. *On the Horizon*, *22*(2), 110–126.	Malaysia / 50 lecturers and deans / Action research foresight workshop	Presents recommendations from a 5-day foresight workshop in 8 categories: establishment of a pilot project; enhancement of digital teaching and learning processes; customization of degrees; changing of the culture in higher education; enhancing collaboration; supporting research activities; rethinking of dominant frames of reference; anticipating upcoming futures trends.
King and Boyatt (2015). Exploring factors that influence adoption of e-learning within higher education. *British Journal of Educational Technology*, *46*(6), 1272–1280.	UK / single HEI / phenomenological approach, faculty-based focus groups and individual interviews	Identifies factors influencing the adoption of e-learning: institutional infrastructure, staff attitudes and skills, perceived student expectations, the importance as perceived by participants of an institutional strategy which provides sufficient resources and guidance. Recommends that such a strategy needs to be supported by a staff development programme and opportunities for sharing practice.
Livingstone (2015). Administration's perception about the feasibility of elearning practices at the University of Guyana. *International Journal of Education and Development Using Information and Communication Technology (IJEDICT)*, *11*(2), 65–84.	Guyana / single HEI, administrators / mixed methods case study, online survey analysed quantitatively and qualitatively	Explores the perceptions of the University's administration regarding the feasibility of developing elearning. Concludes that the perceptions are generally favourable but that educational practices in general need to be improved, and that issues regarding technical infrastructure and support need to be addressed.
Ng'ambi and Bozalek (2013). Leveraging informal leadership in higher education institutions: A case of diffusion of emerging technologies in a southern context. *British Journal of Educational Technology*, *44*(6), 940–950.	South Africa / 22 HEIs, educators and non-academics (n=259) / online survey analysed qualitatively (and quantitatively at a superficial level)	Studies the uses of emerging technologies to transform the teaching and learning practices and the nature of institutional support. Refers to diffusion of innovation theory (Rogers, 2003; Rogers & Scott, 1997). Concludes the need for more transformative and less transactional leadership. Proposes a wheel model for accelerating the diffusion of innovation and emerging technologies in HEIs, recommending that formal leaders work with opinion leaders and change agents.

Table 2 Results: Empirical studies *(Continued)*

Empirical studies 2013-2017	Location / population / methodology	Findings
Roushan et al. (2016). The Kaleidoscope of Voices: An Action Research Approach to Informing Institutional e-Learning Policy. *Electronic Journal of E-Learning, 14*(5), 293–300.	UK / single HEI / two-spiral action research approach	Concludes that the success of TEL integration depends on strong research and technological leadership, building internal alliances with key stakeholders, focusing on the 'middle out' and a partnership approach to working with students, all of which contribute to a transformational and shared approach to institution-wide change.
Sheiladevi and Rahman (2016). An Investigation on Impact of E-Learning Implementation on Change Management in Malaysian Private Higher Education Institutions. *Pertanika Jouornal of Science and Technology, 24*(2), 517–530.	Malaysia / HE educators (n=487) / Quantitative analysis of survey data	Finds that variables of change management ("stakeholders involvement", "system view", "evolving mindset", "understanding transition", "system design" and "system evaluation") influence three aspects of e-learning implementation: "ownership and control", "academic transform", and "service and satisfaction". Concludes with the need to construct a vision and a mission that resonate with teachers, relating it to teaching and learning.
Singh and Hardaker (2017). Teaching in Higher Education Change levers for unifying top-down and bottom- up approaches to the adoption and diffusion of e- learning in higher education. *Teaching in Higher Education, 22*(6), 736–748.	UK / 5 HEIs / qualitative exploratory case studies, interview with senior e-learning leaders, heads of academic departments, faculty, e-learning and IT staff	Applies Giddens' (1984) structuration theory to analyse change levers, identified as using a collaborative, participatory approach, creating social networks for potential adopters to learn from peers, combining mass and interpersonal communication, endorsing bottom-up engagement, recognising cultural differences between faculties and departments.
Spackman et al. (2015). What Can the Business World Teach Us About Strategic Planning. *Online Journal of Distance Learning Administration, 18*(2).	USA / single HEI, administrators / authoethnography	Demonstrates that the Balanced Scorecard (BSC), widely used in the business world but still largely unknown to the distance and continuing education community, can help the latter face the challenges of increasing government regulation and accreditation, competition and accountability in a context of declining funding. However, the BSC methodology requires understanding and support on the part of senior administrators.
Stoddart (2015). Using educational technology as an institutional teaching and learning improvement strategy? *Journal of Higher Education Policy and Management, 37*(5), 586–596.	Australia / single HEI / case study	Explores how educational technology can be used to drive institutional-level learning and teaching strategy. Concludes that although change was measurable, it did not occur at a systemic level, and identifies the need for take-up and mobilisation of the affordances of technology in order to impact teaching and learning. Also identifies the decisive role of human factors in the success or failure of a particular educational strategy, and focuses on inflection points or levers such as collaborative rather than individual approaches.

Table 2 Results: Empirical studies *(Continued)*

Empirical studies 2013-2017	Location / population / methodology	Findings
Tay and Low (2017). Digitalization of learning resources in a HEI – a lean management perspective. *International Journal of Productivity and Performance Management, 66*(5), 680–694.	Singapore / 1 HEI / qualitative exploratory case study	Identifies key factors from a lean management perspective for the conversion of print-based materials to e-learning resources: common vision, top management support, timely information sharing, relationship management.
Trevitt et al. (2017). Leading entrepreneurial e-learning development in legal education: A longitudinal case study of "universities as learning organisations." *The Learning Organization, 24*(5), 298–311.	Australia / 1 HEI / longitudinal case study, interviews and reflective analysis	Examines learning organisation attributes in the context of introducing distance learning within a research-intensive HEI. Analyses from the point of view of the iron triangle (cost-access-quality). Finds that entrepreneurialism resulted in growth (150 -> 2000 students over 15 years, 2 new programmes). Concludes that organisational learning in HE takes time (decades). Keys to success: business logic and internal networking.
Zhu (2015). Organisational culture and technology-enhanced innovation in higher education. *Technology, Pedagogy and Education, 24*(1), 65–79.	China / 684 teachers from six universities / quantitative survey	Studies seven dimensions of organisational culture: goal orientation, participative decision making, innovation orientation, structured leadership, supportive leadership, shared vision and formal relationships with respect to e-learning and computer-supported collaborative learning. Results indicate the importance of goal orientation, innovation orientation, formal relationship among members and structured leadership.
Zhu and Engels (2014). Organizational culture and instructional innovations in higher education. *Educational Management Administration & Leadership, 42*(1), 136–158.	China / 6 HEIs (186 teachers and 865 students)/ quantitative survey	Examines teachers' and students' perceptions of organisational culture together with opinions about teaching and learning innovations (student-centred learning, collaborative learning, use of educational technologies). Highlights the importance of an innovative, open and supportive organizational culture, clear goals, collaborative spirit and shared vision. Most influential organisational culture dimensions: goal orientation and collegial relationship.

Table 3 Results: Theoretical analyses

Theoretical analyses 2013-2017	Location and/or context / method	Approach / theories covered / arguments
Boyd and Sampson (2016). Foundation versus innovation: developing creative education practitioner confidence in the complex blended learning landscape. *Professional Development in Education*, *42*(3), 502–506.	UK / two arts institutions, reflection	Reflects on initiatives aimed toward developing staff digital confidence. Key to these initiatives is the issue of engaging practitioners with the importance of sound pedagogical design whilst developing familiarity with appropriate forms of technology.
Brown et al. (2016). *Curriculum for Digital Education Leadership: A Concept Paper. Commonwealth of Learning.*	Commonwealth / Concept paper	Introduces challenges faced in terms of digital education leadership. Presents conceptions of digital literacy, digital education and digital education leadership and motivations for the conceptualisation of a proposed curriculum framework for digital education leadership. Argues for Digital Education Leadership as a concept rather than e-leadership.
Gupton (2014). Online Frontiers in Education: Leadership's Role. *International Journal of Arts & Sciences*, *7*(2), 609–616.	Reviews research on Quality and Leadership of Online Education	Examines the crisis of leadership in HE in times of great change and the need for leadership as the online delivery of education develops. [NB. Uses emotional and value-laden language.]
Khanna (2017). A conceptual framework for achieving good governance at open and distance learning institutions. *Open Learning: The Journal of Open, Distance and E-Learning*, *32*(1), 21–35.	Proposes a good governance framework for ODL institutions	Based on 7 basic principles for ODL institutions: performance, transparency, accountability, participation, leadership, consensus orientation, fairness. Leadership considered from the perspective of direction and strategic vision.
Markova (2014). A Model of Leadership in Integrating Educational Technology in Higher Education. *Online Journal of Distance Learning Administration*, *17*(4).	Literature review on Educational Technology and Instructional Design, Leadership, Faculty Development, faculty attitudes to educational technology	Proposes a model of TEL leadership in HE and considers the impact educational technologies have on instruction itself and why many faculty members view the technology as being too difficult to apply to existing technology infrastructure. Model not applied.
McCutcheon (2014). A Leadership Framework to Support the use of E-Learning Resources. *Nursing Management*, *21*(3), 24–28.	Application of NHS nursing leadership framework to e-learning for postgraduate nursing education	Proposes the application of the NHS nursing leadership framework to structure and guide the process of e-learning development. Frame work organised into 7 dimensions around the central aim of delivering the service: demonstrating personal qualities, working with others, managing services, improving services, setting direction, creating the vision, delivering the strategy.
Mishra et al. (2016). E-Leadership and Teacher Development using ICT. In R. Huang & J. K. Price (Eds.), *ICT in Education in Global Context* (pp. 248–266). Berlin, Heidelberg, DE: Springer-Verlag.	Analysis of e-leadership in business, applied to education (schools)	Takes e-leadership as understood in the business context and relates it to the field of education, using the RAT (Replace, Amplify, Transform) framework (Hughes, Thomas, & Scharber, 2006).
Mukerjee (2014). Agility: a crucial capability for universities in times of disruptive change and innovation. *Australian Universities' Review*, *56*(1), 56–60.	Australia / organisational agility	Explores the concept of agility as applied to HE institutions: in terms of strategic, business, cultural, customer and partnering agility. Concludes the need to break down silos, to foster both organisational and individual agility and to ensure

Table 3 Results: Theoretical analyses *(Continued)*

Theoretical analyses 2013-2017	Location and/or context / method	Approach / theories covered / arguments
		IT departments take a central strategic role.
Murphy (2016). The future of Technology Enhanced Learning (TEL) is in the hands of the anonymous, grey non-descript mid-level professional manager. *Irish Journal of Technology Enhanced Learning, 2*(1), 1–9.	Ireland / discussion paper as an aside to a literature review, part of a doctoral thesis looking at the management of blended learning courses in HE	Reflects on the changing role of the academic in a new managerialist TEL HE sector and argues for the recognition of the i mportance of the mid-level professional manager in transitioning bottom-up to institute-wide TEL initiatives.
Orr and Cleveland-Innes (2015). Appreciative leadership: Supporting education innovation. *International Review of Research in Open and Distributed Learning, 16*(4), 235–241.	Application of Appreciative Inquiry to educational leadership	Suggests that appreciative leadership can support innovation by rejecting problem-based and deficit models in favour of freeing staff to generate new and innovative solutions, mobilising organisational member participation as a co-constructor of present and future possibilities. Refers to K12 context, but has potential for application in HE.
Phelps (2014). "So much technology, so little talent"? Skills for harnessing technology for leadership outcomes. *Journal of Leadership Studies, 8*(2), 51–56.	Literature review, focus = leadership educators	Reviews the literature on e-leadership and technology-centred fields, and provides recommendations and implications for leading in online environments.
Salmon and Angood (2013). Sleeping with the enemy. *British Journal of Educational Technology, 44*(6), 916–925.	Australia, joint reflection from a Pro Vice-Chancellor of Learning Transformations and an IT director	Explores the reasons for conflict between IT and faculty and formulates 16 (actually 15) recommendations for constructive collaboration leading to organizational changes, grouped into three strategic themes: Behavioural, Organisational, Facilitation.
Sutton and DeSantis (2017). Beyond change blindness: embracing the technology revolution in higher education. *Innovations in Education and Teaching International, 54*(3), 223–228.	Theoretical analysis – diffusion, tech acceptance, TPACK	Explores three foundational educational technology theories: Rogers' (1962, 2003) diffusion model, Davis' (1989) technology acceptance model and Mishra and Koehler's (2006) technological, pedagogical and content knowledge (TPACK) model. Recommends that HE leadership integrate implications of these in design of Continuous Professional Development.
Tintoré and Arbós (2013). Identifying the stage of growth in the organisational learning capacity of universities. *Universities and Knowledge Society Journal (RUSC), 10, No 2*(2013), 375–393.	Analysis of existing questionnaires, final version validated by 8 experts	Proposes a tool (Organisational Capacity Model questionnaire) for identifying the stage of growth in the organisational learning capacity of a university. Covers individual learning, institutional learning (teamwork, leadership and vision, culture and values, structures, resources, openness to the environment, barriers to learning). Tool not applied.
Van Wart et al. (2017). Integrating ICT adoption issues into (e-)leadership theory. *Telematics and Informatics, 34*(5), 527–537.	Analysis of different related fields of research to propose integrated framework	Studies ICT adoption through the lens of technology adoption literature, enterprise resource planning literature and leadership change management. Widens the

Table 3 Results: Theoretical analyses *(Continued)*

Theoretical analyses 2013-2017	Location and/or context / method	Approach / theories covered / arguments
		notion of e-leadership from leading in virtual environments to that of choosing, recommending and sup porting the implementation of ICT in organisations.

Table 4 Results: Opinion pieces

Opinion pieces 2013-2017	Location (if relevant) / method	Approach / theories covered / arguments
Beaudoin (2016). Issues in Distance Education: A Primer for Higher Education Decision Makers. *New Directions for Higher Education*, (173), 9–19.	Opinion piece, exploring distance education issues in HE from a leadership point of view	Presents an overview of current issues related to distance learning in HE. Identifies central questions, issues, challenges and opportunities to be addressed by decision makers, as well as 15 key attributes of effective leaders.
Brown (2014). Reenvisioning Teaching and Learning: Opportunities for Campus IT. *Libraries and the Academy*, *14*(3), 383–391.	Opinion piece, IT et educational technology	Explores the role of IT departments in relation to educational technology and argues for IT to play a strategic role in the development of teaching and learning innovation, implying rethinking the roles of the chief information officer (CIO) and the academic technologist.
Chow (2013). One Educational Technology Colleague's Journey from Dotcom Leadership to University E-Learning Systems Leadership: Merging Design Principles, Systemic Change and Leadership Thinking. *TechTrends*, *57*(5), 64–75.	Opinion piece, personal reflexion on attempts to bring about change as a learning technology leader	Concludes the need to develop systems thinking and to focus on the human aspects, bringing stakeholders together to discuss issues and find solutions. Proposes an e-learning systems change model around ends, means and processes. Main issues: define the vision and assess whether support unit has the appropriate competences.
Moccia (2016). Managing Educational Reforms during Times of Transition: The Role of Leadership. *Higher Education for the Future*, *3*(1), 26–37.	Opinion piece based on personal experience as HE leader	Presents a strategy summarised in six points to help HE leaders reinvent their industry: be global, financially sustainable, value-added, technological-oriented, a strategic local partner, substance more im portant than form.
Persichitte (2013). Leadership for Educational Technology Contexts in Tumultuous Higher Education Seas. *TechTrends*, *57*(5), 14–17.	Opinion piece based on personal experience and some theoretical references. Guiding principles for educational technology leadership	Importance of history and legacy, knowing when to lead from the front and from behind, using iterative data collection for shared problem-solving, awareness of policy and politics, horizon scanning, taking calculated risks, being prepared to take the hard decisions.
Watson and Watson (2013). Exploding the Ivory Tower: Systemic Change for Higher Education. *Tech Trends*, *57*(5), 42–46.	Opinion piece, educational technologists as change agents	Argues for the need for the systemic change of higher education and presents educational technologists as particularly well placed to lead this change.

Empirical studies 2013-2017

In terms of location, the spread across geographical regions was reasonably equitable, as shown in Table 5 below:

It should be noted that four of the six European studies were located in the UK and one other covered three European countries (Finland, Spain and the Czech Republic) as part of an ERASMUS+ project.

Turning now to populations, three main clusters of focus were identified:

1) governance and senior leaders: 9 results,
2) non-governance stakeholders (teachers, teachers and students, instructional designers): 8 results,
3) holistic multi-stakeholder approaches at different levels (project, faculty, single institution, multiple institution): 10 results.

Cluster 1 consists of studies focussed on leadership from the perspective of formal leaders: faculty governance (Ciabocchi, Ginsberg, & Picciano, 2016), university administrators (Livingstone, 2015; Spackman, Thorup, & Howell, 2015), senior leaders (Akcil, Aksal, Mukhametzyanova, & Gazi, 2017; Holt, Palmer, Gosper, Sankey, & Allan, 2015), online education administrators (Burnette, 2015) or through the mobilisation of local and international experts (Davis & Higgins, 2015; Díaz & Báez, 2015).

Cluster 2 results studied leadership from the perspective of stakeholders who are not themselves in TEL leadership roles: change management from teachers' perspective (Sheiladevi & Rahman, 2016); teachers' perceptions of organisational culture (Zhu, 2015), related to a previous study involving both teachers and students (Zhu & Engels, 2014); futures visioning with deans and lecturers (Inayatullah & Milojevic, 2014); instructional designers and e-learning production staff (Ashbaugh, 2013; Tay & Low, 2017) students' perceptions of leadership in online instructors (Bogler, Caspi, & Roccas, 2013).

Cluster 3 studies took a holistic multi-stakeholder approach at project-level (Brown, 2013; Garrison & Vaughan, 2013; Stoddart, 2015), faculty or department level (King & Boyatt, 2015; Trevitt, Steed, Du Moulin, & Foley, 2017) or institution-wide, with one focussing on a single institution (Roushan, Holley, & Biggins, 2016) and four taking a multiple-institution approach (Cifuentes & Vanderlinde, 2015; Domingo-Coscollola, Arrazola-Carballo, & Sancho-Gil, 2016; Ng'ambi & Bozalek, 2013; Singh & Hardaker, 2017).

A variety of methodologies were also mobilised:

- 16 qualitative studies, taking different approaches such as semi-structured interviews, action research, phenomenology, community of inquiry and narrative inquiry;

Table 5 Empirical studies by geographical region

Region	Number of studies
North America	5
Central and South America	3
Africa and Middle East	3
Asia	5
Australasia	4
Europe	6

- 9 quantitative studies;
- 2 mixed methods approaches.

Five of the qualitative approaches were presented as case studies, as was one of the mixed methods studies. It should be noted here that the latter (Livingstone, 2015) relied solely on an online survey and included personal criticism of the institution with value-laden language. A further case study (Brown, 2013) makes no explicit reference to the methodology used and it was not possible to determine this from a detailed reading of the article.

If we now compare the methodologies used to the populations studied, we find that nine of the ten holistic multi-stakeholder approaches used or included qualitative methods (Table 6).

Finally, taking into account Jameson's observation of a lack of dialogue between the two fields of education technology research and education management research, it is worth looking at the type of journal in which these empirical studies have been published:

- 15 studies were published in education technology journals,
- 6 studies were published in education management journals.

The remaining studies were distributed among journals focusing on science and technology education (3), media education (1), education and teaching (1), productivity and performance (1).

Interestingly, one of the studies by Zhu (Zhu & Engels, 2014) was published in an education management journal, the other (Zhu, 2015) in an education technology journal, perhaps showing the will to bridge this divide between the two fields.

Theoretical analyses 2013-2017

Three of the results provide an analysis of leadership theories in relation to the integration of technology for teaching and learning, taking e-leadership as understood in

Table 6 methodologies and research design by population scope (holistic studies)

Scope	Number	Methodology	Research design	Reference
Multi-institution	5	MMR	semi-structured interviews, focus groups, document analysis, survey (n=348)	(Cifuentes & Vanderlinde, 2015)
		QUANT	online survey, (n=259)	(Ng'ambi & Bozalek, 2013)
		QUAL	Document analysis, focus groups	(Domingo-Coscollola et al., 2016)
		QUAL	Multiple case studies	(Brown, 2013)
		QUAL	Exploratory case studies	(Singh & Hardaker, 2017)
Single institution	1	QUAL	Action research	(Roushan et al., 2016)
Faculty level	2	QUAL	Phenomenology: focus groups, individual interviews	(King & Boyatt, 2015)
		QUAL	Interviews	(Trevitt et al., 2017)
Project level	2	QUAL	practical inquiry and community of inquiry	(Garrison & Vaughan, 2013)
		QUAL	case study	(Stoddart, 2015)

business and relating it to the field of education (Mishra, Henriksen, Boltz, & Richardson, 2016), or developing a model of TEL leadership (Markova, 2014).

Others focus on the acceptance of technology by HE teaching staff with recommendations for HE leadership to integrate the implications of different models of technology acceptance (Rogers' (1962, 2003) diffusion model, Davis' (1989) technology acceptance model and Mishra and Koehler's (2006) technological, pedagogical and content knowledge TPACK model) in Continuous Professional Development (Sutton & DeSantis, 2017).

In particular Van Wart, Roman, Wang, and Liu (2017) propose widening the notion of e-leadership from leading in virtual spaces to include the act of choosing, recommending and supporting the implementation of ICT for an organisation, and propose a framework for connecting the different literatures in the fields of e-leadership and technology adoption.

Boyd and Sampson (2016) reflect on initiatives aimed toward developing staff digital confidence, an approach which is also found in Brown et al. (2016), who present conceptions of digital literacy and digital education as motivations for the conceptualisation of a proposed curriculum framework for digital education leadership.

Of significant interest is the approach proposed by McCutcheon (2014). This entails applying the UK National Health Service (NHS) Nursing Leadership Framework to structure and guide the process of developing e-learning for postgraduate nursing education. This framework is organised into seven dimensions around the central aim of delivering the service: demonstrating personal qualities, working with others, managing services, improving services, setting direction, creating the vision, delivering the strategy.

In reviewing research on Quality and Leadership of Online Education, Gupton (2014) examines the need for leadership as the online delivery of education develops, but uses emotional and value-laden language. Mukerjee (2014) explores the concept of organisational agility, while Murphy (2016) formulates an argument for the recognition of the importance of the mid-level professional manager in transitioning bottom-up to institute-wide TEL initiatives.

Finally, in the field of Organisational Learning, Tintoré and Arbós (2013) propose an Organisational Capacity Model questionnaire for identifying the stage of growth in the organisational learning capacity of a university, covering individual learning and institutional learning (teamwork, leadership and vision, culture and values, structures, resources, openness to the environment, barriers to learning). As with Khanna's (2017) good governance framework, Díaz and Báez's (2015) instrument for exploring leadership capabilities for ICT in education, Markova's (2014) TEL leadership model and Jameson's (2013) e-leadership framework for TEL, no evidence of the application of this tool in empirical studies has been identified.

Opinion pieces 2013-2017

The six opinion pieces identified in the literature view are presented briefly here to provide a picture of the preoccupations of HE leaders and other stakeholders who are taking an interest in the question of leadership for TEL in HE. Beaudoin (2016) presents an overview of current issues related to distance learning in HE, identifying central questions, issues, challenges and opportunities to be addressed by decision makers, as well as key attributes of effective leaders, which can be classified as leadership style and vision (transformational, change-management rather than technology as the priority, tolerance for ambiguity and risk); critical (assessment of situations, using data, resisting fashion, focus on both micro and macro perspectives); pedagogical (sound knowledge of distance education and theory, advocacy, decide and act as learner-centered educator); networking (to share ideas, strategies and resources).

Based on personal experience as an HE leader, Moccia (2016) presents a six-point strategy to help HE leaders reinvent their industry: be global, financially sustainable, value-added, technological-oriented, a strategic local partner, substance more important than form. Similarly, Persichitte (2013) builds on personal experience to present TEL leadership recommendations terms of context, behaviours and skills. Chow (2013) gives a detailed and honest account of the adaptation necessary in his move from Dotcom leadership to a HE environment, in particular the need to develop systems thinking and to focus on the human aspects, bringing stakeholders together to discuss issues and find solutions.

From the Information Technology (IT) perspective, Brown (2014) argues for IT departments to play a strategic role in the development of teaching and learning innovation, implying rethinking the roles of the chief information officer (CIO) and the academic technologist, the latter group also being reflected in Watson and Watson's (2013) argument for educational technologists to be seen as key change agents.

Leadership theories

While the purpose of this paper is not to provide a comprehensive review of leadership theory itself, it is still important to look more closely at which leadership theories and concepts are being referred to in the results identified in this literature review. As can be seen from the graph below (Fig. 4) the main theories cited are transformational leadership, distributed leadership and e-leadership.

Stewart (2006) provides a detailed account of the evolutions in transformational leadership theory, tracing it back to its origins in the seminal work of Burns (1978) who identified two types of leadership: transactional and transformational. While transactional leadership involves the leader exchanging something of value with the follower, transformational leadership "looks for potential motives in followers, seeks to satisfy higher needs, and engages the full person of the follower" (Burns, 1978, p. 4). In this case there is a search for mutually beneficial solutions with an increase in commitment and capacity to achieve mutual purposes.

Transactional and transformational leadership are not necessarily diametrically opposed, as can be seen in the development of Full Range Leadership Theory or FRLT (Bass & Avolio, 1997) where leaders mobilise a variety of behaviours in order to obtain greater commitment from followers.

Distributed leadership theory first emerged as a concept in the mid 1950s (Gibb, 1954) and a significant body of work on distributed leadership of educational organisations has been developed since the beginning of the 2000s (Bolden, 2011; Bolden, Gosling, & Petrov, 2009; Gronn, 2002, 2008; Harris, 2008; Harris & Spillane, 2008; Spillane, 2012; Spillane, Halverson, & Diamond, 2004). However, as Tian, Risku, and Collin (2016) point out, there is no universal accepted definition, proposing that "distributed leadership be defined and studied in terms of leadership as a process that comprises both organisational and individual scopes; the former regards leadership as a resource and the latter as an agency. Both resource and agency are considered to emerge and exist at all organisational levels." (Tian et al., 2016, p. 158).

As mentioned in the introduction to this study, e-leadership theory refers to "a social influence process embedded in both proximal and distal contexts mediated by AIT that can produce a change in attitudes, feelings, thinking, behavior, and performance" (Avolio et al., 2014). The different understandings of e-leadership in relation to TEL are discussed later in this article.

The results also cite other concepts associated with leadership which are not necessarily theories in their own right: top-down, bottom-up, middle-out, formal, informal, structured, supportive, passive (the latter coming under the umbrella of FRLT).

The following chart (Fig. 4) shows the frequency of occurrence of each of these theories and concepts according to the type of result.

It should be noted here that the 'distributed' label also encompasses other terms, such as 'distributive', 'collaborative', participatory', 'participative' and that these concepts may not necessarily always refer to the same theory or understanding. Furthermore, the concepts of supportive and structured leadership were only used in two articles relating to the Chinese context (Zhu, 2015; Zhu & Engels, 2014). Finally, several articles, including empirical studies, make no mention of the underlying leadership theory, as is the case of Garrison and Vaughan (2013), despite references to both collaborative and distributed leadership, and of Watson and Watson (2013), who refer to universities as complex systems yet do not make any reference to complexity leadership theory (Arena & Uhl-Bien, 2016; Clarke, 2013; Hazy & Uhl-Bien, 2015; Uhl-Bien, Marion, & McKelvey, 2007).

Other theories not directly related to the field of leadership are used to shed light on the question. In particular Singh and Hardaker (2017) apply Giddens' (1984) Theory of Structuration to identify a set of change levers at the intersection of bottom-up and top-down initiatives, namely the promotion of a collaborative, participatory approach,

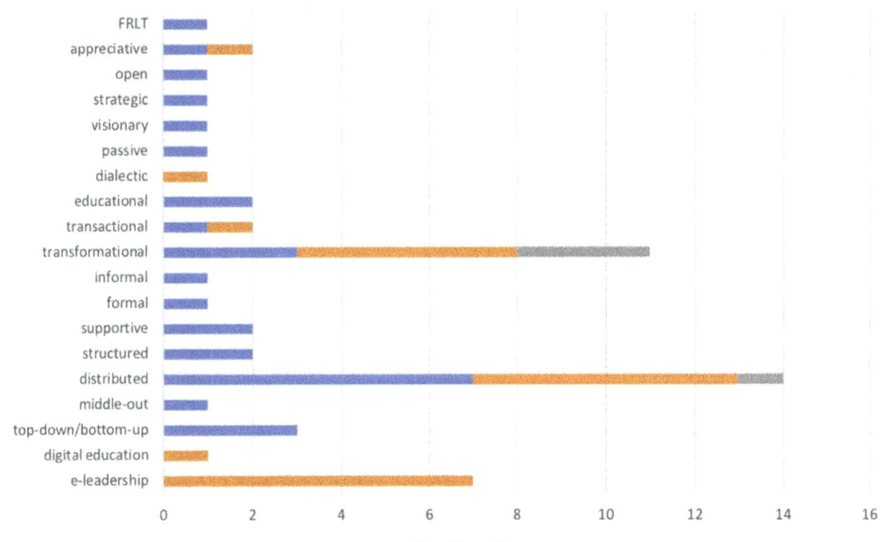

Fig. 4 Number of results per category 2013-2017 citing a particular leadership theory or concept

helping to form social networks so that potential adopters learn from peers, combining mass and interpersonal communication, endorsing bottom-up engagement and recognising the cultural specificity of faculties and departments.

Van Wart et al. (2017) and Sutton and DeSantis (2017) draw on the technology adoption literature, while Ng'ambi and Bozalek (2013) refer to Rogers' diffusion of innovation theory (Rogers, 2003; Rogers & Scott, 1997). Brown (2013) and Shieladevi and Rahman (2016) take a change management perspective. Other theories taken from the management field include learning organisations (Trevitt et al., 2017) and lean management (Tay & Low, 2017).

Perhaps the most significant observation here is that none of the empirical studies actually refer explicitly to e-leadership. We can thus conclude that there is a distinct lack of empirical research in e-leadership for TEL in HE. In those results which did cite e-leadership, the most widely used theories associated with e-leadership were again distributed and transformational, as can be seen in Fig. 5 below.

Discussion

This exploratory literature review was conducted in order to determine the extent to which the concept of e-leadership has taken off a lens through which to study leadership for technology-enhanced learning in higher education. Both the prevalence and the relevance of the use of this concept are discussed below. Trends are identified with respect to Jameson's (2013) e-leadership framework for TEL. Finally, recommendations for further research are formulated to bridge the gaps identified by the interrelated secondary research questions of populations studied, methodologies applied and levels of analysis, as well as in terms of (inter)disciplinarity.

(Re-)defining e-leadership

As we have already noted, none of the empirical studies identified in the search actually cite e-leadership, although there is a certain amount of interest among the theoretical papers. We might conclude that e-leadership for technology-enhanced learning in higher education has not taken off as a field of research, but before jumping to such a conclusion it is worth taking a closer look at the concept of e-leadership itself. If we

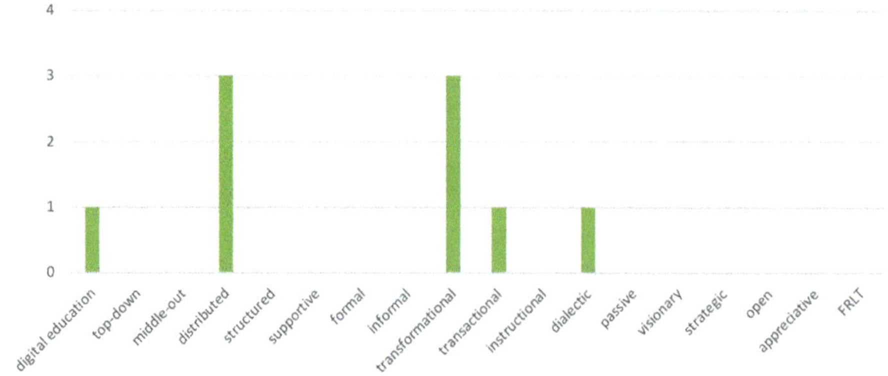

Fig. 5 Other theories or concepts cited alongside e-leadership

take the strict definition of e-leadership as referring to "a social influence process embedded in both proximal and distal contexts mediated by AIT that can produce a change in attitudes, feelings, thinking, behavior, and performance" (Avolio et al., 2014) and then unpack it, we can see that one of the elements in particular, the notion of 'social influence processes... mediated by AIT', might not always be present in the leadership relationships we are studying.

We can take the teaching and learning process to be mediated by AIT in TEL, and therefore see that the application of e-leadership theory is relevant to the topic of leading in online environments (Phelps, 2014). However, the leadership interventions, behaviours and attitudes of higher education governance and academic leaders in strategic thinking and decision-making around TEL are themselves not necessarily mediated by technology, although they may be. One perspective which shows promise in this respect is that put forward by Van Wart et al. (2017), of bringing together the literatures on e-leadership and technology adoption within the following wider definition of e-leadership as "the ability to effectively select and use ICTs for both personal and organizational purposes" (Van Wart et al., 2017, p. 529). While the focus here is on ICT adoption from a general organisation perspective, the further application of this approach to TEL in a higher educational setting is a logical next step, resonating with another educational leadership definition of e-leadership, namely as "the effective promotion and integration of technological learning and literacy into and within [educational] environments" (Preston et al., 2015, p. 991).

In analysing online education administrators' struggles for authority in the higher education landscape, Burnette (2015) quotes Beaudoin's (2002) definition of distance education leadership, namely as "a set of attitudes and behaviors that create conditions for innovative change, that enable individuals and organizations to share a vision and move in its direction, and that contribute to the management and operationalization of ideas" (Beaudoin, 2002, p. 132). This definition could in fact apply to leadership for change in general, although certain components of it are reflected in the some of the main trends identified in the present study (see also Fig. 6 below), in particular e-leadership visioning, change management and strategic planning.

Some authors accept the concept of e-leadership as multifaceted and conceptually ambiguous (Gurr, 2004; Salmon & Angood, 2013). Others go further, proposing a new concept of 'Digital Education Leadership' to mark the shift in focus from emphasising leadership in educational technology to "the fostering of leaders who have the qualities to lead in a digital culture" (Brown et al., 2016, p. 8) where "Digital education leadership is concerned with providing direction in terms of digital education by enhancing access, capacitating peers, making informed decisions and cultivating innovation, to achieve the learning goal (digital literacy)." (Brown et al., 2016, p. 10). However, as can be expected with the introduction of a new concept, a search in the three main databases (ISI Web of Science, Scopus and ERIC) for peer-reviewed papers using the search terms "Digital Education Leadership" AND "Higher Education" produced no results. This would thus not have been useful for our literature review at this stage, but should be included in future searches alongside the combinations already used.

Trends

Looking back at some of the major themes emerging from Jameson's 2013 study, we can see that the majority are still prevalent, to differing degrees. Comparisons of transformational versus transactional leadership are still present (3 results) although there is a clear development of studies focusing on distributed or shared leadership, with 26% of the empirical studies and 38% of the theoretical analyses referring to this concept.

Figure 6 below shows the number and distribution of occurrences of the main themes from Jameson's e-leadership framework, where these themes were present in 5 or more results.

Jameson's framework (Fig. 2) is structured around three major dimensions: Purpose, People and Structures & Social Systems. In the "Purpose" dimension, e-Leadership visioning, Strategic planning and Learning & Teaching are the three most cited themes among the results in this 2013-2017 study. For the "People" dimension, we find Collaboration and collegiality; Values, behaviour and culture; Interpersonal skills; Training and Continuous Professional Development (CPD). Finally, for the "Structures & Social Systems" dimension, the three most cited themes are Distributed leadership, Change management and Resource allocation.

Other emerging themes, over and above those covered in Jameson's framework, are identified as:

- the application of technology acceptance and adoption models (Akcil et al., 2017; Boyd & Sampson, 2016; King & Boyatt, 2015; Livingstone, 2015; Markova, 2014; Sutton & DeSantis, 2017; Van Wart et al., 2017);
- the application of tools and methods from the business world, as suggested by Sangrà (2009), with the caveat of the necessary cultural adaptation to HE (Chow, 2013; Mishra et al., 2016; Spackman et al., 2015; Tay & Low, 2017);
- using data for decision-making (Brown et al., 2016; Burnette, 2015; Persichitte, 2013);

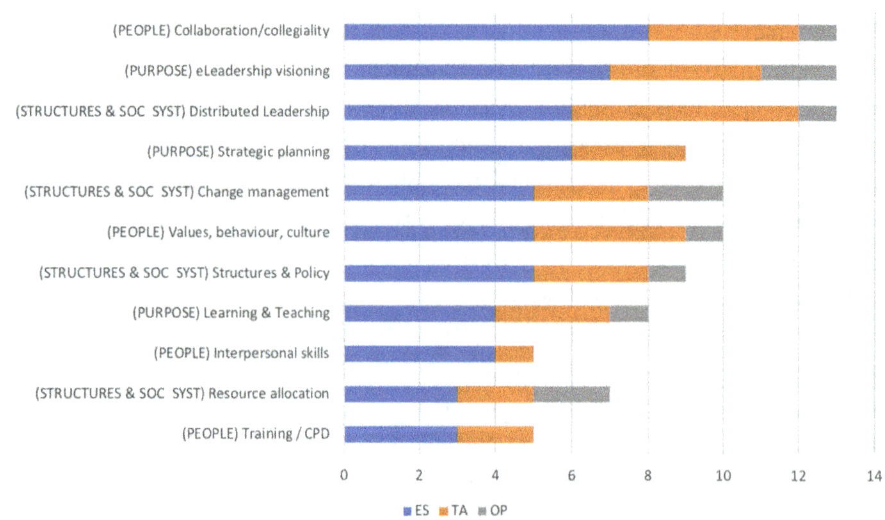

Fig. 6 Thematic analysis of results 2013-2017 compared to Jameson's (2013) e-Leadership framework

- studying TEL adoption from the point of view of organisational learning (Tintoré & Arbós, 2013; Trevitt et al., 2017);
- personal digital competence / literacy / confidence, of both leaders and staff (Akcil et al., 2017; Boyd & Sampson, 2016; Brown et al., 2016; Domingo-Coscollola et al., 2016).

Recommendations

This paper identifies four main gaps in the current research. These can be expressed in terms of populations studied, methodologies used, the disciplines to which these studies are related and the application of models and frameworks.

The first gap is defined as a lack of research at a holistic level, linking leadership to strategy and organisation. As Alvesson (2017) states: "Leadership is not a simple original source of much influencing, but needs to be placed in a broader context of hierarchical and vertical divisions of work, labour processes and cultural and material pressures from various interest groups" (Alvessson, 2017, p. 12). If we are looking to support HE leaders in developing strategic thinking, vision and action to improve the way technology is used for teaching and learning, then the focus of research needs to go beyond the analysis of leadership at project level, with more empirical studies addressing the question of leadership for TEL from a holistic, multi-stakeholder perspective at institutional level. The six results identified in this literature review would benefit from comparison with further studies taking such an approach to build up a much more comprehensive literature base.

Bridging the second gap involves employing robust research designs to take into account the complexity of such a holistic approach. Mixed Methods Research is particularly relevant for this as it "offers richer insights into the phenomenon being studied and allows the capture of information that might be missed by utilizing only one research design, enhances the body of knowledge, and generates more questions of interest for future studies that can handle a wider range of research questions." (Caruth, 2013). Furthermore, given the complex nature of leadership research, mixed methods enable the scholar to provide the most complete analysis, "extending beyond mere quantitative numbers or qualitative words" (Creswell & Plano Clark, 2011; Stentz, Plano Clark, & Matkin, 2012). Such an approach should also contribute to reducing researcher bias and avoid the limitation which Roushan et al. (2016) identify in their study, in that the researchers being themselves advocates of TEL may have meant that some opposition to change was under-reported.

The third gap concerns a distinct lack of interdisciplinary research. Given that this research takes place at the intersection of different disciplinary fields - education technology and management studies - insights from both fields are required. It is thus recommended that interdisciplinary teams collaborate on such research in order to reinforce synergies and ensure the best possible understanding of both worlds. In this respect, much can be learnt from the HE leadership and management literature, for example H. Davis' work on Leadership Literacies (Davis, 2012, 2014; Davis & Jones, 2014), and by continuing to develop the connections between leadership and change management for TEL (Martins & Baptista Nunes, 2016; Risquez & Moore, 2013). Further efforts to publish in education management journals should also be made, in order to increase the awareness of issues relating to the integration of technology for teaching and learning at HE governance level.

The final gap concerns the need to test existing models and frameworks through application in empirical studies. As we have seen, a number of models have been developed, either through empirical or theoretical studies (Díaz & Báez, 2015; Jameson, 2013; Khanna, 2017; Markova, 2014; McCutcheon, 2014). It would thus appear timely to test the validity of these frameworks in the field, through case studies focusing on qualitative contextual data as well as quantitative analysis.

Specific research lines should thus be fostered at meso (institutional) level, focusing on values, strategy, organisation and leadership interactions, while at the same time taking into account macro factors such as the economy and public policy, as well as teaching and learning at the micro level. Attention should be paid to making explicit any underlying assumptions about TEL, on the part of both the researchers themselves and the populations being studied (Bayne, 2015). A further focus should be placed on studying leadership development with specific reference to TEL, exploring the learning ecologies (Esposito, Sangrà, & Maina, 2015) of HE leaders who are making decisions about technology for teaching and learning. In other words, what formal and informal learning do they engage in and what influences their world views with respect to the changing technology landscape and its impact on teaching and learning? Related to this, studies could focus specifically on the relationships between HE leaders' own (critical) digital literacies (Belshaw, 2014), their awareness of the affordances of technology for teaching and learning, and their leadership attitudes and behaviour with respect to TEL.

Conclusion

Given the relative paucity of empirical results in this update of Jameson's 2013 literature review, at a time when HE leaders still need to develop their capacity for strategic thinking with respect to the integration of technology for learning and teaching, we conclude that further research into (e-)leadership for TEL in higher education would be welcome, just as Jameson herself did. The question of how we define e-leadership also needs to be addressed. Rather than hide behind arguments of conceptual ambiguity, it would be preferable for scholars in the field to draw on emerging proposals for including decision-making for TEL adoption at organisational level in the definition or to place e-leadership firmly within the original scope of leading in virtual environments and to adopt another concept such as that of "Digital Education Leadership".

There are of course limitations to this study in that it is intended as an update to that carried out by Jameson and thus covers a relatively short period (2013-2017). Further regular searches will be carried out, including citation analysis.

Finally, we argue for more collaboration between the disciplinary fields of educational technology and educational management. The sun may not yet have fully dawned on e-leadership as the 5th age of educational technology research in higher education, but there is both the potential and the need for this age to emerge at the intersection of these disciplines.

Abbreviations

AIT: Advanced information technology; CIO: Chief Information officer; CPD: Continuous professional development; ES: Empirical studies; FRLT: Full range leadership theory; HE: Higher education; ICT: Information and communication technology; IT: Information technology; MMR: Mixed methods research; NHS: National health system (UK); ODL: Open and distance learning; OP: Opinion pieces; QUAL: Qualitative research; QUAN: Quantitative research; TA: Theoretical analyses; TEL: Technology-enhanced learning; TPACK: Technological, pedagogical and content knowledge

Authors' contributions
This is a fully co-authored paper. Both authors read and approved the final manuscript.

Authors' information
DA is a PhD student on the Education & ICT doctoral programme at Universitat Oberta de Catalunya
AS is director of the UNESCO Chair in Education & Technology for Social Change and associate professor at Universitat Oberta de Catalunya

Competing interests
The authors declare that they have no competing interests.

References

Akcil, U., Aksal, F. A., Mukhametzyanova, F. S. M., & Gazi, Z. A. G. (2017). An Examination of Open and Technology Leadership in Managerial Practices of Education System. *EURASIA Journal of Mathematics Science and Technology Education, 13*(1), 119–131 https://doi.org/10.12973/eurasia.2017.00607a.

Alvesson, M. (2017). Waiting for Godot: Eight major problems in the odd field of leadership studies. *Leadership*, 174271501773670. https://doi.org/10.1177/1742715017736707

Arena, M. J., & Uhl-Bien, M. (2016). Complexity Leadership Theory : Shifting from Human Capital to Social Capital. *People and Strategy, 39*(2), 22–27.

Ashbaugh, M. L. (2013). Expert Instructional Designer Voices: Leadership Competencies Critical to Global Practice and Quality Online Learning Designs. *Quarterly Review of Distance Education, 14*(2), 97–118.

Avolio, B. J., Kahai, S., & Dodge, G. E. (2001). E-Leadership : Implications for Theory, Research, and Practice. *The Leadership Quarterly, 11*(4), 615–668.

Avolio, B. J., Sosik, J. J., Kahai, S. S., & Baker, B. (2014). E-leadership: Re-examining transformations in leadership source and transmission. *The Leadership Quarterly, 25*(1), 105–131.

Barber, M., Donnelly, K., & Rizvi, S. (2013). *An Avalanche is Coming: Higher Education and the Revolution Ahead*. London: *Institute for Public Policy Research.*

Bass, B. M., & Avolio, B. J. (1997). *Full range leadership development: Manual for the Multifactor Leadership Questionnaire.* Mind Garden.

Bälter, O. (2017). Moving Technology-Enhanced-Learning Forward: Bridging Divides through Leadership. *The International Review of Research in Open and Distributed Learning*, 18 (3).

Bates, A. W. Tony. (2015). Teaching in a Digital Age. Retrieved January 8, 2017, from http://www.tonybates.ca/teaching-in-a-digital-age

Bates, A. W. T., & Sangrà, A. (2011). *Managing technology in higher education: Strategies for transforming teaching and learning*. Hoboken: Wiley.

Baydas, O., Kucuk, S., Yilmaz, R. M., Aydemir, M., & Goktas, Y. (2015). Educational technology research trends from 2002 to 2014. *Scientometrics, 105*(1), 709–725.

Bayne, S. (2015). What's the matter with "technology-enhanced learning"? *Learning. Media and Technology, 40*(1), 5–20 https://doi.org/10.1080/17439884.2014.915851.

Beaudoin, M. (2002). Distance Education Leadership: An Essential Role For The New Century. *Journal of Leadership Studies, 8*(3), 131–144 https://doi.org/10.1177/107179190200800311.

Beaudoin, M. (2016). Issues in Distance Education: A Primer for Higher Education Decision Makers. *New Directions for Higher Education, 173*, 9–19 https://doi.org/10.1002/he.

Belshaw, D. (2014). The Essential Elements of Digital Literacies. https://doi.org/10.1007/s13398-014-0173-7.2.

Bervell, B., & Umar, I. N. (2017). A Decade of LMS Acceptance and Adoption Research in Sub-Sahara African Higher Education: A Systematic Review of Models, Methodologies, Milestones and Main Challenges. *EURASIA Journal of Mathematics, Science and Technology Education*, 13(11), 7269–7286.

Bogler, R., Caspi, A., & Roccas, S. (2013). Transformational and Passive Leadership. *Educational Management Administration & Leadership, 41*(3), 372–392 https://doi.org/10.1177/1741143212474805.

Bolden, R. (2011). Distributed leadership in organizations: A review of theory and research. *International Journal of Management Reviews, 13*(3), 251–269 https://doi.org/10.1111/j.1468-2370.2011.00306.x.

Bolden, R., Gosling, J., & Petrov, G. (2009). Distributed leadership in higher education: Rhetoric and reality. *Educational Management Administration & Leadership, 37*(2), 257–277.

Boyd, V., & Sampson, A. (2016). Foundation versus innovation: developing creative education practitioner confidence in the complex blended learning landscape. *Professional Development in Education, 42*(3), 502–506 https://doi.org/10.1080/19415257.2015.1024800.

Boyer, A. (2016). Guidelines for governance of HE institutions, D-Transform. Retrieved January 13, 2017, from http://www.dtransform.eu/resources/#O1-A4

Brown, C., Czerniewicz, L., Huang, C.-W., & Mayisela, T. (2016). Curriculum for Digital Education Leadership: A Concept Paper. Retrieved October 30, 2017, from http://oasis.col.org/handle/11599/2442

Brown, M. (2014). Reenvisioning Teaching and Learning: Opportunities for Campus IT. *Libraries and the Academy, 14*(3), 383–391.

Brown, S. (2013). Large-scale innovation and change in UK higher education. *Research in Learning Technology, 21*, 1–14 https://doi.org/10.3402/rlt.v21i0.22316.

Burnette, D. (2015). Negotiating the mine field: Strategies for effective online education administrative leadership in higher education institutions. *The Quarterly Review of Distance Education, 16*(3), 13–35.

Burns, J. M. (1978). Leadership. New York, NY: Harper & Row.

Caruth, G. D. (2013). Demystifying Mixed Methods Research Design: A Review of the Literature. *Mevlana International Journal of Education (MIJE), 3*(2), 112–122.

Chow, A. S. (2013). One Educational Technology Colleague's Journey from Dotcom Leadership to University E-Learning Systems Leadership: Merging Design Principles, Systemic Change and Leadership Thinking. *TechTrends, 57*(5), 64–75 https://doi.org/10.1007/s11528-013-0693-6.

Ciabocchi, E., Ginsberg, A. P., & Picciano, A. G. (2016). A Study of Faculty Governance Leaders' Perceptions of Online and Blended Learning. *Online Learning, 20*(3), 52–73.

Cifuentes, G., & Vanderlinde, R. (2015). ICT Leadership in Higher Education : A Multiple Case Study in Colombia. *Media Education Research Journal, 23*, 133–141.

Clarke, N. (2013). Model of complexity leadership development. *Human Resource Development International, 16*(2), 135–150.

Craig, R. (2015). *College disrupted: The great unbundling of higher education*. New York: St. Martin's Press.

Creswell, J. W., & Plano Clark, V. L. (2011). Designing and Conducting Mixed Methods Research. Thousand Oaks, CA: SAGE.

D'Emidio, T., Dorton, D., & Duncan, E. (2015). Service innovation in a digital world. *McKinsey Quarterly*. Retrieved from http://www.mckinsey.com/business-functions/operations/our-insights/service-innovation-in-a-digital-world

Davis, F. (1989). Perceived Usefulness, Perceived Ease Of Use, And User Acceptance of Information Technology. *MIS Quarterly, 13*(3), 319 https://doi.org/10.2307/249008.

Davis, H. (2012). *Leadership Literacies for Professional Staff in Universities*. (Doctoral thesis). Retrieved from https://researchbank.rmit.edu.au/view/rmit:160335.

Davis, H. (2014). Towards leadingful leadership literacies for higher education management. *Journal of Higher Education Policy and Management, 36*(4), 371–382.

Davis, H., & Jones, S. (2014). The work of leadership in higher education management. *Journal of Higher Education Policy and Management, 36*(4), 367–370 https://doi.org/10.1080/1360080X.2014.916463.

Davis, N., & Higgins, A. (2015). Researching Possible Futures to Guide Leaders Towards More Effective Tertiary Education. *Journal of Open, Flexible and Distance Learning, 19*(2), 8–24.

Díaz, Y., & Báez, L. (2015). Exploración de la capacidad de liderazgo para la incorporación de TICC en educación: validación de un instrumento. *RELATEC - Revista Latinoamericana de Tecnología Educativa, 14*(3), 35–47 https://doi.org/10.17398/1695.

Domingo-Coscollola, M., Arrazola-Carballo, J., & Sancho-Gil, J. M. (2016). Do It Yourself in Education : Leadership for Learning across Physical and Virtual Borders. *International Journal of Educational Leadership and Management, 4*(1), 5–29 https://doi.org/10.17583/ijelm.2016.1842.

Esposito, A., Sangrà, A., & Maina, M. (2015). Emerging learning ecologies as a new challenge and essence for e-learning. *The case of doctoral e-researchers. International Handbook of E-Learning, 1*, 331–342 https://doi.org/10.4324/9781315760933.

Garrison, R., & Vaughan, N. (2013). Institutional change and leadership associated with blended learning innovation: Two case studies. *The Internet and Higher Education, 18*, 24–28.

Gibb, C. A. (1954). Leadership. In G. Lindzey (Ed.), Handbook of social psychology, Vol 2 (pp. 877–917). Reading, MA: Addison-Wesley.

Giddens, A. (1984). *The Constitution of Society: Outline of the Theory of Structuration*. Berkeley: University of California Press.

Gronn, P. (2002). Distributed leadership as a unit of analysis. *The Leadership Quarterly, 13*(4), 423–451 https://doi.org/10.1016/S1048-9843(02)00120-0.

Gronn, P. (2008). The future of distributed leadership. *Journal of Educational Administration, 46*(2), 141–158 https://doi.org/10.1108/09578230810863235.

Gupton, S. L. (2014). Online Frontiers in Education : Leadership's Role. *International Journal of Arts & Sciences, 7*(2), 609–616.

Gurr, D. (2004). ICT, Leadership in Education and E-leadership. *Discourse: Studies in the Cultural Politics of Education, 25*(1), 113–124.

Harris, A. (2008). Distributed leadership: according to the evidence. *Journal of Educational Administration, 46*(2), 172–188 https://doi.org/10.1108/09578230810863253.

Harris, A., & Spillane, J. (2008). Distributed leadership through the looking glass. *Management in Education, 22*(1), 31–34 https://doi.org/10.1177/0892020607085623.

Hazy, J. K., & Uhl-Bien, M. (2015). Towards operationalizing complexity leadership: How generative, administrative and community-building leadership practices enact organizational outcomes. *Leadership, 11*(1), 79–104.

Holt, D., Palmer, S., Gosper, M., Sankey, M., & Allan, G. (2015). Framing and enhancing distributed leadership in the quality management of online learning environments in higher education. *Distance Education, 35*(3), 382–399.

Hughes, J., Thomas, R., & Scharber, C. (2006). Assessing Technology Integration: The RAT – Replacement, Amplification, and Transformation - Framework. In C. Crawford, R. Carlsen, K. McFerrin, J. Price, R. Weber, & D. Willis (Eds.), *Proceedings of SITE 2006-, USA: Association for the Advancement of Computing in Education (AACE)*.

Inayatullah, S., & Milojevic, I. (2014). Augmented reality, the Murabbi and the democratization of higher education: alternative futures of higher education in. *On the Horizon, 22*(2), 110–126 https://doi.org/10.1108/OTH-08-2013-0029.

Jameson, J. (2013). E-Leadership in higher education: The fifth "age" of educational technology research. *British Journal of Educational Technology, 44*(6), 889–915.

Keeble, H., & Kirk, R. (2007). Exploring the existing body of research. In A. Briggs & M. Coleman (Eds.), Research Methods in Educational Leadership and Management. Sage Thousand Oaks, CA.

Khanna, P. (2017). A conceptual framework for achieving good governance at open and distance learning institutions. *Open Learning: The Journal of Open, Distance and E-Learning, 32*(1), 21–35 https://doi.org/10.1080/02680513.2016.1246246.

King, E., & Boyatt, R. (2015). Exploring factors that influence adoption of e-learning within higher education. *British Journal of Educational Technology, 46*(6), 1272–1280 https://doi.org/10.1111/bjet.12195.

Livingstone, K. A. (2015). Administration's perception about the feasibility of elearning practices at the University of Guyana. *International Journal of Education and Development Using Information and Communication Technology (IJEDICT), 11*(2), 65–84.

Lucas Jr., H. C. (2016). *Technology and the Disruption of Higher Education*. Singapore: World Scientific.

Markova, M. (2014). A Model of Leadership in Integrating Educational Technology in Higher Education. *Online Journal of Distance Learning Administration, 17*, 4.

Martins, J. T., & Baptista Nunes, M. (2016). Academics' e-learning adoption in higher education institutions: a matter of trust. *The Learning Organization, 23*(5), 299–331.

McCutcheon, K. (2014). A Leadership Framework to Support the use of E-Learning Resources. *Nursing Management, 21*(3), 24–28.

Mishra, P., Henriksen, D., Boltz, L. O., & Richardson, C. (2016). E-Leadership and Teacher Development using ICT. In R. Huang & J. K. Price (Eds.), ICT in Education in Global Context (pp. 248–266). Berlin, Heidelberg, DE: Springer-Verlag. https://doi.org/10.1007/978-3-662-43927-2

Mishra, P., & Koehler, M. J. (2006). Technological pedagogical content knowledge: A framework for teacher knowledge. *Teachers College Record, 108*(6), 1017–1054 https://doi.org/10.1111/j.1467-9620.2006.00684.x.

Moccia, S. (2016). Managing Educational Reforms during Times of Transition: The Role of Leadership. *Higher Education for the Future, 3*(1), 26–37 https://doi.org/10.1177/2347631115611278.

Moreau, F. (2013). The Disruptive Nature of Digitization: The Case of the Recorded Music Industry. *International Journal of Arts Management, 15*(2), 18–31.

Mukerjee, S. (2014). Agility : a crucial capability for universities in times of disruptive change and innovation. *Australian Universities Review, 56*(1), 56–60.

Murphy, T. (2016). The future of Technology Enhanced Learning (TEL) is in the hands of the anonymous, grey non-descript mid-level professional manager. *Irish Journal of Technology Enhanced Learning, 2*(1), 1–9 https://doi.org/10.22554/ijtel.v2i1.14.

Ng'ambi, D., & Bozalek, V. (2013). Leveraging informal leadership in higher education institutions: A case of diffusion of emerging technologies in a southern context. *British Journal of Educational Technology, 44*(6), 940–950 https://doi.org/10.1111/bjet.12108.

Öchsner, A. (2013). Types of Scientific Publications. In A. Öchsner (Ed.), *Introduction to Scientific Publishing. SpringerBriefs in Applied Sciences and Technology*, (pp. 9–21). Berlin, Heidelberg: Springer Berlin Heidelberg https://doi.org/10.1007/978-3-642-38646-6_3.

Orr, T., & Cleveland-Innes, M. (2015). Appreciative leadership: Supporting education innovation. *International Review of Research in Open and Distributed Learning, 16*(4), 235–241.

Persichitte, K. A. (2013). Leadership for Educational Technology Contexts in Tumultuous Higher Education Seas. *TechTrends, 57*(5), 14–17 https://doi.org/10.1007/s11528-013-0686-5.

Phelps, K. C. (2014). "So much technology, so little talent"? Skills for harnessing technology for leadership outcomes. *Journal of Leadership Studies, 8*(2), 51–56 https://doi.org/10.1002/jls.

Preston, J. P., Moffatt, L., Wiebe, S., McAuley, A., Campbell, B., & Gabriel, M. (2015). The use of technology in Prince Edward Island (Canada) high schools. *Educational Management Administration & Leadership, 43*(6), 989–1005 https://doi.org/10.1177/1741143214535747.

Pretto, G., & Curró, G. (2017). An Approach for Doctoral Students Conducting Context-Specific Review of Literature in IT, ICT, and Educational Technology. *New Review of Academic Librarianship, 23*(1), 60–83 https://doi.org/10.1080/13614533.2016.1227861.

Risquez, A., & Moore, S. (2013). Exploring feelings about technology integration in higher education. *Journal of Organizational Change Management, 26*(2), 326–339.

Rogers, E. M. (1962). Diffusion of innovations. New York, NY: Glencoe Free Press.

Rogers, E. M. (2003). *Diffusion of innovations*, (5th ed.,). New York: Free Press.

Rogers, E. M., & Scott, K. L. (1997). The Diffusion of Innovations Model and Outreach from the National Network of Libraries of Medicine to Native American Communities. Retrieved November 25, 2017, from https://nnlm.gov/archive/pnr/eval/rogers.html

Rogers, J. (2013). *The death and life of the music industry in the digital age*. New York and London: Bloomsbury Academic.

Roushan, G., Holley, D., & Biggins, D. (2016). The Kaleidoscope of Voices: An Action Research Approach to Informing Institutional e-Learning Policy. *Electronic Journal of E-Learning, 14*(5), 293–300.

Salmon, G., & Angood, R. (2013). Sleeping with the enemy. *British Journal of Educational Technology, 44*(6), 916–925 https://doi.org/10.1111/bjet.12097.

Sangrà, A. (2009). La integració de les TIC a la universitat: models, problemes i reptes. (Doctoral thesis). Retrieved from http://www.tdx.cat/handle/10803/8947.

Selwyn, N. (2013). Discourses of digital "disruption" in education : a critical analysis. In *Fifth International Roundtable on Discourse Analysis, City University Hong Kong, May 23-25, 2013*, (pp. 1–28).

Sheiladevi, S., & Rahman, A. (2016). An Investigation on Impact of E-Learning Implementation on Change Management in Malaysian Private Higher Education Institutions. *Pertanika Jouornal of Science and Technology, 24*(2), 517–530.

Shirky, C. (2012). Napster, Udacity, and the academy. Retrieved January 8, 2017, from http://www.shirky.com/weblog/2012/11/napster-udacity-and-the-academy/.

Singh, G., & Hardaker, G. (2017). Teaching in Higher Education Change levers for unifying top-down and bottom- up approaches to the adoption and diffusion of e- learning in higher education. *Teaching in Higher Education, 22*(6), 736–748 https://doi.org/10.1080/13562517.2017.1289508.

Spackman, J. S., Thorup, J., & Howell, S. L. (2015). What Can the Business World Teach Us About Strategic Planning. *Online Journal of Distance Learning Administration, 18*, 2.

Spillane, J. P. (2012). *Distributed leadership*, (vol. 4). San Francisco: Wiley.

Spillane, J. P., Halverson, R., & Diamond, J. B. (2004). Towards a theory of leadership practice: A distributed perspective. *Journal of Curriculum Studies* (Vol. 36). https://doi.org/10.1080/0022027032000106726.

Staley, D. J., & Trinkle, D. A. (2011). The changing landscape of higher education. *Educause Review, 46*(1), 16–32.

Stentz, J. E., Plano Clark, V. L., & Matkin, G. S. (2012). Applying mixed methods to leadership research: A review of current practices. *The Leadership Quarterly, 23*(6), 1173–1183.

Stewart, J. (2006). Transformational leadership: An evolving concept examined through the works of Burn, Bass, Avolio and Leithwood. *Canadian Journal of Educational Administration and Policy, 54*(54), 1–29.

Stoddart, P. (2015). Using educational technology as an institutional teaching and learning improvement strategy? *Journal of Higher Education Policy and Management, 37*(5), 586–596.

Sutton, K. K., & DeSantis, J. (2017). Beyond change blindness: embracing the technology revolution in higher education. *Innovations in Education and Teaching International*, *54*(3), 223–228 https://doi.org/10.1080/14703297.2016.1174592.

Suzor, N., & Wikstrom, P. (2016). Paper 1: The disruptive forces of the sharing economy. The Innovation Paper, 1–5.

Tay, H. L., & Low, S. W. K. (2017). Digitalization of learning resources in a HEI – a lean management perspective. *International Journal of Productivity and Performance Management*, *66*(5), 680–694.

Tian, M., Risku, M., & Collin, K. (2016). A meta-analysis of distributed leadership from 2002 to 2013. *Educational Management Administration & Leadership*, *44*(1), 146–164 https://doi.org/10.1177/1741143214558576.

Tintoré, M., & Arbós, A. (2013). Identifying the stage of growth in the organisational learning capacity of universities. *Universities and Knowledge Society Journal (RUSC)*, *10. No*, *2*(2013), 375–393.

Trevitt, C., Steed, A., Du Moulin, L., & Foley, T. (2017). Leading entrepreneurial e-learning development in legal education: A longitudinal case study of "universities as learning organisations.". *The Learning Organization*, *24*(5), 298–311.

Uhl-Bien, M., Marion, R., & McKelvey, B. (2007). Complexity Leadership Theory: Shifting leadership from the industrial age to the knowledge era. *The Leadership Quarterly*, *18*(4), 298–318.

Van Wart, M., Roman, A., Wang, X. H., & Liu, C. (2017). Integrating ICT adoption issues into (e-)leadership theory. *Telematics and Informatics*, *34*(5), 527–537 https://doi.org/10.1016/j.tele.2016.11.003.

Watson, W. R., & Watson, S. L. (2013). Exploding the Ivory Tower: Systemic Change for Higher Education. *Tech Trends*, *57*(5), 42–46 https://doi.org/10.1007/s11528-013-0690-9.

Webster, J., & Watson, R. T. (2002). Analyzing the past to prepare for the future: Writing a literature review. *MIS Quarterly*, 26(2), xiii–xxiii. https://doi.org/10.2307/4132319.

Weller, M., & Anderson, T. (2013). Digital Resilience in Higher Education. *European Journal of Open, Distance & E-Learning*, *16*(1), 53–66.

Wheeler, S. (2012). e-Learning and digital learning. In *Encyclopedia of the sciences of learning*, (pp. 1109–1111). Berlin: Springer.

Winn, W. (2002). Current trends in educational technology research: The study of learning environments. *Educational Psychology Review*, *14*(3), 331–351.

Zawacki-Richter, O., & Naidu, S. (2016). Mapping research trends from 35 years of publications in Distance Education. *Distance Education*, *37*(3), 245–269.

Zhu, C. (2015). Organisational culture and technology-enhanced innovation in higher education. *Technology, Pedagogy and Education*, *24*(1), 65–79 https://doi.org/10.1080/1475939X.2013.822414.

Zhu, C., & Engels, N. (2014). Organizational culture and instructional innovations in higher education. *Educational Management Administration & Leadership*, *42*(1), 136–158 https://doi.org/10.1177/1741143213499253.

9

Unfitting, uncomfortable, unacademic: a sociological reading of an interactive mobile phone app in university lectures

Christopher Drew* and Amandeep Mann

* Correspondence: c.drew@tees.ac.uk
Department of Education, School of Social Sciences, Humanities and Law, Teesside University, Middlesbrough TS1 3BX, UK

Abstract

Scholarly literature on education technology uptake has been dominated by technological determinist readings of students' technology use. However, in recent years there has been a move by sociologists of education to highlight how the contexts in which educational technologies are introduced are not *tabula rasa* but socially and culturally complex. This study approaches technology as a social construct, arguing that students *construct* discursive meaning of, rather than simply *respond to*, technologies for learning. The study explores students' constructions of a mobile learning app that was introduced into lectures during a year-long university course. Students largely rejected the app, constructing it as unfitting for the context, a socially uncomfortable experience and an unacademic way of learning. The paper highlights the limitations of technological determinism and closes by arguing for readings of educational technologies that pay close attention to students' voices.

Keywords: M-learning, Technological determinism, Social construction of technology, Lectures

Introduction

Mobile technologies are an increasingly integral part of young adults' lives. Social networking apps on mobile devices like Instagram and Facebook have become online spaces in which users interact, make plans, share experiences, engage in politics and create their identities (Boyd, 2014; Davis & Gardner, 2013). Aware of contemporary university students' familiarity with online spaces, we introduced a smartphone app to our lectures and encouraged students to use the app to engage in formal synchronous online learning during lectures. The app we chose was Collaborate Ultra, which enabled students to 'chat' online during lecture time and write directly onto the shared lecture slides. It thereby facilitated opportunities for sociable and (inter)active lecture experiences. However, the students broadly rejected the online space, framing it variously as 'unacademic', 'unfitting' and 'uncool'.

This paper explores the students' decisions to reject the online space created for them. The research question was:

> What are a selection of first-year undergraduate students' constructions of an interactive educational app within lectures?

Data was collected through focus group interviews with 38 students randomly selected out of the 106-student cohort. The data was analysed using a sociology of education technology perspective (Jones & Bissell, 2011; Oliver, 2013; Selwyn, 2012), wherein we examined the data not for exploring how the app 'acted upon' the students, but rather how the students *constructed* the app as suitable or otherwise for their learning needs (Oliver, 2013). Such a study enables us to highlight how educational technologies are not introduced into a learning scenario that is a *tabula rasa* ripe to be acted upon; rather, they are introduced into complex social learning environments (Chan, Walker, & Gleaves, 2015) in which students have expectations, desires and anxieties that should be acknowledged by educators.

Thus, while our year-long interactive app project was originally designed as an opportunity to turn the lecture into something that was more palatable to both our own social-constructivist pedagogical perspectives (Chi, 2009) and students' increasingly tech-engaged ways of interacting (Boyd, 2014), the results render much richer sociological insights. We came to learn that our assumption that students would be enthusiastic about the online spaces *if only we provided them* was somewhat naive. Indeed, the students widely constructed this interactive mobile app as undesirable for their learning, for a variety of nuanced reasons. The interactive mobile app that we developed was neither how this cohort wanted to utilise their personal mobile technologies nor what they necessarily wanted out of their higher education experience.

Literature review: the case for a sociology of educational technologies

Sociology of education technology scholarship critiques the dominant 'technological determinist' approach to educational technologies. Through a technological determinist lens, educational technologies are perceived as 'acting upon' student cohorts (Jones & Bissell, 2011; Kear, Jones, Holden, & Mark, 2016; Oliver, 2011; Selwyn, 2012; Selwyn & Facer, 2014; Webster, 2013). Such an approach presumes that the agency to effect change is broadly in the hands of technologies that can coerce students into learning, if only they are set up appropriately. As Selwyn (2012, p. 83) argues,

> Throughout the 1980s and 1990s the majority of academic writing was content to imbue educational technologies such as the television and computer with a range of inherent qualities. These qualities were then seen to 'impact' (for better or worse) on young users in ways which were consistent regardless of circumstance or context.

This technological determinism is evident in arguments that accuse games of making youths more violent and overweight; and in arguments selling the transformative effects of gifting students tablet computers at the beginning of a school year. Such claims imply technologies unilaterally act upon learners and often turn out to be overreach.

Studies of the efficacy of mobile learning devices such as web-connected smartphones, tablets and laptops for education have also tended to embrace technological determinist approaches (Chan et al., 2015; Smith, 2016; Wu et al., 2012). Indeed, Wu et al.'s (2012) influential systematic review of mobile learning studies emphasised that literature on mobile learning skews towards positivist and cause-and-effect analyses. This has left some scholars to argue for the need for sociological approaches to mobile learning that engage with "cultural and social perspectives" that might "better theorize the phenomenon of smartphone use in learning contexts" (Chan et al., 2015, p. 96).

Thus, recent scholars within the area of the sociology of educational technologies (Selwyn & Facer, 2014) have called for studies to pursue analyses that recognises the ways that students who are situated within social and cultural contexts approach educational technologies. Sociological analyses of educational technologies can, for example, show that technological artefacts tend to be approached with "interpretative flexibility" (Bijker & Pinch, 1984, p. 419) inasmuch as technologies are interpreted in different ways in different contexts. Similarly, Oliver (2013) invokes the concept of 'construction' of technologies to highlight how technologies garner meaning only through their contextualised interpretations. Thus, the sociology if educational technology literature takes neither an individualising nor a universalising approach (Zerubavel, 1997) to educational technologies. Agency over the success and failure of technological interventions is seen neither as belonging to individual learners or the technologies themselves. Rather, contextualised understandings of technology usage are required in order to render visible the ways social and cultural factors feed into students' agentive constructions of technology (Selwyn, 2012).

By paying attention to social and cultural implications of educational technologies, scholars have highlighted how educational technologies exist within complex classroom ecologies. As Pedro, Barbados and Santos (Pedro, Barbosa, & Santos, 2018, p. 11) argue, new technology in a classroom "does not mean that we have the old environment plus one element." Rather, the success of technology integration is associated with a host of contextual challenges. Similarly, Sung, Chang, and Liu (2016) invoke the metaphor of technology 'orchestration' to highlight how technology integration is not as simple as fitting the technology into an existing classroom environment. Instead, ongoing processes of negotiation and collaboration are required in order for the integration to suit the contextualised learning needs of students.

The study's context

In response to our university's technology enabled learning agenda which encouraged exploration of educational technologies in our classes, we implemented an educational app for use in our weekly lectures. We invited a full cohort of students to log into the Collaborate Ultra app using mobile technologies such as smartphones, tablets or laptops during each lecture for 20 weeks. The students in the study were a largely white working-class female cohort with minimal experiences of university education, studying an introduction to research methods course within the university's Department of Education. The cohort of 106 students was typical of the department's student age demographic, with most students aged 18–24. As we had expected from these young university students, there was no indication throughout the project that any student lacked access to mobile technologies to participate in the study, although students were encouraged to share their screens with others who may not have brought their own devices. Reliable university Wi-Fi was made available to all students.

The app selected for the study was Collaborate Ultra. This app was selected as it enabled students to scrawl directly onto the lecture slides using touch screen capabilities of personal smartphones or tablets. Students' scrawlings on their personal devices was automatically projected onto the main lecture slide at the front of the lecture, making the slides a shared space onto which students could make their contributions. Students were also able to type on a shared chat board, which was also projected onto a chat thread on the right-hand side of the slides on the main lecture screen. The lectures, delivered by Author A, spaced four slides of content with two slides of activities. On the activities slides, students were encouraged to collaboratively solve problems and project their answers onto the shared screen. The scrawling option was generally used to draw concept maps or otherwise circle elements of the slide to which they wanted to draw attention. The chat stream was used to make comments or ask questions of the lecturer. Of the 106 students in the course, only an average of 36 students logged onto the software in the first 1 weeks. Logon rates steadily slid from Week 4, until weekly uptake plateaued at 6 students per week from Week 9 onwards.

Methodology

Given that a sociology of education technology perspective approaches data from an interpretivist paradigm, qualitative semi-structured interviews were selected for the study. Following Smith (2016), we saw interviews with students as the most valuable method for this analysis because it enabled us to gather detailed discussions about how the students constructed the interactive app. At the end of the second semester, 38 students were randomly selected for participation in 8 Focus Groups for semi-structured interviews lasting 20–35 min (Longhurst, 2003). Students were not selected based on their usage patterns but instead were randomly selected so that we could get a broad range of student perspectives of the app. The interviews were conducted by a research assistant (Author B) rather than the lecturer to encourage students to give frank opinions on the topic. Stimulus questions were separated into three categories: students' perceptions of the app's ease of use; students' perceptions of the use of the app's value for learning; and students' perceptions of the app's suitability for lectures. As the interviews were semi-structured and themes were to be induced from the students' conversations, we also encouraged students to 'chat' about the experience in order that the data could emerge through the flow of conversation wherever possible (Vaismoradi, Jones, Turunen, & Snelgrove, 2016).

The transcriptions of the Focus Group interviews were then analysed. During coding, pseudonyms were used to protect students' privacy, as per the university's research ethics standards. We conducted thematic network analysis (Attride-Stirling, 2001; Clarke & Braun, 2013; Vaismoradi et al., 2016), which involved three passes over the transcripts. During the first pass, key quotes were highlighted and coded, which were coagulated into themes during the second and third passes over the data. From the transcript analysis, we found three key organising themes that emerged as dominant across the cohort, which are discussed below.

Results

Three themes emerged from the analysis. Firstly, the students constructed the interactive app as being an awkward fit within a lecture context. The students dominantly saw the ideal lecture as an opportunity to engage in didactic learning (Brown & Race, 2014; Covill, 2011), which led them to direct their attention towards note-taking, and subsequently construct the interactive app as unfitting for the context. Secondly, the students constructed the app as being an 'uncomfortable' risk to their social subjectivties. Students recognised technology users as occupying 'marked' (Brekhus, 2007) social subjectivities that were conspicuously uncomfortable and socially risky. They therefore widely constructed the interactive app as somewhat uncomfortable to use. Thirdly, the students constructed the app as a threat to their sense of themselves as 'good' academic subjects. Many students saw the app as going against their academic sensibilities, seeing it as an unprofessional and distracting device.

Unfitting: interactives apps as unsuitable for a lecture context

A key pedagogical rationale for our introduction of the interactive app within lectures was to engender a shift from passive to (inter)active learning. Our motivation to introduce technology is consistent with a compelling amount of educational technology iterature that highlights the potential of educational technologies for supporting social- and cognitive- constructivist learning (Jonassen & Reeves, 1996; Oliver, 2002; Woo & Reeves, 2007). While we positioned the use of the online space as offering a new and beneficial learning approach, many students were less convinced, appearing to favour a traditional lecture approach. As Covill (2011, p. 98) warns, educators' assumptions about learning in lectures may not match student experiences:

> Professors who advise students that they are going to switch to a method that will increase students' engagement and deepen their learning is likely to be met with confusion by students who already believe they are getting these benefits from traditional lectures

Consistent with Covill's (2011) study, many of the students also responded with discomfort and resistance to the interactive app in the lectures. Here, the students saw the lecture as an "island of meaning" (Zerubavel, 1997, p. 11). The lecture was a concept dominantly understood as having a distinctive cultural value and meaning that was not going to be easily changed. For example, several students discussed what they wanted out of lectures:

> In the lectures I want to get knowledge. It's information for my assignments that I want. In the seminars we can then talk about it, but in the lectures I want to just be told what I need to know. [Focus Group 1]

> In the lectures I just want more information about the subject. But I hope to gain more in-depth knowledge from the seminars so I can speak to the tutor about anything I am concerned about. It is different from the lecture, I just want to get, like, the new information [in the lecture] [Focus Group 2]

In another group, the students rallied around one particular comment about how the app interfered with the traditional notion of the lecture:

> I don't prefer using the app in the lectures. I prefer being told things instead of you doing it yourself. [Focus Group 5]

To this comment, her peers responded enthusiastically:

> Yeah, I do as well.

> Yeah, I prefer someone just speaking at me giving me factual information.
> [Focus Group 5]

Similarly, Focus Group 6 started out their discussion emphasising that they value getting "information from friends" and "group work" [Focus Group 6] in seminars, but quickly shut down the suggestion that the interactive app could help facilitate similar learning situations in lectures. This was not the sort of learning that they ideally wanted for the lecture experience:

> But in lectures It's a hassle isn't it
>
> You only have ten minutes to set up
>
> Yeah, I prefer just old school teaching
>
> [...]
>
> Wouldn't you do [interactive learning] in a seminar, though?
>
> Yeah, it's better in a seminar than a lecture.
>
> It's just better. [Focus Group 6]

Here, it appears that many students believe that they may learn well through interactive tasks involving active knowledge construction but are nonetheless reluctant to redefine their learning role within lectures. It is ironic that these students reported using technology as a hassle, given the extent to which students can go out of their way to use their mobile phones for social purposes during class time (Wallace, 2011). Nonetheless, the theme of technology getting in the way of their idealised view of the lecture was sustained in multiple focus groups.

We contend that there is a broad *socio-cultural* factor at play in this scenario. The concept of the lecture is a longstanding "island of meaning" (Zerubavel, 1997, p. 11) that is well sedimented in academic and cultural discourse (Brown & Race, 2014; Di Leonardi, 2007; Wilson & Korn, 2007). The lecture is not only a pedagogical activity, then, but also a cultural one. It is something students *anticipate*, and that often induces thrill in students who have looked forward to the experience of this 'grown up learning' for several years prior to making it to university. Sitting in a lecture receiving information from the 'sage on the stage' is an image that exists in popular culture and remains dominant across educational institutions (Covill, 2011). It also exists as an image of prestige designed to lure students on university prospectuses and websites (Drew, 2013). Thus, introducing the interactive app in a way that subverts this image was met with resistance from students who can see cultural as well as pedagogical value in the didactic lecture.

Given the continued dominance of this traditional construction of the lecture across courses at universities, a lone course in which an interactive app is introduced to disrupt this model may do little to subvert the dominant model (Gikas & Grant, 2013). Again following Covill (2011, p. 98), we see that:

> ...it would be highly difficult for a professor to sustain an active approach in an institution where the lecture method prevails. Imagine trying to convince students that a particular teaching method is superior when all of the other professors that these students have appear to be contentedly using an "inferior" method. To be working against the predominant culture, is not realistic.

Furthermore, the notion that listening to an educator lecture while students take notes is not necessarily perceived by students to be passive per se (Covill, 2011; Wilson & Korn, 2007). Indeed, students could be very active sorting, organising and classifying *in their minds* without necessarily needing to physically interact with their environments. This approach is highlighted, for example, in the literature on multimedia design, which emphasises the role of lecture slides in signalling, directing and segmenting information in order to support lecture participants' active internalisation of data (Mayer, 2009; Moreno & Mayer, 2007). In other words, these Piagetian *lone scientist* students appeared to find non-interactive lecture presentations valuable for developing their mental schemata, and were uncomfortable with their lecturer unsettling this through the introduction of the interactive app.

Furthermore, there is a challenge in using educational technologies to build upon or supplement a traditional approach. We focused in this study on how to integrate an app into a traditional on-campus course structure. Here, we provided a lecture *with* an educational app. As others have argued (Pedro et al., 2018) there is a risk here in assuming that a technology can be augmented into a traditional classroom in a way that does not disturb its overall ecosystem. Perhaps, there is a need to approach app integration in a way that does not merely supplement traditional education, but rather develops an educational ecosystem in which the app is integral to how learning takes place. As Author 1 has argued elsewhere (2017), the placement of technologies in supplemental roles creates a situation in which educators and students use technologies for augmenting traditional learning, rather than wholesale re-considering how learning might take place. This is, indeed, all the more relevant given that the very app that we selected for this study – Collaborate Ultra – is designed primarily for lectures to take place remotely, not in-person.

Thus, successful integration of educational technologies is significantly more difficult than simply introducing opportunities for (inter)active mobile learning. We contend that educational technologists and educators must acknowledge that a challenge for introducing educational technologies exists within cultural discourse itself (Chan et al., 2015; Covill, 2011). Solitary attempts to introduce an interactive app and reconstruct the pedagogical concept embedded in the notion of 'the lecture' ignore the fact that there exist pre-conceived ideas and legitimate student desires about what *should* be involved in a lecture, and what students *want* to be taking place during this time. Students, therefore, tended to construct the interactive app as *unfitting* for their idealised notions of the lecture, and rejected it on those grounds.

Uncomfortable: the interactive app as a risk to social status

A second salient theme that emerged out of the interviews was students' constructions of the app as being *uncomfortable*. Students had social anxieties about having their questions and responses publicly visible to peers. Many therefore resisted using the technologies out of a fear of having their responses scrutinised by both lecturer and peers. In social media studies, the user who is reluctant to make their presence visible is labelled the 'lurker' (Dennen, 2008; Preece, Nonnecke, & Andrews, 2004). A lurker might browse through the social media space, but resists contributing due to factors including shyness, desire for privacy, fear of aggressive respondents, and lack of interest (Preece et al., 2004). Similarly, in our study, students consistently highlighted the social risks of posting. This discussion emerged in all eight focus group interviews.

We argue that what was emergent during these discussions was students' concerns about what Brekhus (2007, 1998) labels 'marked' and 'unmarked' subjectivities. A marked subjectivity is one that is set apart, and therefore made more conspicuous than safer, and privileged, unmarked subjectivities. Following Brekhus, students saw the educational technology users as being marked subjects. They became members of the cohort who stood out as being *different* and *abnormal*. This difference was widely seen as an undesirable trait because it carried with it certain social risks:

> You feel like you are on your own when you are told to get on [the app ...]. Also, when people answer the name comes up [on the lecture screen] and they don't want to be wrong. I feel like some people don't want their name put up there so it wouldn't matter what they say [Focus Group 8]

> People laugh at you if you do the activities where you write on the screen. [Focus Group 7]

Similarly, Focus Group 8 discussed what they saw to be jostling to appear 'cool' and 'aloof' taking place within the lecture theatre:

> You know when you are in school and you have the cool kids and then they take the mick out of other people? Whatever workplace you are at you have people that are really popular and people that are not in most schools and whatever...

> ...Like, some think they are too cool to use the app...

> ...Yeah. To do it is like something the geeks want to do, and things like that [Focus Group 8]

Focus Group 1 corroborated these claims:

> You know you're not the only person doing it. Like, I hate being the first person to like answer one of the questions, because...

> ...Oh nah I don't like that...

> ...It's like, oh she's a nerd. [Focus Group 1]

Avoiding using the interactive app altogether, or being a silent technology 'lurker', is therefore seen as a socially safe activity. Returning to Brekhus, we can see here that "the 'marked' holds far more social weight than the 'unmarked' in identity attribution" (Brekhus, Brunsma, Platts, & Dua, 2010, pp. 64–65). Here, then, there are high-stakes consequences for using the app. Socially, students may find themselves as losing – or failing to gain – social capital as a result of being marked as 'losers', 'wrong' or 'nerds'. Loss of social capital impacts not only students' sense of their ability to interact with peers in social and academic settings, but also indicates the possibility that they might miss future opportunities for further building valuable social capital amongst academic equals if they become marked.

Thus, remaining unmarked enables students to preserve their social capital. Unmarked students can learn under the radar and exist within the larger cohort without being noticed or pointed out as abnormal. There are certain privileges that extend from this normativity – the privilege of moving through the lecture space without being singled out and the privilege of being able to learn without scrutiny. Students who occupy a normative and therefore 'unmarked' learner subjectivity when avoiding the app use garner access to these privileges, and this provides social incentive to avoid the interactive app in the lecture theatre.

This construction of the interactive app as being an 'uncomfotable' tool that positions students as 'vulnerable' challenges the idea that technology use is an activity that youths naturally gravitate towards (Prensky, 2001; Selwyn, 2012). While being on social networking is an almost compulsory element of mainstream western youth culture in the twenty-first century, social networking is usually a youth-led practice that takes place for social rather than educational reasons (Boyd, 2014; Pachler, Seipold, & Bachmair, 2012). By contrast, our educational technology intervention was teacher-led, and not on the students' terms. Secondly, even in youth-led social networking spaces, it is now widely recognised that youths are heavily involved in risk management, inasmuch as their social media posts are carefully curated to project a particular self-image (Boyd, 2014; Davis & Gardner, 2013). In creating an academic online space, we inadvertently created a social space that students constructed as *uncomfortable* and *risky*, which significantly influenced students' choices to reject the interactive app.

Unacademic: the interactive app as a disruption of students' sense of themselves as 'good' students

A significant amount of literature on mobile learning highlights that mobile phones can be seen as a distraction from learning (Liu, Li, & Carlsson, 2010; Gikas & Grant, 2013; Kuznekoff & Titsworth, 2013; Thomas & O'Bannon, 2013; Pedro et al., 2018). There is an assumption from many educators that mobile phones in class interrupt learning, creating student hesitance to be seen on the devices (Kuznekoff & Titsworth, 2013). Similarly, many students have highlighted how they can find mobile phones a distraction, particularly when push notifications appear on screen. Furthermore, the ability for the devices to emit loud noises such as the ringing from incoming calls and screen brightness means they have the capacity to distract not only the phone user, but surrounding students as well (Thomas & O'Bannon, 2013). While there appears to be some evidence that proficient students can multitask while using the devices (Kuznekoff & Titsworth, 2013), there nonetheless remains an undercurrent of resistance to mobile phones for learning within university discourse.

It is no surprise, then, that several students also saw the use of interactive apps as contravening their sense of themselves as 'good' academically inclined learners. Building upon the students' constructions of 'ideal' lectures as didactic learning experiences, several students discussed that the use of mobile phones was not the 'right' way for them to behave in lectures and seminars. Several students, for example, discussed how the right way to behave was instead to dedicate focus upon the lecturer's presentation:

> So, I always get side tracked if I'm doing something else so if I focus on [the lecturer] then I won't, like, I'll do the right thing [Focus Group 3]
>
> I won't concentrate on my work if I'm busy doing the activities. [Focus Group 7]
>
> If I'm on the phone I'm worried [the lecturer] will think I'm not paying attention and doing the wrong thing [Focus Group 8]
>
> People usually hide their phones under the desk. It's weird just having it out for the lecturer to see [Focus Group 3]

Kasworm (2005) argues that the ideal academically inclined student image tends to be linked to notions of being serious, committed, purposeful, and attentive. These ideals are reinforced through education institutions' cultures; cultures that often continue to actively work to *dissuade* students from using mobile technologies in classrooms (Liu et al., 2010). Idealised notions of the 'committed' and 'attentive' student could indeed conflict with perceptions that phones are a distraction and procrastination tool. Indeed, the above quotes show how some students in this study continued to see mobile technologies as unacademic, even when the interactive apps were encouraged by the lecturer.

Furthermore, academically inclined students can indeed be very active and busy during lectures *before* interactive apps are introduced. With a lecturer talking at the front of class, students often feel compelled to 'keep up' by both note taking and actively listening (Boyle, 2011). Indeed, scholars from information processing theories (Mayer, 2009; Moreno & Mayer, 2007) tend to highlight the ways in which lecture slides, lecturer speech and note taking combined can lead to cognitive overload and the subsequent forgetting of key information. Introducing an interactive app could *add to* the information being provided (Pedro et al., 2018) and therefore *interrupt* a student's note taking – which they may find more important (Boyle, 2011; Di Leonardi, 2007). Here, whereas we valued in-time participation in a learning activity, the students may have valued record keeping more highly, so that they could engage in study at a later date.

We are not implying that the phones are necessarily negative for learning, or indeed necessarily a distraction for students. Instead, we are highlighting how they have the capacity to be *constructed* (Brekhus et al., 2010; Zerubavel, 1997) by both students and educators as unacademic devices, which can feed into students' hesitance to embrace them in lectures. Even when students are encouraged to use interactive apps on mobile devices, they can continue to treat them with caution. The apps could either be seen as a potential 'lure' away from learning, an added degree of work on top of the work they already do during a lecture, or indeed a device seen to be used by people less interested in being academically inclined students.

Conclusions

We see interactive mobile apps not as *causing* change across a cohort; instead, we see the students *constructing* the educational technologies in complex ways in relation to their own desires, anxieties and contexts (Oliver, 2013). Given the opportunity to interact with an interactive mobile app in lectures, a plurality of our students resisted for many complex reasons beyond the mere technological affordances or use values they saw in the technologies. In this study, many students remained very concerned about diverging from the learning identities that they were comfortable with in this sort of space, because it didn't seem *fitting* for a lecture experience, socially *comfortable*, or *academically* appropriate.

We therefore consider the introduction of an interactive mobile app in our lectures for this study to be something of a false start. We came up against resistance that we did not expect, which we found to be very complex and multifaceted. To be sure, we see significant failings in many areas of our implementation. Technologically, the software we settled on turned out to be a drain on students' batteries, and despite several attempts to 'teach' students how to log-on, several students continued to note that they were still unsure how to do so.

However, in this paper, we have focussed on some of the underlying social and cultural aspects of the experience that led students to construct the interactive mobile app as unfitting, uncomfortable and unacademic. Indeed, we believe that students used their *social* and *cultural* perspectives when *choosing* to construct the technological intervention in the ways they did, which leads us to reject a technological determinist approach to educational technologies. By examining the social and cultural dimensions of technology interventions, scholars can open up debate about how and why students construct educational technologies in the ways they do, which may lead to more effective and sensitive uses of technologies for education.

On a closing note, we believe examining the social dimensions of educational technologies also highlights the limitations of the *imposition* of change. In taking up a technological determinist approach, educators can undervalue students' agency to construct educational technologies in ways that are meaningful to their own lived experiences. Perhaps through consulting students, educators can deconstruct what Fielding (2004, p. 295) calls "the presumptions of the present" in order that students and teachers can work together in co-creating meaningful educational technology experiences. As Pedro, Barbados and Santos (Pedro et al., 2018, p. 13) recently argued, there is a need for "a shift from a data-driven use of m-learning to collaborative-driven practices". Thus, we see it fitting to conclude with the students' voice. By co-constructing the meaning of educational technologies with students, we might in the future be able to come to more mutually beneficial teaching and learning arrangements:

> I think he should ask us if we want to do it...
>
> Yeah, before...
>
> I feel like if he asks everybody in the lecture then most people would prefer not to have it. [Focus Group 5]

Authors' contributions

CD was project lead. CD delivered the lectures and was first author on the paper. AD was research assistant. AD developed the interview questions and conducted the interviews. AD was second author on the paper. Both authors read and approved the final manuscript.

Competing interests

The authors declare that they have no competing interests.

References

Attride-Stirling, J. (2001). Thematic networks: an analytic tool for qualitative research. *Qualitative Research, 1*(3), 385–405.

Bijker, W., & Pinch, T. (1984). The social construction of facts and artefacts: or how the sociology of science and the sociology of technology might benefit each other. *Social Studies of Science August, 14*(3), 399–441.

Boyd, D. (2014). *It's complicated.* New Haven: Yale University Press.

Boyle, J. R. (2011). Thinking strategically to record notes in content classes. *American Secondary Education, 40*, 51–66.

Brekhus, W. (1998). A sociology of the unmarked: redirecting our focus. *Sociological Theory, 16*(1), 34–61.

Brekhus, W. (2007). The Rutgers school: a Zerubavelian culturalist cognitive sociology. *European Journal of Social Theory, 10*(3), 448–464.

Brekhus, W., Brunsma, D., Platts, T., & Dua, P. (2010). On the contributions of cognitive sociology to the sociological study of race. *Sociology Compass, 4*(1), 61–76.

Brown, S., & Race, P. (2014). *500 tips for further and continuing education lecturers.* London: Routledge.

Chan, N., Walker, C., & Gleaves, A. (2015). An exploration of students' lived experiences of using smartphones in diverse learning contexts using a hermeneutic phenomenological approach. *Computers & Education, 82*, 96–106.

Chi, M. T. (2009). Active-constructive-interactive: a conceptual framework for differentiating learning activities. *Topics in Cognitive Science, 1*(1), 73–105.

Clarke, V., & Braun, V. (2013). Teaching thematic analysis: overcoming challenges and developing strategies for effective learning. *The Psychologist, 26*(2), 120–123.

Covill, A. E. (2011). College students' perceptions of the traditional lecture method. *College Student Journal, 45*(1), 92–102.

Davis, K., & Gardner, H. (2013). *The app generation: how today's youth navigate identity, intimacy, and imagination in a digital world.* New Haven: Yale University Press.

Dennen, V. P. (2008). Pedagogical lurking: student engagement in non-posting discussion behavior. *Computers in Human Behavior, 24*(4), 1624–1633.

Di Leonardi, B. C. (2007). Tips for facilitating learning: the lecture deserves some respect. *The Journal of Continuing Education in Nursing, 38*(4), 154–161.

Drew, C. (2013). Elitism for sale: promoting the elite school online in the competitive educational marketplace. *Australian Journal of Education., 57*(2), 174–184.

Fielding, M. (2004). Transformative approaches to student voice: theoretical underpinnings, recalcitrant realities. *British Educational Research Journal, 30*(2), 295–311.

Gikas, J., & Grant, M. M. (2013). Mobile computing devices in higher education: student perspectives on learning with cellphones, smartphones & social media. *The Internet and Higher Education, 19*, 18–26.

Jonassen, D. H., & Reeves, T. C. (1996). Learning with technology: using computers as cognitive tools. In D. H. Jonassen (Ed.), *Handbook of research for educational communications and technology*, (pp. 693–719). New York: Macmillan.

Jones, A., & Bissell, C. (2011). The social construction of educational technology through the use of authentic software tools. *Research in Learning Technology, 19*, 285–297.

Kasworm, C. (2005). Adult student identity in an intergenerational community college classroom. *Adult Education Quarterly, 56*(1), 3–20.

Kear, K., Jones, A., Holden, G., & Mark, C. (2016). Social technologies for online learning: theoretical and contextual issues. *Open Learning, 31*(1), 42–53.

Kuznekoff, J., & Titsworth, S. (2013). The impact of mobile phone usage on student learning. *Communication Education, 62*(3), 233–252. https://doi.org/10.1080/03634523.2013.767917.

Liu, Y., Li, H., & Carlsson, C. (2010). Factors driving the adoption of m-learning: an empirical study. *Computers & Education, 55*(3), 1211–1219.

Longhurst, R. (2003). Semi-structured interviews and focus groups. In Clifford, N., Cope, M., Gillespie, T. & French, S. (Eds.), *Key Methods in Geography*, 117–132. London: SAGE.

Mayer, R. (2009). *Multimedia learning*, (2nd ed.,). Cambridge: Cambridge University Press.

Moreno, R., & Mayer, R. (2007). Interactive multimodal learning environments. *Educational Psychology Review, 19*(3), 309–326.

Oliver, M. (2011). Technological determinism in educational technology research: some alternative ways of thinking about the relationship between learning and technology. *Journal of Computer Assisted Learning, 27*(5), 373–384.

Oliver, M. (2013). Learning technology: theorising the tools we study. *British Journal of Educational Technology, 44*(1), 31–43.

Oliver, R. (2002). The role of ICT in higher education for the 21st century: ICT as a change agent. Perth Australia: Edith Cowan University Press.

Pachler, N., Seipold, J., & Bachmair, B. (2012). Mobile learning: some theoretical and practical considerations. In K. Friedrich, M. Ranieri, N. Pachler, & P. Theux (Eds.), *The "My Mobile" handbook. Guidelines and scenarios for mobile learning in adult education*, (pp. 11–16). London: European Union: Lifelong Learning Programme.

Pedro, L., Barbosa, C., & Santos, C. (2018). A critical review of mobile learning integration in formal educational contexts. *International Journal of Educational Technology in Higher Education., 15*(10), 1–15.

Preece, J., Nonnecke, B., & Andrews, D. (2004). The top five reasons for lurking: improving community experiences for everyone. *Computers in Human Behavior, 20*(2), 201–223.

Prensky, M. (2001). Digital natives, digital immigrants part 1. *On the Horizon, 9*(5), 1–6.

Selwyn, N. (2012). Making sense of young people, education and digital technology: the role of sociological theory. *Oxford Review of Education, 38*(1), 81–96.

Selwyn, N., & Facer, K. (2014). The sociology of education and digital technology: past, present and future. *Oxford Review of Education, 40*(4), 482–496.

Smith, E. (2016). "A real double-edged sword:" undergraduate perceptions of social media in their learning. *Computers & Education, 103*, 44–58.

Sung, Y., Chang, K., & Liu, T. (2016). The effects of integrating mobile devices with teaching and learning on students' learning performance: a meta-analysis and research synthesis. *Computers & Education, 94*, 252–275.

Thomas, K., & O'Bannon, B. (2013). Cell phones in the classroom: preservice teachers' perceptions. *Journal of Digital Learning in Teacher Education, 30*(1), 11–20.

Vaismoradi, M., Jones, J., Turunen, H., & Snelgrove, S. (2016). Theme development in qualitative content analysis and thematic analysis. *Journal of Nursing Education and Practice*, *6*(5), 100.

Wallace, P. (2011). M-learning: promises, perils, and challenges for k-12 education. *New Horizons Online Journal* http://archive.education.jhu.edu/PD/newhorizons/Journals/Winter2011/Wallace. Accessed 24 Aug 2018.

Webster, A. (2013). Digital technology and sociological windows. In N. Prior, & K. Orton-Johnson (Eds.), *Digital sociology*, (pp. 227–233). Basingstoke: Palgrave.

Wilson, K., & Korn, J. H. (2007). Attention during lectures: beyond ten minutes. *Teaching of Psychology*, *34*(2), 85–89.

Woo, Y., & Reeves, T. C. (2007). Meaningful interaction in web-based learning: a social constructivist interpretation. *The Internet and Higher Education*, *10*(1), 15–25.

Wu, W. H., Wu, Y. C. J., Chen, C. Y., Kao, H. Y., Lin, C. H., & Huang, S. H. (2012). Review of trends from mobile learning studies: A meta-analysis. *Computers & Education*, *59*(2), 817–827.

Zerubavel, E. (1997). *Social mindscapes: an invitation to cognitive sociology*. Cambridge: Harvard University Press.

10

Using comparative judgement and online technologies in the assessment and measurement of creative performance and capability

Pina Tarricone and C. Paul Newhouse*

* Correspondence:
p.newhouse@ecu.edu.au
Centre for Schooling and Learning Technologies (CSaLT), School of Education, Edith Cowan University, 2 Bradford St, Mount Lawley, 6050 Western, Australia

Abstract

In this paper we argue that comparative judgement delivered by online technologies is a viable, valid and highly reliable alternative to traditional analytical marking. In the past, comparative judgement has been underused in educational assessment and measurement, particularly in large-scale testing, mainly due to the lack of supporting technologies to facilitate the large number of judgements and judges. We describe the foundations of comparative judgement and dispel many of the old issues regarding its use in regards to time, cost and training for large-scale assessment. Studies in the use of comparative judgement and online technologies for the assessment and measurement of practical performance conducted by Edith Cowan University provide a context for further promoting its use in educational testing.

Keywords: Comparative judgement, Paired comparison, Pairwise comparison, Online assessment, Creative performance, Relative judgements, Absolute judgements

Background

Assessment is influenced by numerous factors including the teacher's expertise in the design and application of a measurement instrument, such as a test, and their judgement of student performance. Inferences and judgements are made about a student's learning development based on the evidence provided by a student's performance; and judgement making uses evidence in comparison to a standard, or another performance (e.g. by another student). Performance evidence, its quality, and judgements made are crucial to reliable assessment and have formed the problem of our research. In this paper we argue for the increased use of comparative judgement in the assessment of performance, particularly where creative expression is an integral component of that performance. Initially the concept of comparative judgement is defined and explained, then a range of literature is used to provide a rationale for its application to assessment, the important role of digital technologies is explained, and finally our own research journey over the past decade in the Centre for Schooling and Learning Technologies (CSaLT) is used to illustrate the potential.

Comparative judgement

The fundamental principle of measurement involves comparison, whether between two objects or performances or between a performance and a theoretical standard (e.g. marking criteria). Comparison provides the basis upon which measurement instruments are developed. Measurement instruments, assessment tasks, are deliberately designed and developed to measure ability and to classify performance relative to another performance. Essential to measurement is the construction of the task and its categories, which are used to compare, classify and identify ability through performance in relation to a well-defined outcome space (Humphry & Heldsinger, 2007; Wilson, 2005). Therefore, the basis of measurement is comparison, based on a specific outcome space and developed criteria that identify what performance outcomes are being measured and the categories of the performance (Andrich, 1988; Rasch, 1961; Wilson, 2005).

Comparative judgement, comparative pairs, pairwise comparison or paired comparison are terms that are used to describe a measurement method, which involves making inferences based on specific task criteria about one student's performance compared with another's, in contrast to comparison with a theoretical standard in analytical methods. This means that through comparison, items, objects or performances are measured with reference to another item, object or performance (Andrich, 1988; Rasch, 1961; Thurstone, 1927). Arguably comparative judgement began when Fechner (1860) first introduced the psychophysical method which involved ranking objects of physical magnitude; this method was later investigated and extended by Thurstone (1927, 1954). Comparative judgement was originally used for the pairing of psychophysical stimuli, such as weight, height and for measuring values and attitudes (Andrich, 1988; Bramley et al. 1998; Fechner, 1860; Jones & Alcock, 2014; Jones et al. 2015; Thurstone, 1927, 1954). The original conception of comparative judgement was that repeated comparisons of pairs of items, objects or performance used for an immediate perception with minimal cognitive processing. A comparison for quality takes more time than a comparison for magnitude. An example of an early study applying comparison for quality was by Bradley and Terry (1952), who investigated the feasibility of using comparative judgement to determine the quality of pork meat. Inferences of quality are made based on the criteria and this informs the estimation of the scale location. The process and outcome of the comparison involves estimating or inferring the scale location of the performances/instances, not based on the origin being relative to an absolute zero (Bond & Fox, 2001; Humphry & Heldsinger, 2007).

Measurement of ability (i.e. latent trait) from performance relies upon comparison to infer thresholds and form an interval scale (Andrich, 1988; Andrich & Luo, 2003). Thresholds, classifications or intervals on the latent-trait continuum represent a range of abilities. But differences in ability are not necessarily equal, and therefore the thresholds or intervals on the continuum cannot be proportioned equally. The location of a student's ability on the continuum is inferred by the judgment of their performance on a task or tasks in a specific knowledge domain. A foundation of the latent-trait continuum is that learning is cumulative and prior knowledge becomes the basis for the development of new knowledge and understandings (Humphry & Heldsinger, 2007). Inference and subsequent probabilistic mapping of ability and growth on a continuum, or 'underlying growth continua,' is fundamental to the Rasch (1980) latent-trait theory (Andrich, 1988). Andrich (1988) argued that "ability is a latent trait, whereas performances are the observable manifestations of ability ... in making observations that reflect properties, the actual properties are abstractions based on the patterns of observations" (p. 14). Based on Andrich's conception, the latent nature of ability means that comparisons cannot be deterministic, but are probabilistic.

Deterministic classifications involve comparisons that are determined with certainty (Andrich, 1988). However, comparisons cannot be deterministic if they are measuring ability because it is difficult to determine with certainty the classification of abilities as they are not necessarily fully observable. Therefore, the comparisons are probabilistic; meaning that the outcomes of the comparisons are based on frequency, or some likelihood and qualitative judgment. In addition, invariance of classification is essential to measurement in a two-way frame of reference, such as in comparative judgement (Andrich, 1988). The Guttman structure provides a two-way observational frame of reference where comparisons are made between two items, objects or performances in a process of classification (Andrich, 1988; Bond & Fox, 2001; Humphry & Heldsinger, 2007). The outcomes of such comparisons are labelled dichotomous as they involve two outcomes represented by the integers of 0 or 1. Student work samples are compared to each other in this two-way frame of reference to identify which has achieved the criteria of the assessment at a higher or lower level. Therefore, comparison is used to determine whether each work sample is better (1) or worse (0) than another work sample. Hence, the ordering or comparison process is not deterministic but is probabilistic (Humphry & Heldsinger, 2007).

Referring to Thurstone's work on comparative judgements, Pollitt (2012a), who we understand initially collaborated with Andrich in the 1970's, argued that comparisons can be made with any kind of object including educational performances. Essentially, assessors' holistic judgements provide a shared contribution to the development of a measurement interval scale. The scale represents the outcomes of the assessors' cumulative comparative judgments of the quality of the psychometric latent trait being measured (Bramley, 2007; Pollitt, 2012a).

Relative and absolute judgements

"There is no absolute judgment. All judgments are comparisons of one thing with another" (Laming, 2004, p. 9). Absolute and relative judgements are terms that have been used to describe analytical and comparative judgement assessment methods respectively. Absolute judgements, analytical traditional marking/scoring, refers to the allocation of marks/score points or a grade (Gill & Bramley, 2013; Pollitt, 2012a). It has been contended by researchers that relative, comparative judgements are highly reliable, more so than absolute, analytical judgements (see Jones & Alcock, 2012, 2014; Laming, 2004; Pollitt, 2012b). Jones and Alcock (2012) argued that "people are far more reliable when comparing one thing with another than when making absolute judgements" (p. 64). Pollitt has also consistently supported the argument that comparative judgements, specifically adaptive comparative judgements, can generate "extremely reliable scores, far higher than traditional marking" with little training (Pollitt, 2012a, p. 168). For example, a study investigating absolute and relative judgements and standard-setting by Gill and Bramley (2013) considered the accuracy of holistic comparative judgements in relation to the original analytical marks of examination scripts that were 'close together in overall mark' in a standard-setting exercise. The assessors made absolute (mark/grade of each script), relative (script quality compared to another script) and confidence judgements (how confident they were of their judgements). Gill and Bramley found that in the standard setting/awarding process, the assessors made more accurate relative judgements than absolute judgements, and that the judgements that were described by the judges as 'very confident' had higher accuracy than other judgements.

Heldsinger and Humphry (2013) identified some advantages of analytical marking including that the use of criterion marking rubrics provide specific information for assessors reducing subjectivity. Their review of the literature also suggested that there have been arguments highlighting concerns regarding the "assumption that using rubrics increases inter-rater reliability and validity, and the overall accuracy and quality of assessment" (p. 221). Finally, they concluded that assessors may mark leniently, harshly, to a different standard to others, and may value quality differently leading to a need for a substantial amount of time allocated to training and moderation. And Pollitt (2012a) argued that "a marker may award the same average mark, yet discriminate more finely amongst the objects, in effect being more generous to the better ones and more severe to the poorer—or vice versa" (p. 168). Therefore, one major downside of absolute, analytical marking is that ensuring reliability is challenging and costly to monitor. Whereas, relative judgements can be constantly monitored as they are made, and decisions can be made if additional judges or judgements are needed to increase reliability. Overall, there is agreement amongst researchers in the field with Jones and Alcock's (2012) argument "that people are far more reliable when comparing one thing with another than when making absolute judgements" (p. 64). Comparative judgement ensures that individual judge severity is overcome because the judgement process is focused on the 'relative merit' of each performance and not the individual judge's standard (Bramley, 2007, p. 265; Pollitt, 2012a). Also, if judges are making different quality discrimination decisions, the process of comparative judgment, after multiple rounds of judgements, can accurately rank performance quality (Pollitt, 2012a).

One of the main reasons for high reliability of relative comparative judgements compared to absolute analytical judgements is that, relative judgements require larger numbers of judges. Absolute analytical marking uses just one or two markers whereas comparative judgement requires more than two judges, e.g. ten judges (Pollitt, 2012a). For example, Pollitt (2012b) refers to his work with Richard Kimbell on the e-scape study of the assessment of e-portfolios as an example of the high reliability coefficients that can be achieved with digital assessment and the comparative judgement method. Pollitt posited that in Kimbell et al.'s (2009) study the high reliability coefficient of 0.96 generated by 28 judges assessing 352 e-portfolios with 3067 judgements was higher than any analytical marking system could achieve. Studies by Heldsinger and Humphry (2010), (2013) found that highly reliable comparative judgements of writing scripts by a large number of judges were made using calibrated exemplars as referents, as suggested by Thurstone (1928). They argued that comparative judgement, using calibrated exemplars, were successfully used as a highly reliable method to validate results from large-scale testing programs without the extensive assessor training and moderation processes that were required for absolute analytical judgements. In their 2010 study they found a high level of internal consistency of the teacher judgements and that the comparative judgements were highly correlated with the results of analytical marking from an Australian large-scale test for the same students, providing evidence of concurrent validity. These researchers were motivated by concerns about the accuracy of teacher judgements, the quality of information, including very little diagnostic information, provided by standardized testing. They found that complex rubrics used for analytical marking required extensive training, whereas, comparative judgement required little training. So they found that the assessors' judgements of writing performance were highly internally consistent and highly reliable, considering that initially the teachers were concerned about making judgements across ability ranges with which they were not familiar. In a follow-up study Heldsinger and Humphry (2013) used calibrated writing exemplars as the referents for comparative judgements of scripts to assess student writing performance. The analysis showed a very high reliability and internal consistency.

Several researchers have found that judgements based on quality, using specified holistic criteria, resulted in a more valid assessment of performance (Bramley, 2007; Heldsinger & Humphry, 2010; Pollitt, 2012a). According to Pollitt (2012a) the high reliability of comparative judgement is a "consequence of the constant focus on validity" (p. 168) and this "demands and checks that a sufficient consensus exists amongst the pool of judges involved" (p. 167). Comparative judgements are independent and additional judgements increase reliability (Bramley et al., 1998; Pollitt, 2012a). Thus, judge bias and misfitting scripts can be easily identified during the judgement process, and reliability can be improved by increasing the number of judges and/or the number of judgements (Bramley, 2007). Additional judgements of work at grade cut-offs can help to improve and consolidate the ranking of works and improve reliability (Pollitt, 2012a). However, Bramley (2007) has argued that it is 'implausible' that each comparison is independent as the judges would remember particular scripts. We believe that it may be the case if the comparative judgements were being conducted with a small number of hard copy scripts or performances but it would be unlikely with large numbers of scripts and judgements being made when using online software systems, because judges may not encounter individual scripts in subsequent comparisons.

Time, cost, training and large-scale testing

Researchers have identified several limitations of comparative judgement. One is the time that it takes to make the large number of judgements and the number of judges required to reach the high levels of reliability that can be achieved with comparative judgement (Bramley et al., 1998; Heldsinger & Humphry, 2013; Jones & Alcock, 2014). Heldsinger and Humphry (2013) explained that although comparative judgement was an efficient assessment method complex scripts required additional time to complete the number of judgements needed for reliability. Bramley (2007) used the term psychological validity to describe the additional cognitive requirements to make valid and reliable judgements of complex performances, such as scripts, because of the amount of time taken to make the judgement. Bramley's psychological validity may have some connection with what Thurstone (1927, 1954) described as the "discriminal process" (p. 48). According to Thurstone during comparative judgement the discriminal process encompasses the different reactions to each work sample, item or task as it is being compared to the next work sample, item or task. Thus the discriminal process leads to the comparative judgement and affects the time taken.

The issue of time in making comparative judgements was highlighted in a study by McMahon and Jones (2014), who investigated the use of comparative judgement in the assessment of a secondary school chemistry experiment. The researchers found that the comparative judgement was highly reliable, consistent across judges and the judgements correlated with the analytical marking testing data. The study involved 154 test scripts and five teachers from a secondary school in Ireland. Altogether they made 1550 judgements using the 'No More Marking' online system. All of the scripts were also analytically marked by two of the five teachers. The researchers found that the comparative judgements totalled approximately 14 h (3 h per judge) and the analytical marking totalled approximately 3 h to mark all 154 tests. The two teachers who analytically marked the tests reported that they each took one and a half hours to mark the tests without providing feedback. The estimated reported marking time seems short for the number of scripts that were marked. Although the comparative judgements were more time consuming than the analytical marking, McMahon and Jones acknowledged that other studies, including our own, have shown otherwise (see Jones et al., 2015; Kimbell, 2012; Newhouse, 2011). Our review of the test instrument revealed that a possible reason for this time discrepancy, not identified by the authors, was that it was not conducive to making holistic judgements. Most of the questions required students to list responses rather than provide a descriptive response. These questions required the judge to assess each individual response rather than to make a holistic judgement of the script.

Another time and cost issue is assessor training. Several researchers have found that assessors needed little training in the use of comparative judgement systems and the process, including those in which judges had not had specific assessor training (see Heldsinger & Humphry, 2013; McMahon & Jones, 2014; Pollitt, 2012a). Training generally involves understanding the holistic performance criteria and assessors gaining an understanding of the quality of the evidence presented in a range of work samples (Kimbell et al., 2009). For example, in one study Heldsinger and Humphry (2010) found that training for comparative judgements took approximately half an hour, whereas, analytical marking rubric training needed a full day. In terms of judgement making, Heldsinger and Humphry (2013) found that with little training assessors using calibrated exemplars were able to efficiently judge 29 writing performances, one every three minutes, in one and half hours. Although they specifically did not refer to the lower cost of comparative judgement they did consistently argue the efficiency of the method, in terms of training and judgement making, in contrast to traditional, analytical marking. Pollitt (2012b) has consistently argued that comparative judgment can be conducted at a comparable or lower cost to analytical, traditional marking and that comparative judgement provides consistently high reliability. Jones and Alcock (2014) asserted that the larger number of judges in comparative judgement can be more costly than analytical marking, but this is offset by the greater reliability in the comparative judgment process.

Use of technology and comparative judgement

It has been noted by Heldsinger and Humphry (2013) that until recently there has been little use of comparative judgement methods for educational purposes, probably because it has been considered time consuming, tedious and laborious (see Bramley et al., 1998). The recent increase in the use of comparative judgment may be largely due to the availability and use of online software systems, using digitised student works, by small groups of researchers in the UK and in Western Australia. These online systems, such as the Adaptive Comparative Judgement System (ACJS) (Pollitt, 2012b) and the Pair-Wise Web Software

(Humphry et al. 2013–2015), are based on Thurstone's (1927) law of comparative judgement and have dealt with many of the issues, that in the past inhibited the use of comparative judgement in assessment (Jones & Alcock, 2012; Pollitt, 2012a). These online systems provide a platform for making comparative judgements of digitised works such as scripts, recorded performances and portfolios.

The recent use of these digital comparative judgment systems have been for standard setting (Bramley, 2007; Bramley et al., 1998; Gill & Bramley, 2013), moderation and marking of scripts and portfolios in areas such as writing (Heldsinger & Humphry, 2010, 2013; Pollitt, 2012b), mathematical problem solving (Jones et al., 2015), science (McMahon & Jones, 2014), design and visual arts (Newhouse & Tarricone, 2014), design and technology e-portfolio assessment (Kimbell et al., 2009), scientific and technology enquiry e-portfolio assessment (Davies et al. 2012), oral language assessment (Newhouse, 2011; Pollitt & Murray, 1996), and peer assessment (Jones & Alcock, 2012, 2014; Seery et al. 2012). These studies have provided evidence of the efficacy in using digital assessment systems for relative comparative judgement. Many researchers have also investigated the effectiveness of, and correlation between, absolute analytical marking and relative comparative judgements. For example, research by Jones, Swan and Pollitt (2015) investigated the use of comparative judgement, as an alternative to analytical criterion marking methods, to assess constructs such as mathematical problem solving, that can be somewhat difficult to capture and describe in analytical marking criteria. Their research involved two studies and two groups of mathematics education experts in the UK (Group 1 $N = 12$, Group 2 $N = 11$). The first study investigated the suitability of comparative judgements to assess the General Certificate of Secondary Education (GCSE) final examinations in the UK to determine whether comparative judgement could replicate the analytical marking using specific criteria. In the first study, Group 1 completed 151 judgements in 105 min, and Group 2 completed 150 judgements in 100 min, and showed that comparative judgement could be used to assess the GCSE. The second study used comparative judgement to assess mathematical problem solving skills, using 18 scripts from three tasks. The judgements were correlated with scripts' grades to determine the validity and reliability of comparative judgements as a measure to assess summative examinations and problem solving in mathematics. The groups of assessors, in both studies, produced ranked measurement scales with high reliability.

The CSaLT journey to comparative judgements

The Centre for Schooling and Learning Technologies (CSaLT) was formed in 2003 at Edith Cowan University, Perth Western Australia, with a mission to conduct research into, and promote the use of, digital technologies to improve schooling. The premise was that technologies could be used for teaching, learning and assessment (Newhouse, 2010). Increasingly, research in the Centre has found that the technologies were readily available in educational institutions but seriously underused especially in high-stakes assessment. In response to this situation, researchers in CSaLT decided to partner with the Western Australian curriculum and examination authority in testing the use of digital technologies in high stakes assessments for tertiary entrance. This decision resulted in three major studies from 2006 to 2014. Detailed descriptions of the methodologies and results have been previously reported (e.g., Newhouse, 2011; Newhouse & Tarricone, 2014).

The first study, from August 2006 to December 2007, was funded by a University collaborative research grant, and involved collaboration between CSaLT and the School Curriculum and Standards Authority (Newhouse, 2010). The researchers sought to investigate using digital technologies to support alternative forms of external assessment of student performance in tertiary entrance courses that included a major practical component (Newhouse, 2008). The focus of this study was the use of digital technologies to 'capture' and score performance on practical tasks in an engineering and an applied IT course. The study involved 13 small teacher-class case studies. During this study Professor Richard Kimbell from London University was a visiting scholar at the centre; he introduced the e-scape project, assessing complex practical performance using evidence collected in digital forms, and the use of comparative judgements for generating scores (Kimbell, 2012). As a result one of the outcomes of this study was the successful application of a comparative judgements method of scoring to the assessment of digital posters created by students under exam conditions. To facilitate this an online database tool was custom-designed using Filemaker Pro to allow judges to view pairs of student work and enter their judgements. On completion of all judgements, the researchers exported and analysed the data using RUMMcc software.

The first study was then used as a pilot for a more extensive three-year study investigating the feasibility of using digital representations of work for authentic and reliable performance assessment in foreign language, engineering, information technology, and physical education tertiary entrance courses (Newhouse, 2011). The study was funded by an Australian Research Council Linkage grant, with the local curriculum authority as the partner again, and also involved collaboration with researchers in the British e-scape project (Kimbell et al. 2007). For each course, digital forms of assessment were devised to improve on the standard form of assessment used at the time, with the evidence (e.g. student work, recording of performance) stored in digital files within online systems. Assessors accessed these files using online scoring tools to facilitate analytical marking and comparative judgement. By the second year of the study a commercial system had been developed by TAG Learning for the e-scape project (eventually known as ACJS), so this system was used for comparative judgements. It not only displayed the assessment evidence and captured assessor judgements, it also included the Rasch mathematical calculations to progressively provide scores and reliability statistics. As a result, assessors no longer had to make a set number of judgements before completing the exercise; completion was determined by reaching a required level of reliability.

Rasch measurement was used to analyse all scoring data to determine reliability coefficients and related statistics. The comparative judgement method, for all four courses, generated highly reliable sets of scores, with Cronbach's Alpha and Separation Index coefficients exceeding 0.9. For all four courses the comparative judgment method showed higher levels of reliability than analytical marking, but the comparative judgement scores and rankings were typically moderately to highly correlated with the scores from traditional analytical marking (Newhouse, 2011). Issues related to the time taken to complete comparative judgments when compared with analytical marking, were mainly related to file size, download time and the amount of text and pages of the digital evidence, rather than the time it took to make the comparative judgment. Overall, the study demonstrated the feasibility of using Rasch measurement with analytical marking and comparative judgements for the digital assessment of performance as a reliable and valid alternative to paper-based high-stakes examinations. Ultimately the researchers found that the comparative judgment method of scoring was more reliable than analytical marking.

In the third study, which began in 2011 and was completed in 2014 (Newhouse & Tarricone, 2014) the researchers sought to investigate the efficacy of digitisation for online analytical marking and comparative judgement methods by building on Dillon and Brown's (2006) use of e-portfolios. This study involved three phases; the first two phases investigated the efficacy of digitisation of student practical work and the effectiveness of comparative judgement of portfolios for the purpose of summative assessment in the Visual Arts and Design tertiary entrance courses. Once again the ACJS was used to facilitate the comparative judgements. In the first phase the researchers explored the potential of representing practical work in the two courses, whereas the second phase concerned whether it was feasible for students to create and submit such representations. The third phase focused solely on the online scoring of Visual Arts digital portfolios for the purpose of moderation to ensure consistent standards. The researchers believed that this may be efficiently and effectively accomplished using the approach used in this study to the online scoring of digital portfolios.

In all three phases of the study the researchers demonstrated that the digitised student work could be efficiently and effectively assessed using online marking systems. For both courses, there was low consistency between the assessors for analytical marking, although the combined scores using a Rasch polytomous model exhibited good reliability. For both there was a high level of internal consistency for the results of the comparative judgements. For all three phases and for both Visual Arts and Design, the comparative judgement method generated highly reliable sets of scores, with Cronbach's Alpha and Separation Index coefficients for the first two phases exceeding 0.9. However, in the third phase a reliability coefficient of only 0.88 was achieved, with the most likely explanation being a lack of a consensus understanding of the criteria among some of the Visual Arts teachers who were inexperienced with marking these submissions.

Conclusion

In this paper we have used a range of literature and CSaLT's eight-year research journey to argue that the authenticity, validity and reliability of high-stakes summative assessment may be enhanced through the use of the comparative judgement method of scoring using digital representation of evidence and online tools to facilitate scoring and feedback. The changing requirements of tertiary courses necessitate that students be proficient in using a variety of digital technologies to support their learning. The potential for these technologies to be used for high-stakes assessment is fast becoming a reality, with the added capacity to use comparative judgement for scoring and Rasch modeling to analyse the data. The time is now to embrace digital technologies for high-stakes assessment and consider comparative judgement for scoring as a viable and reliable alternative to analytical marking, particularly for creative performances that rely on highly subjective judgements.

Authors' information

Paul is an Associate Professor at Edith Cowan University in Western Australia where he is the director of the Centre for Schooling and Learning Technologies (CSaLT) in the School of Education. His aim is to improve the opportunities for children to develop their potential through engaging and relevant schooling.

Pina's PhD in educational/cognitive psychology won the 2007 Edith Cowan University Research Medal. Psychology Press published her thesis research as a book titled The Taxonomy of Metacognition. She has a M Ed in Interactive Multimedia. In 2014 she completed a M Ed in Educational Measurement with Honours from the University of Western Australia. Her interests include educational psychology constructs, psychometrics and the use of technologies for assessment.

Acknowledgements

The study discussed in this paper was the work of a research team led by Paul Newhouse and included researchers Jeremy Pagram, Lisa Paris, Mark Hackling, Martin Cooper, Pina Tarricone, Alistair Campbell, Alun Price and many research assistants. The work of everyone in this team, particularly Martin Cooper and Pina Tarricone, and the teachers and students involved, contributed to the research outcomes presented in this paper.

References

Andrich D (1988) Rasch models for measurement. Sage Publications, Newbury Park

Andrich D, Luo G (2003) Conditional pairwise estimation in the Rasch model for ordered response categories using principal components. J Appl Meas 4(3):205–221

Bond, T. G., & Fox, C. M. (2001). *Applying the Rasch model: Fundamental measurement in the human sciences*. Mahwah, N.J. ; London: L. Erlbaum

Bradley RA, Terry ME (1952) Rank analysis of incomplete block designs: I. The method of paired comparisons. Biometrika 39(3/4):324–345

Bramley T (2007) Paired comparison methods. In: Newton P, Baird J-A, Goldstein H, Patrick H, Tymms P (eds) Techniques for monitoring the comparability of examination standards. QCA, London, pp 264–294

Bramley T, Bell JF, Pollitt A (1998) Assessing changes in standards over time using Thurstone paired comparisons. Education Res Perspectives 25(2):1–24

Davies D, Collier C, Howe A (2012) Assessing Scientific and Technological Enquiry Skills at Age 11 using the e-scape System. Int J Technology Design Education 22(2):247–263

Dillon SC, Brown AR (2006) The art of ePortfolios : insights from the creative arts experience. In: Ali J, Kaufman C (eds) Handbook of Research on ePortfolios. Idea Group Reference, Hershey, pp 420–433

Fechner, G. T. (1860). *Elements of psychophysics* (H. E. Adler, Trans. Holt, Rinehart & Winston Eds.)

Gill T, Bramley T (2013) How accurate are examiners' holistic judgements of script quality? *Assessment in Education: Principles*. Policy Practice 20(3):300–324

Heldsinger S, Humphry SM (2010) Using the method of pairwise comparison to obtain reliable teacher assessments. Australian Educational Res 37(2):1–19

Heldsinger S, Humphry SM (2013) Using calibrated exemplars in the teacher-assessment of writing: an empirical study. Educational Res 55(3):219–235

Humphry SM, Heldsinger S (2007) Using measurement principles in developing assessment processes. In: Educational Assessment and Measurement Series. University of Western Australia, Perth

Humphry SM, Wray WH, Wray FW (2013–2015) Pair-Wise Web Software. The University of Western Australia, Perth

Jones I, Alcock L (2012) Summative peer assessment of undergraduate calculus using adaptive comparative judgement. In: Iannone P, Simpson A (eds) Mapping university mathematics assessment practices. University of East Anglia, East Anglia, pp 63–74

Jones I, Alcock L (2014) Peer assessment without assessment criteria. Studies in Higher Education 39(10):1774–1787

Jones I, Swan M, Pollitt A (2015) Assessing mathmatical problem solving using comparative judgement. Int J Science Mathematics Education 13:151–177

Kimbell R (2012) Evolving project e-scape for national assessment. Int J Technology Design Education 22:135–155

Kimbell R, Wheeler T, Miller A, Pollitt A (2007) e-scape: e-solutions for creative assessment in portfolio environments. Technology Education Research Unit, Goldsmiths College, London

Kimbell R, Wheeler T, Stables K, Sheppard T, Martin F, Davies D, Whitehouse G (2009) e-scape portfolio assessment: Phase 3 report. Technology Education Research Unit: Goldsmith College, London

Laming D (2004) Human judgment: The eye of the beholder. Thomson Learning, London

McMahon, S., & Jones, I. (2014). A comparative judgement approach to teacher assessment. *Assessment in Education: Principles, Policy & Practice*. doi: 10.1080/0969594X.2014.978839

Newhouse CP (2008) Digital forms of performance assessment. In: Paper presented at the Australian Computers in Education. ACT, Canberra

Newhouse CP (2010) Aligning assessment with curriculum and pedagogy in applied information technology. Australian Educational Computing 24(2):4–11

Newhouse CP (2011) Comparative pairs marking supports authentic assessment of practical performance within constructivist learning environments. In: Cavanagh RF, Waugh RF (eds) Applications of Rasch Measurement in Learning Environments Research. Sense Publisher, Rotterdam, pp 141–180

Newhouse CP, Tarricone P (2014) Digitizing practical production work for high-stakes assessments. Canadian J Learning Technology 40(2):1–17

Pollitt A (2012a) Comparative judgement for assessment. Int J Design Education 22:157–170

Pollitt A (2012b) The method of Adaptive Comparative Judgement. Assessment Education 19(3):281–300

Pollitt A, Murray NL (1996) What raters really pay attention to. In: Milanovic M, Saville N (eds) Studies in language testing 3: Performance testing, cognition and assessment. Cambridge University Press, Cambridge, pp 74–89
Rasch G (1961) On general laws and the meaning of measurement in psychology. In: Neyman J (ed), Proceedings of the fourth Berkeley symposium on mathematical statistics and probability, Berkeley, California, 1961 (Vol. IV: Contributions to biology and problems of medicine). University of California Press, Berkeley, California, pp. 321-333
Rasch G (1980) Some probabilistic models for the measurement of attainment and intelligence. MESA Press, Chicago
Seery N, Canty D, Phelan P (2012) The validity and value of peer assessment using adaptive comparative judgement in design driven practical education. Int J Technology Design Education 22:205–226
Thurstone LL (1927) A law of comparative judgement. Psychol Rev 34:278–286
Thurstone LL (1928) Attitudes can be measured. American J Sociology 33(4):529–554
Thurstone LL (1954) The measurement of values. Psychol Rev 61(1):47–58
Wilson M (2005) Constructing Measures: An Item Response Modelling Approach. Lawrence Erlbaum Associates, Mahwah

11

Do calculus students demand technology integration into learning environment? case of instructional differences

Eyüp Sevimli

Correspondence:
eyup.sevimli@gop.edu.tr
Faculty of Education,
Gaziosmanpaşa University, 60150
Tokat, Turkey

Abstract

This study evaluated how calculus students' attitudes towards usage of technology changes according to their learning environment and thinking types at the undergraduate level. Thus, the study attempted to determine the place and importance of technological support in the process of attaining the aimed and obtained acquisitions by students. Participants of the study consist of forty-three calculus students who are studying in traditional or CAS-supported teaching environments, and have different thinking types. Pre-and post-assessment tools were used in the data gathering process, and the data were evaluated with descriptive statistics. The results of the study showed that students in the traditional group place more importance on procedural skills, while students in the CAS group attach more importance to conceptual skills in terms of instructional objects. It also determined that acquisitions, which students think developed differ according to learning environment and thinking types. The main implications of the study were discussed in terms of the related literature and teaching practice.

Keywords: Technology, Higher Education, Calculus, Thinking Types

Introduction

Regardless of the fact that it has been more than 30 years since the introduction of technology into mathematics classes, debates relating to the role and effectiveness of technology in the teaching–learning process are continuing without slowing down. Debates gained a new dimension, especially with the increase of computer software programs, graphing calculator interface, and learning objects (e.g., graphing, numerical algorithms, calculations, modelling) which were developed for certain instructional objectives; technology's compatibility with a student, concept, and teacher objectives was also studied. According to Tall et al. (2008), of all the areas in undergraduate mathematics, calculus has received the most interest and investment in the use of technology with an increased number of innovative approaches. The fact that technology's integration into calculus is prioritized by research and software developers can be explained in two ways: Since calculus is not just a part of mathematics, it is also a core curriculum in engineering, science, and some social science departments, it creates a bigger market for software developers; more than half of the students taking the course fail and students who have difficulty in traditional environments are the main factors that direct researchers to search for alternative and innovative teaching-learning approaches (Tokpah 2008). The pioneers of the "calculus reform movement" known as the Harvard Calculus Consortium defended the necessity of conceptual understanding against procedural understanding; for this reason, they suggested that instructional context should be enhanced with multiple representations and should be supported with technology (Hughes-Hallett 1991; Vlachos & Kehagias, 2000). However, despite all of the developed sophisticated instruments and alternative teaching approaches in calculus, the number of lecturers who integrated technology into the learning process remained limited (Marshall et al. 2012). While instructional technology is greeted more warmly in the departments that use mathematics as a tool, in the mathematics departments there are still prejudices against the usage of such technologies. Even though some of the lecturers stated that they are optimistic about mathematical software, the general opinion leans towards the idea that the use of technology in mathematics teaching will weaken the basic skills required for advanced mathematics (Nabb, 2010). Another situation which is worth mentioning at this point is the students' demands and attitudes towards technology. Although there is a large amount of research in literature which includes usage of technology in mathematics classrooms, especially calculus classrooms, the effectiveness of these studies is limited because the expectations and demands of students are not taken into account (Marshall et al. 2012; Samuels, 2010; Swidan & Yerushalmy, 2014). In other words, nowadays, while technology has been trying to find its place in learning environments, there is a shortage of research in literature that considers the needs of the students who are basic components of didactic environments. In this study, opinions of calculus students about technology integration into learning environments were discussed within the context of teaching environments and thinking type differences. For this purpose, answers were sought for the research question below: "How do the calculus students' attitudes towards technology change regarding the following variables: teaching environments and thinking type differences?" Thus, the effect and role of technology in the process of attaining the goals and acquisitions of the course are brought forth. Besides, this study is important because it brings a new perspective on how the need for technology is shaped according to instructional differences.

Theoretical framework

The researchers have placed particular importance on undergraduate mathematics and especially the issue of technology integration in calculus compared to the other teaching levels and disciplines (Marshall et al. 2012; Rasmussen et al. 2014; Tall et al. 2008). A macro-framework for understanding the place of technology in the teaching and learning of calculus has been prepared by Rotman (1995) to evaluate the students' mathematical reasoning (cited in Meagher, 2011). According to this framework, subject, agent, and person are three core elements for integrating technology into the classroom environment. The effectiveness of the teaching-learning process is measured by the strength of the ties between these three components. In his technology integration model which was specially used in calculus, Meagher (2011) changed these three components to be calculus, CAS, and students. As shown in Fig. 1, in the designed technology-supported learning environment, necessities and differences of individuals

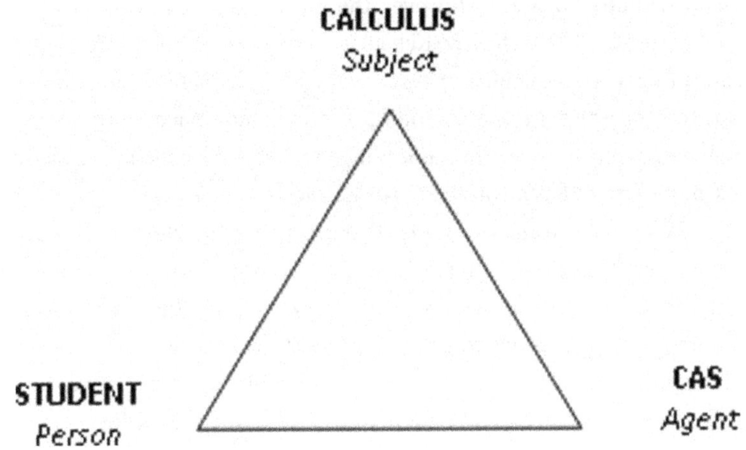

Fig. 1 The Adapted Didactic Triangle (Meagher, 2011)

(person) should be taken into consideration. Some of those individuals are lecturers, and lecturers teaching paradigms also shape expectations of students.

There are several studies in literature that explain the interaction between teacher and technology on the basis of the pedagogical content knowledge and course objectives (Cavin, 2007; Kendal, 2002; Marshall et al. 2012; Tokpah, 2008). Kendal (2002) mentions that technology-supported teaching carried out by a lecturer who lacks technological content knowledge will not yield the expected results. Another reason why lecturers' remain distant from the usage of technology is related to the objectives of the course and to the limited interactive activities of the software. Furthermore; epistemological beliefs between traditionalists and reformist mathematicians can also affect the use of technology at the undergraduate level (Tokpah, 2008). Hung (2001) discusses lecturers' opinions on the basis of philosophical approaches to mathematical teaching while stating that traditionalist mathematicians are less likely to use technology; he also observed that lecturers who prefer technology are more likely to choose software that emphasizes the importance of drill-and-practice (cited in Tokpah, 2008). The calculus reform movement is one of the reformist approaches which points out that knowledge in calculus courses should be learned by students conceptually. But, some mathematicians think that technology-supported reformist-teaching approaches harm the nature of mathematics and simplify the mathematical content (Wilson, 1997). They claim that while some textbooks which were restructured according to the calculus reform movement emphasized the use of technology, mathematical realities are ignored (Chappell & Kilpatrick, 2003). However, Quesada et al. (2008) found that use of graphical teaching via the graphing calculator aids not only visual reasoning but also student understanding of the formal definition in calculus. The discussion about the calculus reform movement and thus the place of technology in calculus classes is ongoing.

The use of CAS in teaching and learning of calculus

Three types of instructional technologies are seen more frequently in undergraduate level mathematics. These are graphing calculators, a Computer Algebra System (CAS), and Dynamic Geometry Software. However, the most practical instructional technology among them is the CAS (Vlachos & Kehagias, 2000). Since each CAS has interfaces that can execute algebraic calculus operations such as derivative, integral, matrix, and determinant, they can be regarded as a kind of calculating machine that provides convenience for mathematicians. At the same time, a CAS is an effective visualization tool with menus providing different projections like plotting 2-D or 3-D graphs (Brown & Steele, 2014; Swidan & Yerushalmy, 2014). The technology-supported teaching environments, as enhanced by the use of a CAS, can help connect symbolic and visual representations of mathematical concepts so that students can utilize from the visual or analytic reasoning in the problem-solving process (Nishizawa et al. 2014; Sevimli, 2013). The findings obtained from a literature review (of 326 papers) regarding the purpose of CAS usage, showed that CAS tools were most widely used for experimentation (63 %) and visualization (59 %) in tertiary mathematics education (Buteau et al. 2010). Vincent et al. (2010) claim that the web based-platforms such as Wolfram|Alpha are more useful than a standard CAS software because of their advantages such as natural language processing always being up-to-date, and the "*show details*" feature. However, simply bringing the software into the teaching environment does not mean that the teaching is now technology assisted. Teachers' technological content knowledge and students' expectations must be taken into consideration. For instance, the study carried out by Eichler and Erens (2014) showed that only a few teachers (2 out of 29) integrate technology into their intended curricula in a sophisticated way to improve students' understanding, whereas most of the teachers used to reduce students' investment in calculations. It is unclear how much CAS-supported teaching is able to fulfil the expectations of students and how these expectations change according to individual differences. It is important to determine the expectations of students and examine whether or not the capacities of technological tools meet these expectations. However, there are very few studies in the literature which can be related to this topic. Several studies show that one of the differences that could help determine priorities of calculus students is a mathematical way of thinking (Haciomeroglu et al. 2010; Presmeg, 1985).

Students thinking differences in calculus

Mathematical thinking should not be regarded as a kind of mathematical skill; it should be regarded as a preference of how mathematical skills are used (Borromeo-Ferri, 2010). Poincare (1900/1907), while pointing out the thinking process in the nature of mathematics, stated that students and mathematicians have two different minds which are "*logical*" and "*intuitive*" and these minds refer to the these two types of thinkers as geometers and analysts, respectively (cited in Galindo-Morales, 1994). Presmeg (1985) associated mathematical ways of thinking with the usage of visualization when attempting to solve mathematical problems and she distinguished students as visualizers and non-visualizers. Visualizers are individuals who prefer to use visual methods like drawing graphs, using diagrams or depicting the spatial information when attempting mathematical problems and non-visualizers are individuals who prefer not to use visual methods when attempting such problems. The nature of calculus also frequently requires the use of both these methods. In many studies in calculus, individuals who use non-visual solution methods are referred to analytical thinkers (Borromeo-Ferri, 2010;

Sevimli, 2013). Lean and Clements (1981) found that the problem- solving success of analytical thinkers is relatively higher than visual thinkers. On the other hand, Lowrie and Kay (2011) observed that when students apply visual strategies to understand the data in problems that they found complex, they tend to use the analytical strategies in easier problem types. It is also known that students make more effort by managing the visual processes than the analytical processes (Presmeg, 2006). Many of the researchers studying students' thinking differences in Calculus have stated that the teaching environment must be structured by supporting the different thinking strategies for conceptual understanding (Galindo-Morales, 1994; Sevimli, 2013). Students with different types of thinking benefit differently from traditional and CAS-supported learning environments (Galindo-Morales, 1994). For instance, Sevimli (2013) found that visual students benefit more from the opportunities of a CAS-supported classroom than the other thinkers in the classroom in terms of transitioning between different representations of a concept. Literature findings outlined above prompted researchers to investigate how demands of students which are related to technology change according to learning environments.

Methods

This study is a part of a long-term, large-scale project, which includes research designs such as pre-field research and teaching experiments in its background. The aim of the study was to maximize information and critical cases (diversity) when examining calculus students' technology demands, not to facilitate generalization (Haciomeroglu et al. 2010; Lincoln & Guba, 1985). Thus, the embedded case study method, one of the qualitative designs, was used in the study.

Research group

The research group of this study consists of forty-three freshmen students who are studying mathematics in the science faculties of a university in Turkey. The university in which the study was conducted is one of Turkey's leading educational institutions with more than 65,000 students, and calculus is taught in the mathematics department and alongside many science and engineering departments. Students in the research group took Calculus-I before the implementation and this study were conducted under Calculus-II course. The research group has different characteristics according to the teaching environment. Two teaching environments have been created as part of the study, which are traditional and CAS-supported teaching environments. In this study, thinking types of students were also taken into account in order to diversify differences in learning environments. Details of the thinking types are explained under the "data collection" sub-heading.

Setting

Students in the study group were randomly assigned to traditional (25 students) or CAS (18 students) groups and teaching processes lasted for six weeks. Since the legal permission given by the institution foresees that the study will be completed in six weeks, the study has been conducted for six hours each week for a total of 36 h (6×6 = 36).

Traditional environment

At the first researchers tried to understand the nature of the teaching environment in a traditional calculus classroom with pre-field research which he conducted by using observation and content analysis techniques. The findings of this research are: *a)* Calculus-I, which was given to students studying mathematics in the fall semester, was taught by a mathematics professor by following traditional textbooks; *b)* Symbolic language and algebraic representations were predominantly used in lectures; *c)* It was observed that students often tried to write down the lecture notes on the board; *d)* Lectures are taught using the expository teaching approach and question-answer techniques. In light of the information above, there was no interference in traditional group lectures and the same instructor continued to give lectures.

CAS-supported environment

In this study, the concept of "*integration technology into the teaching environment*" is limited with the CAS-supported teaching process. While designing the CAS-supported teaching environment, Meagher's (2011) model containing phases of technology integration into teaching environments are taken into consideration. In this context, first of all it should be explained for what purpose technology is going to be used in teaching environments. Since Calculus-II is a course which has theoretical and applied content received in the mathematics department, CAS-supported teaching processes are followed, not CAS-based. The CAS was used as a tool for creating, viewing and/or modifying graphical renderings of mathematical objects to enhance conceptual discussions and support visualizations (Buteau et al. 2010). In the theoretical parts of lectures, a CAS software program was used limitedly to visualize some proofs and to discover different meanings of a concept. While there is a large number of instructional software which can be used in calculus courses, some of the software functions that simplify calculation operations of engineering departments are predominant, and in others visualization tools are limited and software language is complex (Sevimli, 2013). In the *LiveMath* study, (previously known as Theorist), a CAS software program was preferred because of "a unique user interface that allows one to perform 'natural' algebraic manoeuvres even more 'naturally' than one can achieve them on paper" (Kaput, 1992; p.534). This software also allows the students to perform symbolic manipulation, to drag-spin in the 3-D graph, to use easy syntax and interactive animation). The computerized learning environment has included the interactive *LiveMath* activities which encourage the students in the context of visualization, translating between representations and making contact between disciplines. Figure 2 includes an example based on graphical and numeric calculations with which students can answer with the Limits of Riemann Sums.

Technology is used in the group following a CAS-supported teaching process according to the operation steps below: *a)* The learning process in the CAS group was conducted by a mathematics lecturer who has technological-pedagogical content knowledge and has years of experience in teaching calculus; *b)* Before the implementation, the features of the software were introduced to the CAS group to ensure that students are accustomed to technology-supported environment; *c)* The theoretical part of the course was given in a lecture hall and additionally, CAS content which supports visual reasoning in related topics were included; *d)* The practical part of the course was given in computer lab and active participation of students in the usage of technology

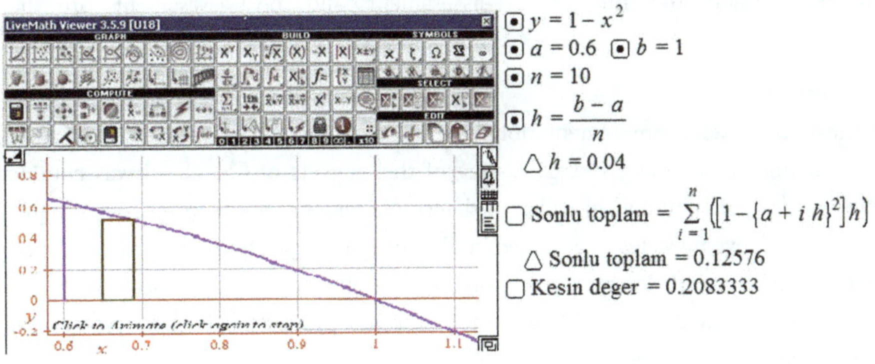

Fig. 2 An Animated Approximation of $\int_{0.6}^{1} (1-x^2)dx$ with Right Riemann Sums in CAS Group

was supported with an activity-based approach, *e)* In contrast to traditional groups, technology support is used to present different representations related to problem situations in the CAS group.

Data collection and analysis process

Three types of data collecting tools were used in the study consisting of tests, questionnaires, and interviews. Tests are auxiliary instruments which are used in order to determine differences in a teaching environment before implementation. The main data is collected by questionnaires and interviews, and after administering the questionnaire, semi-structured interviews were conducted with four respondents for a deeper understanding of the views on integration technology into calculus. The data collection process is summarized in Fig. 3. Information about the process of data analysis, which

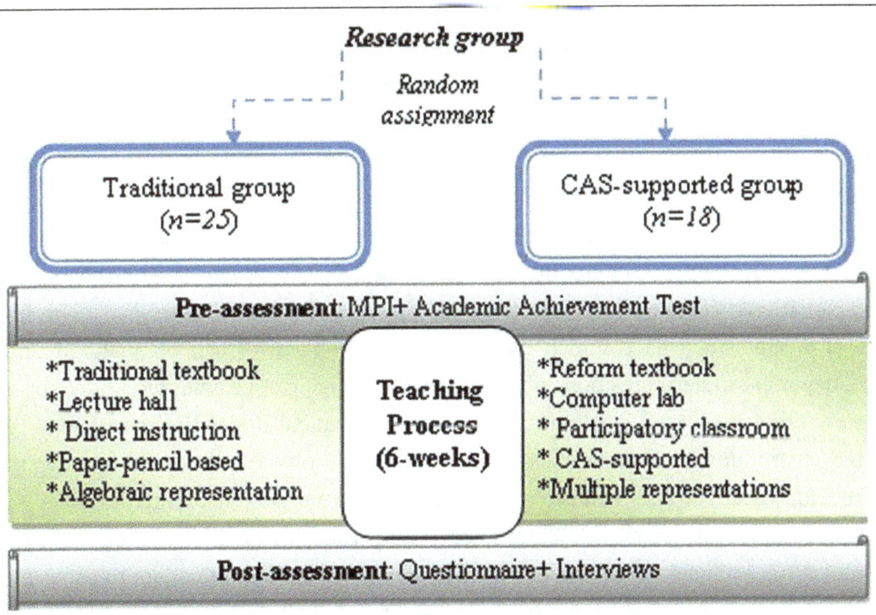

Fig. 3 Flow Chart of Data Collection Process

is gathered under the titles of "pre-assessment" and "post-assessment" are shared below.

Pre-assessment

The tests used before implementations are an academic achievement test and an MPI. An academic achievement test consisting of the subjects of Calculus-I was conducted before the implementation in order to determine whether study groups were equal or not. The achievement test contained multiple choice questions on subjects such as limit, continuity, and differentiation, which were all evaluated on a scale of 100. The test findings revealed that students in the traditional group and the CAS group showed similar performances before the implementation process and no statistically significant differences among the groups were found for academic achievement ($\overline{X}_{Tra} = 68.5$, $\overline{X}_{CAS} = 66.9$, $Sd = 41$, $t = -0.04$, $p = 0.94$).

Another test which was used before implementation was The Mathematical Process Instrument (MPI). The instrument was used to categorize the participants as analytical or visual according to their mathematical thinking types. MPI was developed by Suwarsono (1982), and Presmeg (1985) modified this instrument to be used at higher education level. As the participants of this study were university students, the modified version of MPI was preferred in the study, which had a total of 18 questions. Each problem in the MPI could be solved using either visual or non-visual methods. For the analysis of MPI scores, Presmeg's (1985) analysis framework was used. Regardless of whether the answer was correct or incorrect, each visual solution received 2 points and each non-visual solution received 0. Therefore, each participant had a total score between 0 and 36. Thus the ones who had points between 0-12 were coded and categorized as participants who use analytical thinking (preferences of non-visual methods) and the ones who had points between 22-36 were coded and categorized as participants who use visual thinking (preferences of visual methods).

Post-assessment

After the implementation, a questionnaire was used to evaluate the learning outcomes. The questionnaire used in this study has been developed based on the results of a pilot study and has been formed with the categorization of frequently encountered answers. In the pilot study, students were asked to write an answer to the questions "*what should be the instructional objectives of calculus, which objectives do you expect is going to develop with the course?*" and that "*what are the competencies that you think you have developed end of the teaching process?*" For example, the indicator words in the written answers such as finding integral, knowing the rules of derivate or solving algebraic equations were labelled and categorized under "*procedural flexibility*". The findings of a pilot study have shown that instructional objectives can be analyzed under five categories, while acquisitions obtained end of course can be analyzed under six categories. The categorized data were presented with a table under the two themes: expected instructional objectives and obtained acquisitions. While forming categories related to objectives and acquisitions in calculus, opinions of mathematics professors were consulted who teach this course for a long time. In addition to the researcher classification, each answer was coded individually by two different coders to achieve reliable categorization. When the agreement was not initially achieved, differences were discussed and the final code was agreed upon with a common classification. High compliances were achieved between second coders and researchers in the classification process. In the questionnaire, which is carried out after the implementation process, students are asked to select one or more of the categories and explain why these categories were specially selected. The categories given in the questionnaire are: instructional objectives and acquisitions that the students aimed to achieve during the course. A formal definition of the each category was presented in the questionnaire to ensure that different participants interpreted a category in a similar manner. The students are also encouraged to write (if there is any) different objective and acquisition except those categories. Quotes from the students' written answers were also included for each topic as proof of an argument.

The interviews have been used to evaluate how the outputs of the teaching process change according to thinking types. Semi-structured interviews were conducted with the four selected students and were audio recorded. Describing who will be selected for the interview and the principles that affect the selection will make it easy to interpret the findings. Considering the fact that along with types of thinking, differences in teaching environments might also affect the demands of students regarding technology; students who have sufficied to represent these differences were chosen. For this reason, participants in the interviews were selected using a purposeful sampling technique from voluntary students. The main selection criteria were that each participant had a different thinking type in each environment (CAS or Traditional). Interviews were conducted with visual and analytical thinkers (contrasting cases) in order to determine the similarities and differences between the technological demands of students (Haciomeroglu et al. 2010). Participants were coded with a formulization in the form of environment and thinking types. Analytic participants who are in traditional and CAS-supported environments were coded with Tra-A and CAS-A, respectively. Also, Tra-V and CAS-V codes were used to define visual participants who are in traditional and CAS-supported environments. MPI points (out of 36) of the participants are shown below: CAS-A was 7, CAS-V was 25, Tra-A was 5 and Tra-V was 22. Each participant's interview lasted approximately 40 min, and each of them was transcribed. During interviews, participants were asked to explain their attitudes towards the usage of CAS in calculus considering their expectations of the course. Interview data were analyzed with an open coding method, which consists of identifying, naming, categorizing, and describing phenomena found in the text for the thematic analysis (Strauss & Corbin, 1998). During the open coding process, semi-structured interview data were transcribed, and responses to the same interview questions of the participants who had different thinking types and settings were coded in terms of previously identified categories. The findings obtained by usage of frequently-repeated objectives and acquisitions in the interviews were summarized in the table (Table 2). Some selected quotes (for each participant) were also shared in the text to be able to characterize the participants' attitudes towards usage of CAS.

Findings

The findings of the study were presented in two steps. First of all, general findings were presented in terms of acquisitions, which were thought to be aimed and obtained by calculus students with respect to setting differences. Afterwards, the role of thinking types was particularly taken into consideration while evaluating the attitudes towards CAS integration into calculus.

Objectives and acquisitions of the calculus

In the findings of the questionnaire gathered under this title, students were asked to explain the knowledge or skills they aimed to achieve at the end of the course. The findings of the questionnaire that were analyzed according to their content showed that instructional objectives which are associated with calculus could be gathered under four categories (Table 1). Procedural flexibility, among one of the categories was the most associated instructional objective with calculus by students. When findings are interpreted with respect to variables of teaching environment by taking into account the clustering remarks, it can be seen that students in the CAS group consider *"conceptual understanding"* and students in traditional group consider *"procedural flexibility"* more important. While students in the CAS group also take *"interdisciplinary relation"* into account, 40 % of the students in traditional group also stated that they were aiming to improve their *"abstract thinking"* after the calculus course. Direct quotations of some of the interview contents supporting this implication are presented below. Emphasis was placed on procedural and conceptual skills by one participant from each group (CAS and traditional) as seen in the quotations.

> *Students in traditional group: It is important to be able to do derivative or integral operations quickly and correctly, the primary objectives of the course could be, knowing how to use rules and technique.*

> *Students in CAS group: Unlike in high school, it is required to interpret different meanings of a new mathematical concept at the university level. For example, rates of change of derivatives are more important than finding a derivative.*

Another aim of the questionnaire is to evaluate the implemented teaching processes from the student's perspective. In this context, students in the CAS group and students in the traditional group evaluated CAS-supported teaching process and traditional teaching process in terms of learning outcomes, respectively. Findings indicated that students developed themselves in five mathematical acquisitions. The most apparent of them are *"algebraic thinking"* and *"computation"*, which students think they achieved at the end of the calculus course (Table 1).

The findings of the questionnaire showed that acquisitions, which students think developed differ according to types of teaching environments. While acquisitions, which were pointed out by students in the CAS group, but never mentioned in traditional group are *"using representations"*, the only acquisitions pointed out in the traditional group but never mentioned in the CAS group are *"proving theorems"*. Two explanations in the questionnaire which were evaluated within the categories of *"using representations"* and *"proving theorems"* separately are shared below.

> *Students in traditional group: We run the course on the basis of definition-theorem and proof. I thought I was going to deal with numbers when I came to this department, however, my lecture notes are full of letters and symbols like a literature*

Table 1 Instructional objectives and obtained acquisitions regarding to the students

		Instructional objectives[a]				Obtained acquisitions[a]				
		Procedural flexibility	Conceptual understanding	Abstract thinking	Interdisciplinary relation	Algebraic thinking	Computation	Proving theorems	Using representation	Visualization
CAS	*f*	*7*	*10*	*4*	*6*	*3*	*5*	*4*	*12*	*11*
	%	39	56	22	33	17	28	22	67	61
Traditional	*f*	*14*	*3*	*10*	-	*11*	*8*	*8*	-	*2*
	%	*56*	*12*	*40*	-	*44*	*32*	*32*	-	*8*

[a]The categories in the table contain the most frequently encountered written answers. Because the students can choose more than one category, total categories exceed 100 %

student, which shows that for mathematicians, proofs are much more important acquisitions than examples or any special situation.

Students in CAS group: CAS-supported learning process contributed mostly to my skills of interpreting derivative and anti-derivative graphics. I can switch from derivative equations to primitive function graphics easier by using CAS, and I can interpret the meaning of rise and fall in graphics in derivative equations.

Attitudes towards usage of CAS

Thinking type differences were taken into consideration while attitudes towards the usage of CAS were evaluated within the context of objectives and acquisitions in calculus. For this purpose, the interviews have been conducted with a participant who can represent the teaching environment and has different thinking types. While evaluating reasons of participants about demanding or refusing CAS integration into calculus classrooms, each participant was asked to answer the following question: "What are the roles of CAS support in accomplishing the objectives of the course and carrying on the acquisitions which were gained after a learning period?"

Some participants' (CAS-A, CAS-V and Tra-V) opinions about the usage of CAS are evaluated under the category of "*positive but limited*". These participants converged on the idea that CAS can be used in calculus, but boundaries should be determined. While CAS-A and CAS-V pointed out that technology support is important for the objective of "*conceptual understanding*" and "*interdisciplinary relation*" respectively, a reservation of the participants is the negligence of the abstract nature of mathematics when used with technology.

CAS-A: I am standing with the idea that boundaries of technology support should be well determined. I think technology support will contribute to relational understanding, but CAS is not necessary all the time. First, you should know the concept, have theoretical background and then we can pass on to computer application... I do not find it meaningful to visualize everything, mathematics is abstract, and thinking skills in this aspect should be developed more.

CAS- V: Although, the software (LiveMath) is not useful for proving theorems; I could understand and interpret the definition of integral at numerical and graphical perspectives... Solving real world problems which require interpreting graphical or tabular data is so easy. The software we use encourages me not just for that moment, but to think visually about other problems too.

A common drawback of participants is that the usage of CAS will affect procedural fluency negatively. Participants who evaluated under "*positive but limited*" categories demanded that the software which mathematical-symbolic language can be used flexibly should take place more frequently in the process, while referring to the acquisitions of the course (Table 2). For instance, Tra-V stated that teaching calculus with the traditional method supports calculation skills more. Although Tra-V did not take place in a

CAS-supported teaching environment before, he demands CAS integration on the grounds that technology support brings more visual elements to the learning environment.

Tra-V: Teaching the course with computer support and showing graphic during the course brings to a successful conclusion in terms of concretization. For example, it would be better if technologies supporting visual quality were used in slope of secant line which is the interpretation of the derivative as geometrically... Frequently usage of CAS during the calculation process may decrease our procedural capability. This is why CAS support should be limited in the mathematics classroom.

The only participant with a negative attitude about the usage of CAS is Tra-A. This participant stated that the rules and formulas learned in the traditional classroom are recognized and recalled more easily, and formulas can be used more flexibly in related problem situations. On the other hand, it was observed that the opinion of Tra-A was shaped by a perception of mathematicians in society.

Tra-A: In computer-supported environment, student may not be able to develop a basic level of procedural knowledge. What's important is administrating the process and this type of tools wear down this ability over time. I am pleased with traditional content and running of the course. For the most part, I understand lecture notes on the board and at least I can browse through them at home... Mathematicians cannot carry a computation tool which can do differential–integral calculus and perception of mathematicians in society requires doing operations with paper and pencil or mentally.

It is also determined that CAS-V and Tra-A are the two participants who think they obtained more acquisitions according to the teaching environment variable. While CAS-V pointed out that after CAS-supported teaching process their competences of "*using representations*", and "*visualization*" have developed; Tra-A pointed out that their competences of "*algebraic thinking*", "*calculation*" and"*proving theorems*" have developed. Additionally, according to the participants with analytical thinking, in order to attain the objectives of the calculus course and retaining acquisitions, CAS-supported contents which do not conceal procedural steps and damage calculating ability should be included in the learning process. However, participants with visual thinking suggested that technologies such as CAS should be used as a means of visualization and concretization in order to form interdisciplinary relation.

Table 2 Impact of CAS-supported teaching on the objectives and acquisitions of the calculus

		Attitude	*Objectives*[a]	*Acquisitions*[a]
Participants	*CAS-A*	Positive but limited	(↑) Conceptual understanding	(↔) Algebraic thinking
	CAS-V	Positive but limited	(↑) Interdisciplinary relation	(↔) Proving theorems
	Tra-A	Negative	(↓) Abstract thinking	(↓) Computation
	Tra-V	Positive but limited	(↔) Interdisciplinary relation	(↓) Computation

[a] (↑) Positive impact, (↔) Neutral impact, (↓) Negative impact

Discussion

The interaction between students and technology are quite important in the process of integration technology into teaching-learning environments (Marshall et al. 2012; Meagher, 2011). Students' expectations and demands on CAS integration in calculus were evaluated in this study. Findings showed that students set different limits on usage of CAS in learning environments. Consequently, while some of the students in the study stating that technologies such as CAS should be used limitedly in learning environments; they tried to explain the reason for this statement by citing the objectives and acquisitions of the course. Some students hold prejudices about the nature of calculus knowledge and technology compatibility in terms of visualization, especially students who are in the traditional group. It was noted that there were similar prejudices in the related literature. In one of these studies Eisenberg and Dreyfus (1991) claimed that most of the visual proofs are not accepted as real mathematical proofs by lecturers and students. However, it is injudicious to think that visualization harms the abstract nature of mathematics. Visualization of a mathematical concept does not mean concretization of it, it means establishing relationships between the analytical and the geometric nature of the concept. Therefore, students are making more effort while managing visual processes and they are able to make higher cognitive acquisitions (Presmeg, 2006). Traditional contents and approaches without visual elements prompt students to rule-based thinking and rote learning (Alcock & Inglis, 2010). Aims of students in the traditional group regarding the calculus might be affected by the previous learning experiences and/or paradigm of lecturers. Because a great majority of students in the traditional group attributed to the importance of using symbolic language for "*procedural skills*" and "*proving theorems*", which explains the reason why they remained distant on technology usage. Giving more attention to the procedural competence in the traditional group can be explained based on the "*community of practice*" phenomena. For instance, Sofronas et al. (2011) stated that mathematicians trust formal notation language more in the process of proving theorems, interpreting findings, making inferences, and generalization. Besides, Pierce (1999) interprets students' finding traditional environments more reliable as a result of their lack of confidence about technological content knowledge. Similar inferences were obtained in Hung's (2001) research, and he found that lecturers who are not capable of using technology are more likely to choose programs that concentrate on calculation modules (cited in Tokpah, 2008). The fact that less usage of visual elements in the teaching process of the traditional group may have prompted students to use algebraic solutions is another reason why students in the mathematics department remain distant about CAS usage in learning environments is related to epistemological beliefs. It can be concluded from opinions of participants such as "*real mathematicians do calculations with paper and pencil*" or "*nature of mathematics is symbolic, there is no need for visualization*" that they are under the influence of lecturers' epistemological beliefs (Muis, 2004).

Another component whose effects on usage of technology in calculus have been researched is thinking type differences. The findings of the study show that it would not be correct to make inferences about demands on CAS usage according to the thinking types; but some inclinations could be appointed if teaching environment and thinking types were considered together. Participants who have the most positive and negative attitudes towards CAS usage are visual participants in the CAS group (CAS-

V) and analytical participant in traditional group (Tra-A), respectively. CAS might be considered scaffolding tools, which will bring different perspectives with multiple representations and visualization interface (Pierce, 1999). Thus, technology enriches learning environment provides alternative contents for students with different thinking types. In one of the studies that support this inference Sevimli (2013) stated that CAS-supported teaching approaches, provides students an environment which enables students to choose appropriate content based on their cognitive preferences. In this study, especially the participants with visual thinking type stated that they could observe numerical, geometrical and algebraic interpretations of derivative and integral with the support of CAS, explicitly (CAS-V, p. 18). On the other hand, thinking of the technology only as a device of visualization would mean ignoring the other capabilities of technology such as modelling and developing strategies. Therefore, enriching learning environments where technology is used with activities containing real-life problems and cognitive relations can be established can fulfil the expectations of visual students better.

Participants who are analytical thinkers remain more distant to CAS usage than visual participants in calculus, and the fact that acquisitions, which were thought to be accomplished by the end of the course were limited, might have affected the attitudes of analytical participants regarding CAS usage. At this point, analytical participants in the traditional group remain distant to CAS usage on account of the fact that procedural skills might be negatively affected. Tra-A has bias towards a learning environment which he has not experienced before (e.g., the usage of CAS negatively affects calculation skills and conceals the procedural steps). When opinions of the participants were gathered together it was discovered that using instructional technologies which are computer or calculator-based and which do not show intermediate steps to calculations (e.g., works with the result-oriented principle), were perceived as technology integration. In fact, it has been known that analytical thinkers are able use rule-based approaches more flexibly and they rely on algebraic representations more. Hughes-Hallett (1991) stated that for many calculus lecturers and students being competent in calculus are equal to the ability of manipulating symbols and numbers. In another study, Sofronas et al. (2011) determined that after the negotiations with calculus textbook authors and well-known professors in the US, for a great majority of participants, procedural skills are the leading acquisitions of calculus, and the rate of the participants who mention technology support was limited. Based on the related literature and concordantly with the course objectives it can be understood why analytical participants remain distant to mathematics software that conceals procedural steps. However, regarding mathematical software only as an input-output system by analytical participants in the traditional group limits the usage of technology and brings out the opinion that in traditional classrooms doing calculations with paper and pencil is more instructive. Thus, with the opinion of Tra-A "*we made this commands meaningful for computers and we make a bid for computers to do this handwork instead of us*" confines technology usage to "crosschecking". Analytical participants in the CAS group intend to use technology with the purpose of reducing the burden of operation different from the traditional group. In many studies in the literature, it is pointed out that mathematics software can be used to reduce the time spared for tedious calculations and this time can be used to support conceptual understanding (Harper, 2007; Pierce, 1999; Sevimli, 2013).

The fact that the syntax of instructional software (*LiveMath*) which was used in the study is compatible with mathematical notions (typeset math, not computer code) and software's showing the intermediate steps in the calculation process might have explicitly affected the opinions of the participants. Besides, the fact that visual participants pointed out more acquisitions than analytical participants at the end of the CAS-supported teaching process may show that analytical thinkers are either not aware of acquisitions such as "using representations" and "visualization" or they do not regard these acquisitions as mathematical qualifications. While visual participants demanded CAS support more than analytical ones because of the fact that they obtained their objectives better, participants in the traditional group generally remained distant from the usage of CAS due to epistemological beliefs related to the abstract nature of the calculus.

Conclusion

The results of the study showed that students in the traditional group pay more importance to procedural fluency, while students in the CAS group attach more importance to conceptual competencies in terms of instructional objects. In addition to this, it was stated by students that the traditional teaching environment supports procedural fluency, and the CAS-supported teaching environment assists using multiple representations and visualization aspects more. According to the results obtained from the interview findings, visual participants demanded CAS support more than analytical participants, and the relation between objectives and acquisitions are important in attitudes about integrating technology into calculus. In this sense, it was observed that participants who remain distant to the usage of technology (CAS) in the learning process are mainly in the traditional group, or they are mainly analytical thinkers. For participants in this study, epistemological beliefs related to the abstract nature of the calculus and for participants with analytical thinking type confidence on algebraic solutions and the idea of harming of procedural skills are the reasons for the limited usage of CAS.

The main implication of the study is that the objectives of the course and characteristics of the target audience should be taken into consideration while integrating technology in a learning environment. It seems that technology demands and attitudes of participants with different thinking types in the same learning environment or participants with same thinking types of different learning environments may differ. Undoubtedly the results of this study are limited by the self-assessment capacity of the participants. Therefore, asserting that analytical participants in traditional classrooms or visual participants in CAS-supported classrooms can obtain more acquisitions would be wrong. However, the results of the study bring an important projection regarding self-assessments of participants in different teaching environments, and with different instructional characteristics. The aim of this study is not to reach a generalization, but to thoroughly examine the reasons why students need technology. Consequently, interviews were carried out with a limited number of students. However, a new study, which will be conducted with a larger sample can explain how technology demands of students change according to thinking types and department differences. In other candidate studies which could be follow-ups of this study, it is suggested that researchers analyze the opinions of students about technology usage in didactics of mathematics with samples, discipline, and data collecting tool diversification. For example, compatibilities and incompatibilities between student expectations about different mathematics classrooms in different educational levels (such secondary, high school and higher education) and capabilities of mathematical software could be examined. Moreover, differences in the students' thinking types and course requirements should be taken into account when designing a technology-enhanced learning environment by lecturers and software developers.

Acknowledgements
This paper is a revised and extended version of a paper that was presented at 13th International Congress on Mathematical Education (ICME-13) in July 24 – 31, 2016, in Hamburg/Germany.

Authors' contributions
The author has made substantial contributions to conception and design, analysis and interpretation of data, has been involved in drafting the manuscript and revising it critically and has given final approval of the version to be published. He also read and approved the final manuscript.

Authors' information
Eyup SEVIMLI, Ph.D., is currently an assistant professor in the Department of Mathematics Education of Gaziosmanpaşa University, Tokat, Turkey. His research interests include advanced mathematical thinking, integration technology into mathematics classroom and representational system in mathematics education. He also has experience in university teaching and textbook design.

Competing interests
The author declares that he has no competing interests.

References

Alcock, L., & Inglis, M. (2010). Visual considerations in the presentation of mathematical proofs. *International Journal of Media, Technology and Lifelong Learning, 6*, 43–59.

Borromeo-Ferri, R. (2010). On the influence of mathematical thinking styles on learners' modelling behaviour. *Journal für Mathematik-Didaktik, 31*, 99–118.

Brown, M., & Steele, C. (2014). MathExplorer: exploring maths for engineering students. *Teaching Mathematics and Its Applications, 33*, 65–80.

Buteau, C., Marshall, N., Jarvis, D., & Lavicza, Z. (2010). Integrating Computer Algebra Systems in post-secondary mathematics education: preliminary results of a literature review. *International Journal for Technology in Mathematics Education, 17*, 57–68.

Cavin, M. (2007). *Developing technological pedagogical content knowledge in preservice teachers through microteaching lesson study. Ph.D. thesis.* USA: Florida State University.

Chappell, K., & Kilpatrick, K. (2003). Effects of concept-based instruction on students' conceptual understanding and procedural knowledge of calculus. *PRIMUS, 13*, 17–37.

Eichler, A., & Erens, R. (2014). Teachers' beliefs towards teaching calculus. *ZDM—The International Journal on Mathematics Education, 46*, 647–659.

Eisenberg, T., & Dreyfus, T. (1991). *On the reluctance to visualize in mathematics. Visualization in Teaching and Learning Mathematic (W. Zimmermann & S. Cunningham eds.).* Washington: MAA.

Galindo-Morales, E. (1994). *Visualization in the calculus class: Relationship between cognitive style, gender, and use of technology. Ph.D. thesis.* USA: Ohio State University.

Haciomeroglu, E., Aspinwall, L., & Presmeg, N. (2010). Contrasting cases of calculus students' understanding of derivative graphs. *Mathematical Thinking and Learning, 12*, 152–176.

Harper, L. (2007). *The use of Computer Algebra Systems in a procedural algebra course to facilitate a framework for procedural understanding. Ph.D. thesis.* USA: Montana State University.

Hughes-Hallett, D. (1991). *Visualization and calculus reform. Visualization In Teaching and learning mathematics (W. Zimmermann & S. Cunningham eds.)* (pp. 121–126). Washington: MAA.

Hung, D. (2001). Theories of learning and computer-mediated instructional technology. *Education Media International*, 38(4),282–286.

Kaput, J. (1992). *Technology and mathematics education. Handbook of Research on Mathematics Teaching and Learning (D. Grouws ed.)* (pp. 515–556). NY: Macmillan.

Kendal, M. (2002). *Teaching and learning introductory differential calculus. Ph.D. thesis.* Australia: University of Melbourne.

Lean, G., & Clements, M. A. (1981). Spatial ability, visual imagery, and mathematical performance. *Educational Studies in Mathematics*, 12(3), 267–299.

Lincoln, Y., & Guba, E. (1985). *Naturalistic inquiry*. Beverly Hills, CA: Sage.

Lowrie, T., & Kay, R. (2001). Task representation: The relationship between visual and nonvisual solution methods and problem difficulty in elementary school mathematics. *Journal of Educational Research*, 94, 248–253.

Marshall, N., Buteau, C., Jarvis, D., & Lavicza, Z. (2012). Do mathematicians integrate computer algebra systems in university teaching? Comparing a literature review to an international survey study. *Computers & Education, 58*, 423–434.

Meagher, M. (2011). Students' relationship to technology and conceptions of mathematics while learning in a Computer Algebra System environment. *International Journal for Technology in Mathematics Education, 19*, 3–16.

Muis, K. (2004). Personal Epistemology and mathematics: A critical review and synthesis of research. *Review of Educational Research, 74*, 317–377.

Nabb, K. (2010). CAS as a restructuring tool in mathematics education. Proceedings of the 22nd International Conference on Technology in Collegiate Mathematics. (see http://www.keithnabb.com/yahoo_site_admin/assets/docs/CAS_As_A_Restructuring_Tool_in_Mathematics_Education.28990404.pdf) [accessed 16 May 2014].

Nishizawa, H., Kimura, K., Ohno, W., & Yoshioka, T. (2014). Interactive worksheets for connecting symbolic and visual representations of 3D vector equations. *Teaching Mathematics and Its Applications, 33*, 52–64.

Pierce, R. (1999). *Computer Algebra Systems facilitate positive learning strategies. (J. Truran & K. Truran eds.), Making the Difference. Proceedings of the 22nd Annual Conference of the Mathematics Education Research Group of Australasia.* Sydney: MERGA.

Presmeg, N. (1985). *The role of visually mediated processes in high school mathematics: A classroom investigation. Ph.D. thesis*. UK: University of Cambridge.

Presmeg, N. (2006). Research on visualization in learning and teaching mathematics. In A. Gutierrez (Ed.), *Handbook of Research on the Psychology of Mathematics Education: Past, Present and Future*. Rotterdam: Sense.

Quesada, A., Richard, L., Wiggins, & M. (2008). The impact of the graphical approach on students' understanding of the definition of limit. *International Journal for Technology in Mathematics Education*, 15, 95-102

Rasmussen, C., Marrongelle, K., & Borba, M. (2014). Research on calculus: what do we know and where do we need to go? *ZDM—The International Journal on Mathematics Education, 46*, 507–515.

Samuels, J. (2010). *The use of technology and visualization in calculus instruction. Ph.D. thesis*. USA: Columbia University.

Sevimli, E. (2013). *The effect of computer algebra system supported teaching on students' processes of transition of representations in integral with the thinking type differences (English abstract). Ph.D. thesis*. Turkey: University of Marmara.

Sofronas, K., De Franco, T., Vinsonhaler, C., Gorgievski, N., Schroeder, L., & Hamelin, C. (2011). What does it mean for a student to understand the first-year calculus? Perspectives of 24 experts. *The Journal of Mathematical Behavior, 30*, 131–148.

Strauss, A., & Corbin, J. (1998). *Basics of qualitative research: Techniques and procedures for developing grounded theory* (2nd ed.). Thousand Oaks, CA: Sage.

Suwarsono, S. (1982). *Visual imagery in the mathematical thinking of seventh-grade students. Ph.D. thesis*. Australia: Monash University.

Swidan, O., & Yerushalmy, M. (2014). Learning the indefinite integral in a dynamic and interactive technological environment. *ZDM—The International Journal on Mathematics Education, 46*, 517–531.

Tall, D., Smith, D., & Piez, C. (2008). Technology and calculus. In M. K. Heid & G. W. Blume (Eds.), *Research on technology and the teaching and learning of mathematics* (pp. 207–258). USA: NCTM, Publications.

Tokpah, L. (2008). *The effects of Computer Algebra Systems on students' achievement in mathematics. Ph.D. thesis*. USA: Kent State University.

Vincent, E., Andrew, S., Lang, D., & Locke, L. (2010). Teaching calculus with Wolfram|Alpha. *International Journal of Mathematical Education in Science and Technology, 41*, 1061–1071.

Vlachos, P., & Kehagias, A. (2000). A Computer Algebra System and a new approach for teaching. *Journal of Computer Algebra in Mathematics Education, 7*, 87–104.

Wilson, R. (1997). A decade of teaching "reform calculus" has been a disaster, critics charge. *The Chronicle of Higher Education, 4*, 12–l3.

12

Integration of learning technologies into teaching within Fijian Polytechnic Institutions

Shalendra Kumar and Ben Kei Daniel*

* Correspondence:
ben.daniel@otago.ac.nz
University of Otago, Dunedin,
Otago, New Zealand

Abstract

In the 21st century, learning technologies have increasingly become pervasive within various forms of learning environments. Institutions of higher education are increasingly turning to these technologies to resource and support their teaching and learning environments under distributed circumstances, face-to-face or blended. Recently, the Fijian Ministry of Education systematically introduced learning technologies into Fiji's technical colleges to support teaching and learning. However, prior to the widespread deployment of these technologies, little information was available on educators' perception of the value of these technologies, and the extent to which this could influence adoption. The purpose of this study was to gain a better understanding of lecturers' perceptions of the value of learning technologies and factors likely to influence their decisions to adopt and integrate these technologies into teaching as well as challenges they are likely to face. A survey was administered to fifty five self-selected lecturers involved in teaching within three Polytechnics in Fiji. Although overall findings suggested that lecturers strongly valued the contribution of learning technologies in enhancing student learning, a number of factors likely to influence the rapid adoption of these technologies were identified. These included attitude towards technology and perceived usefulness of technology in teaching, the institutional cultural environment, as well as resources available to support uptake. This research contributes to the growing significance of individual, contextual and cultural influences in the adoption of learning technologies into teaching.

Keywords: Learning technologies, Attitude, Perceived usefulness, Ease of use, Compatibility, Perceived behavioural control, Self-efficacy, Behavioural intention, Subjective norms

Introduction

Learning technologies refer to as e-Learning, refers to a suit of technologies to support teaching or learning. These also include technological platforms that support virtual learning environments (VLEs) (Sife, Lwoga, & Sanga, 2007). Sife, et. al, (2007) identified different types of educational technologies, ranging from those that are used as supplementary learning support tools and environments, those that support classroom (PowerPoint), and others that are used as hybrid or blended, supporting face-to-face and fully online instruction (Arabasz & Baker, 2003). In the last few decades there has been an increasing integration of Learning Technologies (LTs') into teaching and learning within the higher education sector (Laurillard, 2013). LTs' in this study is referred to software's' (word processing, spreadsheets, databases, PowerPoint, virtual learning), hardware (PCs, laptops, multi-media projectors, interactive whiteboard), as well as to internet applications (search engines, for example Google, Wikipedia, and social media sites such as Facebook, and Twitter).

There is a widespread belief that such technologies will transform teaching and learning practices, making them more significant, interesting and relevant to the students, and thereby radically changing the quality of learning students experience (Karasavvidis & Kollias, 2014). Institutions in higher education are making a substantial investment in technologies to support teaching and learning (Bebell, Russell, & O'Dwyer, 2004). The rapid advancement of learning technologies in higher education is attributed to the realisation that learning technologies can support, and innovate teaching (Fernández-Ferrer & Cano, 2016) and enhance various forms of assessments (Farrell & Rushby 2016). Drent and Meelissen (2008) argue that the deployment of learning technologies into the teaching and learning environment brings benefits for students, such that they are able to develop skills for searching and assessing information, collaboration, communication and problem solving. Research also shows that technologies can be used to improve the quality of teaching through the provision of professional development opportunities for teachers (Levin & Wadmany, 2008; Mends-Brew, 2012; Peters, 2009; Ruhizan, Norazah, Mohd, Faizal, & Jamil, 2014). Further, disruptive technologies such as Massive Open Online Courses (MOOCs) provide flexible online education for teachers, as well as opportunities for them to repurpose and adapt content to their own teaching (Conole, 2013; Kay, Reimann, Diebold & Kummerfeld, 2013). Proponents of the use of technology in education suggest that technology will make education more accessible, more affordable, and more effective, whereas opponents of the use of technology in education claim that there is no significant difference in learning when technology is used in the education process (Abrahams, 2010).

Despite a growing enthusiasm in introducing these LTs' within the higher education environment, successful deployment and adoption is highly dependent on the provision of adequate resources (Pelgrum, 2001), and ability to address individual, contextual and cultural dynamics within a particular country. In addition, Karasavvidis and Kollias (2014) argue that the past three decades of research on technology use in teaching has failed to transform teaching and learning practices. The authors further stated two major reasons for the failure. First, there has been a low rate of technology usage in classrooms. Second, even though educators embrace technology, it gets integrated in ways which reinforces the status-quo rather than bringing innovation in teaching. Past research has also shown that institutional reforms led by technology have also failed (Zhao & Frank, 2003). The connection between technology and learning can be seen as multifaceted phenomena, but research indicates that particular uses of technology can improve students' learning (Moeller & Reitzes, 2011). Integration of technology into teaching allows faculty to accept individual differences in students' achievements, learning approaches and abilities, and at the same time providing students and faculty better flexibility in different learning modes (Massy & Zemsky, 1995).

On individual level, educators are likely to face a number of challenges when adopting new technologies for the first time. These challenges often concern economic, technical, socio-political, attitudinal, and pedagogical issues (Shohel & Kirkwood, 2012). Literature also mentions that, in order to effectively and efficiently embrace learning technologies, it is necessary to consider technical factors (Al-Senaidi, Lin, & Poirot, 2009); teacher competencies (Samarawickrema & Stacey, 2007), teachers' roles and pedagogical concerns (Kirkwood, 2015), organizational and financial support (Drent & Meelissen, 2008), and safety and privacy concerns (Mitzner et al., 2010).

In order for successful integration of LTs, we need to better understand the factors that determine why some individuals adopt new technologies while others prefer to resist. The purpose of this study was to gain a better understanding of Fiji's Technical College lecturers' perceptions of the value of learning technologies and factors likely to influence their decisions to adopt and integrate these technologies into teaching. The research also aimed to identify educators' views on particular opportunities afforded by these technologies in enhancing student learning, as well as possible adoption challenges.

Literature review

Hall and Khan (2003) describe technology adoption as a consistent process that enables hesitant users to successfully adopt and use technology for a particular purpose. They pointed out that technology adoption occurs when users engage in a series of decisions that are outcomes of comparison of the advantages and disadvantages associated with the use of particular technologies. In the higher education sector, it is critical to understand the circumstances and conditions necessary for educators to embrace new technologies such as economic, socio-political, attitudinal, as well as pedagogical (Arenas, 2015; Shohel & Kirkwood, 2012). Further, there is a general consensus in the literature suggesting that understanding technical issues, teacher competencies, teacher's role, pedagogical concerns, organisational and financial support, safety and privacy concerns are critical enablers of technology adoption (Alazam, Bakar, Hamzah, & Asmiran, 2013; Bonsu, Duodu, JA, & Djang-Fordjour, 2013; Buabeng-Andoh, 2012a; Peters, 2009). This body of research also stated that although technologies have the potential to make teaching and learning more interesting, it requires considerable input of teacher training, preparation and production of appropriate materials.

Alazam et al. (2013) identified a close relationship between having technology usage skills and level of technology integration in classroom. Similarly, other studies pointed out that better technology integration into the classroom is dependent on users' level of knowledge and technological skills (Buntat, 2010; Paryono & Quito, 2010; Saud et al., 2010; Sukri, 2010). Further, Alazam et al. (2013) revealed that teachers' lack of technological skills was due to limited provision of pre-service and in-service training opportunities on the effective use of technology in the classroom.

In some studies, the lack of computers and access to them, lagging ICT infrastructural development, cost of training materials, and poor ICT competency skills are identified as significant barriers to technology adoption (Bonsu et al., 2013). Early research on uptake of ICT in Fiji pointed out that inadequate infrastructure, lack of awareness of the value of technologies poor skills, and cultural challenges were barriers to adoption (Lynch, Szorenyi, & Lodhia, 2002). Similarly, Al-Senaidi, Lin and Poirot (2009) pointed out that the lack of equipment, institutional support, disbelief in ICT benefits, and lack of time, are some of the factors that cause barriers to technology integration. Shohel and Kirkwood (2012) pointed out that resistance to technology adoption can be attributed to risk perception and uncertainty, which can limit teachers' ability to make full evaluations of technology integration (Howard, 2013). Within some faculty, lack of time commitment contributed to poor integration of technology into teaching (Amanortsu, Dzandu, & Asabere, 2014).

Analysis of various factors likely to influence educators' adoption of learning technology and the subsequent integration into teaching is critical. In this study we employ Decomposed Theory of Planned Behaviour (DTPB) as proposed by Taylor and Todd (1995b) to guide our analysis. According to Taylor and Todd (1995b), DTPB offers more transparency and clear relations among beliefs, attitudes and intentions. It can be applied to examine issues in a range of situations, offers a generic framework for identifying specific factors that lead to adoption and use of new technology. In the DTPB attitudinal beliefs are deconstructed into three concepts; namely, perceived usefulness, ease of use and compatibility (Taylor & Todd, 1995a). Normative beliefs are also important constructs within the DTPB framework, and they are associated with difference between the opinions of key reference groups in an organisational setting (supervisors, colleagues, and friends). Moreover, control beliefs are broken down into two groups: self-efficacy and resource facilitating conditions. Self-efficacy relates to perceived ability of using a new technology. Facilitating conditions refers to the availability of time, money and technological resources for technology adoption. DTPB suggests that the clearer the perceptions of both self-efficacy in the new technology and the existing facilitating conditions, the more likely is the intention to adopt the innovation (Taylor & Todd, 1995a).

Fiji higher education system

Fiji is a country made up of about 360 Islands in the Pacific Ocean. It is inhabited by an estimate of 895,825 people. Despite the presence of numerous Islands, the majority of the population (80 %) live in only two prominent Islands of Viti Levu and Vanua Levu. The Ministry of Education (MOE) is the responsible for the administration of the educational system. English is the official language of instruction in schools. The tertiary and the higher education sector is relatively small, with three universities: the University of the South Pacific, University of Fiji, and Fiji National University and a number of technical vocational education and training (TVET).

TVET has been in existence in Fiji from early 1950's with the aim of providing skills training for youths, as well as the working population wanting to attain higher skills and competencies. Until 2010 the structure of TVET in Fiji comprised three main organizations: school-based TVET under the Ministry of Education (MOE), the Fiji Institute of Technology (FIT), and non-formal training provided by the Training and Productivity Authority of Fiji (TPAF). However, TVET structure and curriculum programmes have undergone many changes in the last five years including the establishment of Fiji National University (FNU) in 2010. This came about as a result of a merger between six higher education institutions in Fiji, namely the Fiji Institute of Technology, Fiji School of Nursing, Fiji College of Advanced Education, Lautoka Teachers College, Fiji School of Medicine and Fiji College of Agriculture. In addition to

FNU there are two more universities in Fiji called University of the South Pacific and University of Fiji.

Furthermore, as part of continued education reforms Fiji plans the closure of 71 TVET Centres attached to high schools within a two year period and establish 10 hi-tech technical colleges around the country by the year 2016 (Ministry of Education, 2014). There are three such colleges already established in early 2015 which are also chosen for this research. The Colleges offer qualifications under the newly established Fiji Qualifications framework with the aim to enhance skills based training for greater employment opportunity and economic growth (Ministry of Education, 2015). In the Ministry of Education Fiji vision for 'Quality Education for Change, Peace and Progress' that emphasises its role in delivering quality education for the betterment of the country and people in order to be globally competitive, it was stipulated that Fiji needs to develop highly skilled and knowledgeable workforce in order to compete in the globalised world.

In order to realise its vision, the Annual Business Plan 2015 saw a need to improve access to technology in education with the aim to improve teaching and learning through integration of technologies (Ministry of Education, 2015). This necessitates a need for educators in Fiji to embrace learning technologies in their daily teaching. While many of the new initiatives were mostly focused on primary, high schools and universities, not much evidence to show that polytechnic education also gets a similar preference. TVET lecturers' technology adoption and integration became an important initiative but remained unexplored. While, on the surface this seems an obvious way to align education within the national goal of progress and growth, the act of technology integration is fraught with challenges (Al-Senaidi et al., 2009; Alazam et al., 2013; Bonsu et al., 2013; Buabeng-Andoh 2012a, b; Drent & Meelissen, 2008; Howard, 2013). The aim of this study was to explore Fiji's Technical Colleges lecturers' experiences and beliefs and values around the contribution of new learning technologies to enhance teaching and better student learning.

Method and procedures

Research reported in this article utilised a survey design. A questionnaire adapted from (Hartshorne & Ajjan, 2009) was used a s a main instrument for gathering data about the types of technologies respondents have used, usage frequencies, value accrued to the use of technology, opportunities afforded by the integration of learning technologies into teaching as well as possible challenges. According to Teddlie and Tashakkori (2009), researchers employ questionnaire to gather self-report data about attitudes, beliefs and feelings towards an issue of interest.

The survey instrument consisted of: technology adoption, nature of technology/applications used, participants attitude towards technology use for teaching and learning, perceived ease of use, and usefulness of technology in teaching, current technology usage challenges, subjective norms, perceived behavioural control, self-efficacy, resources and support, intention of usage, and participants demographics. The instrument was tested for reliability and revealed a high Cronbach's Alpha ($\alpha = .832$); ($n = 55$). Results of the test indicated a good acceptability level considering that .70 is normally the cut-off value for being acceptable (Cortina, 1993). Formal approval for administrating the survey was obtained from the Research

Unit of Fiji's Ministry of Education. Courtesy phone calls were made to the Director of the Technical College Fiji and the Senior Education officers informing about the study and also to seek their assistance in order to increase participation from the target population.

The survey was then made available online for the respondents in early August 2015. Data were collected within a two-week timeframe. There are only three Technical Colleges established this year with a total teaching staff population of 72. However, questionnaire was only distributed to 63 staff members as some of the lecturers were away. A total of 55 respondents completed the survey. Sample Error: 5.5 %. In order to ascertain sample representativeness of sample from the population surveyed. Standard error of the sample was computed, revealing ($n = 55$; 95 % confidence, margin of error 5.5 %).

Data analysis and respondents' characteristics

Data was analysed using Statistical Package for Social Science (SPSS) software. Descriptive statistics such as median, frequency, and percentage are used for analysis. Furthermore, factor analysis was also performed to identify key factors that are likely to influence adoption. The desired sample size was 63 but the actual number of respondents who took part in the study was 55, yielding a high response rate of 76.3 %. Most of the respondents identified as male (37, 67 %), and reported a variety of academic positions, (44, 80 %) lecturers and (8, 14 %) heads of department in a variety of disciplines. Participant age range was normally distributed with the majority falling between the maximum of 31–40, (20, 36.4 %); followed by those within the age range of 20–30, (18, 33 %). Further, majority of respondents (34, 63 %) rated their computer competence as intermediate; (15, 27.8 %) mentioned advanced level knowledge and skills and only (5, 9.3 %) were beginners. Competence in the use of technology can be attributed to a prior requirement to take pre-service computer related courses or to the lecturers' own effort to upgrade their technology handling skills.

Factor analysis

In order to determine factors likely to influence respondents' decisions in integrating technology into their teaching, principal axis factor analysis with varimax rotation was conducted to examine the underlying structure for 52 factors. A Kaiser–Meyer–Olkin (KMO) and principal component factor analysis were performed. The value of KMO was 0.7, which suggests that the sample was adequate to proceed with principal component factor analysis. In addition, the value for Bartlett's test showed significance ($p < .000$) indicating high correlation among variables for factor analysis. The assumption of independent sampling, normality, linear relationship between pairs of variables, and variables being correlated at a moderate level were met. Furthermore, to examine construct validity, VARIMAX rotation was carried out with results (see Table 1). Table with rotated component Matrix is presented in Table 2. There were only 11 items whose loading values are ≥ 0.04.

Fifty-one items loaded above accepted 0.60 threshold, which were then mapped to the items describing the decomposed theory of planned behavior. After rotation the first factor accounted for 35.3 % of the variance (see Table 2). The items that loaded

Table 1 Rotated Component Matrix

Item	Component										
	1	2	3	4	5	6	7	8	9	10	11
I use computer technology hardware and software that are designed to meet specific learning objectives	0.8										
Working with learning technologies is fun	0.8										
I use technology to facilitate students learning	0.7										
I will recommend the idea of using technologies in teaching to my colleagues	0.7										
I use technology to promote creativity	0.7										
I use technologies into teaching to increase the productivity of my lessons	0.7										
Any learning technology makes work more interesting for me	0.6										
I use computer technologies for exam preparations	0.6										
I look forward to those aspects of teaching that involves technologies	0.6				0.4						
I use computer technologies for exam analysis and reports	0.6										
I believe it is important for technical college lecturers to use technologies in teaching	0.6		−0.5								
I am confident in using technologies in practical lessons		0.8									
I am confident in using technologies in both theory and practical lessons		0.8									
I get enough time to incorporate technologies in teaching		0.6									
I am confident in my ability to use technologies in practical lessons		0.6									
I am confident in using technologies in theory lessons	0.4	0.6									
My colleagues think I should use technologies in my teaching		0.5				0.4					
My peers/colleagues are using technologies in teaching		0.4									
There is not enough institutional help for teachers to use technologies for teaching			0.9								
There are no incentives provided by my institution for integrating technologies in teaching			0.8								
Most teaching staff are not interested in using any forms of technologies in their teaching			0.8								
I find use of technologies in teaching difficult			0.7								
There are not enough computers and technologies available for teaching in my institution			0.7						−0.5		
Using technologies for teaching is entirely within my control				0.8							
I would like to use technologies for teaching				0.7							
I have knowledge to use technologies in my teaching				0.7							
I have resources to use technologies in my teaching				0.7					0.4		
I would feel comfortable learning about new technologies on my own				0.5		0.4					
I intend to learn and adopt more about technologies in my teaching practices					0.8						
The advantages of using technologies in teaching outweigh the disadvantages	0.4				0.8						

Table 1 Rotated Component Matrix *(Continued)*

I feel that future teaching demands will require me to be well versed with computer and other learning technologies					0.6						
I am aware that my students should be trained on using equipment and machines of latest model and make so that they can perform well at their workplace					0.6						
In general, I follow my friends' advice in making decisions						0.8					
When it comes to matters of teaching, I want to be like my friends						0.7					
My students think I should use technologies in class						0.7					
I do not have departmental/instructional supported time to learn about technology usage			0.4			0.5					
My institution provides adequate time for professional development							0.8				
My institution provides me the training I need to confidently use technologies in teaching							0.7				
I try to identify benefits of technology to maximize learning	0.5						0.7				
My institution provides staff with sufficient information towards using technologies in teaching							0.6				
Thanks to my resourcefulness, I know how to handle unforeseen situations								0.8			
No matter what comes my way, I'm usually able to handle problems								0.8			
I can manage to solve difficult problems if I try hard enough	0.4							0.7			
I would feel comfortable using technologies on my own				0.4				0.4			
There are sufficient technological resources for my teaching and learning in my institution		0.5							0.7		
My institution provides me with appropriate equipment to use technologies									0.7		
My institution gives recognition to staff who use technologies in their teaching									0.6		
When it comes to matters of teaching, I want to do what my supervisor thinks I should do										0.8	
My immediate supervisor thinks I should use technologies in my teaching										0.6	
I often lack time in using technologies in my teaching											0.7
Extraction Method: Principal Component Analysis.											

Rotation Method: Varimax with Kaiser Normalization

into this factor include attitudes towards technology and usefulness of technology in teaching. The second factor explained 9.7 % of the variance. Items that loaded into this factor describe perceived ease of technology use. The third factor explained about 6.7 % variance, describing technology usage challenges. The fourth factor explained 5.8 % of the variance and was used to explain perceived behavior control. The fifth factor accounted for 4.5.1 % of the variance and was used to describe intention to use technology. The sixth factor which accounted for only 4.0 % described subjected norms. The seventh factor described resources and support. The rest of the factors are presented in Table 1, each with an Eigenvalue >1. Further, items used to capture self-efficacy poorly loaded into the factors.

Table 2 Total Variance Explained

	Total	% of Var	Cum %	Total	% of Var	Cum %	Total	% of Var	Cum %
1	16.5	34.3	34.3	16.5	34.3	34.3	6.8	14.1	14.1
2	4.9	10.3	44.6	4.9	10.3	44.6	4.7	9.7	23.8
3	3.2	6.6	51.2	3.2	6.6	51.2	4.0	8.2	32.0
4	2.9	6.1	57.3	2.9	6.1	57.3	3.8	7.9	39.9
5	2.1	4.4	61.6	2.1	4.4	61.6	3.6	7.6	47.5
6	1.8	3.8	65.4	1.8	3.8	65.4	3.4	7.1	54.6
7	1.7	3.6	69.0	1.7	3.6	69.0	3.2	6.6	61.2
8	1.5	3.1	72.1	1.5	3.1	72.1	3.1	6.5	67.7
9	1.3	2.8	74.9	1.3	2.8	74.9	2.1	4.3	72.0
10	1.2	2.4	77.3	1.2	2.4	77.3	1.8	3.8	75.8
11	1.0	2.2	79.5	1.0	2.2	79.5	1.8	3.7	79.5
12	1.0	2.0	81.5						
13	0.9	1.9	83.4						
14	0.8	1.7	85.1						
15	0.8	1.6	86.7						
16	0.7	1.5	88.2						
17	0.7	1.4	89.7						
18	0.6	1.2	90.9						
19	0.5	1.1	91.9						
20	0.5	1.0	92.9						
21	0.4	0.9	93.8						
22	0.4	0.8	94.7						
23	0.4	0.7	95.4						
24	0.3	0.6	96.0						
25	0.3	0.6	96.6						
26	0.2	0.5	97.1						
27	0.2	0.4	97.6						
28	0.2	0.4	97.9						
29	0.2	0.4	98.3						
30	0.1	0.3	98.6						
31	0.1	0.3	98.8						
32	0.1	0.2	99.0						
33	0.1	0.2	99.2						
34	0.1	0.2	99.4						
35	0.1	0.2	99.5						
36	0.1	0.1	99.6						
37	0.0	0.1	99.7						
38	0.0	0.1	99.8						
39	0.0	0.1	99.9						
40	0.0	0.0	99.9						
41	0.0	0.0	99.9						
42	0.0	0.0	100.0						
43	0.0	0.0	100.0						
44	0.0	0.0	100.0						

Table 2 Total Variance Explained *(Continued)*

45	0.0	0.0	100.0
46	0.0	0.0	100.0
47	0.0	0.0	100.0
48	0.0	0.0	100.0

Extraction Method: Principal Component Analysis.

Results

Utilisation of technology

A large number of respondents indicated that they were generally competent in the use of available learning technologies (36, 67 %), and stated that they value the integration of technology into their teaching. Some stressed that their use of technology increased their creativity in teaching. In addition, (9, 16 %) respondents reported using computers between two to three hours per day, while close to (15, 27 %) respondents mentioned they spent between three to four hours per day. We asked respondents to indicate whether they had taken pre-service computer training. Three quarters of respondents (41, 75 %) reported that they were required to take some form of formal computer training during their tertiary studies. It was also observed that (29, 53.7 %) of participants did not participate in any formal technology training after joining the teaching profession. However, variations were observed in other institutions as nearly half of the respondents (25, 46.3 %) indicated that they were required to undertake some computer related courses.

Web usage

Respondents were also asked about their engagement with resources on the web. Figure 1 shows that between the years 1992 to 1998 8 (15 %) respondents used the web for the first time.

However, between the years 2000 to 2009 the number increased by 61 % (see Fig. 2). Furthermore, from 2005 there was an increased adoption of social network sites such as YouTube and Facebook. This could have been attributed to more lecturers using the web for research and teaching purposes. Results also showed that 47 (88.7 %) lecturers fall in the combined intermediate and advance skills categories of web usage.

Technology for teaching purpose

As seen in Fig. 3 above, there seems to be a steady increase in the integration of technology into teaching from 2005 to 2009 representing 11 (20 %) respondents. From 2010 to 2015, there was a significant increase of 57 %, representing 55 % of the total population who reported integrating technology into their teaching.

Respondents mentioned access to different forms of technologies which they either owned or were provided to them by their institutions, with an overall preference for laptops over iPads (19, 26 %), which might be attributed to the fact that most of the institutions had only a few iPads available for the staff members compared to laptops. Nearly all respondents (51, 93 %) also reported proficiency in the use of office productivity software (e.g. Excel, Word, PowerPoint, etc.)

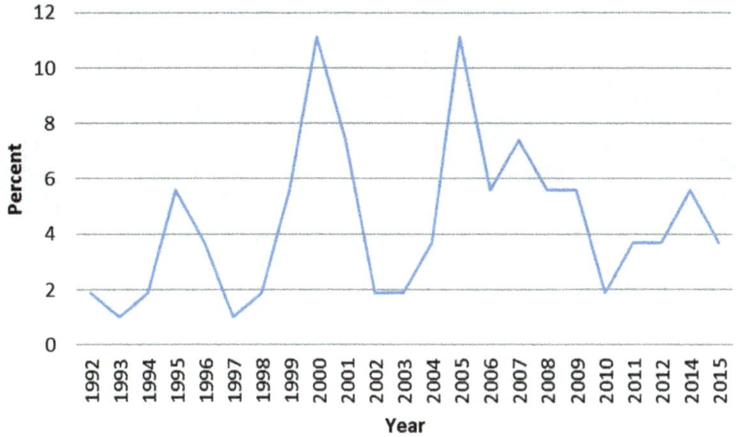

Fig. 1 First year of Web usage by respondents

Social media

Social media utilisation in teaching is an emerging area that has not been thoroughly investigated in the literature. In our analysis the vast majority of respondents (50, 93 %) reported using YouTube, followed by Facebook (47, 87 %). There was a shared view among respondents in support of the use of social media for teaching. It was believed that the current generation of students had wider exposure to many aspects of social media outside of class, therefore they could also use such media for their own learning. Furthermore, some respondents mentioned that

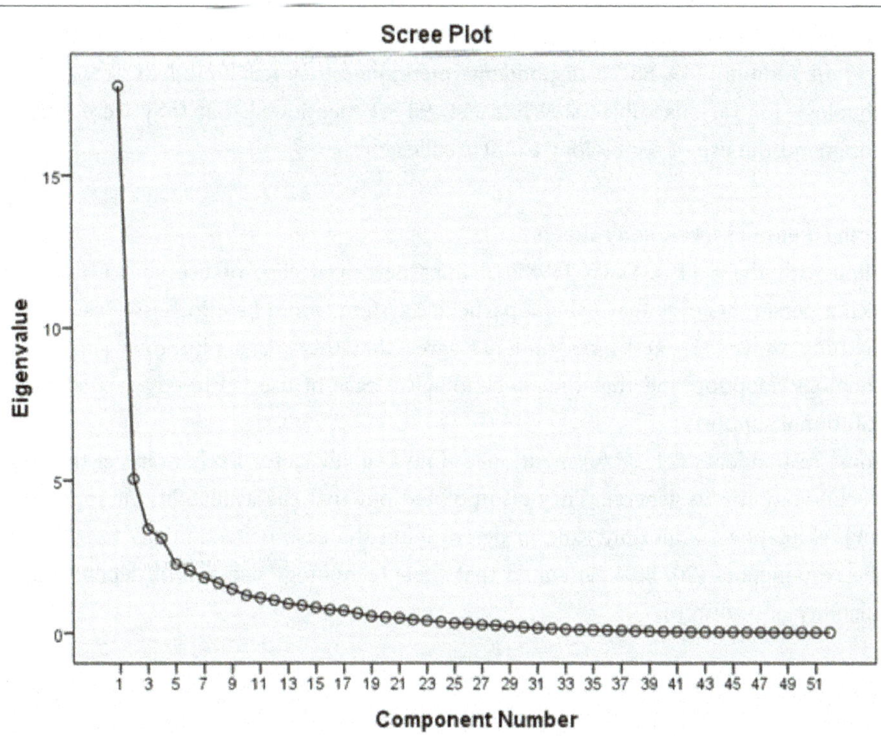

Fig. 2 Shows the factors extracted

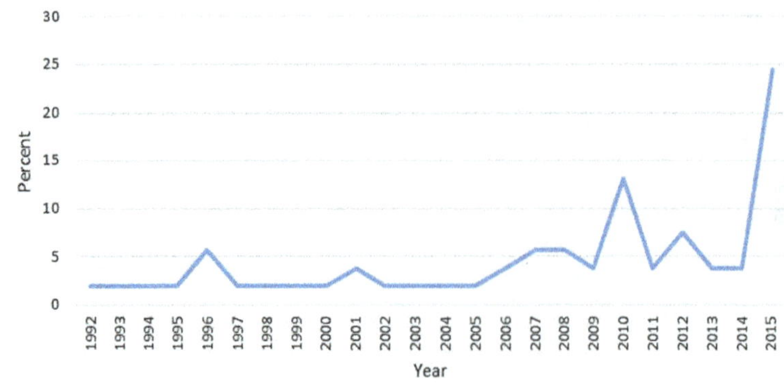

Fig. 3 Computers for teaching purpose

social media also allows them to share teaching and learning resources with their students and also with their colleagues.

Factors likely to influence technology adoption

Technology adoption in teaching is influenced by a number of factors. Some of the factors are associated with the environment, the nature of the technology, and personal attributes and preferences.

Attitude towards technology adoption

Almost all respondents reported that the use of technology makes their work easier (52, 94 %). Some indicated that employing technology in teaching can help them effectively manage their time, especially during lecture preparation and presentation. A significant number (54, 98 %) mentioned that they have been using technologies in teaching and that the utilisation of technology for teaching helps engage students (53, 96 %). In addition, (49, 88 %) respondents mentioned they feel confident in integrating technology for various subjects. While (54, 98 %) mentioned that they were likely to recommend the use of technology to their colleagues.

Perceived ease of technology usage

In line with the DTPB, Davis (1989) defines perceived ease of use as the degree to which a person believes that using a particular system would be effortless. Results from this study show (35, 60 %) respondents agree that there is institutional support for technology adoption and that their technological ease of use is directly related to this institutional support.

Some respondents (21, 38 %) mentioned time as a key factor likely to affect their ease of technology use in general. They also pointed out that the availability of appropriate resources plays an important role in determining the ease of technology use. Further, some respondents (20, 36.4 %) stated that their technology use would depend on the availability of resources.

Subjective norms

DTPB suggests that subjective norms such as influence from peers and supervisors play can influence the degree to which people can embrace or reject integration of technology into their practices. The survey results indicated that majority of respondents (52, 96 %) were aware their colleagues were using various forms of technologies in their teaching. They indicated that their colleagues are more likely to support their adoption of technology. In addition, majority of respondents mentioned their decision to integrate technology into teaching is likely to be influenced by their immediate supervisors' beliefs about the efficacy of technology in delivering better teaching outcomes. Additionally, almost three quarters (41, 74.6 %) of respondents cited that they would follow what their supervisor thought was right for them. Similarly, almost (40, 73 %) mentioned that possibility of integrating technology can also be influenced by views their students hold.

Perceived behavioural control

According to the DTPB perceived behavioural control refers to individuals' perceptions of their ability to accomplish a given behaviour and it is influenced by the availability of skills, resources, and opportunities that influence adoption of technologies in teaching. A large number of respondents (48, 87 %) believed that the use of technology in teaching is within their control, and the availability of adequate resources and sufficient knowledge of technology significantly contributes to future adoption.

Self-efficacy

Self-efficacy is the belief in one's ability to successfully perform a technologically sophisticated new task. It does not focus on the skills one has, but rather the judgments of what one can do with his or her skills. In our analysis respondents (49, 89 %) demonstrated a great deal of self-efficacy, in that they can find solutions to problems if they try hard enough. Some pointed out that (52, 95 %) they are more likely to handle unexpected situations with the current resources they have. In general respondents showed a high level of confidence in finding solutions to problems, and remaining confident solving complex problems involving technology in teaching. More than three quarters of (48, 87 %) reported that they comfortably use existing technologies on their own.

Resources and support

Respondents were asked about the availability of resources and support in the use of technology in their institutions. More than half of the respondents 34 (62 %) believed they had adequate institutional support in possible integration of learning technologies into their teaching. In addition, (40, 73 %) believed that they were provided with adequate infrastructure. Furthermore, three quarters (41, 75 %) stated that their institutions recognise and likely to reward staff members who use technology in their teaching. They also mentioned that professional development was made available for them.

Intention to use technology

Intention to use technology is an aspect that captures the extent of willingness by individuals to use technological tools (Ajzen, 1991). The survey explore individuals' willingness to adopt technology in teaching. Results suggest that a vast majority (51, 93 %) agreed that they were aware of the future need and significance of integrating learning technologies into their teaching. They also mentioned that to train students using technology offers more advantages than disadvantages. As such many (54, 98 %) indicated they intend to continue with future integration of technology into their teaching. The survey also examined perceived challenges of integrating learning technology into teaching. Some (32, 58 %) identified timed needed for better integration of learning technologies into teaching. Though some variation was observed across participating institutions as some respondents seemed to differ (23, 42 %) that time is not an issue for them when integrating technology in their teaching.

Discussion and conclusion

The purpose of this study was to gain a better understanding of lecturers' perceptions of the value of learning technologies and factors likely to influence their decisions to adopt and integrate these technologies into teaching. The research also aimed to identify opportunities afforded by these technologies in enhancing student learning, as well as possible adoption challenges. Overall, results suggested that respondents strongly valued the contribution of learning technologies in enhancing student learning. Further, results revealed almost all respondents from the three technical colleges in Fiji were in the process of technology adoption. As mentioned earlier this research identified a number of factors likely to influence the rapid adoption of these technologies.

According to Pelgrum (2001), the success of any innovation is largely dependent on the skills and knowledge of the educators. Further, Buabeng-Andoh (2012b), mention that success of an educational technology programme in any institution depends on the teachers' support, and their attitudes as well as the beliefs they hold about the potentials of a particular technology in transforming their teaching practice, and enhancing student learning. Majority of respondents in this study believed that using learning technologies would significantly contribute to the efficacy of their teaching. More specifically, they stressed that integrating learning technologies into their teaching would offer a greater opportunity for student engagement, which confirms the views in the literature suggesting that educational technology provides prospects for students to develop their creativity and enhance reasoning skills, critical thinking skills, communication skills and other higher order thinking (Chigona & Chigona, 2010; Trucano, 2005). Respondents who are already currently employing learning technologies in their teaching said they use them for creativity, to facilitate students' learning, to meet specific learning objectives, and to perform academic tasks.

Another key findings in this research is that lectures value the contribution of learning technologies to student learning. Research currently suggest that users attitude and perceived usefulness of technology are the key factors necessary in supporting the possible integration of learning technologies into teaching The observations reported here are consistent with outcomes of similar studies, noting that attitude was a key factor in determining technology adoption (Shiue, 2007; Teo, 2008, 2012; Taylor & Todd, 1995). Further, attitude, behavioural controls, self-efficacy, perceived usefulness and intention to use technology are key factors identified, that are likely to influence future adoption and integration of learning technologies into teaching. In addition, related factors such as ease of use, knowledge, and confidence in handling technologies were also viewed important. Similar to previous work, analysis of the data revealed that majority of respondents believed that the use of technology in teaching was within their control, these results are in line with the literature (Ajzen & Madden 1985).

An individual intention to experiment with new technologies in general is an important predictor for future adoption of technology. Further, Teo (2012) examined the intention to use technology among pre-service teachers and found that subjective norms have a significant influence on teachers' behavioural intentions to use technology. In the survey, respondents mentioned that they keen to integrate technologies into their teaching. Within the DPBT, peer and supervisory influence were additional important strong predictors of future adoption. Peer and supervisory influence as predictors of technology adoptions are both culturally bounded. In the case of Fiji, collective cultural practices and strong hierarchical power structures have direct influence on the extent of subjective, peer and supervisory factors for adoption of technologies (Lynch, Szorenyi, & Lodhia, 2002; Schepers & Wetzels, 2007; Venkatesh & Davis, 2000). Further, institutional level factors such as resources, funding, incentives, supervisors' influence, and technology related professional opportunities were also identified as critical.

Generally, respondents were fully aware of the opportunities afforded by learning technologies and expressed their willingness to adopt and integrate these technologies into their teaching. Respondents also acknowledge the challenges likely to interfere with future adoptions, and stressed the role of institutions to overcome systemic barriers to adoption. On the other hand, Mumtaz (2000) noted that institutions can only go so far in providing up-to-date technology, related support, and encouragement for technology usage but the actual take-up depends largely on individuals' personal feelings, skills and attitudes.

The results of this study showed that respondents have a high level of self-efficacy, which is likely to help them overcome issues they might face during technology integration. However, as new technologies continue to permeate the higher education landscape, for effective integration there will be a need for many lecturers to familiarise themselves with various technologies, to develop confidence. Respondents reported possible barriers to effective integration of learning technologies into teaching include a lack of knowledge and skills, inadequate resource and support from administrators and the institutions, and the sociocultural dynamics within the Fijian context. This particular finding is consistent with Lynch, Szorenyi and Lodhia (2002) analysis of cultural differences and how this would likley influence technology adotpion. This research contributes to the growing significance of individual, contextual and cultural influences in the adoption of learning technologies into teaching.

Study limitations

Even though this research has contributed to contextual and institutional factors likely to influence the integration of learning technologies into teaching in Fiji, it was conducted in technical colleges, results of which might not apply in other higher institutions in Fiji. Moreover, the sample was self-selected and might already be influenced by social desirability bias in that only those interested in the use of technology in teaching might have contributed. Future research need to deploy a systematic observation, including focus group and critical analysis of institutional documents such as curriculum plans, and technology inventory records. Furthermore, results would have been more meaningful and richer if students and administrators were also involved in the study.

Acknowledgement

The research reported in this article was part of a Master's thesis funded by NZAid. The researchers would like to acknowledge scholarship support from NZ for Shalendra Kumar, and postgraduate writing grant from the department of Higher Education, at the University of Otago, New Zealand.

Authors' contribution

Both authors contributed equally towards this article.

Authors' information

Mr. Shalendra Kumar is the head of department and the acting principal of a Fiji Higher Education Commission (FHEC) registered TVET institute. He is also a registered accessor and evaluator of TVET programs with FHEC. His research interest is looking at ways to enhance the teaching and learning of TVET in Fiji, particularly focusing on on use of learning technologies by lecturers. Dr. Ben Kei Daniel is a Senior Lecturer in Educational Technology and Research Methodologies, in Higher Education. He currently leads an Educational Technology Group, at the University of Otago—New Zealand. His research is focused on understanding the value of Big Data and learning analytics in highereducation. He is also investigating theories and praxis of teaching Research Methodologies for Academia and Business.

References

Abrahams, D. A. (2010). Technology adoption in higher education: a framework for identifying and prioritising issues and barriers to adoption of instructional technology. *Journal of Applied Research in Higher Education, 2*(2), 34–49.

Ajzen, I., & Madden, T. (1985). From intentions to action: a theory of planned behaviour. In J. Kuhl & J. Beckmann (Eds.), *Action control: from cognition to behaviour.* New York: Springer Verlag.

Ajzen, I. (1991). The theory of planned behavior. *Organizational behavior and human decision processes, 50*(2), 179–211.

Alazam, A.-O., Bakar, A., Hamzah, R., & Asmiran, S. (2013). Teachers' ICT skills and ICT integration in the classroom: the case of vocational and technical teachers in Malaysia. *Creative Education, 3*(8), 70–76.

Al-Senaidi, S., Lin, L., & Poirot, J. (2009). Barriers to adopting technology for teaching and learning in Oman. *Computers & Education, 53*(3), 575–590.

Amanortsu, G., Dzandu, M. D., & Asabere, N. Y. (2014). Towards the access to and usage of information and communication technology (ICT) in polytechnic education. *International Journal of Computer Applications, 66*(1), 23–33.

Arabasz, P., & Baker, M. B. (2003). Evolving campus support models for e-learning courses. *Educause Center for Applied Research Bulletin*, 1–9. Retrieved 10 September 2016 from: http://net.educause.edu/ir/library/pdf/ers0303/ekf0303.pdf.

Arenas, E. (2015). Affordances of learning technologies in higher education multicultural environments. *Electronic Journal of E-Learning, 13*(4), 217–227. Retrieved from http://0-search.proquest.com.cataleg.uoc.edu/docview/1697674722?accountid=15299.

Bebell, D., Russell, M., & O'Dwyer, L. (2004). Measuring teachers' technology uses: Why multiple-measures are more revealing. *Journal of Research on Technology in Education, 37*(1), 45–63.

Bonsu, K., Duodu, A., JA, A., Bonsu, K., Duodu, A., Ansere, J. A., & Djang-Fordjour, K. (2013). The challenges and prospects of ICTs in teaching and learning in sunyani polytechnic, Ghana. *Capa Scientific Journal, 1*(1), 12–17.

Buabeng-Andoh, C. (2012a). Factors influencing teachers' adoption and integration of information and communication technology into teaching: A review of the literature. *International Journal of Education and Development using Information and Communication Technology, 8*(1), 136.

Buabeng-Andoh, C. (2012b). Factors influencing teachers' adoption and integration of information and communication technology into teaching: A review of the literature. *International Journal of Education and Development using Information and Communication Technology, 8*(1), 136–155.

Buntat, Y. (2010). Computer technology application and vocational education: a review of literature and research. *European Journal of Social Sciences, 14*(4), 645–651.

Business Plan 2015 Ministry of Education, Heritage and Arts: Retrieved 15 September 2016 from http://www.education.gov.fj/images/AnnualBusinessPlans/2015_ABP.pdf.

Chigona, A., Chigona, W., Kayongo, P., & Kausa, M. (2010). An empirical survey on domestication of ICT in schools in disadvantaged communities in South Africa Agnes Chigona, Wallace Chigona, Patrick Kayongo and Moses Kausa University of Cape Town, South Africa. *International Journal of Education and Development using Information and Communication Technology, 6*(2), 21–32.

Conole, G. (2013). MOOCs as disruptive technologies: strategies for enhancing the learner experience and quality of MOOCs. *RED. Revista de Educación a Distancia*, (39), 1–17. Retrieved 10 September 2016, from http://revistas.um.es/red/article/view/234221/179941.

Cortina, J. M. (1993). What is coefficient alpha? an examination of theory and applications. *Journal of Applied Psychology, 78*(1), 98.

Davis, F. D. (1989). Perceived Usefulness, Perceived Ease Of Use, And User Accep. *MIS Quarterly, 13*(3), 319.

Drent, M., & Meelissen, M. (2008). Which factors obstruct or stimulate teacher educators to use ICT innovatively? *Computers & Education, 51*(1), 187–199.

Farrell, T., & Rushby, N. (2016; 2015). Assessment and learning technologies: An overview. *British Journal of Educational Technology, 47(1)*, 106–120. doi:10.1111/bjet.12348

Fernández-Ferrer, M. & Cano, E. (2016). The influence of the internet for pedagogical innovation: using twitter to promote online collaborative learning. *International Journal of Educational Technology in Higher Education*, 13(22). doi:10.1186/s41239-016-0021-2

Hall, B. H., & Khan, B. (2003). *Adoption of new technology (No. w9730)*. National Bureau of Economic Research. Retrieved on 10 September 2016 from: http://www.nber.org/papers/w9730.

Hartshorne, R., & Ajjan, H. (2009). Examining student decisions to adopt Web 2.0 technologies: theory and empirical tests. *Journal of Computing in Higher Education, 21*(3), 183–198.

Howard, S. K. (2013). Risk-aversion: understanding teachers' resistance to technology integration. *Technology, Pedagogy and Education, 22*(3), 357–372.
Karasavvidis, I., & Kollias, V. (2014). Technology integration in the most favorable conditions: findings from a professional development training program. In C. Karagiannidis (Ed.), *Research on e-learning and ICT in education* (pp. 197–224). New York: Springer.
Kay, J., Reimann, P., Diebold, E., & Kummerfeld, B. (2013). MOOCs: So many learners, so much potential. *Technology, 52*(1), 49–67.
Kirkwood, A. (2015). Teaching and learning with technology in higher education: blended and distance education needs 'joined-up thinking'rather than technological determinism. *Open Learning: The Journal of Open, Distance and e-Learning, 29*(3), 1–16.
Laurillard, D. (2013). Teaching as a Design Science: Building Pedagogical Patterns for Learning and Technology. New York: Routledge, Taylor & Francis Group.
Levin, T., & Wadmany, R. (2008). Teachers' views on factors affecting effective integration of information technology in the classroom: developmental scenery. *Journal of Technology and Teacher Education, 16*(2), 233–263.
Lynch, T., Szorenyi, N., & Lodhia, S. (2002). *Adoption of information technologies in Fiji: issues in the study of cultural influences on information technology acceptance. Paper presented at the ITIRA conference.* Rockhampton: Central Queensland University.
Massy, W. F., & Zemsky, R. (1995). *Using information technology to enhance academic productivity.* Washington, DC: Inter-University Communications Council, Inc.
Mends-Brew, E. (2012). Enhancement of ICT in polytechnics for accelerated development. *Natural and Applied Science, 3*(3), 99–107.
Ministry of Education, H. a. A. (2014). Annual Corporate Plan. Government of Fiji reports: Available at: http://www.education.gov.fj/index.php/resources/photo-movies.
Ministry of Education, H. a. A. (2015). Annual Corporate Plan. Government of Fiji reports: Available at: http://www.education.gov.fj/index.php/resources/photo-movies.
Mitzner, T. L., Boron, J. B., Fausset, C. B., Adams, A. E., Charness, N., Czaja, S. J., & Sharit, J. (2010). Older adults talk technology: technology usage and attitudes. *Computers in Human Behavior, 26*(6), 1710–1721.
Moeller, B., & Reitzes, T. (2011). *Integrating technology with student-centered learning. A report to the Nellie Mae education foundation.* Retrieved from http://www.nmefoundation.org/getmedia/befa9751-d8ad-47e9-949d-bd649f7c0044/integrating.
Mumtaz, S. (2000). Factors affecting teachers' use of information and communications technology: a review of the literature. *Journal of Information Technology for Teacher Education, 9*(3), 319–342.
Paryono, & Quito, B. G. (2010). Meta-analysis of ICT integration in vocational and technical education in southeast asia. In *An International Conference on VTET Research and Networking.* SEAVERN Research Report. SEAMO VOCTECH Regional Centre, Brunei Darussalam. From: http://www.voctech.org.bn/conference/papers/[VOCTECH]%20Paryono%20&%20Ben.pdf.
Pelgrum, W. J. (2001). Obstacles to the integration of ICT in education: results from a worldwide educational assessment. *Computers & education, 37*(2), 163–178.
Peters, L. (2009). *Global education: using technology to bring the world to your students.* Washington, DC: International Society for Technology in Education.
Ruhizan, M., Norazah, M., Mohd, B. R., Faizal, A., & Jamil, A. (2014). Vocational education readiness in Malaysia on the use of e-portfolios. *Journal of Technical Education and Training, 6*(2), 157–171.
Samarawickrema, G., & Stacey, E. (2007). Adopting Web-based learning and teaching: a case study in higher education. *Distance Education, 28*(3), 313–333.
Saud, MS., Rajuddin, B., Ismail, S., Nordin, MS., Minghat, AD., Subari, K., & Arsat, M. (2010). ICT application in vocational and technical education and training (VTET) institutions in Malaysia. *SEAVERN journals, 2*(1). Retrieved 15 September, 2016 from http://s3.amazonaws.com/academia.edu.documents/25676036/64-35-1-SM.pdf?AWSAccessKeyId=AKIAJ56TQJRTWSMTNPEA&Expires=1473889551&Signature=y7DVe%2FjbIPRJmefpdwW4ID790Fg%3D&response-content-disposition=inline%3B%20filename%3DICT_Application_in_Vocational_and_Techni.pdf.
Schepers, J., & Wetzels, M. (2007). A meta-analysis of the technology acceptance model: Investigating subjective norm and moderation effects. *Information & Management, 44*(1), 90–103.
Shiue, Y.-M. (2007). Investigating the sources of teachers' instructional technology use through the decomposed theory of planned behavior. *Journal of Educational Computing Research, 36*(4), 425–453.
Shohel, M. M. C., & Kirkwood, A. (2012). Using technology for enhancing teaching and learning in Bangladesh: challenges and consequences. *Learning, Media and Technology, 37*(4), 414–428.
Sife, A., Lwoga, E., & Sanga, C. (2007). New technologies for teaching and learning: Challenges for higher learning institutions in developing countries. *International Journal of Education and Development using ICT, 3*(2), 57–67.
Sukri, M. (2010). *ICT application in vocational and technical education and training (VTET) institutions in Malaysia.* Paper presented at the An International Conference on VTET Research and Networking. SEAVERN Research Report. SEAMO VOCTECH Regional Centre, Brunei Darussalam. Retrieved from http://www.voctech.org.bn/conference/papers/[MY]% 20Dr.% 20Sukri% 20Saud% 20&% 20Prof.% 20Rashid. pdf.
Taylor, S., & Todd, P. (1995). Decomposition and crossover effects in the theory of planned behavior: a study of consumer adoption intentions. *International Journal of Research in Marketing, 12*(2), 137–155.
Teddlie, C., & Tashakkori, A. (Eds.). (2009). Foundations of mixed methods research: Integrating quantitative and qualitative approaches in the social and behavioral sciences. Sage Publications Inc
Teo, T. (2008). Pre-service teachers' attitudes towards computer use: a Singapore survey. *Australasian Journal of Educational Technology, 24*(4), 413–424.
Teo, T. (2012). Examining the intention to use technology among pre-service teachers: an integration of the technology acceptance model and theory of planned behavior. *Interactive Learning Environments, 20*(1), 3–18.
Trucano, M. (2005). *Knowledge maps: ICTs in education.* Washington, DC: InfoDev/World Bank.
Venkatesh, V., & Davis, F. D. (2000). A theoretical extension of the technology acceptance model: four longitudinal field studies. *Management Science, 46*(2), 186–204.
Zhao, Y., & Frank, K. A. (2003). Factors affecting technology uses in schools: an ecological perspective. *American Educational Research Journal, 40*(4), 807–840.

13

Initial evidence to validate an instructional design-derived evaluation scale in higher education programs

Tania Moreira-Mora* and Julia Espinoza-Guzmán

* Correspondence: tmoreira@itcr.ac.cr
Costa Rica Institute of Technology, P.O. Box: 159 7050, Eastern District, Cartago, Costa Rica, Central America

Abstract

Instructional design has been a key strategy in ensuring the quality of higher education; therefore, it is essential to evaluate its effects on learning processes through the use of tools that comply with defined technical standards. Hence, the purpose of this study is to validate a scale used to evaluate the degree to which the students perceive the five aspects of instructional design: objectives, curricular content, learning activities, educational resources, and the existing evaluation strategy at the Costa Rica Institute of Technology (TEC). Through the use of an analytical and descriptive study, as well as qualitative and quantitative techniques, a Likert evaluation scale was designed. According to the results, the final version of the instrument consisted of 33 items and had a confidence coefficient of 0.923. In regards to the evidence associated to its validity, it was possible to verify the representability and relevance of the instructional design components and their factorial structure. The main conclusion obtained from this study is the importance of measuring, from a systemic perspective, the instructional design components, in classroom, blended learning and virtual courses with tools that are properly validated in order to guarantee the confidence level and valid interpretation of the results.

Keywords: Instructional design, Higher education, Validation, Learning environments

Introduction

In higher education, instructional design has been a basic planning strategy used to ensure that the pedagogic development of courses is organized and coherent. Indeed, one of the reasons for selecting this topic is that, in various studies that analyze and propose quality models, instructional design is considered a decisive factor in the educational experience of the students (Cabero, 2006a, 2006b; Correa & Paredes, 2009; Gil, 2004; Khlaisang, 2010). Instructional design is a tool that guarantees that there will not be any improvisation during course execution and, furthermore, it constitutes a guide that will also allow decisions to be made and actions taken related to unforeseen events that tend to occur in educational processes (Cabero, 2006a, 2006b). Other authors agree that instructional design is a success factor for a virtual or blended learning course (Bates & Sangrà, 2011; Jung, 2011; Sun, Tsai, Finger, Chen, & Yeh, 2008; Williams, Schrum, Sangrà, & Guárdia, 2004).

Thus, in 2011, the Costa Rica Institute of Technology (TEC) developed – on its technological platform – an application used to execute instructional design that included the five components thereof: objectives, curricular content, learning activities, educational resources, and evaluation strategy. The overall aim of doing so was to improve the pedagogic planning of the courses (Francesa, Espinoza-Guzmán, & Chacón-Rivas, 2012). This application was designed for use with the different study methods available at the university: face-to-face, blended and virtual courses. It was precisely within this context that the need to validate a tool for the evaluation of the instructional design components from the students' point of view was detected.

At higher education level, there are many studies on learning and instructional design evaluation. Rovai, Wighting, Baker, and Grooms (2009), based on the meta analysis of 232 comparative studies performed by Bernard et al. (2004) indicated that there is a broad variability in the results achieved by students on distance (online) learning courses and classroom courses. Also, they established that there are different elements associated with educational effectiveness: pedagogic techniques, student characteristics and instructional models, among other factors. These researchers developed the Perceived Learning Scale tool consisting of 9 items used to measure the cognitive, psychomotor and affective aspects related to learning in face-to-face and virtual courses.

Other researchers developed a scale to compare demographic indicators and analyze the difference in the performance and satisfaction of the students on classroom courses as well as on virtual courses. The analyzed components corresponded to the students' perceptions of their own learning processes, the experience obtained in the courses, and the instructor evaluation (Driscoll, Jicha, Hunt, Tichavsky, & Thompson, 2012).

Reyes (2012), on the other hand, presented a study that evaluates the quality of the online learning environment from the college students' perspective; to achieve this, a Constructivist On-Line Learning Environment Survey (COLLES) was used, since it measures relevance, reflection and support from the tutors, support from classmates and interpretation of the learning process. The most relevant results obtained are related to significant learning strategies and learning objects and how these factors ensure knowledge acquisition.

Santoveña (2010) describes the process of creating a scale to measure the quality of online courses through the use of criteria such as general environment quality, didactic methodology, and technical quality when navigating the page and the technical quality and design of multimedia resources.

Considering that instructional design is a process, there is a series of steps that allow for the definition of key aspects. First, what must be learned, the materials to use and the quality of instruction must be determined. Second, the learning requirements, the goals, and the instructional materials and activities must be designed, as well as the follow-up strategies that have to be specified (Berger & Kam, 1996; Yakavetsky, 2003).

At TEC, the administrative office of "TEC Digital" has used the model proposed by Gil (2004) and Coronado L (2010): Presentación del Proceso del Diseño Instruccional del Tecnológico de Costa Rica, unpublished) to guide this process, as shown in Fig. 1.

TEC's instructional design includes two components: a) the context or characterization of the course and the targeted student population, and b) the planning process for the instructional design. Within this context, aspects such as the number of participants; requirements; specific characteristics such as age, gender, knowledge and skills, among

Instructional design development process for TEC-Digital

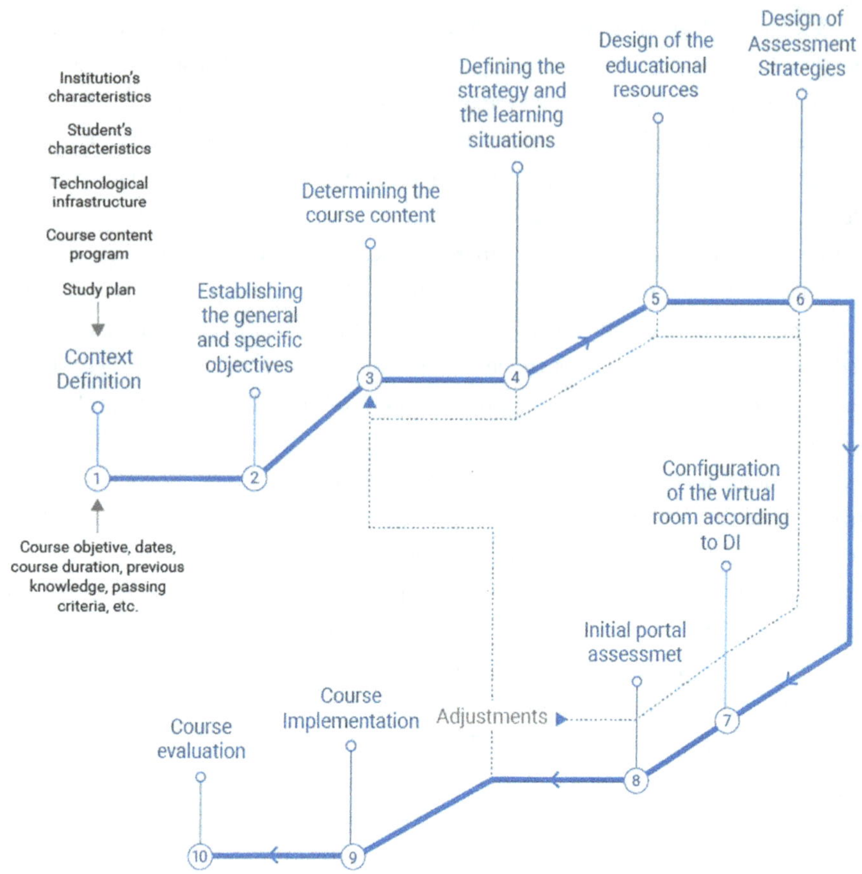

Design by: Visual Communication TEC-Digital

Fig. 1 Development process of TEC Digital's instructional design, based on the proposals by Gil (2004) and Coronado L (2010): Presentación del Proceso del Diseño Instruccional del Tecnológico de Costa Rica, unpublished

others; the course mode – classroom, blended or virtual; course characteristics – theory, theory-practical, laboratory work or fieldwork; level or degree at which the course must be taken; whether it is part of a study plan or if it is a course for continued professional training. In the second component, the instructional design is structured by objectives: content, learning activities, educational resources and evaluation strategies, which, when merged, create course content that aims to generate satisfactory learning experiences (Arjona & Blando, 2007). Although the available literature on virtual environments highlights the importance of instructional design when planning a virtual or blended learning course, its development must not be overlooked in face-to-face education.

Background

In the current standards for educational and psychological tests established by the American Educational Research Association (AERA), American Psychological Association (APA) and National Council on Measurement in Education (NCME), Sireci and Padilla (2014) determined that the validation of a tool requires a global effort, where different types of evidence that integrate a valid argument must be trusted, in order to support the use of the test for a particular objective.

As pointed out by Pérez-Gil, Chacón, and Moreno (2000), from a unified validity perspective, the meaning of the scoring used is what provides the rational base to arrive at relevant and representative criteria of the test's content and establish a predictive hypothesis that can contribute to understanding the nature of the tool constructed. Within this context, for Carretero and Pérez (2005), the phases for a study focusing on the construction or adaptation of a test should be:

- Study justification
- Conceptual delimitation of the construct to be evaluated
- Development and qualitative evaluation of the items
- Statistical analysis of the items
- Dimensioning study for the test developed (internal structure)
- Reliability coefficient
- Gathering external evidence to obtain test validity

In regards to the conceptual delimitation of this study, the following operational components of the instructional design were considered: objectives, curricular content, learning activities, educational resources and evaluation. According to Gil (2004), the instructional design is the scheme that allows the different processes involved in distance education to be organized, which detail the required technology and infrastructure, the necessary methods to provide the instruction based on the educational requirements; it should also allow for content selection and organization, and for the design of the learning and evaluation situations that satisfy these needs, always taking into account the learners' characteristics and the expected learning outcomes. Additionally, Gustafson and Branch (2002) indicate that instructional design is a systemic, planned, synergic and structured process, which must be executed before providing a course or an educational activity.

The instructional design objectives consider the specific abilities and skills that the students will have developed by the time the educational program concludes: cognitive or intellectual, motor function, affective, social action and interaction. These are the start and end points of the educational process, because they constitute the foundations for developing evaluation processes (Gil, 2004).

Cabero (2006a) proposes that curricular content must be analyzed from a three-fold perspective – quality, quantity and structure – in order to ensure the content is pertinent, relevant and from a trustworthy source. In terms of quantity, there must be enough content for the target group, and it must be based on the established objectives. The structure corresponds to the way the content is displayed in the correct design and formats.

In learning activities, Herrera (2006) suggests that interventions should promote cognitive imbalance, high-level interaction and the development of thinking skills. This would encourage the students to go through the different learning stages of knowledge acquisition, skills development and critical thinking abilities.

Educational resources correspond to the series of resources used to encourage the teaching and learning process, as explained by Blázquez and Saénz (1988), in such a way that the resources and the learning means become the tools in this process.

Educational resources affect educational process efficiency, as their development and creative use enhances the probability of students learning better.

According to Salinas (2008), the design of evaluation strategies is closely related to the learning methodology used. Depending on how the evaluation is proposed and designed, it can be either a judgment tool or a learning opportunity. From the latter perspective, evaluation is an educational intervention action focusing on improving and reconstructing knowledge, in a way that is aimed at reaching the proposed learning objectives.

These concepts and empirical evidence from previous studies formed the basis for the development of the evaluation tool, which also considered the characteristics of the higher education students.

Methodology

This is an analytical-descriptive study, in which the data collection process was based on quantitative and qualitative techniques, as established in the following procedure:

First stage

The design of a tool based on a Likert-type scale with five values, according to the operation matrix of the instructional design components. As per Wang, Willett, and Eccles (2011), the development and selection of the items was executed through the use of theoretical concepts as well as the revision made by experts, in order to obtain higher variability in the responses.

Second stage

The application of the judging technique to determine the level of representation and relevance of the variables to be measured. As explained by Sireci and Faulkner-Bond (2014), this is the most common method and it consists in the evaluation of matching answers, used to measure the degree to which the items correctly represent specific and significant content. As defined by Sireci and Faulkner-Bond (2014), the evidence obtained is one of the five ways validated by APA, AERA and NCME to establish the level to which the content of a test is congruent with its purposes. In order to ensure that the measured content represents the construct that is being measured, four aspects are considered: conceptuality, representativeness, relevance and appropriateness of the development process.

In this procedure, five experts from computer sciences, e-learning, education and psychology were selected through the snowball strategy. Each was trained individually and they were provided with an instruction guide, an evaluation sheet, and a matrix, similar to the one found in Table 1, so that they could judge the items based on the following categories: 1) coherent, keep without making any adjustments; 2) partially coherent, keep after making some adjustments and 3) incoherent, delete the item.

Third stage

The use of a student focus group with the aim of exploring the meaning of different terms, ensuring the understanding of the instructions, outlining format errors and estimating the time required to apply the tool. As evidenced by Hamui-Sutton and

Table 1 Operational matrix for the measurement tool used for instructional design (2012)

Dimensions	Indicators	Items	Matching percentage
Objectives	Degree of development for the procedural, cognitive and attitudinal objectives.	3, 4, 5, 6 and 7	1: 30 % 2: 55 % 3: 15 %
	Degree of satisfaction for the students' needs and expectations.	1 and 2	1: 37.5 % 2: 12.5 % 3: 50 %
Curricular content	Level of congruence with the course objectives.	9	1: 0 % 2: 75 % 3: 25 %
	Compliance level based on the quality criteria.	8, 10, 11, 12, 13 and 14	1: 29.2 % 2: 54.2 % 3: 16.6 %
Learning activities	Level of congruence with the course objectives.	15, 16 and 19	1: 8.3 % 2: 66.7 % 3: 25 %
	Compliance level based on the quality criteria.	17, 18, 20, 21, 22 and 23	1: 29,2 % 2: 45.8 % 3: 25 %
Educational resources	Level of congruence with the course objectives and activities.	25 and 28	1: 37.5 % 2: 50 % 3: 12.5 %
	Compliance level based on the quality criteria.	24, 26 and 27	1: 25 % 2: 50 % 3: 25 %
Evaluation strategies	Level of congruence with the course objectives and content.	31, 34, 35 and 36	1: 50 % 2: 37.5 % 3: 12,5 %
	Compliance level based on the quality criteria.	29, 30, 32 and 33.	1: 37.5 % 2: 50 % 3: 12.5 %

Varela-Ruiz (2013), the technique promotes discussion and must therefore be developed within a study protocol in accordance with the objective. An interview guide and the required logistics must be established in order to successfully develop this technique. In it, the selected participants complied with being registered on blended and on-site courses from different degree programs.

Fourth stage

The pilot implementation of the first version of the tool was executed in October and November 2012 with a group of 58 students having characteristics similar to those of the target group. Later, a second test of the tool, in its enhanced version, was performed with another sample of 64 students in 2013. In both tests of the tools, the groups were selected considering the representation of face-to-face and blended courses from different degree programs.

For the statistical analysis of the results, IBM SPSS Statistics 0.19 software was used. In the test to determine the dimensionality of the tool, an inductive estimate with exploratory factorial analysis, also considered by Díaz and Fuentes (2007), was considered the most appropriate test. The main objective if this analysis was to find the combination of observed variables in a lower number of latent variables; therefore, it was necessary to reduce the dimensionality of the original variables while retaining most of the information provided (Cea, 2004). The author indicates that the analyses are important only when there is a correlation between the variables that is greater or equal to 0.30.

The second analysis of the results corresponded to a reliability coefficient, that is, determining the Cronbach Alpha coefficient (interclass correlation), which is defined as the accuracy of a test or measuring tool when applied to the same subject twice, that is, the results are consistent and coherent (Hernández, Fernández, & Baptista, 2010). This index is calculated through a variance-covariance matrix obtained from the values of the items, where the diagonal of the matrix provides the variance of each item while the rest of the entries represent the internal covariance between the groups of items (Cea, 1998; Oviedo & Campos-Arias, 2005). This is an index used to measure the internal consistency of a scale, in order to evaluate the level to which the items are correlated (Oviedo & Campos-Arias, 2005).

Results

In the first stage of the validation, two qualitative techniques were used – a panel of judges and a focus group – and the information was merged with the conceptual framework of reference. As explained by Hamui-Sutton and Varela-Ruiz (2013), this technique allows for the integration of bibliographical resources and evidence from previous studies.

Considering the criteria generated by the judges, changes were made to the way the items were phrased; also, two of the items were deleted and other items were reorganized. For example, the item: "Appropriate development based on the course program" was deleted from the evaluation tool, when the following observation was made by judge 4: "Will this be evaluated by the end of the course? If not, it cannot be properly evaluated by the student unless the student is retaking the course." In order to verify the matching percentage between the observations made by the judges, Kendall's Tau_b test, which measures the range of correlation, was used. The results showed a correlation of 0.277, with a confidence level of 0.05 % between judges 2 and 4 only (there was no statistical evidence for the rest of the experts).

Through the feedback provided by the focus groups, it was possible to substantially improve the accuracy of the items. For instance, terms like academic education, proficiencies, ethical principles, feedback, self-evaluation and self-learning, among other terms, were not well understood by the students. Hence, by discussing these concepts with the focus group, it was possible to come up with more comprehensive terms, such as academic studies required for the degree, capabilities, values, error analysis and deficiencies, value individual accomplishments and learning. On the other hand, it was determined that broadening the response range from a 5-level scale to a scale from 1 to 10 was necessary for the tool to be better accepted in the educational context and also for maximizing the response variability when using it.

In the second validation stage, a trial test was performed with 58 students, who were given the tool in October and November 2012. In the different studies focusing on the items and the tool's measurement properties, reliability was estimated using the Cronbach Alpha coefficient. This analysis was performed using IBM SPSS Statistics 0.19 software, whose range varies between 0.0 and 1.0 (perfect confidence level). The initial coefficient of the scale was 0.841 and, following these results, two items were removed: item 27 with a correlation level of 0.04, and item 24 with a value of 0.08 (both items from the educational resources category). Therefore, the final version of the tool consisted of 33 items and presented a confidence coefficient of 0.923, resulting from a second trial test. According to Morales (2012), a high coefficient is clearly desirable when the differences between the subjects tested are legitimate and expected. For research purposes, as emphasized by Hernández et al. (2010), this value is acceptable, since it corroborates that the items are highly correlated.

In order to include additional valid evidence in this tool design, the principal axis method of factor extraction was performed, to test whether the five components of the design were represented in the proposed items, as shown in the scree plot graphs the eigenvalue against the factor number (Fig. 2).

This analysis also explained the variance with a lower number of factors when compared to the initial factors tested (Nunnally & Bernstein, 1995). The rotation method used was orthogonal (Varimax) and, according to the results from the second trial run, the variance percentage obtained from the five factors evaluated was 65.21 %. By grouping the items based on the factorial results for the factors (over 0.30), it was possible to detect several multidimensional items. This means that an item can be associated to more than one factor; however, all items were kept in the scale due to the significance of their content. As detailed by Carretero and Pérez (2005), the choice of

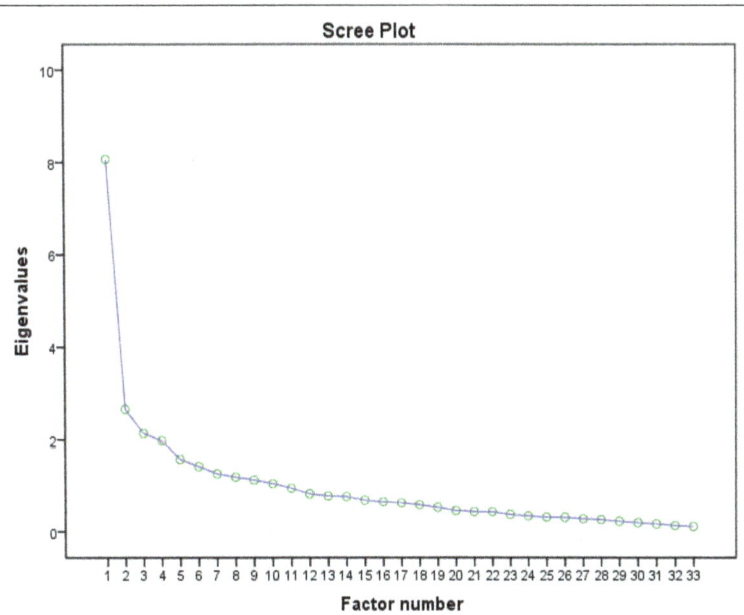

Fig. 2 Scree plot for the instructional design scale

keeping or removing an item must be based on a joint evaluation of all the statistical indices, and also considering the conceptual interests of the tool designed.

Finally, two statistical adjustment tests were used. First, the KMO (Kaiser-Meyer-Olkin) measure of sampling adequacy used to compare the magnitude of the correlation coefficients observed with the magnitude of the partial coefficients (Pardo & Ruiz, 2002), obtaining a value of 0.627. According to the authors, values under 0.6 are considered insignificant. Second, Bartlett's Test of Sphericity, which allowed the null hypothesis to be rejected, establishing that the factors are correlated and that the model is appropriate for explaining the data obtained.

Discussion and conclusions

In the evaluation for higher education learning, under any teaching modality, it is essential to consider all the factors involved in instructional design, regardless of the methodology used to develop it. This is so because, when the course ends, it is necessary to have indicators to evaluate course quality and to improve any deficiencies that may be found (Williams et al., 2004). As determined by earlier studies, there are scales such as COLLES (Reyes, 2012) and the one developed by Santoveña (2010) that incorporate diverse instructional design elements in order to rate the general quality of the course. While the proposed scale in this article focuses on measuring all the components or factors of the instructional design, understood as the systematic process organized according to course objectives, curricular content, learning activities, didactic resources and evaluation strategies.

This particular property of the designed scale is due to the absence of specific technological terms and to its focus on the educational process itself, which allows the comparison of different course modalities, as outlined by Berridi, Martínez, and García (2015), and Motii and Sanders (2014). Additionally, as with any other tool, it can be adjusted to the context of any institution, without altering the systemic vision of day-to-day pedagogic activities, and the instructor can obtain relevant information, from the students' perspective, about the effectiveness of the general design and its specific components.

As established by Bolívar (2008), despite the fact that the positive perception of blended learning courses has increased over the years, it is still not possible to visualize a clear and definitive trend regarding the effectiveness of the instructional strategy. This justifies the need to continue researching into this field in order to remove any doubts and enhance the knowledge available on this subject matter. With this scale, educators can gather relevant information from the students' point of view about the effectiveness of the general design and its specific components. As indicated before, and like any other tool, this one can be placed in the context of each institution, along with a protocol in order to standardize the requirements for its use, to obtain an appropriate interpretation of the results.

The experience of validating an evaluation scale for students' perceptions of the instructional design, following a rigorous procedure, was important in order to guarantee the confidence of the results and valid interpretation. The relationships between the concepts of each component used in the design and the empirical data obtained from both trial runs were also demonstrated. The main limitation is the lack of evidence of external validation, due to the sampling size as well as its non-probabilistic selection. However, as with every validation process, it is possible to continue obtaining more evidence of the tool's psychometric properties in order to strengthen its interpretation and, hence, its impact on the higher education environment. Finally, the researchers involved in this study consider it important to share this research outcome, which, together with its protocol for use, can be accessed via the following link: http://tecdigital.tec.ac.cr/servicios/investigacion/?q=protocolo_escala_percepcion_componentes_diseno_instruccional.

About the authors

Tania Elena Moreira-Mora

Tania Elena Moreira-Mora has a PhD in Education. She is currently working in the Psychology and Orientation Department of Costa Rica Institute of Technology as researcher and evaluator in the Admission Examination Committee. Additionally, she is an instructor in the Postgraduate Program in Education at the State Distance University of Costa Rica (UNED).

Julia Espinoza-Guzmán

Julia Espinoza-Guzmán, Computer Engineer at Costa Rica Institute of Technology, graduate in Education from UNED, Costa Rica, Master in Project Management at Universidad Politécnica de Cataluña and Master in Educational Technologies at the Instituto Tecnológico de Monterrey. At Costa Rica Institute of Technology, she coordinates the e-learning training processes, and she is a researcher and professor for the Computational Engineering and Information Technologies Management career programs.

References

Arjona, M., & Blando, M. (2007). *Diseño Instruccional, elemento clave en el desarrollo de cursos para Ambientes Virtuales de Aprendizaje*. Retrieved from http://bibliotecadigital.conevyt.org.mx/colecciones/documentos/somece/51.pdf

Bates, T., & Sangrà, A. (2011). *Managing technology in higher education: Strategies for transforming teaching and learning*. San Francisco: John Wiley & Sons.

Berger, C., & Kam, R. (1996). *Education 626: Educational Software Design and Authoring*. Retrieved from http://www.umich.edu/~ed626/define.html

Bernard, R. M., Abrami, P. C., Lou, Y., Borokhovski, E., Wade, A., Wozney, L., Fiset, M., & Huang, B. (2004). How does distance education compare to classroom instruction? A meta-analysis of the empirical literature. *Review of Educational Research, 74*(3), 379–439. doi:10.3102/00346543074003379

Berridi, R., Martínez, J. I., & García, B. (2015). Validación de una escala de interacción en contextos virtuales de aprendizaje. *Revista electrónica de investigación educativa, 17*(1), 116–129.

Blázquez, F., & Sáenz, O. (1988). *Didáctica General*. España: Editorial Anaya.

Bolívar, C. (2008). El blended-learning: evaluación de una experiencia de aprendizaje en el nivel de postgrado. *Investigación y Postgrado, 23*(1), 11–36.

Cabero, J. (2006a). Bases pedagógicas del e-learning. *Universities and Knowledge Society Journal, 3*(1), 1–10. Retrieved from http://www.redalyc.org/articulo.oa?id=78030102

Cabero, J. (2006b). *La calidad educativa en el e-Learning: sus bases pedagógicas. Educación Médica* (p. 9). Retrieved from http://scielo.isciii.es/pdf/edu/v9s2/original1.pdf

Carretero, H., & Pérez, C. (2005). Normas para el desarrollo y revisión de estudios instrumentales. *International Journal of Clinical and Health Psychology, 5*(3), 521–551. Retrieved from http://www.aepc.es/ijchp/articulos_pdf/ijchp-158.pdf

Cea, M. (1998). *Metodología cuantitativa: Estrategias y técnicas de investigación social*. S.A, Madrid: Editorial Síntesis.

Cea, M. (2004). *Análisis multivariable: teoría y práctica en la investigación social*. S.A, Madrid: Editorial Síntesis.

Correa, J., & Paredes, J. (2009). Cambio Tecnológico, Uso de plataformas e-learning y Transformación de la Enseñanza en las Universidades Españolas: una perspectiva de los profesores. *Revista de Psicodidáctica, 14*(2), 261–277. Retrieved from http://www.redalyc.org/pdf/175/17512724007.pdf

Díaz, C., & Fuentes, I. (2007). Validación de un cuestionario de razonamiento probabilístico condicional. *Revista Electrónica de Metodología Aplicada, 12*(1), 1–15. Retrieved from http://www.unioviedo.es/reunido/index.php/Rema/article/viewFile/9774/9517

Driscoll, A., Jicha, K., Hunt, A. N., Tichavsky, L., & Thompson, G. (2012). Can online courses deliver in-class results? A comparison of student performance and satisfaction in an online versus a face-to-face introductory sociology course. *Teaching Sociology, 40*(4), 312–331. Retrieved from http://tso.sagepub.com/content/40/4/312.full.pdf+html

Francesa, A., Espinoza-Guzmán, J., & Chacón-Rivas, M. (2012). *Hacia una herramienta para el diseño instruccional en educación superior*. Madrid, Spain: Work presented in VII Conferencia Ibérica de Sistemas y Tecnologías de Información.

Gil, M. C. (2004). Modelo de Diseño Instruccional para programas Educativos a Distancia. *Revista Perfiles Educativos, XXVI*(104), 93–114. Retrieved from http://www.redalyc.org/pdf/132/13210406.pdf

Gustafson, K. L., & Branch, R. M. (2002). *What is instructional design. Trends and issues in instructional design and technology* (pp. 16–25).

Hamui-Sutton, A., & Varela-Ruiz, M. (2013). La técnica de grupos focales. *Metodología de investigación en educación médica, 2*(1), 55–60. Retrieved from http://apps.elsevier.es/watermark/ctl_servlet?_f=10&pident_articulo=90219695&pident_usuario=0&pcontactid=&pident_revista=343&ty=95&accion=L&origen=zonadelectura&web=www.elsevier.es&lan=es&fichero=343v02n05a90219695pdf001.pdf

Hernández, R., Fernández, C., & Baptista, M. P. (2010). *Metodología de la investigación* (5th ed.). Lima: McGraw Hill.

Herrera, M. (2006). Consideraciones para el diseño didáctico de ambientes virtuales de aprendizaje: una propuesta basada en las funciones cognitivas del aprendizaje. *Revista Iberoamericana de Educación, 38*(5), 2.

Jung, I. (2011). The dimensions of e-learning quality: from the learner's perspective. *Educational Technology Research and Development, 59*(4), 445–464.

Khlaisang, J. (2010). Proposed Models of Appropriate Website and Courseware for E-Learning in Higher Education: Research Based Design Models. In J. Sanchez & K. Zhang (Eds.), *Proceedings of World Conference on E-Learning in Corporate, Government, Healthcare, and Higher Education 2010. Association for the Advancement of Computing in Education (AACE), Chesapeake* (pp. 1520–1529).

Morales, P. (2012). *Análisis de ítems en las pruebas objetivas*. Retrieved from http://educrea.cl/wp-content/uploads/2014/11/19-nov-analisis-de-items-en-las-pruebas-objetivas.pdf

Motii, B. B., & Sanders, T. J. (2014). An Empirical Analysis of Student Learning Outcomes in an Introductory Microeconomics Course: Online Versus Face-To-Face Delivery Methods. *Global Education Journal, 3*

Nunnally, J. C., & Bernstein, I. J. (1995). *Teoría psicométrica*. Madrid: McGraw-Hill.

Oviedo, H., & Campos-Arias, A. (2005). Aproximación al uso del coeficiente alfa de Cronbach. *Revista Colombiana de Psiquiatría, XXXIV*(4), 572–579. Retrieved from http://www.scielo.org.co/pdf/rcp/v34n4/v34n4a09.pdf

Pardo, A., & Ruiz, M. A. (2002). *SPSS 11. Guía para el análisis de datos*. Madrid, Spain: McGraw-Hill.

Pérez-Gil, J. A., Chacón, S., & Moreno, R. (2000). Validez de constructo, el uso de análisis factorial exploratorio-confirmatorio para obtener evidencias de validez. *Psicothema, 12*(2), 442–446. Retrieved from http://www.psicothema.com/psicothema.asp?id=601

Reyes, N. (2012). Los Entornos Virtuales: Valoración de la Calidad desde la Perspectiva del Estudiante. In I. Mogollón (Ed.), *Educación a Distancia: Encuentros* (pp. 144–162). Sevilla: Protagonistas y Experiencias. GITE Univesidad de Sevilla.

Rovai, A. P., Wighting, M. J., Baker, J. D., & Grooms, L. D. (2009). Development of an instrument to measure perceived cognitive, affective, and psychomotor learning in traditional and virtual classroom higher education settings. *The Internet and Higher Education, 12*(1), 7–13.

Salinas, J. P. (2008). *Metodologías centradas en el Alumno para el Aprendizaje en Red*. Barcelona: Editorial Síntesis S.A.

Santoveña, S. (2010). *Cuestionario de evaluación de la calidad de los cursos virtuales de la UNED. Revista de Educación a Distancia* (p. 25). Retrieved from www.um.es/ead/red/25/

Sireci, S., & Faulkner-Bond, M. (2014). Evidence based on test content. *Psicothema, 26*(1), 100–107. doi:10.7334/psicothema2013.256

Sireci, S., & Padilla, J. L. (2014). Validating assessments: introduction to the special section. *Psicothema, 26*(1), 97–99. doi:10.7334/psicothema2013.255

Sun, P. C., Tsai, R. J., Finger, G., Chen, Y. Y., & Yeh, D. (2008). What drives a successful e-learning? An empirical investigation of the critical factors influencing learner satisfaction. *Computers & Education, 50*(4), 1183–1202.

Wang, M.-T., Willett, J. B., & Eccles, J. (2011). The assessment of school engagement: examining dimensionality and measurement invariance by gender and race/ethnicity. *Journal of School Psychology, 49*, 465–480. Retrieved from http://www.sciencedirect.com/science/article/pii/S0022440511000240

Williams, P., Schrum, L., Sangrà, A., & Guárdia, L. (2004). *Fundamentos del diseño técnico-pedagógico. Modelos de diseño instruccional en e-learning*. Barcelona: Universitat Oberta de Catalunya.

Yakavetsky, G. (2003). *La elaboración de un módulo instruccional*. Retrieved from http://www1.uprh.edu/gloria/publicaciones/comoelaborarunmoduloinstruccional.pdf

14

Applying action research in CAD teaching to improve the learning experience and academic level

Veronica Gracia-Ibáñez* and Margarita Vergara

* Correspondence: vgracia@uji.es
Departamento de Ingeniería Mecánica y Construcción, Universitat Jaume I, Avda. Sos Baynat, s/n, E12071 Castellón, Spain

Abstract

A project involving innovation in university education is described in this paper. It was implemented in a Computer-Aided Design (CAD) course on the Bachelor's Degree in Industrial Design and Product Development Engineering. Several studies have been published about CAD curricula, yet to the best of our knowledge nothing on applying Action Research (AR) to CAD teaching. The project was carried out over a two-year period, after detecting that academic results were not very good even when the course was not very demanding. In the first year, an experiment based on the AR methodology was planned and put into practice. We took the figure of the teacher-researcher as our own, owing to our conviction that teachers themselves must study their own work and reflect on it critically. Encouraged by the good results, throughout the following year, more changes were made in order to further improve the learning experience. The main actions were to develop self-learning material and to use rubrics for assessment, together with an increase in the level of difficulty in some parts of the evaluation. A detailed chronological description of the actions that were carried out, the implied motivations and both the expected results and those actually obtained are presented.

Keywords: CAD, improving academic results, level of difficulty, Action Research methodology

Introduction

The teaching of Computer-Aided Design (CAD) is such a broad field of study (Asperl, 2005) that there is no consensus about what to include in the curricula, since these differ depending on the degree and on the level and age of the CAD learners. Furthermore, some studies (Field, 2004) emphasise the importance of continuing evolution in the training and educational needs of users of CAD systems. From the point of view that today's student is tomorrow's engineer, descriptions have also been put forward regarding what CAD curricula should be like depending on the role CAD will play in the student's future (as a user, an application developer, a software developer or a CAD manager) (Ye, Peng, Chen, & Cai, 2004). An analysis of the situation of CAD teaching in Spain (Rubio Garcıa R, Gallego Santos R, Suárez Quirós J, Álvarez Peñın PI, 2005) showed that, since the Organic Law of Universities[1] came into force, each teacher uses different methodologies and tools to teach CAD. In that study, the authors presented the results of a survey about different issues carried out on over 600 teachers. It revealed that, in Spanish universities, there was no agreement on the desirable number of students in the labs, the time to be dedicated to practical sessions, the CAD software to be used or its type (parametric or not) or on the system of evaluation. Hence, the authors classified the ways of assessing students into three groups: by means of practical exercises that are delivered and revised on a weekly base; by means of a final examination in which the student has to solve a problem by using the computer to draw a solution within a given time; or by means of an end-of-year assignment. The tendency seemed to be to give more weight to students' daily work than to the traditional final examinations.

On the other hand, there are also several studies that deal with improving different CAD-related abilities (spatial abilities, visualisation skills or the relationship between 2D drawings and 3D models) using different technologies and methodologies (Contero M, Naya F, Company P, Saorín JL, 2006; Contero M, Naya F, Company P, Saorín JL, Conesa J, 2005; Plumed, Calleja, Varley, & Martin, 2013). Furthermore, Rossignac (2004) presented some particular examples of teaching CAD based on what he calls education-driven research (EDR). In these examples, new concepts are introduced by mean of analogies or metaphors; expressive notation and evocative names are used to facilitate memorisation, and the focus is placed only on essential aspects, thereby simplifying concepts until they are well understood.

One interesting aspect of teaching CAD (Chester, 2007) is the difference between command knowledge (knowing the tools provided by the software and the procedure for using them) and strategic knowledge (knowing the methods that can be used to achieve a specific task and how to choose one of them), with strategic knowledge being more effective in the development of CAD expertise, especially when no previous CAD instruction has been provided.

Another important aspect in teaching CAD (Asperl, 2005) is the choice of software. Often, CAD software applications have limitations (tools fail to work the way they should, the user interface is not appropriate, the software is not affordable for students, and so forth) that impose a specific way of working.

Knowing exactly how knowledge is transferred and what way of teaching is best for each type of competence will almost certainly lead to an improvement in CAD education. Teaching and researching, understood as an integrated activity, gives rise to the figure of the teacher-researcher. This figure was first noted by Stenhouse (Rudduck & Hopkins, 1985), a British pedagogue who argued that action research refers to the research conducted by teachers on their own practice in order to find ways to improve students' learning. Teachers' research, he claimed, should also aim to make a contribution to the theory of education that is accessible to other teachers and enters into the critical discourse of the profession (Groundwater-Smith & Mockler, 2011).

Rudduck and Hopkins (1985) developed a paradigm of action research that aimed to "demystify and democratise research", as a response to their perception that educational research was not contributing effectively to classroom practitioners. It seems pretty clear to us that the best contributions that research in education can make are the contributions that can be transferred to actual educational practice. Although this methodology is well known in the field of Social Sciences, it is still little known in most technological areas such as Engineering (Marqués Andrés & Ferrández Berrueco,

2011). The Action Research (AR) methodology (Marqués Andrés & Ferrández Berrueco, 2011; Riel & Whitehead, 2011; Riel, 2010) implies following five phases throughout its implementation: identifying the focus, i.e., what we want to improve; analysing the problem or the issues than can be improved; developing an action plan with indicators to measure the impact of the action; carrying out the actions; and, finally, observing and reflecting upon it by analysing the data collected. Successful indicators would point out that the planned action has obtained the expected outcome.

This article presents a case study in which the AR methodology was applied to a CAD course in a particular context (available software, degree, size of lab groups, and education programme). The course is taught to students in the second year of the Bachelor's Degree in Industrial Design and Product Development Engineering at Jaume I University (UJI) in Castellón, Spain. It has been taught for three years since the degree started in the 2011/2012 academic year. The project described here was carried out for the two years following the start of the degree, after detecting that the academic results in the first year were not very good even when the level of difficulty of assessment activities was not very high. This situation is not a desirable one for a committed teacher. In the first year of its implementation (2012/2013), an experiment based on the AR methodology was planned and developed. Encouraged by good results, throughout the second year of its implementation (2013/2014), more changes were made in order to improve the learning experience. A detailed chronological description of the actions carried out, the implied motivations and both the expected results and those actually obtained are presented. Our focus was on finding methodologies to improve academic results while increasing the level of difficulty. If academic results improve, despite a higher level of difficulty of the assessment activities, the learning experience will be better and the target competences will be achieved. Even though the applied AR methodology aims to detect local needs, the changes in methodology and evaluation that have been made are based in the principles of the most ingrained pedagogical theory of knowledge: constructivism, in its different forms (Coll, 1996). We have taken from Piaget the idea that humans have to create their own knowledge (Zaphiris & Ioannou, 2014), from Ausubel (1968) that we have to start from prior knowledge for learning to be significant, and from Vygotsky (1978) the idea of scaffolded learning. Consequently, our results can be applied to other subjects or situations to improve the learning experience. The main idea is to provide resources to help students achieve significant learning by working on their own and by making their own efforts.

The action plan was intended to be carried out over two years: in the first academic year, the focus was on the practical part, whereas in the second year, the focus was also on the theoretical part. The indicators employed to decide whether the action implemented worked as expected were the academic results (final marks) and the students' perceptions of the planned actions and the teachers' perceptions of the experiment.

Material and methods

The CAD course is taught in coordination with three other courses of the degree. The global aims of the four coordinated courses, related to Technical Drawing and Graphic Communication, are that students have to develop the following competences and achieve the following learning outcomes:

- Ability to apply spatial representation systems (multiviews and pictorial projections), and graphic representation techniques.
- Knowledge of descriptive geometry and metric geometry.
- Ability to sketch, and ability to draw and model with CAD.
- Skills and capabilities for engineering technical drawings.

The first two competences, the ability to sketch and some skills for engineering technical drawings are worked on intensively in the first year of the degree, through two one-semester courses (Technical Drawing and Graphics I & II). In the second year of the degree, in the CAD I course, the one for which we created the experience described here, students have to develop the abilities needed to draw with CAD applications and to improve their skills and capabilities for engineering technical drawings, using mainly the 2D drawing module of a CAD commercial software package. In the third year, the aim of the CAD II course is to improve those same abilities and skills but instead using 3D modelling (virtual models of products in 3D or virtual prototypes).

The educational programme, or syllabus, of the course must follow certain rules with regard to content, to time dedicated to specific activities (theory and lab classes, personal work) and to evaluation, which were approved in the initial definition of the degree and could not be changed. The content can be summarised as knowledge of CAD tools for generating, editing and sharing engineering drawings, as well as the development of technical drawings with the 2D drafting module of a widely used commercial CAD system. The study load of the course is 6 ECTS credits and Table 1 shows the number of hours set per activity, including both class attendance and personal work. Finally, with regard to the assessment of the students, the degree establishes a maximum weight of 20 % of the final mark for practical assignments carried out at home, which implies that at least 80 % of the final mark has to be achieved through exams.

Within this context, we have detailed the CAD I curricula in a more specific list that includes typical drawing aids of CAD systems, coordinate systems and geometric transformations of figures, primitives in CAD (groups, layers, advanced primitives such as patterns, text and tables), graphic formats, storage and exchange of information, dimensioning and parametric drawing, curves, schematic drawings, project drawings and an introduction to 3D.

Table 1 Activities scheduled for the CAD I course

Activities	Classroom hours	Personal work hours	Specific activity (proposed by teachers)
Theory	12	0	Theory sessions (12 x 1 hours/week)
Practical part (laboratory) and Tutoring	37 + 1	0	Practical sessions (≈13 x 3 hours/week) including project tutoring
Evaluation	10	0	Practical evaluation (2 x 3 hours) + Final Exam (4 hours)
Personal work	0	60	Weekly voluntary exercises (14 weeks x 2.5 hours/week) + Graphic Project (25 hours)
Exam preparation	0	30	Theoretical concepts study, solving previous year's exams
Total hours (number credits * 25) = 150	60	90	

Table 1 also shows the methodology we followed for each time period and activity. Time spent on attending classes consists of theory sessions presenting general concepts of CAD according to the detailed curricula, and the related practical sessions where those concepts can be applied. The software used is AutoCAD©, which is available at the university with a campus licence and students can also have a legal copy through the university. In the practical sessions, certain problems are proposed, the commands of the program needed to solve them are presented, and the different ways of solving them are discussed in terms of efficacy to ensure that strategic knowledge can be achieved. Personal work at home includes weekly voluntary exercises (similar to the problems proposed in the lab session) and a mandatory graphic design project, in which technical drawings of an assigned existing product have to be produced (Fig. 1) as an end-of-year assignment.

Given that the weight of the exams in the final mark is so high, there are two mid-term practical ones and a final theory and practice one. Hence, the final mark is composed of the mark obtained in the exams and the mark for the graphic project.

During the course prior to carrying out the project, several issues were found:

- Listening to the students, it became quite clear that there was a shortage of learning material.
- From the results obtained, especially the graphic design projects handed in, it was easy to deduce that these results were unsatisfactory, even though the level of difficulty of the assessment activities was not very high.

Hence, we felt compelled to do something. It is important to note that we did not feel compelled to do something because of the desire for students to have good grades. Like

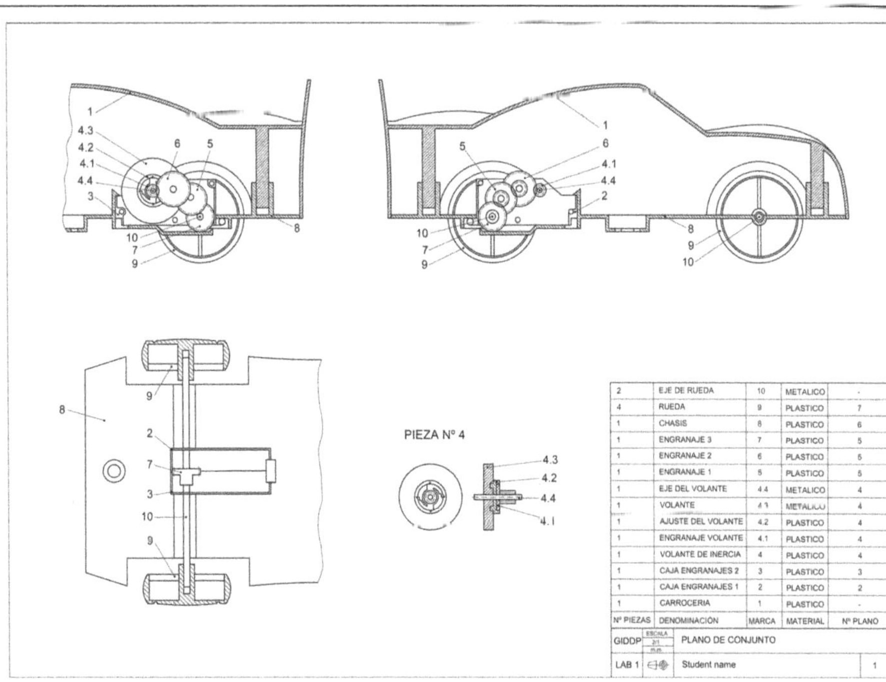

Fig. 1 Example of a technical drawing from a graphic project (reproduced with the student's permission). The product selected is a toy car powered by a friction motor

Ken Bain (Bain, 2007), we do not consider good teachers to be those who prepare their students well for an exam, but instead those who expect their students to achieve valuable learning, and that is what we pursue. In the first year of the experiment, we focused on the practical part and greater importance was given to the graphic project in order to reach the desired competences. Both the practical part and the graphic project bear a closer relationship to real problems that students are likely to find in their professional lives.

Our five AR phases were as follows:

Our aim was to find methodologies to improve academic results while increasing the level of difficulty of the assessment activities. If academic results improve, despite a higher level of difficulty, the learning experience will be better and the target competences would probably be achieved (phase 1).

On analysing the problem (phase 2), the action plan (phase 3) was intended to be developed over two years. In the first year, the focus was on the practical part of the subject, whereas the second academic year also focused on the theory part.

Basically, two actions were carried out (phase 4): making changes in the methodology and increasing the level of difficulty of the assessment activities. From the results obtained, an in-depth reflection was made (phase 5) and the conclusions shown in this work were drawn.

Changes in the methodology were taken into account by providing the students with more learning resources. Throughout the first year, some tutorials (Fig. 2) were developed for the practical sessions as learning support material. More than 25 tutorials

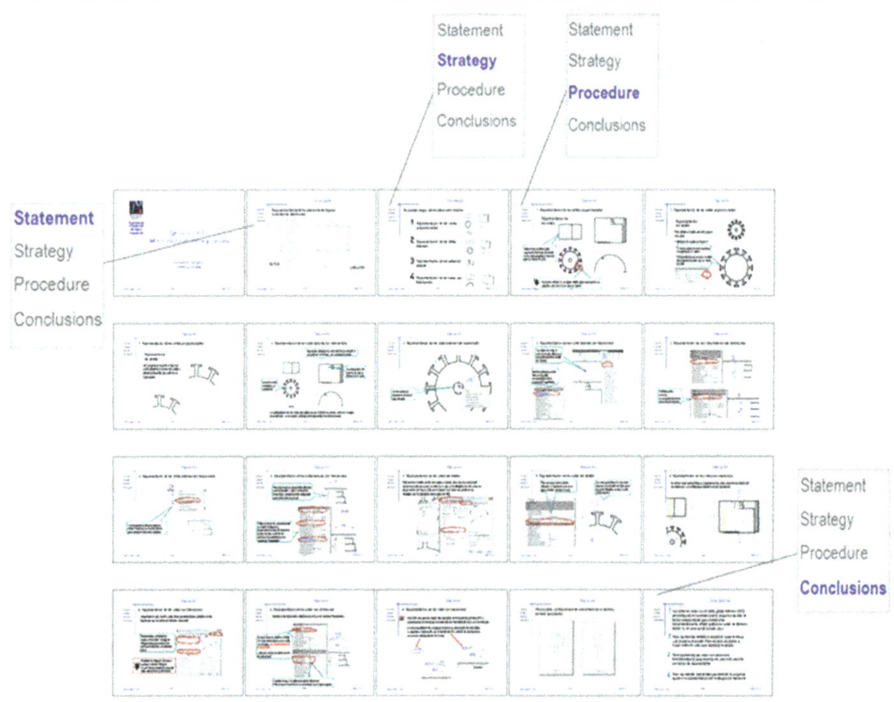

Fig. 2 Example of a tutorial provided for the practical sessions. Content is not relevant due to its specificity on the CAD I subject. It is shown in order to point out the methodology used in solving problems. The steps always follow the same pattern: statement of the problem, strategy to solve the problem, detailed procedure and conclusions to highlight important learned things to remember. The tutorials were provided in pdf format and each rectangle in this figure corresponds to a page of the pdf

were produced, ranging from 9 to 38 pages. Each tutorial formulates a problem and explains a strategy to solve it and how to do it step by step, emphasising the use of the most appropriate tools in CAD software to achieve it in a more efficient way. Thus, the students could work on their own. They could also review those aspects that had been practised in class. Hence, the action developed was aimed at giving students more information to allow them to undertake self-learning. The experiment focused on constructivist learning, self-learning and meaningful learning (Novak, 2004) through solving problems/real cases (Coll, Mauri, & Onrubia Goñi, 2006) as methodologies to produce improvements. This should presumably lead to higher academic performance.

Encouraged by the good results obtained in the practical skills in the first year (for a description, see below under Results), the second year of the study was devoted to improving the theoretical skills, also by creating more material or improving it. More than 15 detailed documents were produced, ranging from 15 to 59 pages. In this case, besides the written support for theoretical classes, weekly online self-correcting questionnaires (Fig. 3) were developed as a support to the continuous learning of theoretical concepts.

Furthermore, as supplementary material to help in focusing on the objectives, in the first year, the assessment criteria for the practical exams were clearly specified and explained to students, and in the second year, a rubric for the assessment of the graphic project was also provided (Fig. 4), together with the formulation of the project in order to better guide its execution. It has already been demonstrated that it is of utmost importance to specify the assessment criteria clearly (Sanmartí, 2007).

Regarding the second action carried out, we increased the level of difficulty in two directions, by means of insisting on higher quality in the graphic project and also by requiring a minimum mark.

In the first year of its implementation, we increased the difficulty of the assessment activities, both in terms of the quality of the graphic design project and in the exams. The level of difficulty for the project was increased by requiring more quality and content and, in the exams, by requiring a minimum mark of 4 out of 10 in each part. In the second year, the requirement of 4 out of 10 was also added in the project.

Mark the correct answer:

○ Technical drawings are produced with CAD, because the geometric information is complete.

○ CAD software is used in conceptual design.

○ Sketching applications are usually integrated within CAD applications.

○ CAD software is not useful for technical drawings.

Blocks are files which are saved either as independent files or within the file itself as an entity or special primitive:

○ True.

○ False.

Fig. 3 Example of some of the questions on the weekly online self-correcting questionnaires (12 questionnaires with 7 to 14 questions in each one)

Project Evaluation Rubric:
Each of these items is evaluated as Perfect / Fair / Incorrect. All the items have the same rating. The items marked with * are optional: they are used only to improve the grade.

Items about paper delivery:
- Order, folding and presentation of drawings
- Title block is fully labelled
- Visibility of lines (colour and selection of visible lines)
- Appropriate sizes and orientations of the paper
- Appropriate thickness and type of lines
- Appropriate size of dimensions and other annotations
- Other representations well done (perspectives) *
- Other representations well done (tolerances) *

Items about explanation of the product:
- Proper explanation of the assembly and how it works
- Photo with identification of parts and all part names

Items about assembly drawings:
- Bill of materials is complete
- Bill of materials is well drawn
- Marks on all parts
- Marks well delineated (sequence and location of marks)
- Views and sections: All parts are shown
- Views and sections: Sketching of section lines is well represented (angle and spacing)
- Views and sections: Lines are well represented

Items about detailed drawings of simple parts (minimum 2 simple parts per student):
- Enough views and sections to define the shape of the parts
- Fully dimensioned to define the dimensions of the parts

Items about detailed drawings of parts with an intermediate level of difficulty (minimum 2 intermediate parts per student):
- Enough views and sections to define the shape of the parts
- Fully dimensioned to define the dimensions of the parts

Items about detailed drawings of difficult parts (minimum 1 difficult part per student):
- Enough views and sections to define the shape of the parts
- Fully dimensioned to define the dimensions of the parts

Items about Electronic delivery:
- Presentations are identifiable and tidy. Content is easily accessible
- No 'trash' in the electronic file
- Organization of layers
- Use of standardized scales

Fig. 4 Rubric for the Graphic Project

To encourage the students, a higher weight was given to the project in the final mark by increasing the percentage up to the maximum allowed, that is to say, 20 %. All these conditions are listed in Table 2.

Objectivity was taken into account by triangulating data when establishing the indicators to decide whether the actions implemented gave the expected results: academic outcomes (final marks), students' perceptions of the planned actions and teachers' perceptions of the experiment.

Table 2 Evolution of assessment over the years of implementation

	First call (January)					Second call (June)				
Year	PE (%)	GP (%)	TP (%)	PP (%)	Additional requirements	PE (%)	GP (%)	TP (%)	PP (%)	Additional requirements
Previous year	10	10	32	48				32	68	
First year	10	20	25	45	TP ≥ 4 PP ≥ 4			25	75	TP ≥ 4 PP ≥ 4
Second year	10	20	25	45	TP ≥ 4 PP ≥ 4 GP ≥ 4		20	25	55	TP ≥ 4 PP ≥ 4

PE Practical exercises during course (2), *GP* Graphic Project
TP Theory part of the final exam, *PP* Practical part of the final exam

In the case of academic outcomes, an increase in the number of students who pass or an increase of marks would indicate that the actions implemented gave the expected results. First, Pearson's Chi Square tests (Siegel, 1988) were applied to check significant differences in the percentage of students who did or did not pass in the different years. Second, the final marks neither follow normal distributions for the years of implementation (before or after the experiment) nor present homogeneity of variances. Therefore, instead of an ANOVA, a Kruskal-Wallis test (Siegel, 1988) was performed to check whether the distribution of the final marks in the three years was significantly different (dependent variable: the final marks obtained [best mark of each call for all the students, those who passed or not]; independent variable: year of implementation).

The students' and the teachers' perceptions were also taken into account. A survey was conducted in order to include the students' perceptions. The questions included dealt mainly with the usefulness of the learning materials provided and their opinions about the methodology as a whole. In particular, three questions asked about the tutorials of the practical sessions, three about the graphic project and three about the on-line self-correcting questionnaires. A Likert scale from 1 to 5 was used. Furthermore, open-ended questions were included for all the three aspects and for the midterm exams. All the teachers of the course (three or four depending on the year) had previous and ongoing meetings to coordinate methodology and evaluation criteria and, above all, a final meeting to discuss their individual perceptions about the implementation of the experiment.

Results

Data obtained from the three viewpoints are presented below.

Figure 5 shows a graph with the percentage of students who passed (out of those who took the exams). An initial Pearson's Chi Square test, with the three years and the number of students who passed or failed, produced a significant value of $p = 0.049$ indicating that a significant statistical difference exists. Therefore, to check which years were different (post-hoc), three subsequent Pearson Chi Square tests were performed including each pair of years (to have 2×2 contingency tables). The significant values were 0.017 for Previous/First Year, 0.724 for Previous/Second Year, and 0.042 for First/Second Year, which means that statistical differences in the percentage of students that passed the exams exist between the first year of implementation and the other two.

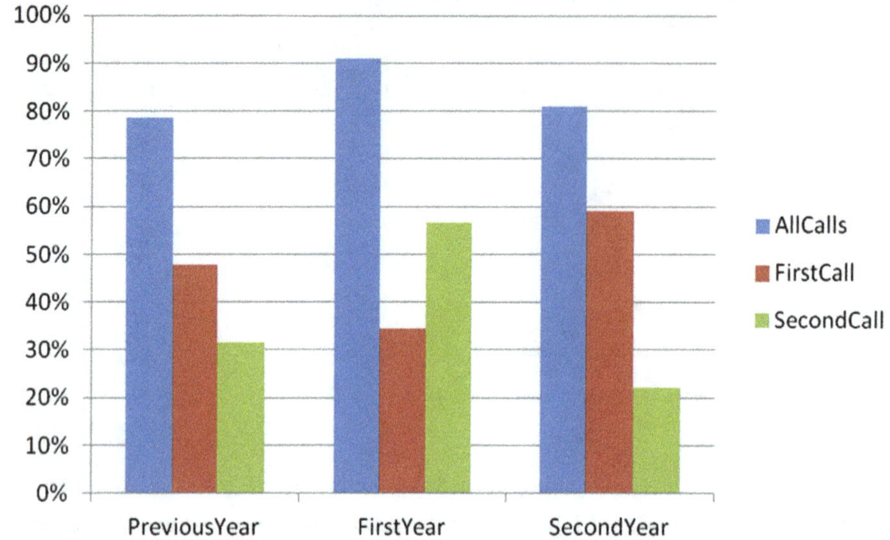

Fig. 5 Graph of the percentage of students (out of those who took the exams) who have passed over the years

Table 3 shows descriptive statistics of marks across the years of implementation. The results of the Kruskal-Wallis test showed significant differences in the statistical distribution of the marks between the previous year and the other two. The significant values were <0.001 for Previous/First Year, <0.001 for Previous/Second Year, and 0.821 for First/Second Year. The existence of significant differences between the previous year and the other two years of implementation can be inferred.

Besides the academic results, especially the final marks, two more indicators were also considered: teachers' observations and students' perceptions.

Figure 6 shows the results of the survey conducted on the students, aggregated by methodology (practical tutorials for practical sessions, graphic project and the questionnaires for theory concepts): the confidence interval of mean opinions over the two years of the implementation of the plan.

The open-ended questions also offered some good insights. The main complaint reflected in them was about the (according to them, still too small) weight of the project in the final mark.

Discussion

From the results obtained and in relation to the first indicator, it can be observed that the percentage of students who passed at all the exam calls increased significantly in the first year of implementation (Fig. 5 and statistical test). However, the percentage of

Table 3 Descriptive statistics of marks: mean and standard deviation, along with quartiles for all students (those who passed and those who did not, considering their best mark in both calls) based on a total of 10 points

Year	Mean	SD	P_{25}	P_{50}	P_{75}
Previous year	5.2	1.2	5.0	5.3	5.9
First year	5.9	1.2	5.1	6.1	6.7
Second year	5.9	1.5	5.0	6.0	7.0

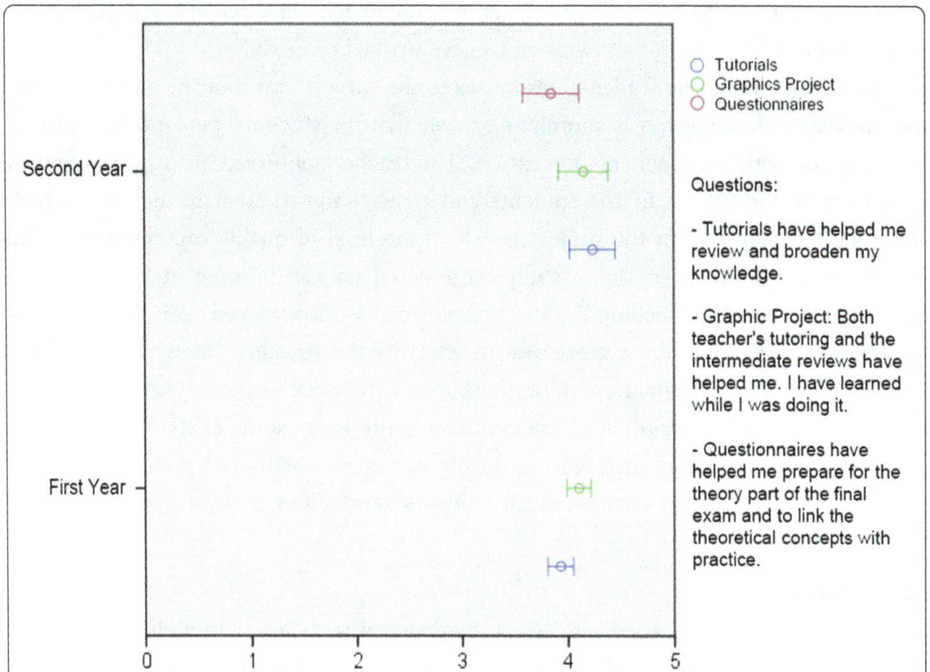

Fig. 6 95 % CI for the mean of the questionnaire. The scale was a Likert scale from 1 to 5

students who passed at the first call in that case was reduced, probably due to the new requirement of the minimum mark of 4 in the theoretical exam without any additional support and the higher level of difficulty in the exam. For the second year of the experiment, the level of difficulty in the theory part was increased, because we expected a better result on the weekly online questionnaires. The number of students who passed increased in comparison to the previous year, but decreased if compared with the first year. This result reinforces the idea that the changes made produced a benefit because of a significant increase of the students who passed among those who took the exam, especially in the first year of the implementation.

Also worthy of note is that despite the more demanding requirements, the percentage of students who passed and the average mark both increased as a result of the implementation of these methodologies. However, what attracts the most attention in this case is that the standard deviation increased in the second year. This may be due to a different reaction of the students when increasing the level of difficulty: those who make a greater effort get higher marks, but those who do not get lower ones; hence there is more variation in the marks. The results from the Kruskal-Wallis test, showing significant differences between marks of the previous year (before the implementation of the experiment) and marks of the first and second years (after the implementation of experiment) reinforces the fact that the experiment carried out produced significant improvements.

The results are in accordance with the ones expected according to literature. The actions carried out tried to support students by means of scaffolding their learning (Vygotsky, 1978) by facilitating ways to create their knowledge. Our purpose was far from simply giving the students knowledge to be accepted and memorised. Instead, it was to give them strategies and resources to make them create their own knowledge and to enable them to use it to solve problems. In Piaget's words: "*... education means* *making creators... You have to make inventors, innovators—not conformists*" (Bringuier, 1980). Actions taken in this sense seem to have worked properly.

If we take a look at the students' responses to the survey, they indicate a clear acceptance of the methodology. It is stimulating to see that the students' perceptions more or less coincide with the teachers' perception. The teachers observed an improvement in receptivity to the subject by the students and a clear improvement in the level, which was reflected above all in the project in which the level of quality increased, as more complicated products were successfully represented (as can be seen in Fig. 1). Obviously, the students' higher implication and effective work achieved with these actions have been accompanied by a great deal of effort by the teachers. We strongly believe that good levels of coordination among teachers, hard work in preparing valuable material or a thorough description of the evaluation criteria are some of the key points for success. However, all this hard work is highly rewarded when an improvement in the quality of learning and an increase in the students' satisfaction are observed.

Conclusions

From the experiments carried out, it can be deduced that the methodology employed has produced the expected effects, which means an improvement in academic results despite a higher level of difficulty of the assessment activities. It is remarkable that the perception that students have of the subject has also been improved. Although the experience has been developed in teaching CAD, the methodology may be applied to any specific subject or country.

As a final conclusion we would say that by:

- Providing varied self-learning material
- Detailing evaluation criteria in each part (including the use of rubrics)
- Requiring a higher level (quality, complexity)
- Demanding minimum marks, but giving a mark for everything

better academic results can be achieved, together with a good level of appreciation by students.

Endnotes

[1]The Organic Law of Universities came into force in 2001 in Spain for defining, among other aspects, the rules for Spanish Universities to adapt their degree courses to the requirements of the European Higher Education Area (Bologna Process).

Authors' information

Verónica Gracia-Ibáñez is a lecturer in Computer-Aided Design at Jaume I University (UJI) in Castellón, Spain. Her professional background has been in the field of industrial engineering projects. Since her engagement as a part-time lecturer in 2011, she has developed an interest in researching both in the field of biomechanics, in which she is currently working on her PhD thesis, as well as in the field of education, as shown by her participation in two educational innovation projects, two publications at international congresses on education and the co-authorship of a textbook.

Margarita Vergara is Full Professor in Computer-Aided Design and Ergonomics at Jaume I University (UJI) in Castellón, Spain. Her professional research interests are biomechanics of the hand and the ergonomic evaluation of product design, as well as ways to improve her teaching. Thus, she has taught Computer-Aided Design and Graphics in different Engineering Degrees for more than 20 years and has authored 18 textbooks. As a result of her interest in improving teaching, she has published one paper in an international peer-reviewed journal and presented 18 communications at congresses and conferences on teaching.

Acknowledgements

The authors are grateful for support from the *Unitat de Suport Educatiu* of Jaume I University through project Ref: 2793/13 and for the comments made by the reviewers, which were very helpful.

References

Asperl, A. (2005). How to teach CAD. *Computer-Aided Design and Applications, 2*(1–4), 459–468. doi:10.1080/16864360.2005.10738395

Ausubel, D. P. (1968). *Educational Psychology: A Cognitive View. Educational psychology a cognitive view.* doi:10.1107/S010827019000508X

Bain, K. (2007). *Lo que hacen los mejores profesores universitarios.* Traducción de Óscar Barberá: Servicio Publicaciones Universidad de Valencia, Valencia (Spain). ISBN 978-84-370-6669-1.

Bringuier, J. C. (1980). Conversations with jean piaget. *Society, 17*, 56–61. doi:10.1007/BF02694634

Chester, I. (2007). Teaching for CAD expertise. *International Journal of Technology and Design Education, 17*, 23–35.

Coll, C. (1996). Constructivismo y educación escolar: ni hablamos siempre de lo mismo ni lo hacemos siempre desde la misma perspectiva epistemológica. *Anuario de Psicología*, 153–178.

Coll, C., Mauri, T., & Onrubia Goñi, J. (2006). Análisis y resolución de casos-problema mediante el aprendizaje colaborativo. *RUSC. Universities and Knowledge Society Journal, 3*(2), 8.

Contero, M., Naya, F., Company, P., & Saorín, J. L. (2006). Learning support tools for developing spatial abilities in engineering design. *International Journal of Engineering Education, 22*, 470–477.

Contero, M., Naya, F., Company, P., Saorín, J. L., & Conesa, J. (2005). Improving visualization skills in engineering education. *IEEE Computer Graphics and Applications, 25*, 24–31. doi:10.1109/MCG.2005.107

Field, D. A. (2004). Education and training for CAD in the auto industry. *Computer-Aided Design, 36*(14), 1431–1437. doi:10.1016/j.cad.2003.10.007

Groundwater-Smith, S., & Mockler, N. (2011). Speaking of Quality and Research that Counts: Making an Impact on Practice. *Action Researcher in Education, 11*, 10–18.

Marqués Andrés, M., & Ferrández Berrueco, R. (2011). *Investigación práctica en educación: investigación-acción.* Escuela Técnica Superior de Ingeniería Informática: Universidad de Sevilla.

Novak, J. D. (2004). La teoría del aprendizaje significativo. *Technology*, 1–10.

Plumed, R., Calleja, P. C., Varley, P. A., & Martin, R. (2013). *From Sketches to CAM Models: Perceiving Pockets and Steps in Single-view Wireframe Sketches of Polyhedral Shapes* (pp. 951–958). In: Proceedings of International Joint Conference on Pervasive and Ubiquitous Computing.

Riel, M. (2010). Understanding action research. *Center for Collaborative Action Research, 43*, 435–437. doi:10.1016/j.pragma.2010.08.016

Riel, M., & Whitehead, J. (2011). *Paper presented at annual meeting of the American Educational Research Association: Action Research Identity Outcomes: Shift in Self-Perception, Professional Role, and Researcher Identity Interactive Symposium.* New: Orleans. A meta-analysis of the outcomes of action research.

Rossignac, J. (2004). Education-driven research in CAD. *Computer-Aided Design, 36*(14), 1461–1469. doi:10.1016/j.cad.2003.10.008

Rubio García, R., Gallego Santos, R., & Suárez Quirós, J. (2005). Present state of CAD teaching in Spanish Universities. *Comparative Education, 44*(3), 201–215. doi:10.1016/j.compedu.2003.09.003

Rudduck, J., & Hopkins, D. (1985). *Research As a Basis for Teaching: Readings from the Work of Lawrence Stenhouse.* London: Heinemann.

Sanmartí, N. (2007). *10 ideas clave.* Graó, Barcelona: Evaluar para aprender.

Siegel, S. (1988). *Nonparametric statistics for the behavioral sciences.* New York: McGraw-Hill.

Vygotsky, L. S. (1978). Interaction between learning and development. *Readings on the Development of Children, 23*(3), 34–41.

Ye, X., Peng, W., Chen, Z., & Cai, Y. Y. (2004). Today's students, tomorrow's engineers: an industrial perspective on CAD education. *Computer-Aided Design, 36*(14), 1451–1460. doi:10.1016/j.cad.2003.11.006

Zaphiris, P., & Ioannou, A. (2014). Learning and Collaboration Technologies. *Designing and Developing Novel Learning Experiences.* doi:10.1007/978-3-319-07482-5

15

Written peer-feedback to enhance students' current and future learning

Georgeta Ion*, Aleix Barrera-Corominas and Marina Tomàs-Folch

* Correspondence:
georgeta.ion@uab.cat
Universitat Autònoma de Barcelona,
Cerdanyola del Vallès, Barcelona,
Spain

Abstract

Spanish universities are engaged in the implementation of the European Higher Education Area (EHEA). This process implies the use of the most effective instructional designs and methodologies in order to achieve deep learning, increase student involvement in their own development, and professional and personal-greater autonomy in the construction of knowledge. Peer-feedback is an effective strategy to reach such requirements. The study aimed to analyze the type of feedback students provide in peer-assessment in group work projects and to investigate students' perception towards peer-assessment for the improvement of the learning process.

The methods were mixed. A semantic analysis of the type of feedback was conducted. A total of 637 feedback units were analysed according to the guidelines developed in the project. In addition, questionnaires to students and teachers involved in the experience were administrated.

The results demonstrate that the great majority of feedback offered by students was related to task development, followed by feedback regarding the motivational aspects of the process and finally the structural and formal aspects of the writing. At the end of the process, both teachers and students declared that the feedback received helped them to better develop the task and support them in future learning.

Keywords: Assessment, Competencies, Peer-Feedback, Feedforward

Introduction

The launch of the European Higher Education Area has placed the student in the central place of the learning process. This approach has emphasised the need to align assessment activities with learning outcomes (Biggs 2003), hence the creation of continuous assessment systems where learning activities are converted into evaluation activities and evidence. However, most students' assessment activities in higher education is designed and conducted by university staff and rarely are students given central responsibility for the evaluative process (Giles et al. 2004).

Scientific literature dedicated to assessment reveals that continuous assessment aims to facilitate student learning, enables students to become active, responsible and reflective practitioners, improves the quality of learning and provides formal accountability and accreditation of knowledge (Orsmond et al. 2000; Wen et al. 2006, among others).

To address these challenges, peer-assessment has been a common practice in higher education involving an important change in assessment procedures (Patri 2002; Wen et al. 2006). It is defined as a way whereby students assess the quality of their colleagues' performance and give feedback to one another (Dochy, Segers, & Sluijsmans 1999; Sluijsmans et al. 2002). It is designed to develop active autonomous learners who can think reflectively and take responsibility (Wen & Tsai 2006). Therefore, peer-assessment is embedded in higher education to help students appraise their own work and that of others, and to adopt a more self-directed attitude towards their learning in preparation for their ongoing professional development and lifelong learning (Jaques 2000; Falchikov 2001).

As part of the constructivist approach of education, feedback is considered to be a key component of the learning and assessment activity for the reflective construction of knowledge and lies in a transformed role for students in feedback and in a variety of forms: in targeting, generating and interpreting feedback and in communicating and engaging with it (Hounsell 2007). Among the different types of procedures and methods, feedback includes qualitative comments involving groups of students or peers and has a series of strengths for students' learning, makes students more responsible for their actions, encourages a reflexive approach to learning, involves learners in judging their performance or that of their peers, and also the developing and using of evaluative expertise, and providing, seeking and utilising feedback.

Among the different types of feedback, peer-feedback appears as especially beneficial for the students' learning being eloquently articulated by Boud, Falchikov and others in a series of studies (Boud 1995; Falchikov 2001; Brew 1999), focusing on the students' involvement in the process of feedback, understanding the substantial role of feedback for higher-quality learning outcomes to be achieved. Peer-feedback is provided by equal status learners and can be regarded both as a form of formative assessment, the counterpart of teacher feedback (Topping 1998), and as a form of collaborative learning (Van Gennip, Segers, & Tillema 2010; among others). Peer-feedback supports the learning process by providing an intermediate check of the performance against the criteria, accompanied by feedback on strengths, weaknesses and/or suggestions for improvement (Falchikov 2001).

The use of peer-feedback is justified from different perspectives: Askew and Lodge (2000) focused on the constructivist theories of learning where feedback is able to engage both teacher and students in a reflexive and collaborative dialog. As assessees, students receive feedback and may make improvements accordingly. Through such processes, peer feedback becomes a strategy for formative assessment and a tool for reflection by students (Cheng & Warren 1999). But, not all feedback leads to performance improvement. Nicol and Macfarlane-Dick (2006) focused on self-regulation in learning which led to the drawing up of a set of principles for a good feedback practice. These authors highlight the students' capacity to self-regulate their learning which can be powerfully facilitated through well-designed feedback and formative assessment and can empower students to generate their own internal feedback in an effective way.

In addition, recent research at universities also demonstrates that the proactive feedback called feedforward (Carless et al. 2006; Boud & Molloy 2013) tends to be more useful in order to enhance students' self-regulation and stimulate the learning process. All these perspectives define an authentic and significant engagement in and with feedback as a condition for sustainability in students' learning. Strijbos et al. (2010) add several conditions under which proactive feedback has a positive influence on future learning. This is focused on the type of writing (mostly syntactic and grammatical) which feedback should provide. In the same line, the proposal of Lilly et al. (2010) is more generic and focuses on three aspects: content, style and clarity and so offers clues as to how feedback has to be with respect to these three axes. The proposal of Nicol (2011) is even more generic or wide, for who written feedback should fulfil some formal characteristics regarding the way in which it is presented but also some characteristics which are much more general, with respect to the purpose, frequency, content, specificity of the feedback that is provided. Nicol proposes a type of feedback that is easy to understand, comprehensive, flexible, contextualised, among other characteristics.

As can be appreciated, some recurring aspects which improve the efficacy of feedback are: sufficient time should be allowed for it; that it should be specific (as demonstrated by Strijbos et al. 2010); and it must be positive and constructive (Shute 2008). There are also recurring aspects with respect to format, clarity, specificity, precision and dimension.

Starting from this background, our research aims to analyse the type of feedback students provide in peer-assessment in group work projects, to investigate students' perception towards peer-feedback for the improvement of the learning process and finally to give suggestions to promote the effective use of peer -assessment in educational programs.

Specifically, the study addresses the following questions:

1. What type of feedback students provide to their peers?
2. What are the benefits of using peer assessment in education from the students and teachers' perspective?
3. What are the shortcomings of using peer assessment in education field from the students and teachers' perspective?

Methods

In order to accomplish these objectives, exploratory research was conducted between September 2014 and June 2015, among a non-random sample of 160 students from the Autonomous University of Barcelona (UAB) undergraduate programmes in Pedagogy and Social Education.[1] The participants were all the students involved in the subject titled: "Organisation and groups" which was imparted in the second year. During the course students have been involved in an experience based on the use of peer-assessment. During this process, students provided peer-feedback to their colleagues. Firstly they rated and commented on two randomly assigned peers' projects, and secondly they were then asked to improve their projects based on the feedback they received. Feedback has been provided in written form, on an academic assignment, using track changes mode of word. In order to implement this task, students received at the beginning of the course specific guidelines on how they have to provide feedback, what kind of feedback they could provide and also they have been trained on the procedure.

At the end of the experience a guideline for the analysis of feedback has been designed. Data was also collected through the administration of two questionnaires: one for students and another one for teachers.

Firstly, data was gathered through the analysis of the content of the feedback provided by peers. For that purpose, a guideline of analysis have been designed based on the proposal of Nicol (2011) which evaluated the feedback through the following categories:

(1) Task development:

a) feedback is centred on the objectives of the task,
b) feedback is oriented towards the learning results,
c) feedback could be transferred to other learning tasks or other practical activities,
d) feedback is balanced between the negative and positive aspects of the assignment,
e) feedback enhances students' reflection,
f) feedback stimulates the students' implication and engagement with the task,
g) feedback refers to the students'' competencies.

(2) Formal aspects:
a) language correctness,
b) structural aspects of the assignment,
c) use of norms of written communication,
d) ability to produce changes.

(3) Motivational aspects:
a) feedback is able to motivate and improve students' self-esteem
b) assertiveness

Each one of these indicators is evaluated with a Likert scale from 1 (less) to 4 (a lot).

The guideline was validates and piloted by the research team and experts and improvements were made on the first version during the process.

This guideline permitted the identification of "feedback units" (the comments with sense elaborated by students in the feedback process). These units were evaluated with the indicators established in the guideline. At the end of the process, all 160 students provided a total of 637 feedback units.

Data gathered through semantic analysis was completed with information obtained through two questionnaires: one for the teachers and the other for the students. Both questionnaires contained closed items, in which each item had to be evaluated in a scale of 1 to 4. The participants could also freely express their opinion in an open section of the questionnaire. These questionnaires were validated through experts' validation

Both questionnaires contain items organised around following aspects:

a. Satisfaction in relation to the activity: satisfaction with regard to the frequency of the feedback, to the workload, to the training received at the beginning of the activity
b. Aspects related to the feedback received: feedback helps to develop competencies, to enhance the learning process, to improve future learning, to improve engagement with learning
c. Aspects related to the feedback provided: feedback helps to develop competencies, to enhance the learning process, to improve future learning, to improve engagement with learning.

All 160 students involved in the experience have answered the questionnaire at the end of the process. In addition, all four teachers in charged with the subject completed the questionnaire.

Results

In spite of the initial exploratory nature of the study, the results presented in this paper include referential statistics to try to reach conclusions beyond the immediate data alone. The results of the analysis of the frequencies of the data grouped in function of the profile of the participants (students and teachers) of the study are presented, as well as the semantic analysis of the qualitative responses obtained in the final evaluation questionnaires that both collectives responded to.

The results are divided in two main sections: on the one hand, a descriptive analysis of the type of feedback that the students have given to their colleagues; and on the other hand, the data of the questionnaires of the students and teachers on their experience of peer-assessment developed in the classroom.

Typology of feedback

Through an analysis of the units of feedback provided by the students, three types of feedback have been identified corresponding to the three types of regulation described by Nicol (2011) within the theoretical framework. These types are: feedback oriented towards the task; that oriented towards motivational and emotional aspects; and the feedback regarding structural aspects of the activity.

With respect to the first type of feedback, 54 % of the units of analysis made reference to indicators related with the task, 25 % was linked to indicators related with motivational and emotional aspects and the remaining 21 % to aspects linked to the structure of the task.

The types of feedback for each one of these categories were distributed in the following way: in the case of feedback that is task-oriented, we note that the bulk of the feedback is related to the learning results linked to the task ($n = 285$), followed by feedback regarding the objectives of the task (relevant: $n = 273$), feedback that fosters reflection and the processes of self-regulation ($n = 228$), feedback that makes reference to the level of implication of the students in the task ($n = 218$), followed by feedback enabling transfer to other tasks ($n = 213$). Finally, the feedback is balanced in that it refers to both positive and negative aspects of the task ($n = 208$) and makes reference to the acquisition of competencies ($n = 185$).

As regards the second category of feedback, which refers to structural elements, we note that most of the feedback encourages the receivers to make changes in their work ($n = 207$), followed by the feedback oriented towards the structure of the work ($n = 205$) and the use of drafting standards and finally, linguistic correction. The third category of feedback, regarding motivational aspects, highlights the texts which reinforce self-esteem ($n = 323$), followed by those that make use of assertiveness to stress the importance of the positive or the negative aspects in the accomplishment of the activity ($n = 286$).

The distribution of the different types of feedback is illustrated in Fig. 1.

Students' perceptions about peer-assessment

When the activity ended, the students were requested to answer the questionnaire to measure their perceptions in relation to three groups of variables: (1) general perception regarding the accomplished activity; (2) evaluation of *feedback* received; and (3) evaluation regarding the intention of the feedback offered.

Whole participants, both students and teachers have expressed their satisfaction with the experience of peer-feedback and they consider that this has helped them to improve the learning process.

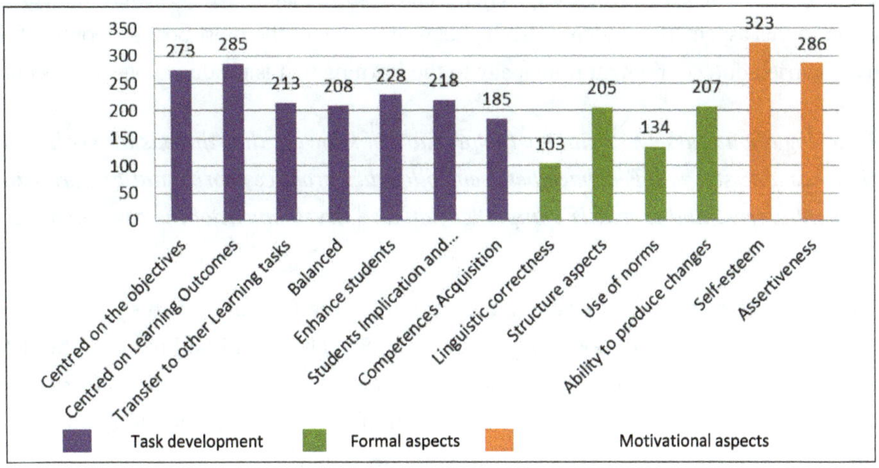

Fig. 1 Distribution of the units of *feedback* according to the indicators of the framework of analysis

From the general perception of the students (Table 1), it can be observed that all the aspects considered have received a very positive assessment, above 2 of a scale of 1 to 4. The participants consider that the feedback has helped them to improve on their future tasks (feedforward) with a score of 3,14, and it has helped them to increase their level of implication in their learning (3,03), followed by the perception that the activity has helped them to improve their competencies (2,97).

The proactive role of feedback in the enhancement of future tasks has been highlighted by the participants in the open-ended section of the questionnaire. They point the fact that the feedback received has been useful given because it permitted them to: *know how to rectify thanks to the help provided by others* (Group 1). It has helped them not only to *accept constructive criticism, but also to know how to do their work better in the future* (Group 2).

With regard to the second most valued aspect linked to a better involvement of the students with the activity that they are developing, the opinions of the participants emphasise this aspect: "*Being able to evaluate all the members of the group so that the participation and implication of all of them are reflected* (Group 3).

Table 1 Perception of the teachers and students in relation to the usefulness of the feedback

Items	Students' perception (means)	Teachers' perception (means)
Feedback has helped to enhance the competencies of the student.	2,97	2,5
Feedback has helped to improve the learning process of the student.	2,86	2,5
Feedback has been useful to improve the future activities of the student.	3,14	3
Feedback has increased the motivation of the student.	2,61	2
Feedback has heightened the involvement of the student in the activities.	3,03	3
The frequency of the Feedback has been appropriate.	2,53	2
The workload for the student has been acceptable.	2,64	2,5
The workload for the teachers has been satisfactory.		2,5

Thirdly, the enhancement of competencies linked to the subject is positively valued. Regarding to this aspect, the students also highlight it as one of the most positive points of the activity carried out, confining it principally to the learning that is produced between peers:

> *Learning about ourselves, without the pressure of knowing that there is an evaluator that has assessed you. Feedback between colleagues produces horizontality, permitting proximity, trust and a greater comprehension and development of the competencies required* (Group 4).

The aspect with the lowest evaluation is related to the frequency of the *feedback* that the students have received, obtaining a score of 2,53. This could be linked to the delay of some groups in forwarding their scores of *feedback* to their colleagues, and the consideration that they would have been more useful if they were returned in good time in order to introduce changes in the work to be undertaken.

> *Perhaps the weakest point has been the timing of the return of feedback* (Group 5).

If we contrast this block of items with the opinion of the teachers, we can see that the results coincide, although the students tend to evaluate all the aspects at a higher level. The teachers coincide that the feedback has contributed to improve the future activities of the students (mean of 3 out of 4) and it has helped them to increase their participation and engagement. On a second level, the assessments are found with respect to the usefulness of the feedback to enhance the competencies of the students, to improve the learning process (2,5) and finally it was assessed that the feedback has contributed to boost the motivation of the students in the activities (2 out of 4). Just as for the case of the students, the teachers coincide that the weak point of the experience has been the frequency of the feedback (2 out of 4). Table 1 systematises the information relative to the usefulness of the feedback according to the perception of the teachers and the students.

The results obtained in the aspects concerning the assessment of *feedback* received on the part of the participants, as well as the assessment of their intentionality with those that offered *feedback* to the rest of the colleagues that participated are outlined in Fig. 2. The first aspect that can be highlighted is the tendency of the students to appraise markedly higher the evaluations that they have offered to the rest of the students in all the indicators posed.

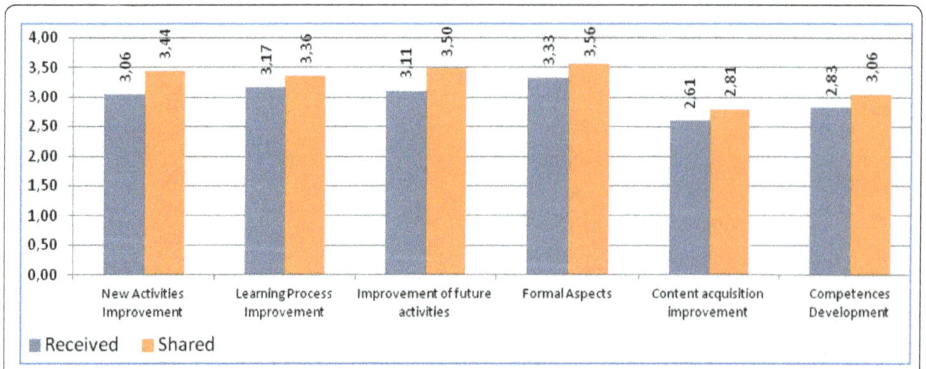

Fig. 2 Average scores of the feedback received and shared

The one that scored highest in both cases is the one which is linked to the formal aspects of the task (drafting, orthography, presentation, linguistic correction, style etc.), which receives a mean score of 3,56 in that offered, and 3,33 in what is received. Hereafter, we can see that a score of 3,50 appears for *feedback* offered, and 3,11 for *feedback* received. The capacity of the indications to motivate to keep working and improve future activities, an aspect that is related with *feedforward*, together with an enhancement of future activities, receives a score of 3,44 in the feedback that is offered, and 3.06 in the assessment of what is received. These two aspects, which are placed in second and third place respectively, are related with the factor which the students have appreciated most of the experience, linked to the capacity of *feedback* received to enhance future activities.

The improvement of the learning process appears to be rated in fourth place in the *feedback* offered (3,36 points on average), and in second place in the feedback received (3,17 points), and this would be linked to the units of *feedback* analysed, 54 % of which is related to the task. The item with the lowest score is related to the capacity of the *feedback* to foster a greater knowledge of the specific content of the subject, which received a score of 2,81 in the feedback offered, and 2,61 in the feedback received.

Finally, the open responses of the students underline the potentialities and the points to be improved with regard to feedback. Among the positive evaluations of the experience, aspects that are linked with peer-learning are emphasised, as well as self-reflection of the actual activity and learning.

> *The strong point is the acquired horizontal learning, integrating different points of view* (Group 7).

Among the negative evaluations of the experience, besides the lack of time to introduce changes once the *feedback* of the colleagues is received, aspects not directly related to the experience of feedback carried out are emphasised, like those of the lack of collaborative working in the team and the low level of involvement of some students.

> *Regardless of the quantity of feedback received, if we are not in a cohesive group and that we don't all collaborate together, it will be difficult to resolve the activities correctly* (Group 10).

Discussion and conclusions

The results of the study demonstrate the role of peer-feedback in the students' learning process. Students were involved in an active way in the feedback process with their peers, declaring that through this process they learned not only how to better solve their tasks but also how to solve similar tasks in the future. This proactive feedback called feedforward has a high potential to enhance students' self-regulation and stimulate the learning process (Carless et al. 2006; Boud & Molloy 2013) and define authentic and significant engagement in and with feedback as a condition for the sustainability in students' learning.

In relation to the types of feedback, as we have observed, feedback offered during the process is mainly oriented to task solving and is characterised by the information on how to improve work and how to take learning further. This proactive dimension of the feedback associated to the self-regulation of learning facilitates students' learning and help them to become active, responsible and reflective practitioners, improve the quality of learning and provide formal accountability and accreditation of knowledge (Wen et al. 2006; Shute 2008). This approach certainly reinforces the positions of many authors, like that of Nicol and MacFarlane-Dick (2006), who defend the formative dimension of feedback in the teaching and learning process, and specifically, for assessment purposes.

The motivational role of the feedback is also an important component in the regulation process. The results show the feedback is characterized by the emotional elements which stimulate the implication of students, in line with Kimbell and Stables (2008) studies that highlight the importance of the support offered to students in order to increase their level of responsibility for their own learning and autonomy.

The research results also demonstrate the high level of satisfaction for both teachers and students with peer-feedback. Students and teachers agreed that feedback helps students to better learn and develop their competencies. In addition, it helps them to get engaged with the learning process and to increase their self-regulation abilities.

Comparing the students' perception through the questionnaires on the intention of their feedback and the perception on the usefulness of feedback received, the results are coherent. They give a critical role to the feedback for future activities, and to feel motivated to continue studying and to improve their learning. These results are also confirmed by the semantic analysis of the feedback units. Moreover, comparing to the type of feedback students really provide, we can observe some divergences. While students perceive feedback they provide is oriented to improve structural aspects of the task, analysing the feedback provided to their colleagues demonstrates that the main type of feedback is oriented to the improvement of task solving. This situation needs further clarification in the future in spite studies as carried out by Simpson and Clifton (2015) reached similar results showing the feedback developed during the peer review process is focused on style and presentation preferentially to content.

The data reveals that students and teachers are highly satisfied with the peer-feedback in the assessment process. The horizontal learning, motivation and implication make students more aware of their learning process represent their arguments supporting the strong points of peer-feedback in order to make it positive and constructive (Shute 2008). The critical points which should be improved are related to the time delivery of the feedback that is too slow in some cases, the amount of work and the difficulties teachers experiment to monitor the changes in the revised task. All these weak points should be improved in order to ensure an authentic and sustainable learning as demonstrated by Strijbos et al. (2010).

In short, the results of the research suggest the benefits of transferring the protagonist role from the teachers to the students in search of a more dialogic feedback, in which students are the judge of their own learning process (Orsmond et al. 2000; Boud & Molloy 2013) and changing the attention of the teachers (as the only ones that offer feedback) towards the students and what they can do (Ruegg 2015).

This has led us to propose future projects of educational innovation and research, analysing in depth the peer-feedback process where students are involved, in which they have a more active role in the processes of feedback and this being self-regulated and dialogic and evidently implicating that the student is involved, knows and applies the standards of work, utilises information that is obtained to improve their work for future occasions and reflects about the quality of it.

We would like to point out some of the limitations of the research which we identify for future lines of study. On the one hand, as we previously explained in the methods section, the results we have obtained only make sense within the frame of the subjects analysed. Therefore it would be interesting to carry out similar research with a larger sample made up of different types of courses. On the other hand, taking into account the feedback conceptualisation proposed by Nicol (2011), other dimensions which define the feedback process could be analysed; for example, the forms of feedback proposed by Guasch et al. (2013): corrective, suggestive, epistemic, and informative and to analyse in-depth the consequences of the feedback provided through longitudinal studies.

To conclude, we want to emphasise that despite the evidence that peer-feedback has advantages for students, more student and teacher training should be given on this topic. The training in written feedback through digital tools should take into account the developing of strategies for providing teachers and students with knowledge and methodology on the type and characteristics of a good feedback, especially because of its potential to improve students' self-regulation skills and produce sustainable and long term learning.

Endnotes

[1]This research forms part of the innovative project: "Design, implementation and evaluation of sustainable feedforward experiences" (REDICE 2014–966), funded by University of Barcelona

References

Askew S, Lodge C (2000) Gifts, ping-pong and loops – Linking feedback and learning. In: Askew S (ed) Feedback for Learning. Routledge Falmer, London, pp 1–18

Biggs J (2003) Calidad del aprendizaje universitario. Cómo aprenden los estudiantes. Narcea, Madrid

Boud D, Molloy E (2013) Rethinking models of feedback for learning: the challenge of design. Assess Eval High Educ 38(6):698–712

Boud D (1995) Enhancing learning throught self assessment. Kogan Page, London

Brew (1999) Towards autonomous assessment: using self -assessment and peer assessment. In: Brown S, Glasner A (eds) Assessment matters in higher education: choosing and using diverse approaches. Society for Research into Higher education and Open University Press, Buckingham, pp 48–63

Carless D, Joughin G, Mok MMC (2006) Learning-oriented assessment: principles and practice. Assess Eval High Educ 31(4):395–398

Cheng W, Warren M (1999) Peer and teacher assessment of the oral and written tasks of a group project. Assess Eval High Educ 24(3):301–314

Dochy F, Segers M, Sluijsmans D (1999) The use of self-, peer- and co-assessment in higher education: A review. Studies in Higher Education 24:331–350

Falchikov N (2001) Learning together. Peer tutoring in higher education. Routledge Falmer, London

Giles A, Martin S, Bryce D, Hendry G (2004) Students as partners in evaluation: student and teacher perspectives. Assess Eval High Educ 29(6):681–685

Guasch T, Espasa A, Alvarez IM, Kirschner PA (2013) Effects of Teacher and Peer Feedback on Collaborative Writing in an Online Learning Environment. Distance education 34(3):324–338

Hounsell D (2007) Towards more sustainable feedback to students. In: Boud D, Falchilov N (eds) Rethinking assessment in higher education. Learning for the longer term. Routledge, London, pp 101–113

Jaques D (2000) Learning in groups: A handbook for improving group work, 3rd edn. Kogan Page, London

Kimbell R, Stables K (2008) Researching Design Learning. Springer, London

Lilly J, Richter M, Rivera-Macias B (2010) Using feedback to promote learning: student and tutor perspectives. Practitioner Research in Higher Education 4(1):30–40

Nicol D (2011) Good designs for written feedback for students. In: McKeachie WJ, Svinicki M (eds) McKeachie's Teaching Tips: Strategies, Research, and Theory for College and University Teachers, 13th edn. Wadsworth, Cengage Learning, Belmont USA, pp 108–124

Nicol D, MacFarlane-Dick D (2006) Formative assessment and self -regulated learning: A model and seven principles of good feedback practice. Studies in Higher Education 31(2):199–218

Orsmond P, Merry S, Reiling K (2000) The use of student-derived marking criteria in peer and self-assessment. Assess Eval High Educ 25(1):21–38

Patri M (2002) The influence of peer feedback on self- and peer assessment of oral skills. Language Testing 19(2):109–131

Ruegg R (2015) Differences in the Uptake of Peer and Teacher Feedback. RELC Journal 46(2):131–145

Shute VJ (2008) Focus on formative feedback. Review of Educational Research 78(1):153–189

Simpson G, Clifton J (2015) Assessing postgraduate student perceptions and measures of learning in a peer review feedback process. Assessment & Evaluation in Higher Education. 1–14. doi:10.1080/02602938.2015.1026874

Sluijsmans D, Brand-Gruwel S, Merriënboer J (2002) Peer assessment training in teacher education: Effects on performance and perceptions. Assess Eval High Educ 27(5):443–454

Strijbos J, Narciss S, Dünnebier K (2010) Peer feedback content and sender's competence level in academic writing revision tasks: Are they critical for feedback perceptions and efficiency? Learning and instruction 20(4):291–303

Topping K (1998) Peer assessment between students in colleges and universities. Review of Educational Research 68: 249–276

Van Gennip NAE, Segers MSR, Tillema HH (2010) Peer assessment as a collaborative learning activity: the role of interpersonal variables and conceptions. Learning and Instruction 20(4):280–290

Wen M, Tsai C (2006) University students' perceptions of and attitudes toward (online) peer assessment. Higher Education 51:27–44

Wen M, Tsai C, Chang C (2006) Attitudes towards peer assessment: A comparison of the perspectives of pre-service and in-service teachers. Innov Educ Teach Int 43(1):83–92

Permissions

All chapters in this book were first published in IJETHE, by Springer; hereby published with permission under the Creative Commons Attribution License or equivalent. Every chapter published in this book has been scrutinized by our experts. Their significance has been extensively debated. The topics covered herein carry significant findings which will fuel the growth of the discipline. They may even be implemented as practical applications or may be referred to as a beginning point for another development.

The contributors of this book come from diverse backgrounds, making this book a truly international effort. This book will bring forth new frontiers with its revolutionizing research information and detailed analysis of the nascent developments around the world.

We would like to thank all the contributing authors for lending their expertise to make the book truly unique. They have played a crucial role in the development of this book. Without their invaluable contributions this book wouldn't have been possible. They have made vital efforts to compile up to date information on the varied aspects of this subject to make this book a valuable addition to the collection of many professionals and students.

This book was conceptualized with the vision of imparting up-to-date information and advanced data in this field. To ensure the same, a matchless editorial board was set up. Every individual on the board went through rigorous rounds of assessment to prove their worth. After which they invested a large part of their time researching and compiling the most relevant data for our readers.

The editorial board has been involved in producing this book since its inception. They have spent rigorous hours researching and exploring the diverse topics which have resulted in the successful publishing of this book. They have passed on their knowledge of decades through this book. To expedite this challenging task, the publisher supported the team at every step. A small team of assistant editors was also appointed to further simplify the editing procedure and attain best results for the readers.

Apart from the editorial board, the designing team has also invested a significant amount of their time in understanding the subject and creating the most relevant covers. They scrutinized every image to scout for the most suitable representation of the subject and create an appropriate cover for the book.

The publishing team has been an ardent support to the editorial, designing and production team. Their endless efforts to recruit the best for this project, has resulted in the accomplishment of this book. They are a veteran in the field of academics and their pool of knowledge is as vast as their experience in printing. Their expertise and guidance has proved useful at every step. Their uncompromising quality standards have made this book an exceptional effort. Their encouragement from time to time has been an inspiration for everyone.

The publisher and the editorial board hope that this book will prove to be a valuable piece of knowledge for researchers, students, practitioners and scholars across the globe.

List of Contributors

Angela T. Ragusa
School Humanities and Social Sciences, Charles Sturt University, Albury, NSW, Australia

Laura A. Schindler and Osama A. Morad
University of Liverpool Online, Liverpool, UK

Gary J. Burkholder
Laureate Education, Inc., Baltimore, USA
Walden University, Minneapolis, USA

Craig Marsh
University of Lincoln, Lincoln, UK

Carmen Yot-Domínguez and Carlos Marcelo
Universidad de Sevilla, Pirotecnia s/n C.P, 41013 Sevilla, Spain

Daniel J. Peart, Penny L. S. Rumbold, Karen M. Keane and Linda Allin
Department of Sport, Exercise and Rehabilitation, Faculty of Health and Life Sciences, Northumbria University, Newcastle-upon-Tyne, UK

Jesper Aagaard
Department of Psychology and Behavioral Sciences, Aarhus University, 8000 Aarhus C, Denmark

Cheryl Poth
Department of Educational Psychology, University of Alberta, Edmonton, Alberta, Canada

Joan Ferrés, Maria-Jose Masanet and Julio-César Mateus
Communication Department, Universitat Pompeu Fabra, C/ Roc Boronat, 138, 08018 Barcelona, Spain

Deborah Arnold and Albert Sangrà
Universitat Oberta de Catalunya, Rambla del Poblenou 156, 08018 Barcelona, Spain

Christopher Drew and Amandeep Mann
Department of Education, School of Social Sciences, Humanities and Law, Teesside University, Middlesbrough TS1 3BX, UK

Pina Tarricone and C. Paul Newhouse
Centre for Schooling and Learning Technologies (CSaLT), School of Education, Edith Cowan University, 2 Bradford St, Mount Lawley, 6050 Western, Australia

Eyüp Sevimli
Faculty of Education, Gaziosmanpaşa University, 60150 Tokat, Turkey

Shalendra Kumar and Ben Kei Daniel
University of Otago, Dunedin, Otago, New Zealand

Tania Moreira-Mora and Julia Espinoza-Guzmán
Costa Rica Institute of Technology, Eastern District, Cartago, Costa Rica, Central America

Veronica Gracia-Ibáñez and Margarita Vergara
Departamento de Ingeniería Mecánica y Construcción, Universitat Jaume I, Avda. Sos Baynat, s/n, E12071 Castellón, Spain

Georgeta Ion, Aleix Barrera-Corominas and Marina Tomàs-Folch
Universitat Autònoma de Barcelona, Cerdanyola del Vallès, Barcelona, Spain

Index

www.ingramcontent.com/pod-product-compliance
Lightning Source LLC
LaVergne TN
LVHW080921210926
848485LV00004B/698